THE WYCLIFFITE
OLD TESTAMENT LECTIONARY

EARLY ENGLISH TEXT SOCIETY
O.S. 358

2021

is in filiis: leeke foul ꝯ and
a wise man: be mnꝛfiede ꝯ t þe
holi: be h glouꝛice ꝯ lo t come
soon and my mede wiþ me: to
ȝilde to eche man aftir hise
werkis t am alpha and o:
þe firste and þe laste: bigyn
nynge and ende: blessid be þei
þat waschun her stolis: þat
þe power of hem be in þe tre
of liif: And entre bi þe ȝatis in
to þe citee: for wiþoutforþ hou
dis and wricchis and bel...
men and manquellers and
seruynge to ydolis: and eche
þat loueþ and makiþ leesyng
I þe sente myn aungel to wit
nesse to ȝou þese þingis in chir
chis t am þe root t kynn of da
uiþ: and þe schynynge moꝛwe
sterre: and þe spirit and þe
spousesse: seien come þou: t
he þat heeriþ: seie come þou:
t be þat þirstiþ: come: and
he þat wole: take he freli þe
watir of liif: and I witnesse
to eche man heerynge þe wor
dis of profecie of þis book: if
ony man schal putte to þo þin
gis: god schal putte on hem
þe veniaunnis writun in þis
book: and if ony man do awei
þe woꝛdis of þe book of þis
profecie: god schal take awei

þe part of hym fro þe book
of liif t fro þe holi citee: t fro
þes þingis þat ben writun
in þis book: he seiþ þat beriþ
witnessynge of þese þingis
ȝhe Amen: I come soone: and
come þou lord Ihu: þe graas of
oure lord Ihu crist be wiþ ȝou
alle: Amen. Heere endiþ þe
Apocalips or reuelacioun: And þe
newe testament...þid heer
bigynneþ þe lessouns and pi
stlis of þe oolde lawe þat ben
redde in þe chirche: bi al þe ȝer
þe firste is þe lessoun in þe...

He lord seiþ þese
þingis: þeriþ
...ne ȝe þat suen
...þat: þat is iust
...and seken þe lord
take ȝe heede to þe stoon fro w
...whennes ȝe ben take doun:
to þe caue of þe lake: fro whi
...che ȝe ben kitte doun: take ȝe
heede to abraham ȝoure fadir
t to sare þat childide ȝou: for
clepide hym oon and t y blessi
hi t t multipliede hym: þerfor
þe lord schal coumforte sioun:
he schal coumforte alle þe ki
þingis þerof: and he schal set
þe desert þerof as delices: in
þe wildirnesse þof as a gardyn...

THE WYCLIFFITE OLD TESTAMENT LECTIONARY

EDITED BY

COSIMA CLARA GILLHAMMER

Published for

THE EARLY ENGLISH TEXT SOCIETY

by the

OXFORD UNIVERSITY PRESS

2021

OXFORD
UNIVERSITY PRESS

Great Clarendon Street, Oxford, OX2 6DP,
United Kingdom

Oxford University Press is a department of the University of Oxford.
It furthers the University's objective of excellence in research, scholarship,
and education by publishing worldwide. Oxford is a registered trade mark of
Oxford University Press in the UK and in certain other countries

© Early English Text Society 2021

The moral rights of the author have been asserted

First edition published in 2021

Impression: 1

British Library Cataloguing in Publication Data

Data available

ISBN 978-0-19-284768-3

Typeset by John Waś, Oxford
Printed in Great Britain
on acid-free paper by
TJ Books Limited, Padstow, Cornwall

ACKNOWLEDGEMENTS

The present edition is the result of a one-year postdoctoral research project at the University of Oxford, funded by the John Fell Research Fund and supported by the Faculty of English Language and Literature at Oxford and the Ludwig Humanities Research Fund at New College, Oxford. I would like to express my gratitude to these funding bodies for their support, which enabled me to conduct this research.

I am deeply indebted to Elizabeth Solopova and Anne Hudson for their generous advice, expert guidance, and constant kindness throughout this project. I have benefited enormously from their expertise, and this book would not exist without them. I am most grateful to William Marx for his detailed comments on early versions of this edition; the resulting text is much improved thanks to his suggestions. I am equally grateful to Bonnie Blackburn for her careful and patient copy-editing and Helen Spencer for her guidance through the process of publication. My thanks also go to Daniel Sawyer for his patience in answering my questions and his help in many matters big and small. My doctoral supervisor Daniel Wakelin has been a wise guide and mentor throughout the past years, and I am very grateful for his unceasing generosity in giving me his time, expertise, and help. Among the other colleagues who have helped me through their advice and support, I must especially thank Kantik Ghosh and Simon Horobin. Tristan Franklinos and Elizabeth Davis advised on some particularly difficult issues of Latin translation, and Rebecca Menmuir was kind enough to measure two manuscripts in Cambridge University Library for me. My mentors Ursula Lenker and Hans Sauer at the University of Munich have always been generous with their advice and help.

I am grateful for the kind assistance lent to me by the library staff and archivists at a number of libraries in the UK and elsewhere, particularly at the Bodleian Library, Oxford; Christ Church, Oxford; the British Library; the University Library at Cambridge; the Pepys Library at Magdalene College, Cambridge; Jesus College, Cambridge; Sidney Sussex College, Cambridge; Trinity College, Cambridge; Lambeth Palace Library; the National Library of Scotland; York Minster Library; the Bancroft Library at the University of California at Berkeley; the Beinecke Library at Yale University; the Firestone Library at Princeton University; New York Public Library; and Dunedin Public Library, New Zealand.

On a personal level, I first and foremost want to thank my parents, who were foundational for my love of old books, medieval languages, and liturgical texts. I am also very grateful to my grandparents, and I wish Opa could have seen this book. My thanks go to my friends for their kindness and care while I was working on this edition. Space does not permit me to name everyone, but I would especially like to thank Myriam Burstow née Frenkel, for her endless patience and support when I had lost my way; Claudia De Luca, for laughter and road trips; Cees Carels, for conversations about Bach; Jessica Frazier and Tristan Franklinos, for summer evenings in the Fellows' Garden; Katie Bank, for weekend walks and musical musings; John Kenny, Chris MacMackin, and Alan Miscampbell, for board games and bakery; Magnus Makeschin, for ruminations on the possessive dative; Rebekah Wallace, for exhilarating discussions; Pip Marshall, for being a voice of reason; Jamie Powe, for introducing me to the music of Lang, Dove, and MacMillan; and the Arcadian Singers of Oxford, for bringing so much choral joy to my life.

A. M. D. G.

Trinity College, Oxford
December 2020   C.C.G.

CONTENTS

CONTENTS

LIST OF ILLUSTRATIONS

PLATES

FIGURE

SIGLA

Ar	London, British Library, Arundel 254
As	Oxford, Bodleian Library, Ashmole 1517
Ba	Berkeley, Bancroft Library, 128
Bo	Oxford, Bodleian Library, Bodley 665
Bx	Oxford, Bodleian Library, Bodley 531
Cc	Oxford, Christ Church, 146
Do	Oxford, Bodleian Library, Douce 265-a
Dr	Dresden, Sächsische Landesbibliothek, Od. 83
Du	Dunedin, New Zealand, Public Library, Reed Fragment 20
Eg	London, British Library, Egerton 1171
He	London, British Library, Harley 1029
Hl	London, British Library, Harley 1710
La	London, Lambeth Palace Library, 532
Lm	Oxford, Bodleian Library, Laud misc. 388
Ln	London, British Library, Lansdowne 455
Lt	Warminster, Longleat House, 5
Mo	New York, Morgan Library, M. 362
N	Cambridge, Sidney Sussex College, 99
Ny	New York, New York Public Library, 64
o	London, British Library, Harley 6333
Pl	New York, Columbia University, Plimpton Add. 03
Pr	Princeton, University Library, Scheide Library 13
r	Manchester, John Rylands Library, Eng. 80
Ra	Oxford, Bodleian Library, Rawlinson C. 259
s	Cambridge, Jesus College, 47 (Q. D. 6.)
Se	Oxford, Bodleian Library, Selden supra 51
Si	London, Lambeth Palace Library, Sion College ARC L 40.2/E.2
Ta	Dublin, Trinity College, 75
Tc	Cambridge, Trinity College Library, B. 10. 20
Ty	New Haven, Yale University Library, Takamiya 113
Ua	Cambridge, University Library, Add. 6683
Ub	Cambridge, University Library, Add. 10068
Ul	Cambridge, University Library, Ll. 1. 13
Vk	Orlando, Van Kampen Collection, 641
w	Cambridge, Magdalene College, Pepys 2073
Wo	Worcester, Cathedral Library, Q. 84

x   London, Lambeth Palace Library, 369
Yo   York, Minster Library, XVI. N. 7
ι   Cambridge, University Library, Kk. 1. 8

ABBREVIATIONS

BL	British Library
BLOC	British Library, 'Online Catalogue of Illuminated Manuscripts' ⟨http://www.bl.uk/catalogues/illuminatedmanuscripts/introduction.asp⟩, accessed 10 July 2018
C	Commemorations
CL	Calendar-lectionary
CR	Cross-reference
Digital Scriptorium	'Digital Scriptorium' ⟨https://digital-scriptorium.org/⟩, accessed 15 July 2018
DMLBS	R. K. Ashdowne, D. R. Howlett, and R. E. Latham (eds.), *Dictionary of Medieval Latin from British Sources* (Oxford, 2018)
EV	Earlier Version of the Wycliffite Bible
F&M	J. Forshall and F. Madden (eds.), *The Holy Bible . . . in the Earliest English Versions Made from the Latin Vulgate by John Wycliffe and his Followers*, 4 vols. (Oxford, 1850)
GP	General Prologue
IN	independent translation (used in list of lections in §III of the Introduction)
LALME	Angus McIntosh, M. L. Samuels, and Michael Benskin, 'Linguistic Atlas of Late Medieval English. rev. M. Benskin and M. Laing', 1986 ⟨http://www.lel.ed.ac.uk/ihd/elalme/elalme.html⟩
LV	Later Version of the Wycliffite Bible
MED	Hans Kurath, Sherman M. Kuhn, John Reidy, et al. (eds.), *Middle English Dictionary*, ⟨http://quod.lib.umich.edu/m/med/⟩ (Ann Arbor, 1952–2001)
MS	manuscript
NS	Non-Sarum lections (in Type I OTLs)
NT	New Testament
OT	Old Testament
OTL	Old Testament Lectionary
S	Sanctorale
SM	Sarum Missal

Solopova, *MSS of WB*	Elizabeth Solopova, *Manuscripts of the Wycliffite Bible in the Bodleian and Oxford College Libraries*, Exeter Medieval Texts and Studies (Liverpool, 2016)
SYN	Synthesis of EV and LV (not clearly identifiable as either)
T	Temporale
TOL	Table of Lections
Vu	Vulgate
WB	Wycliffite Bible

INTRODUCTION

The Wycliffite Bible (WB) is a text well known for its extraordinarily large number of surviving manuscripts and the difficulties these present for the modern editor. For the most part scholarship on WB has been devoted to the Middle English translation of the biblical text itself, while less attention has been paid to the plethora of texts closely related to the Bible that survive in manuscripts of WB. These other texts are often liturgical or paraliturgical materials, such as tables of lections, liturgical calendars, or tables to determine the date of Easter. The most sizeable liturgical text found in Wycliffite manuscripts is the Old Testament Lectionary (OTL). This lectionary contains all the readings or lections from the Old Testament which are read at Mass over the course of the liturgical year after the Use of Sarum. It occurs exclusively in Wycliffite manuscripts which contain only a translation of the New Testament rather than the entire Bible, thus complementing these manuscripts from a liturgical point of view. OTL is more than a collection of extracts: it is a continuous structured text with its own titles, rubrics, and complex system of cross-references (see Plate 1 for a typical page layout).

The lections read at Mass after the Use of Sarum followed a set pattern. At every Mass there were at least two readings: first, the reading referred to as the 'epistle', which could be a section taken from the Old Testament, from Acts, the Epistles, or Revelation. Depending on the liturgical occasion, there could be one or several lections from these books. This would be followed by a gospel reading. These lections were fixed for each feast day, and most OTL manuscripts are accompanied by a table of lections (TOL) which provides a summary of which section from which part of the Bible is to be read for each liturgical occasion throughout the year (see Plate 2). Therefore the reader of OTL manuscripts would have had access to a translation of all lections for the Mass. The materials in such manuscripts are intended to be used jointly: those readings which were taken from the New Testament could be found in the full New Testament text itself, while those readings which were derived from the Old Testament were contained in OTL.

This model was evidently successful, as OTL is found in early and later Wycliffite manuscripts and appears in both the Early Version (EV) and the Late Version (LV). With thirty-nine surviving OTL texts and fragments, this text is found in roughly 16 per cent of all extant manuscripts

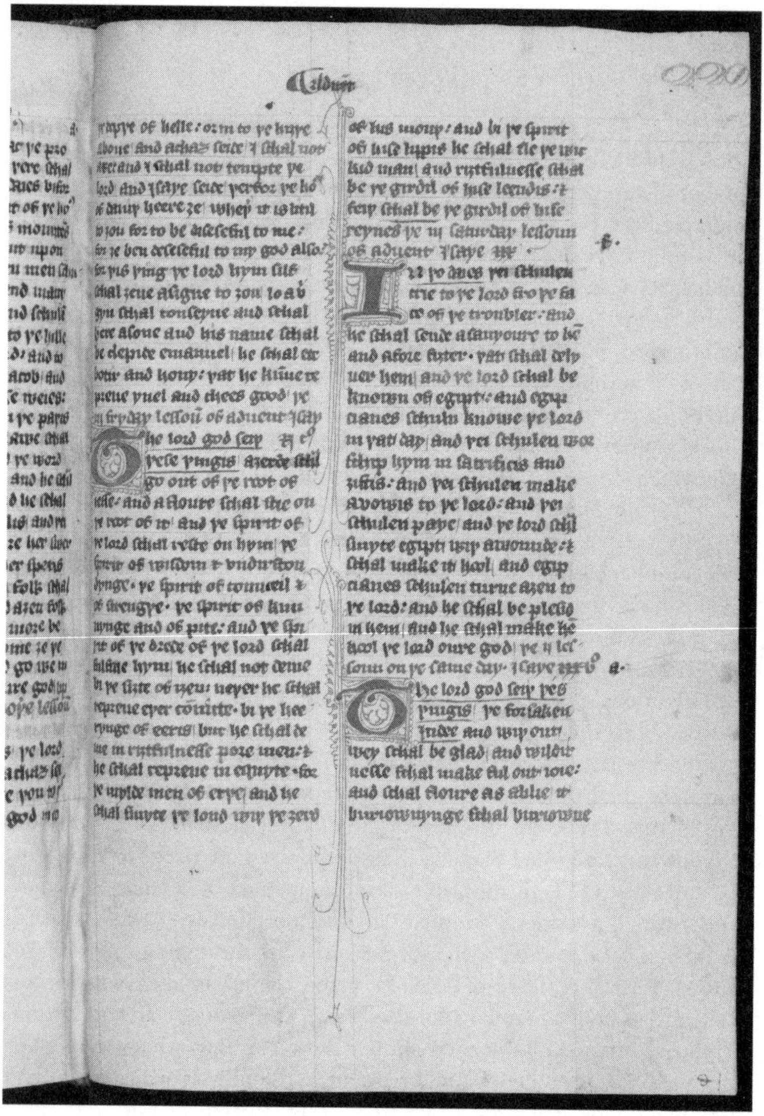

PLATE I. Oxford, Bodleian Library, MS Bodley 665, f. 228ʳ
Reproduced by permission of the Bodleian Libraries, University of Oxford

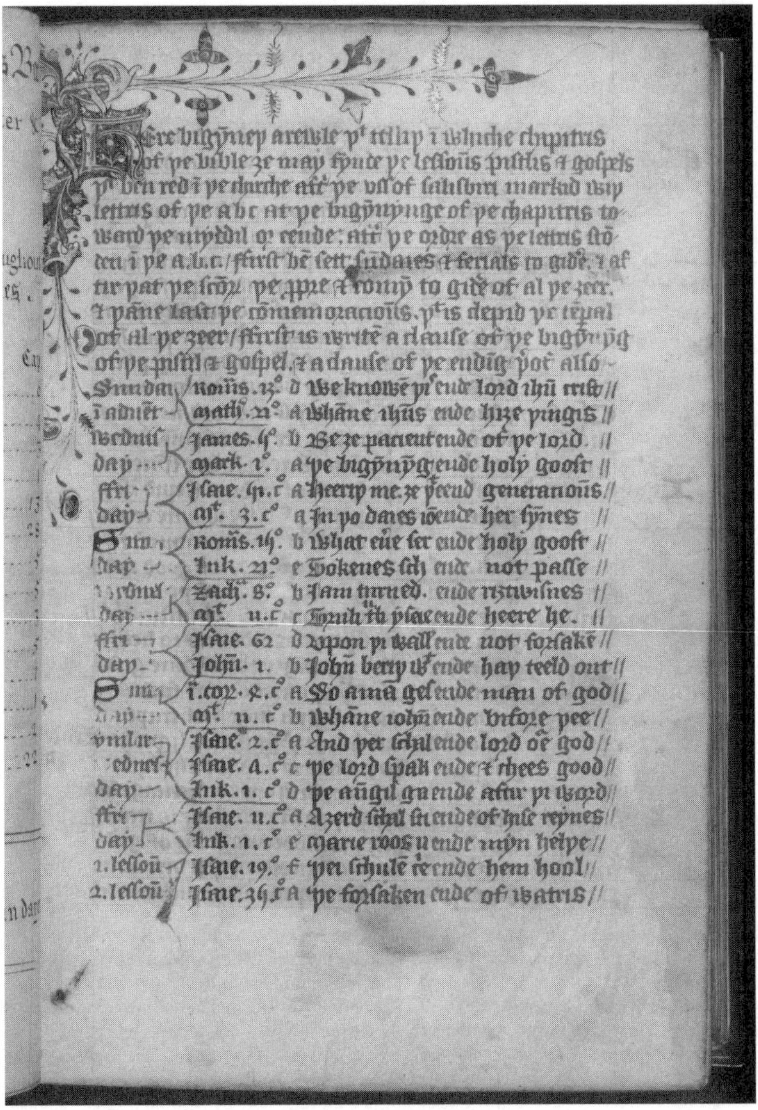

PLATE 2. Manchester, Rylands Library, MS Eng. 80, f. 9ʳ

© The University of Manchester 2021

of WB. Two of the thirty-nine manuscripts are *comites*, full lectionaries which include gospel readings, and as such are exceptions to the typical pattern outlined above.[1] With thirty-seven lectionaries containing Old Testament readings only, and about 109 manuscripts containing complete or partial New Testaments,[2] we arrive at a number of roughly 34 per cent of Wycliffite New Testament translations containing OTL. The popularity of this textual model survived for a long time, as can be seen even in post-Wycliffite translations: Tyndale's translation of the New Testament, printed in several editions, contains a lectionary which follows the Wycliffite OTL very closely in terms of visual presentation, layout, and referencing tools.[3]

The order of lections in OTL follows a distinctive pattern. The lectionary contains two main sections, the Temporale and the Sanctorale.[4] The Temporale includes the moveable feasts of the liturgical year, most of which change their date in relation to the date of Easter, such as Ascension, Pentecost, etc. It includes Sundays as well as weekdays. Another liturgical cycle which runs concurrently with the Temporale is the Sanctorale, which contains the fixed feasts celebrated on the same date every year. Those are typically saints' feast days. The Sanctorale can be further subdivided into the Proper and the Common. While the Proper contains those feasts which have individual readings unique to that feast, such as Candlemas, the Annunciation,[5] St Luke, St Mary Magdalen, etc., the Common contains readings which are used on several feasts. These are

[1] These manuscripts are *He* and *Hl*.

[2] Mary Dove, *The First English Bible: The Text and Context of the Wycliffite Versions*, Cambridge Studies in Medieval Literature, 66 (Cambridge, 2007), 18.

[3] *The Newe Testament yet once agayne corrected by Willyam Tindale; where vnto is added a kalendar and a necessarye table wherin earlye and lightelye maye be founde any storye contayned in the foure Euangelistes and in the Actes of the Apostles*, STC 2830 (1534). Tyndale's lectionary contains only the Temporale and a short Sanctorale (St Nicholas, Conception of Our Lady, Candlemas, Annunciation, Sts Philip and James, Nativity of St John the Baptist, Visitation of Our Lady, St Mary Magdalene, Assumption of Our Lady, Nativity of Our Lady, St Matthew, St Luke, St Catherine), lacking Common and Commemorations. The OTL is accompanied by a TOL which contains the NT lections only.

[4] I use the terms 'Temporale' and 'Sanctorale' in a narrow sense to refer to those feasts which are commemorated in the *Proprium de Tempore* or the *Proprium Sanctorum* in the Use of Sarum. The terms have at times been applied more loosely by Middle English scholars (see, for instance, the summary of the problem in the context of the *South English Legendary* provided by O. S. Pickering, 'The Temporale Narratives of the South English Legendary', *Anglia*, 91 (1973), 425–55 at 427); I do not follow this practice here.

[5] Although some early liturgical books occasionally insert Candlemas and the Annunciation into the Temporale (see, for instance, the Leofric Collectar, as detailed in M. Bradford Bedingfield, *The Dramatic Liturgy of Anglo-Saxon England* (Woodbridge, 2002), 58), the Sarum Use commonly classes them as Sanctorale feasts.

readings for saints who are grouped together based on specific characteristics, for instance the feasts that commemorate a confessor and bishop,
several martyrs or virgins, etc. Lectionaries also frequently contain votive
masses, also termed commemorations, for specific intentions, such as for
peace, for relief from pestilence affecting beasts, for pilgrims, etc. This
basic structure is found in the Latin missal of the Use of Sarum and is
followed in all OTLs, although there is some variation between individual OTL types as to whether the Proper and the Common are presented
separately or together in one section.

In spite of the prominence of OTLs in manuscripts of WB, Forshall
and Madden devoted very little space in their pioneering edition of WB
to the liturgical materials, a decision which is understandable in view of
the enormous editorial challenges they were facing.[6] They did not discuss OTL in any detail, and although they edited a TOL, their edition
is problematic as it is a conflation of different versions of this text. In
recent years there has been an increasing recognition of the importance of
OTL to Wycliffite studies. Anne Hudson repeatedly referred to the significance of the liturgical materials in her seminal work on Wycliffite thought.[7]
The late Mary Dove briefly discussed OTL in one of her major publications on WB, although she was aware of only twenty-nine of the extant
OTL manuscripts.[8] More recently, Elizabeth Solopova has devoted a more
extensive part of her analysis of Wycliffite manuscripts in the Bodleian and
Oxford College libraries to the liturgical texts, making some important
observations as to the visual and textual features of OTL. She identified
two distinct categories of texts, which she termed Type I and Type II,[9]
and this distinction is adopted and further refined in my study. The present edition of OTL takes the next step in these scholarly investigations in
order to provide a basis for further enquiry into this text and its history.

This edition presents, for the first time, one of the main versions of
this important Wycliffite text, together with an analysis of key aspects of
OTL and their significance for our understanding of the Wycliffite textual
enterprise. One of the key difficulties in editing OTL is the complexity
of its textual variation. The thirty-nine extant witnesses fall into distinct
groups, which can be identified in terms of the different sources they use:

---

[6] J. Forshall and F. Madden (eds.), *The Holy Bible . . . in the Earliest English Versions Made
from the Latin Vulgate by John Wycliffe and his Followers*, 4 vols. (Oxford, 1850).

[7] Anne Hudson, *The Premature Reformation* (Oxford, 1988), 198–9.

[8] Dove, *The First English Bible*, 61–5.

[9] Elizabeth Solopova, *Manuscripts of the Wycliffite Bible in the Bodleian and Oxford College
Libraries*, Exeter Medieval Texts and Studies (Liverpool, 2016), 7–17.

these are EV and/or LV, or independent translations of the Latin sources in the Vulgate or the Sarum Missal.

This variation in the use of sources produces great textual variation among the individual groups. At the same time, witnesses within each group are textually closely related and show little variation. In this context the idea of 'version' must be understood as distinct from the idea of 'recension', because, although the different groups share a structure, for the texts each group draws on different sources or different combinations of sources. However, these different versions can be seen as evidence of the chronological development of these translations of liturgical texts, as they are linked to the two Wycliffite translations EV and LV and marked by an increasing uniformity of presentation. The textual tradition of the OTL as a whole presents a difficult problem for an editor aiming to take into account all of the witnesses, and it is doubtful whether collation on this basis would be desirable, as collation is unhelpful in cases where completely different translations of the Latin sources are used. The corpus of variants would become unmanageable and ultimately of little use. The solution that has been adopted here is to use one of the versions as the basis for the edition and not to attempt to produce a critical edition of the OTL in the traditional sense. The version that has been chosen is Type II B because of its particular textual features and because it presents a transitional stage in the development of OTL, sharing features both with Type III and the (probably later) Type I. Variants are given from representative manuscripts of all relevant textual groups, except where collation is not possible owing to the degree of variation. This approach has been chosen in order to give the reader an overview of the textual differences between the various groups and the parameters of the transmission of the text, while keeping the apparatus to a manageable length. As witnesses within each group are textually closely related, through this approach it is possible to show the textual differences between these groups with relative accuracy. At the same time, this approach enables the edition to present a wider range of textual information than would have been the case had the collation been restricted to manuscripts within a single group. In other words, the editorial method followed in this edition is a hybrid method; rather than being a conventional critical edition it aims at being a 'working edition' displaying the breadth of this textual tradition and its development.[10]

The textual features of OTL and their relationship with EV and LV are further discussed in §II below, as well as in the Explanatory Notes. As a

---

[10] This selective editorial approach is somewhat similar to that used by Ralph Hanna in his edition of *Speculum Vitae*, which he calls 'a reading edition' (EETS os 331–2, 2008).

liturgical text, OTL not only uses the biblical text but also gives it a liturgical setting based on the Use of Sarum. The relationship between OTL and the Sarum Missal is further discussed in the Explanatory Notes. For any scholar working with medieval liturgy, the absence of a reliable modern edition of the Sarum Missal presents a significant problem. The two main editions of the Sarum Missal in existence were prepared by J. Wickham Legg[11] and by F. H. Dickinson.[12] However, neither of these is ideal for the scholar working with Wycliffite texts, as Legg's edition is chiefly based on thirteenth-century texts and is therefore too early as a point of comparison, while Dickinson used the early printed Sarum missals, which are too late to represent the Use of Sarum in its fourteenth-century form.[13] In the absence of such an edition, the present study uses both Legg's and Dickinson's editions as points of reference on specific liturgical texts, and notes which one has been adopted in cases where there are significant differences between the two. There are similar problems with establishing the exact form of the Vulgate to which the Wycliffite translators had recourse. The inaccuracies of the 'Paris Bibles' were well known to the Wycliffite translators (as they are to modern scholars), and although there have been some recent attempts at tracing the ways in which the Wycliffites sought to establish a more accurate Latin text,[14] the specific form of the version of the Vulgate which they used as the basis of their translations remains largely unclear, especially in the books of the Old Testament. In the interest of convenience, the present edition uses Weber and Gryson's edition of the Vulgate as a point of reference,[15] while keeping in mind the problems outlined above.

The introductory material to this edition contains a full list of all extant OTL manuscripts, together with information on their type and the translation they use. This section also includes descriptions of these manuscripts, with a focus on the features of OTL in each. This is followed by an explanation of the categorization of the manuscripts into distinct groups and their chronology. The next section contains an extensive table of all lections, the manuscripts within which they appear, and what translation

---

[11] *The Sarum Missal, Edited from Three Early Manuscripts*, ed. J. Wickham Legg (Oxford, 1916).

[12] *Missale ad usum insignis et praeclarae ecclesiae Sarum*, ed. Francis Henry Dickinson (Burntisland, 1861–83).

[13] Richard W. Pfaff, *The Liturgy in Medieval England* (Cambridge, 2009), 357, discusses the problems with these editions in greater detail.

[14] Ralph Hanna, 'The Wycliffite Translators' Vulgate Manuscript: The Evidence from Mark', *Medium Ævum*, 86 (2017), 60–90.

[15] *Biblia Sacra iuxta Vulgatam versionem*, ed. Robert Weber and Roger Gryson, 5th rev. edn., ed. Roger Gryson (Stuttgart, 2007).

they use. This is followed by a discussion of the language of the collated manuscripts, based on linguistic profiles of twenty test items. The section following discusses in greater detail crucial visual and textual features, such as methods of cross-referencing and use of Wycliffite translations, with the aim of drawing conclusions as to OTL's production and use. A part of this analysis is devoted to TOL and its relationship with OTL. Due to the aforementioned problems with F&M's edition of TOL, a new edition of TOL which represents one specific type, rather than a conflation of several types, is presented in the Appendix. The editorial policy for both OTL and TOL is detailed in the last section.

The presentation of parts of the introductory material in the form of extensive tables is intended to make the information more readily accessible. It is the aim of this edition to provide a basis for further investigation of the OTL and its numerous manuscripts within the context of the large number of academic, educational, and scholarly initiatives characteristic of the Wycliffite endeavour. There is scope for a number of future editions of other versions, particularly of the version in Group II D, which is not the main focus of the present study. It is to be hoped that future work will analyse in greater detail the particular features characteristic of that version.

I. MANUSCRIPTS CONTAINING THE OLD TESTAMENT LECTIONARY

The following table contains a list of all thirty-nine extant OTL manuscripts. Details of the type and group of each OTL are also given.[16] The column 'Version' refers to the version used in OTL, which can differ from the version used in the other texts in the same manuscript. Where a version is listed as EV+LV, it means that the OTL uses predominantly EV+LV (in addition to some independent translations, which are not mentioned explicitly in this table and in the manuscript descriptions in §2 but are discussed in detail in §V.6 below). EV OTLs do not use LV. Sigla used in this edition follow F&M; sigla in italics are used for EV manuscripts. Where F&M did not assign a siglum to a manuscript, this edition uses a new siglum, which—in contrast to sigla from F&M—consists of two letters. The last column serves the purpose of cross-referencing the manuscripts with earlier scholarship: it contains numbers given in F&M as well as those by Conrad Lindberg (marked in italics).[17]

---

[16] For further details on this categorization, refer to §II below.

[17] Conrad Lindberg, 'The Manuscripts and Versions of the Wycliffite Bible', *Studia Neophilologica*, 42 (1970), 333–47. Sigla and numbers in this table follow the index of manuscripts of WB in Elizabeth Solopova, 'Index of Manuscripts of the Wycliffite Bible', in Solopova (ed.),

1. List of Manuscripts

MS	Type	Version	Siglum	F&M no.
Berkeley, Bancroft Library, 128	II C	EV+LV	Ba	*226*
Cambridge, Jesus College, 47 (Q. D. 6.)	II B	EV+LV	s	121
Cambridge, Magdalene College, Pepys 2073	I	EV+LV	w	125
Cambridge, Sidney Sussex College, 99	II D	EV	*N*	127
Cambridge, Trinity College Library, B. 10. 20	II A	EV+LV	Tc	135
Cambridge, University Library, Add. 6683	II C	EV+LV	Ua	*176*
Cambridge, University Library, Add. 10068 (British and Foreign Bible Society, Eng 1,2)	II C	EV+LV	Ub	
Cambridge, University Library, Kk. 1. 8	—	EV+LV	ι	110
Cambridge, University Library, Ll. 1. 13	II C	EV+LV	Ul	111
Dresden, Sächsische Landesbibliothek, Od. 83	I	EV+LV	Dr	
Dublin, Trinity College, 75	II A	EV+LV	Ta[18]	151
Dunedin, New Zealand, Public Library, Reed Fragment 20 (fragment)	III	EV+LV	Du	
London, British Library, Arundel 254	II D	EV	*Ar*	30
London, British Library, Egerton 1171	I	EV+LV	Eg	34
London, British Library, Harley 1029	II D	EV	*He*	
London, British Library, Harley 1710	II D	EV	*Hl*	
London, British Library, Harley 6333	I	EV+LV	o	25
London, British Library, Lansdowne 455	II C	EV+LV	Ln	28
London, Lambeth Palace Library, 369	—	EV+LV	x	47
London, Lambeth Palace Library, 532	I	EV+LV	La	38
London, Lambeth Palace Library, Sion College ARC L 40.2/E.2	II B	EV+LV	Si	43
Manchester, John Rylands Library, Eng. 80	II A	EV+LV	r	157
New York, Columbia University, Plimpton Add. 03	II D	EV	*Pl*	*194*
New York, Morgan Library, M. 362 (fragment)	—	EV+LV	Mo	*221*
New York, New York Public Library, 64	II B	EV+LV	Ny	*201*
Orlando, Van Kampen Collection, 641	III	EV+LV	Vk	
Oxford, Bodleian Library, Ashmole 1517	II A	EV+LV	As	89
Oxford, Bodleian Library, Bodley 531	III	EV+LV	Bx	62
Oxford, Bodleian Library, Bodley 665	II B	EV+LV	Bo	63

The Wycliffite Bible: Origin, History and Interpretation, Medieval and Renaissance Authors and Texts, 16 (Leiden, 2017), 484–92.

[18] F&M use the siglum *T* in italics here, since the New Testament in this manuscript uses EV. However, the OTL is predominantly in LV. To reflect this, I have chosen the new siglum Ta, which is not in italics.

Oxford, Bodleian Library, Douce 265-a (fragment)	III	EV+LV Do	
Oxford, Bodleian Library, Laud misc. 388	I	EV+LV Lm	
Oxford, Bodleian Library, Rawlinson C. 259	II C	EV+LV Ra[19]	80
Oxford, Bodleian Library, Selden supra 51	II A	EV+LV Se	69
Oxford, Christ Church, 146	II B	EV+LV Cc	92
Princeton, University Library, Scheide Library 13	II B	EV+LV Pr	169
Warminster, Longleat House, 5	III	EV+LV Lt	*179*
Worcester, Cathedral Library, Q. 84	I	EV+LV Wo	140
New Haven, Yale University Library, Takamiya 113 (fragment)	III	EV+LV Ty	
York, Minster Library, XVI. N. 7	II C	EV+LV Yo	141

2. Manuscript Descriptions

In its prototypical form, the visual presentation of OTL resembles that of many Wycliffite Bibles (see Plate 1 above). The text is typically written in textura of varying levels of formality and laid out in two columns, frequently with running titles which refer to the liturgical season in the Temporale and the months in the Sanctorale. Individual lections are preceded by a rubric referring to the liturgical occasion and the biblical book and chapter, usually followed by an indexing letter, which is often placed in the margin. Initials are executed in red and blue and decorated with red penwork. Extra-biblical material, such as liturgical additions at the start and end of lections, is underlined in red. The end of each lection is frequently indicated by double strokes placed in the margin. There are, however, several manuscripts which deviate from these typical features in a number of ways, as will be apparent from the descriptions below.

The base text of this edition is described first, in some detail. The other extant OTL manuscripts are ordered conventionally (location, repository, shelfmark), preceded by the siglum. These descriptions (necessarily very abbreviated) are principally intended to outline the features of the OTL in each manuscript and bring to the fore similarities and differences between the manuscripts' visual and textual features.[20] The abbreviations used to

---

[19] The siglum used in F&M for this manuscript is *b*. F&M used it only to collate the Prologue to Romans (i, p. xxxvi), and chose a siglum in italics since this text is in EV. The OTL, however, is predominantly in LV, and I have therefore chosen a new siglum for the purposes of this edition.

[20] These features are further discussed in §V.5 below. Wycliffite manuscripts are notoriously difficult to date owing to the predominance of textura in a large majority of surviving manuscripts. No attempt has been made at dating beyond repeating the well-known fact that

describe the order of sections in the OTL are as follows: T = Temporale, S = Sanctorale, C = Commemorations, NS = non-Sarum lections. CL is used to indicate the presence of a Calendar-lectionary, and the relation between CL and TOL is discussed in greater detail in §V.1 below. If a typical textual or visual feature of OTL, such as blue initials with red penwork, is not mentioned in a description, this feature is absent from the manuscript in question.

Bo: Oxford, Bodleian Library, Bodley 665

NT in the later Wycliffite translation (LV), with liturgical materials. Middle English.

169 parchment leaves, 176×118 mm (trimmed in later rebinding), written frame 116×80 mm, ruled in ink in two columns with one vertical and two horizontal bounding lines, 34 lines per page; pricking occasionally survives. Running titles and rubrication throughout. Modern foliation in pencil i–iv+1–169.

DECORATION: 4- to 9-line gold initials at the beginnings of biblical books and some prologues, borders decorated with floral designs in pink, blue, and gold. Three-line blue initials with red penwork at the beginning of chapters. Catchwords decorated with floral designs in black ink, red, and yellow.

SCRIPT: informal textura

COLLATION: (ff. i–iv) i paper and iii parchment flyleaves, (ff. 1–12) I¹², (ff. 13–36) II–IV⁸, (ff. 37–43) V⁸ (3 cancelled), (ff. 44–267) VI–XXXIII⁸, (ff. 268–9) i parchment singleton, i paper flyleaf. Catchwords and occasional leaf signatures (aj, aij, etc.) survive.

CONTENTS

1. (ff. 1ʳ–12ᵛ) Table of lections of Type I, beginning 'Here bigynneþ a reule þat telliþ in whiche chapitris of þe bible 3e may fynde þe lessouns pistlis and gospelis'

2. (ff. 13ʳ–226ᵛ) NT in LV with prologues, beginning 'Matheu þat was of Iudee'

3. (ff. 226ᵛ–266ʳ) OTL of Type II B, beginning 'here endiþ þe apocalips of Ioon and also þe newe testament And here bigynnen þe lessouns and pistlis of þe olde lawe'. Blue initials with red penwork, running titles giving liturgical season, rubrics giving details for each lection, added

most of the manuscripts were produced in the late fourteenth or early fifteenth century. On problems of dating see Ralph Hanna, 'The Palaeography of the Wycliffite Bibles in Oxford', in Solopova (ed.), *The Wycliffite Bible*, 246–65.

material underlined in red. Indexing letters A–L. Order of sections: T–S–C. Introductory liturgical material at the start of lections ('þe lord saiþ þese þingis', etc.)

BINDING: 16th century, leather on wood boards; the front board has become detached. Recesses for clasps which are now missing. Sewn on five cords.

PROVENANCE: English notes by 16th-century owner in the margins and in calendar. Owned by Thomas Bodley and given to the library in 1602.

2° fol. Twelfþe ny3t

BIBLIOGRAPHY

F&M, i, p. xlvii.
Madan and Craster, *Summary Catalogue*, ii, pt. 1, no. 2998.
Ogilvie-Thomson, *Index of Middle English Prose: Handlist VIII*, 17.
Scott, *An Index of Images*, no. 273.
Solopova, 'Manuscript Evidence for the Patronage, Ownership and Use of the Wycliffite Bible', 338 n. 15.
Solopova, *MSS of WB*, 77–83.

Ba: Berkeley, Bancroft Library, 128

OTL Type II C on ff. 226ʳ–261ᵛ. Other contents: TOL, NT (LV). OTL version: EV+LV. Order of sections in OTL: T–S–C. Introductory liturgical material at the start of lections ('þe lord saiþ þese þingis', etc.). Referencing system: indexing letters only on first leaf, then abandoned. TOL Type: I.

280×185 mm. Blue initials with red penwork, some initials illuminated. Running titles giving liturgical season. Rubrics giving details for each lection. Added material underlined in red. Two columns. Script: textura.

BIBLIOGRAPHY

Digital Scriptorium ⟨http://ds.lib.berkeley.edu/BANCMSUCB128_1⟩.

s: Cambridge, Jesus College, 47 (Q. D. 6.)

OTL Type II B on ff. 341ᵛ–394ᵛ. Other contents: Table of contents for NT, TOL, NT (LV). OTL version: EV+LV. Order of sections in OTL: T–S–C. Introductory liturgical material at the start of lections ('þe lord saiþ þese þingis', etc.). Referencing system: indexing letters A–L. TOL Type: I.

165×117 mm. Blue initials with red penwork, illuminated on first leaf. Running titles giving liturgical season. Rubrics giving details for each lection. Added material underlined in red. Two columns. Script: textura.

BIBLIOGRAPHY

James, *A Descriptive Catalogue . . . Jesus College, Cambridge*, no. 47.

w: Cambridge, Magdalene College, Pepys 2073

OTL Type I on ff. 287^r–337^r. Other contents: NT (LV), TOL. OTL version: EV+LV. Order of sections in OTL: T–S–C–NS. Introductory liturgical material at the start of lections ('þe lord saiþ þese þingis', etc.). Referencing system: indexing letters A–L. TOL Type: I.

275×180 mm. Blue initials with red penwork. Running titles giving liturgical season, alternating red (on verso) and blue (on recto). Rubrics giving details for each lection, preceded by blue paraphs. Added material underlined in red. Two columns. Script: textura.

BIBLIOGRAPHY

McKitterick and Beadle, *Catalogue of the Pepys Library*, v, pt. i, no. 2073.

N: Cambridge, Sidney Sussex College, 99

OTL Type II D on ff. 208^r–238^v. Other contents: TOL, NT (EV). OTL version: EV. Order of sections in OTL: T–S–C. No introductory liturgical material at the start of lections. Referencing system: no indexing letters. TOL Type: II (does not agree completely with OTL).

311×216 mm. Blue initials with red penwork. Rubrics giving details for each lection, including Latin incipit, usually preceded by blue paraph. Added material underlined in red. Two columns. Script: textura.

BIBLIOGRAPHY

James, *A Descriptive Catalogue . . . Sidney Sussex College, Cambridge*, no. 99.

Tc: Cambridge, Trinity College Library, B. 10. 20

OTL Type II A on ff. 240^r–272^r. Other contents: Calendar, NT (LV), capitula list, CL, TOL. OTL version: EV+LV. Order of sections in OTL: T–S–C. Introductory liturgical material at the start of lections ('þe lord saiþ þese þingis', etc.). Referencing system: 4 sections A–D in upper margin, references with letters and numbers, e.g. a1, a2, . . . (similar to Se and Tc), indexing letters A–L also given. TOL Type: unclear (S in calendar instead of TOL).

168×114 mm. Blue initials with red penwork. Running titles giving liturgical season. Rubrics giving details for each lection. Added material underlined in red. Two columns. Script: informal textura.

BIBLIOGRAPHY

James, *The Western Manuscripts . . . Trinity College, Cambridge*, no. 231.

Ub: Cambridge, University Library, Add. 10068 (formerly British and Foreign Bible Society, Eng 1,2)

OTL Type II C on ff. 1^r–35^v. Other contents: NT (LV) (bound separately). OTL version: EV+LV. Order of sections in OTL: T–S–C. Introductory liturgical material at the start of lections ('þe lord saiþ þese þingis', etc.). No referencing system, no indexing letters. No TOL.

143×110 mm. Blue initials with red penwork. Rubrics giving details for each lection. Added material underlined (black ink for liturgical additions, red for alternative translations and other additions). Two columns. Script: textura.

BIBLIOGRAPHY

Ker, *Medieval Manuscripts in British Libraries*, i. 7–8.

Ua: Cambridge, University Library, Add. 6683

OTL Type II C on ff. 269^r–312^r. Other contents: TOL, NT (LV). OTL version: EV+LV. Order of sections in OTL: T–S–C. Introductory liturgical material at the start of lections ('þe lord saiþ þese þingis', etc.). Referencing system: column ruled in OTL for indexing letters, but only infrequently added (e.g. f. 275^r), full set of indexing letters in TOL. TOL Type: I (order of sections: T–C–S).

203×143 mm. Blue initials with red penwork, illuminated for first lection. Running titles giving liturgical season. Rubrics giving details for each lection. Added material underlined in red. Two columns. Script: informal textura.

BIBLIOGRAPHY

Ringrose, *Summary Catalogue*, 254.

ι: Cambridge, University Library, Kk. 1. 8

OTL Type: uncategorized. Fragmentary OTL on ff. 182^r–186^v (lacuna on ff. 184^v–185^r). Other contents: GP, TOL, NT (LV), capitula list for NT. OTL version: EV+LV. Christmas lection does not give parts which are sung. Order of sections in OTL: unclear. No introductory liturgical material at the start of lections. No referencing system in OTL, no indexing letters. TOL Type: II.

271×197 mm. Blue initials with red penwork. Details for each lection given in Latin and preceded by red paraphs. Two columns. Script: anglicana in OTL (textura in TOL).

BIBLIOGRAPHY

A Catalogue of the Manuscripts Preserved in the Library of the University of Cambridge, iii, no. 1942 (p. 566).

Ul: Cambridge, University Library, Ll. 1. 13

OTL Type II C on ff. 2^r–56^v (NT epistles and OT lessons until f. 34^r, then only OT lections). Other contents: TOL, NT (LV). OTL version: EV+ LV. Order of sections in OTL: T–S–C. No introductory liturgical material at the start of lections. No referencing system: no indexing letters (in TOL a column is ruled for indexing letters, but has not been filled in). TOL Type: II (without S).

236×175 mm. Blue initials with red penwork. Rubrics giving details for each lection. Added material underlined in red. Two columns. Script: textura.

BIBLIOGRAPHY

A Catalogue of the Manuscripts Preserved in the Library of the University of Cambridge, iv, no. 2142 (p. 7).

Dr: Dresden, Sächsische Landesbibliothek, Od. 83

OTL Type I on ff. 352^v–410^r. Other contents: TOL, NT (LV). OTL version: EV+LV. Order of sections in OTL: T–S–C–NS. Introductory liturgical material at the start of lections ('þe lord saiþ þese þingis', etc.). Referencing system: indexing letters A–L, cross-references for repeated lections using foliation in original hand. TOL Type: I.

170×120 mm. Blue initials with red penwork. Running titles giving liturgical season. Rubrics giving details for each lection. Added material underlined in red. Two columns. Script: textura.

BIBLIOGRAPHY

Schnorr von Carolsfeld and Schmidt, *Katalog der Handschriften der Sächsischen Landesbibliothek zu Dresden*, iii. 142–3.

Ta: Dublin, Trinity College, 75

OTL Type II A on ff. 247^r–281^r. Other contents: Concordance of gospel passages, TOL, NT (EV), GP, Latin letter to Cardinal Henry Beaufort. OTL version: EV+LV. Order of sections in OTL: T–C–S. Introductory liturgical material at the start of lections ('þe lord saiþ þese þingis', etc.). Referencing system: OTL does not have indexing letters; TOL has indexing letters A–G. Folios 1–4 of OTL foliated in original hand, starting at 1. TOL Type: II, incomplete (incipit and explicit for OT lections given only on ff. 4ʳ–5ʳ, indicating that OTL was written separately). 310×225 mm. Relatively small, simple red initials (2 lines deep), without penwork. No running titles. Rubrics giving details for each lection (probably added after main text was written). Added material not underlined. Two columns. Script: secretary (OTL in same hand as GP and Latin letter, with rubricated punctuation marks). GP, Latin letter, and OTL form a unit which is codicologically separate from the rest of the manuscript.

BIBLIOGRAPHY

Abbott, *Catalogue of the Manuscripts in the Library of Trinity College, Dublin*, no. 75 (p. 10).

Colker, *Trinity College Library: Descriptive Catalogue*, i. 119.

Scattergood and Latré, *Dublin, Trinity College Library MS 75*, 163–80.

Scattergood, Pattwell, and Williams, *Trinity College Library Dublin: A Descriptive Catalogue of Manuscripts*, 40–53.

Du: Dunedin, New Zealand, Public Library, Reed Fragment 20

OTL Type III (OTL inserted into TOL). Fragment (one leaf), perhaps from same manuscript as Ty. OTL version: EV+LV. Introductory liturgical material at the start of lections ('þe lord saiþ þese þingis', etc.). Referencing system: indexing letters A–L. TOL Type: III. 210×131 mm. Blue initials with red penwork. Running titles giving liturgical season. Rubrics giving details for each lection. Added material underlined in red. One column. Script: informal textura.

BIBLIOGRAPHY

Manion, Vines, and de Hamel, *Medieval and Renaissance Manuscripts in New Zealand Collections*, no. 83 (p. 98).

o: London, British Library, Harley 6333

OTL Type I on ff. 307ʳ–364ᵛ. Bound in 2 volumes. Other contents: *oon of foure*, NT lections; rest of NT (LV), capitula list of OT, TOL, CL. OTL version: EV+LV. Order in OTL: T–S–C–NS. Introductory liturgical material at the start of lections ('þe lord saiþ þese þingis', etc.). Referencing system: indexing letters A–L, cross-references for repeated lections using foliation in original hand. TOL Type: I (adapted for *oon of foure*).

270×195 mm. Elaborate blue initials with red penwork. Running titles giving liturgical season. Rubrics giving details for each lection. Added material underlined in red. Two columns. Script: textura.

BIBLIOGRAPHY

BLOC ⟨https://www.bl.uk/catalogues/illuminatedmanuscripts/record.asp?MSID=18708&CollID=8&NStart=6333⟩.
A Catalogue of the Harleian Manuscripts in the British Museum, iii, no. 6333.

Ar: London, British Library, Arundel 254

OTL Type II D on ff. 104^r–135^v. Other contents: *oon of foure* and epistles, chapter list, TOL (only gospel lections from *oon of foure*). OTL atelous. OTL version: EV. Order of sections in OTL: T–S (atelous). No introductory liturgical material at the start of lections. No referencing system, no indexing letters. No TOL.

231×145 mm. Blue initials with red penwork. No running titles. Liturgical occasion at the start of each lection underlined in red, preceded by blue paraph, and followed by Latin incipit. Added material occasionally underlined in red. Two columns. Script: anglicana formata.

BIBLIOGRAPHY

BLOC ⟨https://www.bl.uk/catalogues/illuminatedmanuscripts/record.asp?MSID=7274&CollID=20&NStart=254⟩.
Catalogue of Manuscripts in the British Museum, NS, i: *The Arundel Manuscripts*, no. 254 (p. 77).

Eg: London, British Library, Egerton 1171

OTL Type I on ff. 300^r–357^r. Other contents: Calendar, TOL, NT (LV). OTL version: EV+LV. Order of sections in OTL: T–S–C–NS. Introductory liturgical material at the start of lections ('þe lord saiþ þese þingis', etc.). Referencing system: indexing letters A–L. TOL Type: I. Order of sections in TOL: T–C–S (different from OTL).

148×95 mm. Blue initials with red penwork. Running titles giving liturgical season. Rubrics giving details for each lection, preceded by blue paraph. Added material underlined in red. Two columns. Script: textura.

BIBLIOGRAPHY

BLOC ⟨https://www.bl.uk/catalogues/illuminatedmanuscripts/record.asp?MSID=6673&CollID=28&NStart=1171⟩.

A Guide to the Exhibition . . . Egerton Collection of Manuscripts in the British Museum, no. 57.

Thompson, *Wycliffe Exhibition in the King's Library*, no. 50.

He: London, British Library, Harley 1029

OTL Type II D on ff. 2ʳ–212ʳ. Other contents: NT lections (full lectionary, similar to *Hl*). OTL version: EV. Order of sections in OTL: T–S–C. No introductory liturgical material at the start of lections. No referencing system, no indexing letters. No TOL.

241 × 170 mm. Blue initials with red penwork. No running titles. Liturgical occasion at the start of each lection underlined in red, preceded by blue paraph, and followed by rubric giving Latin incipit and biblical book and chapter. Added material underlined in red. One column. Script: informal textura.

BIBLIOGRAPHY

A Catalogue of the Harleian Manuscripts in the British Museum, ii, no. 1029.

Hl: London, British Library, Harley 1710

OTL Type II D on ff. 2ʳ–164ᵛ. Other contents: NT lections (full lectionary, similar to *He*). OTL version: EV. Order of sections in OTL: T–S–C. No introductory liturgical material at the start of lections. No referencing system, no indexing letters. No TOL.

263 × 190 mm. Blue initials with red penwork, one puzzle initial in red and blue on f. 2ʳ. No running titles. Liturgical occasion at the start of each lection underlined in red, preceded by blue paraph, and followed by rubric giving Latin incipit and biblical book and chapter. Added material underlined in black. Two columns. Script: informal textura.

BIBLIOGRAPHY

BLOC ⟨https://www.bl.uk/catalogues/illuminatedmanuscripts/record.asp?MSID=3535&CollID=8&NStart=1710⟩

A Catalogue of the Harleian Manuscripts in the British Museum, ii, no. 1710.

Ln: London, British Library, Lansdowne 455

OTL Type II C on ff. 18ʳ–33ᵛ. Other contents: Lections of the Office, tracts by Richard Rolle, Calendar, TOL, NT (LV). OTL version: EV + LV. Order of sections in OTL: T–S–C. Introductory liturgical material at the start of lections ('þe lord saiþ þese þingis', etc.). Referencing system: indexing letters A–L. TOL Type: I.

369×236 mm. Blue initials with red penwork. Running titles giving liturgical season on a few leaves. Rubrics giving details for each lection. Added material underlined in red. Two columns. Script: textura.

BIBLIOGRAPHY

BLOC ⟨https://www.bl.uk/catalogues/illuminatedmanuscripts/record.asp?MSID=5281&CollID=15&NStart=455⟩.

Hanna, *The English Manuscripts of Richard Rolle: A Descriptive Catalogue*, no. 52.

Thompson, *Wycliffe Exhibition in the King's Library*, no. 44.

x: London, Lambeth Palace, 369

OTL Type II (?) on ff. 251^v–252^v (fragment). Other contents: NT (LV). OTL version: EV(?)+LV. Order of sections in OTL: unclear. Introductory liturgical material at the start of lections ('þe lord saiþ þese þingis', etc.). No referencing system, no indexing letters. No TOL.

245×179 mm. Blue initials with red penwork, illuminated initial on f. 251^v. No running titles. Rubrics giving details for each lection. Added material not underlined. Two columns. Script: textura.

BIBLIOGRAPHY

James, *A Descriptive Catalogue of the Manuscripts in the Library of Lambeth Palace*, no. 369.

La: London, Lambeth Palace Library, 532

OTL Type I on ff. 366^r–430^v. Other contents: TOL, NT (LV), capitula list. OTL version: EV+LV. Order of sections in OTL: T–S–C–NS. Introductory liturgical material at the start of lections ('þe lord saiþ þese þingis', etc.). Referencing system: indexing letters A–L, cross-references for repeated lections using foliation in original hand. TOL Type: I.

173×121 mm. Blue initials with red penwork, one puzzle initial on f. 366^r. Running titles giving liturgical season, preceded by blue paraphs. Rubrics giving details for each lection. Added material underlined in red. Two columns. Script: textura.

BIBLIOGRAPHY

James, *A Descriptive Catalogue of the Manuscripts in the Library of Lambeth Palace*, no. 532.

Si: London, Lambeth Palace Library, Sion College ARC L 40.2/E.2

OTL Type II B on ff. 269^r–316^v. Other contents: NT (LV) and prologues. OTL version: EV+LV. Order of sections in OTL: T–S–C. No introductory liturgical material at the start of lections. No referencing system, no indexing letters. No TOL.

161×115 mm. Blue initials with red penwork. Running titles giving liturgical season, preceded by blue paraphs. Rubrics giving details for each lection. Added material underlined in red. One column. Script: textura.

BIBLIOGRAPHY

Ker, *Medieval Manuscripts in British Libraries*, i. 288.
Pickering and O'Mara, *The Index of Middle English Prose, Handlist 13*, 79–80.

r: Manchester, John Rylands Library, Eng. 80

OTL Type II A on ff. 272^r–316^v (first leaf missing). Other contents: Table of moveable feasts, calendar, table to determine the date of Easter, TOL, NT (LV). OTL version: EV+LV. Order in OTL: T–C–S. Introductory liturgical material at the start of lections ('þe lord saiþ þese þingis', etc.). Referencing system: indexing letters A–L, some supplied by different hand. TOL Type: I (order of sections: T–S–C).

215×147 mm. Blue initials with red penwork. Rubrics giving details for each lection, preceded by blue paraphs. Added material usually not underlined in red. Two columns. Script: informal textura.

BIBLIOGRAPHY

Tyson, *Hand-List of the Collection of English Manuscripts in the John Rylands Library*, no. 80 (p. 18).
Ker, *Medieval Manuscripts in British Libraries*, iii. 406.

Ny: New York, New York Public Library, 64

OTL Type II B on ff. 261^r–308^r. Other contents: TOL, NT (LV). OTL version: EV+LV. Order in OTL: T–S–C. Introductory liturgical material at the start of lections ('þe lord saiþ þese þingis', etc.). Referencing system: indexing letters A–L. TOL Type: I.

187×126 mm. Blue initials with red penwork. Running titles giving liturgical season. Rubrics giving details for each lection. Added material underlined in red. Two columns. Script: informal textura.

BIBLIOGRAPHY

Digital Scriptorium ⟨http://ds.lib.berkeley.edu/NYPLMA064_41⟩.

Pl: New York, Columbia University, Plimpton Add. 03

OTL Type II D on ff. 242ʳ–265ᵛ. Other contents: NT (EV), Lollard Chronicle of the Papacy, Prophecy of St Hildegard, Seven Words of Christ. OTL version: EV. Order in OTL: T–S–C. No introductory liturgical material at the start of lections. No referencing system, no indexing letters. No TOL. 250×170 mm. Blue initials. Rubrics giving details for each lection, followed by Latin incipit in black ink, usually preceded by blue paraph. Added material underlined in red. One column. Script: anglicana formata.

BIBLIOGRAPHY

Digital Scriptorium ⟨http://ds.lib.berkeley.edu/PlimptonAdd.MS03_20⟩.

As: Oxford, Bodleian Library, Ashmole 1517

OTL Type II A on ff. 166ʳ–192ʳ. Other contents: TOL, NT (LV). OTL incomplete. OTL version: EV+LV. Order of sections in OTL: T–C–S. Introductory liturgical material at the start of lections ('þe lord saiþ þese þingis', etc.). Referencing system: 5 sections A–E in upper margin, references with letters and numbers, e.g. a1, a2, . . . (similar to Se and Tc), indexing letters A–L also given. TOL Type: unclear (Sanctorale in calendar?). TOL incomplete, possibly originally preceded by calendar. 280×205 mm. Blue initials with red penwork. Rubrics giving details for each lection. Added material underlined in red. Two columns. Script: informal textura.

BIBLIOGRAPHY

Eldredge, *Index of Middle English Prose, Handlist IX*, 108.
Ogilvie-Thomson, *Index of Middle English Prose, Handlist VIII*, 15.
Scott, *An Index of Images*, no. 83.
Solopova, *MSS of WB*, 37–41.

Bx: Oxford, Bodleian Library, Bodley 531

OTL Type III on ff. 1ʳ–37ᵛ (OTL inserted into TOL). Other contents: NT (LV). OTL incomplete. OTL version: EV+LV. Order of sections in OTL: T–C–S. Introductory liturgical material at the start of lections ('þe lord saiþ þese þingis', etc.). Referencing system: indexing letters A–L. TOL Type: III.

205×142 mm. Blue initials with red penwork. Running titles giving liturgical season. Rubrics giving details for each lection. Added material underlined in red. One column. Script: informal textura.

BIBLIOGRAPHY

Solopova, *MSS of WB*, 66–72.

Do: Oxford, Bodleian Library, Douce 265-a

OTL Type III (OTL inserted into TOL). Fragment (one bifolium); bound with MS Douce 265 by Francis Douce (?). OTL version: EV+LV. Order of sections in OTL: T–C. Does not include Wednesday after 25th Sunday after Trinity. Referencing system: indexing letters A–L. TOL Type: III.
213×147 mm. Blue initials with red penwork. Running titles giving liturgical season. Rubrics giving details for each lection. Added material underlined in red. One column. Script: informal textura.

BIBLIOGRAPHY

Solopova, *MSS of WB*, 112–13.

Lm: Oxford, Bodleian Library, Laud misc. 388

OTL Type I on ff. 257^r–297^v. Other contents: CL, TOL, NT (LV). OTL atelous. OTL version: EV+LV. Order of sections in OTL: T–S–C–NS. Introductory liturgical material at the start of lections ('þe lord saiþ þese þingis', etc.). Referencing system: indexing letters A–L, cross-references for repeated lections using foliation in original hand. TOL Type: I.
220×150 mm. Blue initials with red penwork. Running titles giving liturgical season. Rubrics giving details for each lection. Added material underlined in red. Two columns. Script: textura.

BIBLIOGRAPHY

Ogilvie-Thomson, *Index of Middle English Prose, Handlist VIII*, 42–3.
Scott, *An Index of Images*, no. 666.
Solopova, *MSS of WB*, 186–92.

Ra: Oxford, Bodleian Library, Rawlinson C. 259

OTL Type II C on ff. 205^r–240^v (atelous). Other contents: Calendar, NT (LV), TOL. OTL version: EV+LV. Order in OTL: T–S–C. Introductory liturgical material at the start of lections ('þe lord saiþ þese þingis', etc.). Referencing system: indexing letters A–L. TOL Type: I.
189×122 mm. Blue initials with red penwork. Running titles giving

biblical book and chapter. Rubrics giving details for each lection. Added material underlined in red. Two columns. Script: textura.

BIBLIOGRAPHY

The Earlier Version of the Wycliffite Bible, ed. Lindberg, viii. 274.
Hudson, 'Lollard Book Production', 140.
Scott, *An Index of Images*, no. 863.
Solopova, *MSS of WB*, 211–15.

Se: Oxford, Bodleian Library, Selden supra 51

OTL Type II A on ff. 284^r–326^v (OTL atelous but completed in different contemporary hand). Other contents: capitula list, CL, TOL, NT (LV). OTL version: EV+LV. Order in OTL: T–C–S. Introductory liturgical material at the start of lections ('þe lord saiþ þese þingis', etc.). Referencing system: 5 sections A–E in upper margin, references with letters and numbers, e.g. a1, a2, . . . (similar to As and Tc), indexing letters A–L also given. TOL Type: unclear (S in calendar instead of TOL).

146×208 mm. Blue initials with red penwork. Rubrics giving details for each lection. Added material underlined in red. Two columns. Script: informal textura.

BIBLIOGRAPHY

Hudson, 'Lollard Book Production', 140.
Scott, *An Index of Images*, no. 1015.
Solopova, *MSS of WB*, 223–26.

Cc: Oxford, Christ Church, 146

OTL Type II B on ff. 200^v–231^v. Other contents: TOL, NT (LV), capitula list for NT. OTL version: EV+LV. Order of sections in OTL: T–S–C. Introductory liturgical material at the start of lections ('þe lord saiþ þese þingis', etc.). Referencing system: indexing letters A–L. TOL Type: I.

197×125 mm. Blue initials with red penwork. Running titles giving liturgical season. Rubrics giving details for each lection. Added material underlined in red. Two columns. Script: textura.

BIBLIOGRAPHY

Hanna and Rundle, *A Descriptive Catalogue of the Western Manuscripts, to c. 1600, in Christ Church, Oxford*, 310–13.
Ogilvie-Thomson, *Index of Middle English Prose, Handlist VIII*, 16–17.
Solopova, *MSS of WB*, 235–38.

Pr: Princeton, University Library, Scheide Library 13

OTL Type II B on ff. 204^r–242^v. Other contents: TOL, NT (LV). OTL version: EV+LV. Order in OTL: T–S–C. Introductory liturgical material at the start of lections ('þe lord saiþ þese þingis', etc.). Referencing system: indexing letters A–L. TOL Type: I.

180×130 mm. Blue initials with red penwork, illuminated on first leaf. Running titles giving liturgical season. Rubrics giving details for each lection. Added material underlined in red. Two columns. Script: textura.

BIBLIOGRAPHY

De Ricci and Wilson, *Census of Medieval and Renaissance Manuscripts*, no. 13.

Lt: Warminster, Longleat House, 5

OTL Type III on ff. 1^r–36^v (OTL inserted into TOL). Other contents: NT (LV). OTL incomplete. OTL version: EV+LV. Order in OTL: T–S. Referencing system: indexing letters A–L. TOL Type: III.

Red initials. Running titles giving liturgical season. Rubrics giving details for each lection. Added material underlined in red, but no introductory liturgical material at the start of lections. One column. Script: informal textura.

Wo: Worcester, Cathedral Library, Q. 84

OTL Type I on ff. 248^r–294^r. Other contents: calendar, part of TOL, NT (LV). OTL version: EV+LV. Order of sections in OTL: T–S–C. Introductory liturgical material at the start of lections ('þe lord saiþ þese þingis', etc.). Referencing system: indexing letters A–L in the margins, preceded by blue or illuminated paraph and decorated by red or blue penwork. TOL Type: unclear (fragment).

210×140 mm. Blue initials with red penwork, some initials illuminated. Running titles giving liturgical season on some leaves. Rubrics giving details for each lection. Added material underlined in red. Two columns. Script: textura.

BIBLIOGRAPHY

Thomson, *A Descriptive Catalogue . . . Worcester Cathedral Library*, 178.

Ty: New Haven, Yale University Library, Takamiya 113

OTL Type III (OTL inserted into TOL). Fragment (one leaf), perhaps from same manuscript as Du. OTL version: EV+LV. Referencing system: indexing letters A–L. TOL Type: III.

186×145 mm. Blue initials with red penwork. Running titles, giving the liturgical season (?). Rubrics giving details for each lection. Added material underlined in red. One column. Script: informal textura.

BIBLIOGRAPHY

Clemens, Ducharme, and Ulrich, *A Gathering of Medieval English Manuscripts*, 38.

Yo: York, Minster Library, XVI. N. 7

OTL Type II C on ff. 298^v–344^v. Other contents: TOL (acephalous), NT (LV). OTL version: EV+LV. Order of sections in OTL: T–S–C. Introductory liturgical material at the start of lections ('þe lord saiþ þese þingis', etc.). Referencing system: indexing letters A–L (intermittent; indexing letters missing in parts of the manuscript). TOL Type: I.

204×132 mm. Blue initials with red penwork. Intermittent running titles giving liturgical season (consistent at the start, only occasionally later). Rubrics giving details for each lection. Added material underlined in red. Two columns. Script: textura.

BIBLIOGRAPHY

Ker and Piper, *Medieval Manuscripts in British Libraries*, iv. 751–2.

II. CATEGORIZATION INTO GROUPS

As discussed above, the textual tradition of OTL manuscripts is highly complex and presents several problems for the editor. There is a great deal of variation between the thirty-nine extant witnesses in terms of their inventories of lections and their chosen translations. Different OTLs include different sets of lections, draw on different Wycliffite translations (EV, LV, or both), or go back to the Vulgate or the Sarum Missal and translate the lections independently. The use of different translations in the OTLs can vary from lection to lection, with the result that a collation of witnesses is difficult and in some cases unhelpful, especially where entirely different translations are used. On the other hand, in cases where the same translation is used throughout, there is frequently very little substantive variation between witnesses, so that it is difficult to isolate versions on the basis of textual variants or error. In the face of these problems—great variation on one level, and great uniformity on another—the approach to identification and classification of the different groups of the OTL that has been adopted for this edition is one based on two criteria: (1) inventories of lections and (2) the translation used (EV, LV, both, or independent translations). Such an approach has the potential to yield results that give insight into the history of the OTL.[21] The evidence for this classification—a detailed inventory of lections—is presented in §III below.

1. Characteristics of Individual Groups

Based on the approach explained above, the witnesses have been categorized into several distinct groups, visualized in Figure 1. The features are outlined here. Type I and Type II are categories first identified through Elizabeth Solopova's research.[22] Lectionaries of Type I consist of four parts: the Temporale; a detailed Sanctorale with readings for individual saints, with a rubric indicating that it contains 'þe rule of þe sanctorum boþe of þe propre and comyn togidere'; votive masses termed 'commemorations'; and a short section of readings which are 'not red aftir þe uss of Salisburi'. These 'non-Sarum' lections are, in fact, five lections which usually occur in the Common,[23] but which are not assigned to any of the saints' feasts in the Use of Sarum. The inventory of lections found in Type I manuscripts is very uniform, so that no subgroups can be identified. The only witness that shows marked differences from the others in this group is Wo, which omits the section containing non-Sarum lections—perhaps a deliberate omission due to the fact that inclusion of these lections was not essential for following the readings throughout the liturgical year.

Type I lectionaries are also characterized by fixed incipits and explicits. A representative example of this is the text of Eg, which begins with the rubric 'Here bigynneþ þe lessouns and pistlis of þe olde lawe þat ben red in þe chirche in al þe ȝeer aftir þe uss of Salisburi' (f. 300ʳ) and ends with 'Here eendiþ þe pistlis and lessouns of þe olde testament aftir þe uss of Salisbury of al þe ȝeer' (f. 356ʳ), which is placed after the Commemorations but before the non-Sarum lections. Similarly, the Temporale is concluded with a fixed rubric, 'Here eendiþ the rule of þe dominicals and ferials togidere of al þe ȝeer' (f. 342ᵛ), while the Sanctorale is followed by 'Here eendiþ þe rule of þe sanctorum boþe þe propre and þe comyn togidere. Here bigynneþ þe temperal þat is þe commemoracioun of þe ȝeer'

---

[21] In general rather than specific terms, there is a precedent for this approach in Manfred Görlach's analysis of the witnesses to the *South English Legendary* (*The Textual Tradition of the South English Legendary* (Leeds, 1974)).   [22] Solopova, *MSS of WB*, 6–17.

[23] These lections are nos. 204, 212, 214, 218, and 220 in the list of lections in §III.

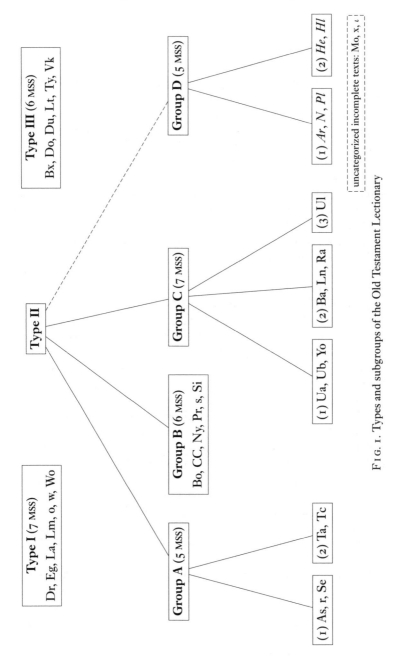

FIG. 1. Types and subgroups of the Old Testament Lectionary

(f. 354ᵛ). These rubrics show greater variation in Types II and III, but are remarkably uniform in Type I.

Like lectionaries of Type I, Type II contains the Temporale, Sanctorale, and the Commemorations. Type II differs from Type I mainly with regard to its Sanctorale, which is subdivided into two parts, the Proper and the Common. The Proper is relatively short and contains a small number of important feasts of widely venerated saints, which can vary according to the different groups and subgroups. The Common contains readings for categories of saints' feasts, such as feasts of several martyrs, a confessor and abbot, a virgin who was not a martyr, etc. The Common can include the non-Sarum lections identified in Type I, but not all manuscripts do so. The order in which these different parts occur can vary between different lectionaries—some place the Commemorations before the Proper and the Common, while others place them at the very end. Incipits and explicits for the individual parts of the lectionaries vary, as opposed to the fixed format found in Type I manuscripts. Some saints' feast days also have titles in Type II lectionaries which are different from those in Type I. For instance, Type II gives two feasts at the end of June as 'Midsomer euyn' and 'Mydsomer day', while the same feasts are listed under their traditional liturgical titles as 'euen of Seint Ioon baptist' and 'þe Natyuyte of Seynt Ioon baptist' in Type I. The feast of the beheading of St John the Baptist typically occurs as 'decollacioun' or 'biheding of Seint Ioon baptist' in Type II, while Type I calls it 'Seint Iones dai in heruest'.

While Type I lectionaries are very uniform in their presentation, Type II shows much greater variation in terms of visual presentation, script, textual aspects, and the overall inventory of lections. The identification of various subgroups as summarized in Figure 1 is based on the inventory of readings as well as the translations used. Although manuscripts which appear to be more closely related have been grouped together, in only a few cases do they present exactly the same inventory. Overall, OT lectionaries of Type II present a remarkable range of inventories, so that even manuscripts within the same textual group can show considerably different inventories.

Group A contains those texts which omit a number of specific lections, namely the Sunday in the Christmas octave, the feast of St Luke, St James Eve, St Lawrence Eve, and the Annunciation. The Commemorations for peace and for battles are also omitted. Apart from Tc, all manuscripts in this group place the Commemorations between the Temporale and the Sanctorale. As, r, and Se are more closely related, with all three additionally omitting the fifth lesson on the Saturday after Pentecost (no. 84) and the fifth lesson on the 17th Saturday after Trinity (no. 92).[24] Ta and Tc fit the pattern less perfectly and show some marked differences between each other as well as from Group A1, as can be seen from the inventory of feasts in §III. Ta shows a greater number of differences from A1 than Tc.

A key feature of Group B is an erroneous cross-reference to the feast of St Lawrence Eve, which occurs in the common in Lection 217 for a virgin and martyr. However, the actual feast of St Lawrence Eve (Lection 157) is misnamed as St Cyriacus in all Group B manuscripts, so that this is effectively an empty cross-reference. A further common characteristic of this group is the fact that all of these manuscripts include the full set of lections in the Common, including the non-Sarum lections.

In contrast to Group B, Group C does include the feast of St Lawrence Eve, so that the cross-reference in the Common has an appropriate counterpart in the Proper. Lectionaries of Group C tend to omit the non-Sarum lections from the Common, although there are subtle differences as to which lections are excluded. Ba, Ua, and Yo are exceptions to this rule and do include the non-Sarum lections. In Group C the most closely related manuscripts are Ua, Ub, and Yo, all of which give both Ecclus. 44 and Ecclus. 50 for the feast of St Silvester (no. 20), with the note that 'þis þistil is rad but on ij. feestis of Seint Edmound bischop'. Group C1 also shows an error in the Common, where the lection for a feast of a confessor and abbot is referred to as a feast of many martyrs (no. 214). Group C2 contains those manuscripts which share the common characteristics of Group C, but which are less closely related to each other than Group C1. Ul has been grouped separately, as it is the only lectionary in this group which contains NT epistles as well as OT ones, until this practice is abandoned halfway through the text.

Group D differs from all other groups in that it uses EV and independent translations exclusively for all lections, while Groups A–C use a mixture of LV, EV, and independent translations, with the majority of lections taken from LV. Group D1 contains those lectionaries which have OT lections in EV only. Group D2 contains the only two extant full OT and NT lectionaries, which have both epistles and gospels for the entire liturgical year. Although *Ha* and *Hl* are very similar in many respects, there are some small differences between their inventories of lections. All Group D lectionaries contain some lections which do not occur in any other groups or types, such as no. 215. It is also noteworthy that all Group D texts

---

[24] Most other OTLs contain a cross-reference for these lessons. Even in the absence of such cross-references, readers of As, r, and Se would probably have been able to find these lections based on the information given in the TOL.

contain Latin incipits for the individual lections, which do not typically occur with texts within the other groups.[25]

Type III is a term used in this edition to refer to those manuscripts which insert the OT lections directly into a table of lections instead of presenting TOL and OTL as two distinct texts (see Plate 3). In these manuscripts, only the OT lections are given in full in the TOL, while NT lections are given in the form of a reference, so that the appropriate sections could be found in the full NT contained in the rest of the manuscript. In terms of structure, Type III lectionaries are similar to Type I insofar as they combine the Proper and the Common into one section, which is preceded by the rubric 'Here . . . bigynneþ þe sanctorum boþe of þe comyne and propre togidre' (Bx, f. 28ʳ). In other aspects, however, Type III lectionaries are closer to Type II than Type I, as they use the headings 'Natiuite day of Seint Iohn Baptist' and 'Biheding of Baptist' rather than those typical of Type I for these feasts. Since three out of the six Type III manuscripts are fragments, it has not been possible to categorize this group further into different subgroups.[26]

There are three further manuscripts, Mo, x, and ι, which cannot be assigned to any of the groups on account of their fragmentary nature. However, it is possible that x is related to Se, since both texts share a similar introductory rubric.

2. Chronology

The identification of distinct groups invites a consideration of the ordering of their relationships. The evidence of the type of translation is used tentatively to suggest a chronology of the groups, as it is likely that EV lectionaries are chronologically earlier than those lectionaries which use LV alongside EV.

Group II D is characterized by the use of the EV text in combination with Latin incipits, which suggests indebtedness to Latin models. Together these features indicate that Group II D is an early version of OTL. It is suggestive that all of these EV lectionaries in Group II D use the headings associated with Type II lectionaries for feasts of St John the Baptist—'Midsomer euyn' and 'Mydsomer day', and 'decollacioun of Seint Baptist'. The connection between earlier lectionaries and these

---

[25] The only exception to this rule is ι, which contains predominantly LV lections with Latin incipits. Because of its fragmentary nature, it was not possible to categorize this manuscript.

[26] Unfortunately, it has not been possible to consult the Van Kampen manuscript Vk for this edition.

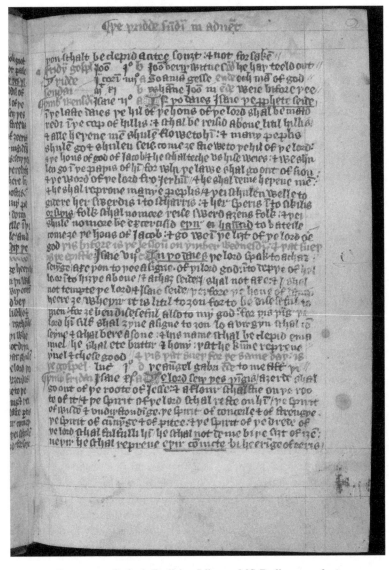

PLATE 3. Oxford, Bodleian Library, MS Bodley 531, f. 2ʳ
Reproduced by permission of the Bodleian Libraries, University of Oxford

characteristic headings may be an indication that the other Type II groups A–C are also earlier than Type I, where the titles of these lections are systematically changed. Type II also contains an independent translation of the lection for the midnight Mass at Christmas (no. 15, translated from *Missa in gallicantu*);[27] in Type I this is an LV translation, which suggests that Type II precedes Type I. Other aspects of Type I further support this hypothesis. In particular, Type I is characterized by a greater sophistication and precision of cross-references and layout, while these aspects are less developed in Type II, and especially so in Group II D, suggesting that Group II D might be the earliest version of OTL.

If we posit a chronology in which Type II is earlier than Type I, it is likely that Type III presents a link between Type I and Type II. As shown above, Type III has features of both the other types, in that its structure is similar to Type I but its headings are similar to those of Type II. It is easy to see how the structure of a TOL, into which the OT lections are inserted in Type III manuscripts, may have provided a model for Type I. In Type I OTLs, the division between Proper and Common, so characteristic of Type II, is given up, and this same structure of a combined Proper and Common is found in Type III. In this sense, Type I very much follows the structure of a TOL and, by extension, the order of lections in Type III manuscripts. The only significant difference in terms of structure is the addition of the non-Sarum lections at the end of Type I manuscripts. This evidence suggests, then, that Type II is the earliest type and Type I the latest, with Type III representing an intermediate stage.[28]

3. Group II D: Textual Characteristics

Group II D is anomalous in comparison with other subgroups of Type II, as the five manuscripts of Group II D use EV for all those lections which use LV in other Type II groups. For this reason this group is excluded from the collation in the present edition. However, a sample collation has been conducted with the five Group II D manuscripts, based on five lections, and can be found below. The lections chosen for analysis were: 3rd Saturday of Advent, the second lesson (no. 8), Thursday in the second week of Lent (no. 42), St Andrew's Eve (no. 95), the lection *Dedit dominus*

---

[27] This lection is discussed in greater detail below, §V.6.

[28] The nomenclature of Types I, II, and III does not reflect this chronological development. The reason for this disjunct is that Types I and II as first identified by Elizabeth Solopova (*MSS of WB*, 7–17) were neutral descriptors of these versions, and were not intended to suggest that Type I precedes Type II chronologically. In this edition I have adhered to Solopova's basic terms of reference while refining and developing this system of classification and establishing a chronology for the different types.

on the feast of one confessor and doctor (no. 211), and the Requiem Mass (no. 232). In other Type II manuscripts, nos. 8 and 42 are straightforward LV lections, no. 211 uses a mixture of LV and independent translation, while no. 232 is preserved as an EV lection in all extant manuscripts and no. 95 uses an independent translation in all extant manuscripts. The lections have been edited below from Hl^{29} and collated with the other four extant II D manuscripts (*Ar, He, N, Pl*).[30]

The sample collation shows that Lections 8 and 42 in Group II D are fairly close to EV as edited in F&M. The variants which can be found are typically minor differences of syntax, inversions of parts of sentences, replacement of conjunctions, and omission or addition of function words. Such variants can be found in LV lections in other groups as well, although they are less frequent in later OTLs than in Group II D. On the whole, the version in *Ar* appears to be somewhat less carefully executed, omitting to provide a translation for *claudus* (the subject of the sentence in Isa. 35: 6) and the future tense in *germinabit* (Isa. 35:2) and *timebit* (Jer. 17: 8)— omissions which are likely to be the result of scribal inattentiveness.

A similar picture emerges for Lection 232, which largely agrees between all II D manuscripts and EV. Perhaps the most notable exception to this rule is 2 Macc. 12: 43, where the liturgical addition 'Iudas þe man most strong' is omitted in *He*, which follows the Vulgate here instead of the Sarum Missal. Even in later Type II and Type I lectionaries, which replace almost all EV lections with LV, the EV version of this lection was preserved without any significant changes to the text apart from the inclusion of the liturgical addition.

Lection 95 for St Andrew's Eve is a composite lection with a translation independent of EV and LV. The most notable variants here are found in *N*, which has an inversion of 'wundris plesing' (Ecclus. 44, D), perhaps to make the syntax more idiomatic, as well as 'an herte and precept' instead of 'hestis' (Ecclus. 44, K). This lection remains unchanged in other Type II groups and Types I and III.

Lection 211 is a composite lection which uses a section from Ecclus. 47, followed by a section from Ecclus. 24. The entire lection in Group II D uses an independent translation, with variants differing markedly from EV. For instance, 'dulces fecit modulos'[31] (Ecclus. 47: 11) is translated as 'he haþ maad swote notis' in Group II D, but as 'he made sweete motetes'

---

[29] The edition follows the principles outlined in the editorial policy below (§VI).

[30] Lections 211 and 232 are missing in *Ar* since the manuscript is atelous.

[31] *The Sarum Missal*, ed. Legg, 375. Some copies of the Vulgate have 'modos' here instead of 'modulos'.

in EV. Interestingly, in the first section of this lection the excerpt from Ecclus. 47 is replaced by an LV translation in Groups II A–C, Type I, and Type III, while the second section from Ecclus. 24 is preserved in the independent translation in all lectionaries. This might have been simply a matter of convenience; since the lection does not follow the biblical text in a linear fashion, it would have taken time and special effort to find the relevant LV passage from Ecclus. 24 for this composite lection. For this reason the translators may have preferred simply to copy the independent translation, which was more easily accessible. Alternatively, the evidence might indicate that only particular parts of the LV translation were available to the translators of OTL at the time of writing. In this case, the reason would not have been convenience but necessity.

In all lections, collation shows that *He* and *Hl*, although they do not agree in all ways, are more closely related to each other than other manuscripts in this group. There is also frequent agreement between the variants in *N* and *Pl*. For instance, *NPl* both have 'will 3e' where *HeHl* have 'wileþ' (Isa. 35: 4), and *NPl* have 'crokyd men' where *HeHl* have 'þe halte' (Isa. 35: 6). It is noteworthy that *N* contains a number of variants which are unique to this manuscript. In particular, *N* inverts the order of the words 'humour seendiþ' (Jer. 17: 8), and has 'salt lond' instead of 'lond of bareyn' (Jer. 17: 6). Most of the variants in *Ar* are unique and frequently consist of omission of articles, prepositions, and forms of *shal* and *to be*.

Sample collations follow, here with lemmata cued to the verse numbers.

3rd Saturday of Advent, the second lesson (Isa. 35, Lection 8)

¹Gladen schal desert and þe wiþouten weye, and ful out schal ioi3en þe wildirnesse and flouren as a lilie. ²Buriounende it schal burioune and ful out ioi3en, ioi3eful and preisende. The glorie of Liban is 3ouen to it, þe fairnesse of Carmel and of Saron, þei schul seen þe glorie of þe Lord and þe fairnesse of oure God. ³Counforteþ þe hondis losid atwynne, and þe feble knees strengþiþ. ⁴Seiþ 3ee kouwardis, or of litil corage, takeþ counfort and wileþ not dreden. Lo, oure God veniaunce of 3elding schal bringe. God, he schal comen and sauen vs. ⁵Than schuln ben openyd þe eien of blynde men and eres of deue men schuln ben openyd, ⁶þan schal lepen as an herte þe halte and opened schal be þe tunge of doumbe men. For kit ben in desert watris and stremys in wildirnesse, ⁷and þat was drie into a pond and þe þristende into wellis of watris, seiþ oure Lord almi3ti.

1 Gladen schal desert] Desert schal gladen *N*   and þe wiþouten weye] in þe weye *NPl* and³] as *Ar*   as] *om. Ar*   2 schal¹] *om. Ar*   3 Counforteþ] Counforte 3e *NPl* strengþiþ] strengþe 3e *NPl*   4 wileþ] will 3e *NPl*   veniaunce of 3elding schal bringe]

schal brynge veniaunce of ȝelding *NPl*   5 ben openyd þe eien of blynde men] scholen þe
iȝen of blynde men ben openyd *NPl*   6 schal lepen] lepen schal *NPl*   þe halte] crokyd
men *NPl, om. Ar*   opened schal be þe tunge of doumbe men] þe tunge of domb men schal
be openyd *NPl*   ben] *om. Ar*   kit ben in desert watris and stremys in wildernesse] watris
and stremys ben kit in desert in wildirnesse *N*   7 þat] *add.* that *N*

Thursday in the second week of Lent (Jer. 17, Lection 42)

⁵Cursid þe man þat trusteþ in man and putteþ flesche his arm and fro þe
Lord his herte goþ awey. ⁶Forsoþe it schal be as Iencian tre or broom in
desert and he schal not seen whan schal comen good, but he schal dwellen in drouȝte in desert in þe lond of bareyn and vnhabitable. ⁷Blissid be
þe man þat trosteþ in þe Lord, and þe Lord schal be his trust ⁸and he
schal ben as a tree þat is ouer plauntid vpon watris, þat at þe humour
seendiþ his rootis and he schal not dreden. Whan schal comen greet hete
and his leef schal be grene and in tyme of drouȝte he schal noȝt be bisy,
ne eny tyme schal cesen to maken fruyt. ⁹Schrewid is þe herte of man
and vnserchable; who schal knowen it? ¹⁰I, þe Lord, sekende þe herte and
preuende renys þat ȝyue to eche man aftir his weie and after þe fruyt of his
fyndynges.

5 Cursid] *add.* be *NPl*   6 tre] *add.* in desert *N*   in desert¹] tree *N*   schal comen good]
god schal come *N*   in³] *om. Ar*   lond of bareyn] salt lond *N*   of] *om. Ar*   7 be¹]
is *N, om. Ar*   trosteþ] *add.* and *Ar*   8 is] *placed after* plauntid *N*   þe] *om. Ar*
humour seendiþ his rootis] sendiþ his humour to þe roote *N*   he²] *om. He*   schal²] *om.*
Ar   schal comen greet hete] greet heete schal come *N*   he³] *om. He*   9 who] whoso
Pl   10 renys] þe reenes *Ar*   þe²] *om. N*   fyndynges] fyndyng *Pl*

St Andrew Eve (Ecclus. 44, Lection 95)³²

The blessynge of þe Lord is ᴬon þe heed of þe riȝtwise man, and þerfore he
hath ȝouen eritage vnto him, and he hath diuisid a part vnto him among
þe twelue kynredis, and ᴮhe haþ founden grace in þe siȝte of alle flesch,
and he haþ magnified him in drede of enemys, and in his wordis he ᶜhaþ
ᴰwundris plesing. He hath glorified him ᴱin ᶠþesiȝte of kynges, and he haþ
schewid his glorie vnto him. In bileue and softnesse of him he haþ maad
ᴳhim holy. And he haþ chosen him ᴴof alle flesch; he haþ ȝouen ᴵvnto him
ᴶhestis and þe lawe of lyf and of lerynge, and he hath mad him ful heyȝ.
ᴷHe sette ᴸto him an euer lastende testament, and he haþ girt him aboute
wiþ a girdil of riȝtwisnesse, and þe Lord hath clad him with þe croune of
glorie.

ᴬ on] vpon *He*   ᴮ he] *om. Ar*   ᶜ haþ] *add.* maad *He*   ᴰ wundris plesing]

---

³² Continuous numbering of verses is not possible in this composite lection. Instead, the
letters of the alphabet are used in superscript and placed immediately before the lemma to
which they refer.

plesid wondris *N*   ᴱ in] *om. Ar*   ꜰ þe] *om. He*   ᴳ him] *om. Pl*   ᴴ of] *om.*
Pl   ᴵ vnto] into *Pl*   ᴶ hestis] an herte and precept *N*   ᴷ He] *add.* haþ *He;* and
he *Ar*   ᴸ to] vnto *ArHePl*

Feast of one confessor and doctor (Ecclus. 47, Lection 211)

⁹The Lord haþ ȝouen knoulechynge to his seynt and vnto þe ful heiȝe in þe
world of glorie. ¹⁰He haþ preisid þe Lord of al his herte and he haþ loued þe
God þat made him and he haþ ȝouen to him myȝt aȝens his enemys, ¹¹and
he made syngers to stonde forn aȝen þe auter, and in þe sounes of hem he
haþ maad swote notis, ¹²and he haþ ȝouen wurschipe to him in halewynges
and he haþ enourned tymes to þe ende of his lif, þat he miȝte preise þe
holy name of God, and þat he myȝte make more bi þe morn þe holynesse
of God. ¹³Crist haþ pergid þe synnes of him, and he haþ heiȝid þe hour of
him into wiþouten ende.

[Ecclus. 24]

¹Wisdam schal preisen his soule and he schal ben honourid in oure Lord,
and he schal be gloried in þe myddis of his peple, ²and he schal openen his
mouþ in þe chirchis of most heiȝ, and in biholdynge of þe vertu of him he
schal be gloried. ³In þe myddis of his peple he schal ben enheiȝid and in
holy fulhede he schal ben merueilid. ⁴In þe multitude of chosene he schal
han preisyng and amongis þe blessid he schal be blessid.

9 to] vnto *He*   10 haþ loued] halowed *Pl*   11 aȝen] *om. N*   12 he
miȝte] þei schulde *N*   he myȝte make more] þei schulden largen *N*   13 into] *om.*
He   Ecclus. 24 2 and¹] *om. HePl*   þe¹] *om. NPl*   heiȝ] *add.* God *N*   þe²] *om. NPl*
3 fulhede] plente *N*

Requiem Mass (2 Macc. 12, Lection 232)

⁴³Collacioun or spekynge togidre maad Iudas þe man most strong, sente
twelue þousende dragmes of siluer to Ierusalem to ben offrid sacrifiȝe
for synnes of dede men, wel and religiousely bithenkende of aȝenrisynge.
⁴⁴Soþli ȝif he hopede not hem þat fellen to risen aȝeen, it was seen superflu and veyn to preiȝen for dede men ⁴⁵and for he biheld þat þei þat token
slepinge or diȝynge wiþ pite hadden best grace kept. ⁴⁶Therfore holy and
helþeful þenkynge is to preȝen for dede men þat þei be vnbounde fro
synnes.

43 Iudas þe man most strong] *om. He*   to] forto *He*   44 risen] rijsenge *He*   to²] forto
He   45 diȝynge] dey *He*   46 þenkynge is] is þe þouȝt *N*   to] forto *He*

III. LIST OF LECTIONS

The following table contains an inventory of lections found in the OTL manuscripts. The manuscripts Do, Du, Mo, Ty, x are excluded on account of their fragmentary nature. It was not possible to examine Vk for the purposes of this study. The lections given in OTL can differ from the TOL which accompanies it in many manuscripts.[33] As will be readily apparent from the list, different manuscripts contain different inventories of lections, and there is no single manuscript which contains all of the lections listed. The list, therefore, is cumulative in nature. For easy reference, the numbering of lections in this edition follows the numbers in this list. However, the base text of this edition (Bo) does not contain all the lections in this cumulative list. This in turn means that the lections in the edited text are not numbered continuously in all places.

The lections listed here are exclusively those which are found in OTL, and not those in TOL. Each individual lection is given a number, which is used throughout this edition for reference. Lections are identified by their title, as well as the biblical chapter and verse from which they are taken.[34] Some lections are not given in full, but rather in form of a cross-reference in the manuscripts. These lections are included in the list here and not specifically marked. Many of the lections in the Common are composite lections, so that they cannot be as easily identified by giving chapter and verse numbers. Since these lections are well-known parts of the Sarum Use and are available in the main editions of the Sarum Missal, the Latin incipits are given in this table to refer to these lections. The reader is referred to Legg's edition of the Sarum Missal for further details on these lections in Latin and their use of biblical verses.

The third column gives details as to the translation used for a particular lection in Bo (the base text of this edition), and thus provides an overview of the translations as they appear in this edition. Where the third column is left blank, this indicates that a specific lesson is not contained in Bo. It is important to note that the information in the third column is specific to Bo and is not representative for all manuscripts, especially not for Group II D,

---

[33] Occasionally, lections which are missing in OTL are given in TOL, for example in As, where the 17th Saturday in the week after Trinity is missing from OTL but is listed in TOL.

[34] The format of this table is in part modelled on the list of lections in Ursula Lenker's detailed study of the West Saxon gospels and their liturgical use (*Die westsächsische Evangelienversion und die Perikopenordnungen im angelsächsischen England* (Munich, 1997), 298–382).

which uses EV and independent translations for all lections. However, it should give a general impression for the pattern according to which the translations were chosen, and this is further discussed below. The abbreviation 'IN' is here used for independent translations, and 'SYN' for lections which are not identifiable as either EV or LV but are indebted to both. If two different types of translation are used within one lection, both are mentioned. Where Bo gives a cross-reference instead of the entire lection, this is noted with the abbreviation 'CR', and the translation type of the lection to which the cross-reference refers is given in the third column.

No.	Lection	transl. in Bo

TEMPORALE

1 **First Friday in Advent** (Isa. 51: 1–8)   LV
   contained in *Ar*, As, Ba, Bo, Bx, Cc, Dr, Eg, *He*, *Hl*, La, Lm, Ln,
         Lt, *N*, Ny, o, *Pl*, Pr, Ra, s, Se, Si, Ta, Tc, Ua, Ub, Ul,
         w, Wo, Yo, *ι*
   acephalous As, r

2 **Second Wednesday in Advent** (Zech. 8: 3–8)   LV
   contained in As, Ba, Bo, Bx, Cc, Dr, Eg, *He*, *Hl*, La, Lm, Ln, Lt,
         N, Ny, o, *Pl*, Pr, Ra, s, Se, Si, Ta, Tc, Ua, Ub, Ul, w,
         Wo, Yo, *ι*
   acephalous r
   omitted *Ar*

3 **Second Friday in Advent** (Isa. 62: 6–12)   LV
   contained in *Ar*, As, Ba, Bo, Bx, Cc, Dr, Eg, *He*, *Hl*, La, Lm, Ln,
         Lt, *N*, Ny, o, *Pl*, Pr, Ra, s, Se, Si, Ta, Tc, Ua, Ub, Ul,
         w, Wo, Yo, *ι*
   acephalous r

4 **First lesson on the third Wednesday of Advent** (Isa. 2: 2–5)   EV+LV
   contained in *Ar*, As, Ba, Bo, Bx, Cc, Dr, Eg, *He*, *Hl*, La, Lm, Ln,
         Lt, *N*, Ny, o, *Pl*, Pr, r, Ra, s, Se, Si, Ta, Tc, Ua, Ub,
         Ul, w, Wo, Yo, *ι*

5 **Second lesson on the third Wednesday of Advent** (Isa. 7: 10–15)   LV
   contained in *Ar*, As, Ba, Bo, Bx, Cc, Dr, Eg, *He*, *Hl*, La, Lm, Ln,
         Lt, *N*, Ny, o, *Pl*, Pr, r, Ra, s, Se, Si, Ta, Tc, Ua, Ub,
         Ul, w, Wo, Yo, *ι*

6 **Third Friday of Advent** (Isa. 11: 1–5)   LV
   contained in *Ar*, As, Ba, Bo, Bx, Cc, Dr, Eg, *He*, *Hl*, La, Lm, Ln,
         Lt, *N*, Ny, o, *Pl*, Pr, r, Ra, s, Se, Si, Ta, Tc, Ua, Ub,
         Ul, w, Wo, Yo

omitted   *ι*

7   **Third Saturday of Advent: First lesson** (Isa. 19: 20–2)   LV
     contained in   *Ar*, As, Ba, Bo, Bx, Cc, Dr, Eg, *He*, *Hl*, La, Lm, Ln,
                    Lt, *N*, Ny, o, *Pl*, Pr, r, Ra, s, Se, Si, Ta, Tc, Ua, Ub,
                    Ul, w, Wo, Yo, *ι*

8   **Third Saturday of Advent: Second lesson** (Isa. 35: 1–7)   LV
     contained in   *Ar*, As, Ba, Bo, Bx, Cc, Dr, Eg, *He*, *Hl*, La, Lm, Ln,
                    Lt, *N*, Ny, o, *Pl*, Pr, r, Ra, s, Se, Si, Ta, Tc, Ua, Ub,
                    Ul, w, Wo, Yo, *ι*

9   **Third Saturday of Advent: Third lesson** (Isa. 40: 9–11)   LV
     contained in   *Ar*, As, Ba, Bo, Bx, Cc, Dr, Eg, *He*, *Hl*, La, Lm, Ln,
                    Lt, *N*, Ny, o, *Pl*, Pr, r, Ra, s, Se, Si, Ta, Tc, Ua, Ub,
                    Ul, w, Wo, Yo, *ι*

10   **Third Saturday of Advent: Fourth lesson** (Isa. 45: 1–8)   LV
     contained in   *Ar*, As, Ba, Bo, Cc, Dr, Eg, *He*, *Hl*, La, Lm, Ln, Lt,
                    N, Ny, o, *Pl*, Pr, r, Ra, s, Se, Si, Ta, Tc, Ua, Ub, Ul,
                    w, Wo, Yo, *ι*
     lacuna   Bx

11   **Third Saturday of Advent: Fifth lesson**   LV
     Dan. 3: 49–88 with text for different seasons
     contained in   As, Ba, Bo, Cc, *He*, *Hl*, Ln, *N*, Ny, Pr, r, s, Se, Si, Ta,
                    Tc, Ua, Ub, Ul, Yo, *ι*
     Dan. 3: 49–52 without text for different seasons
     contained in   *Ar*, Dr, Eg, La, Lm, Lt, o, *Pl*, Ra, w, Wo
     lacuna   Bx

12   **Fourth Wednesday of Advent** (Joel 2: 23–4; 3: 17–21)   EV
     contained in   *Ar*, As, Ba, Bo, Cc, Dr, Eg, *He*, *Hl*, La, Lm, Ln, Lt,
                    N, Ny, o, *Pl*, Pr, r, Ra, s, Se, Si, Ta, Tc, Ua, Ub, Ul,
                    w, Wo, Yo, *ι*
     lacuna   Bx

13   **Fourth Friday of Advent** (Zech. 2: 10–13)   LV
     contained in   *Ar*, As, Ba, Bo, Cc, Dr, Eg, *He*, *Hl*, La, Lm, Ln, Lt,
                    N, Ny, o, *Pl*, Pr, r, Ra, s, Se, Si, Ta, Tc, Ua, Ub, Ul,
                    w, Wo, Yo, *ι*
     lacuna   Bx

14   **Christmas Eve** (Isa. 62: 1–4)   SYN
     contained in   *Ar*, As, Ba, Bo, Cc, Dr, Eg, *He*, *Hl*, La, Lm, Ln, Lt,
                    N, Ny, o, *Pl*, Pr, r, Ra, s, Se, Si, Ta, Tc, Ua, Ub, Ul,
                    w, Wo, Yo, *ι*
     lacuna   Bx

---

[35] Ua, Ub, and Yo give Ecclus. 50 here in addition to Ecclus. 44, with the note that 'þis þistil is rad but on ij. feestis of Seint Edmound bischop' (Yo, f. 305ᵛ).

N, Ny, o, *Pl*, Pr, r, Ra, s, Se, Si, Ta, Tc, Ua, Ub, Ul,
w, Wo, Yo, ι
lacuna   Bx

22 **Sunday in the same week** (Isa. 60: 1–5)   LV (CR)
contained in *Ar*, Ba, Bo, Bx, Cc, Dr, Eg, *He*, *Hl*, La, Lm, Ln, Lt,
N, Ny, o, Pl, Pr, Ra, s, Si, Ta, Ua, Ub, Ul, w, Wo, Yo
omitted   As, r, Se, Tc, ι

23 **Octave of Twelfth Day** (Isa. 25: 1; 28: 5; 35: 1–2, 10; 41: 18; 52: 13;   IN
12: 3–5)
contained in *Ar*, As, Ba, Bo, Bx, Cc, Dr, Eg, *He*, *Hl*, La, Lm, Ln,
Lt, N, Ny, o, Pl, Pr, r, Ra, s, Se, Si, Ta, Tc, Ua, Ub,
Ul, w, Wo, Yo, ι

24 **Ash Wednesday** (Joel 2: 12–19)   LV
contained in *Ar*, As, Ba, Bo, Bx, Cc, Dr, Eg, *He*, *Hl*, La, Lm, Ln,
Lt, *N*, Ny, o, *Pl*, Pr, r, Ra, s, Se, Si, Ta, Tc, Ua, Ub,
Ul, w, Wo, Yo, ι

25 **Thursday after Ash Wednesday** (Isa. 38: 1–6)   LV
contained in *Ar*, As, Ba, Bo, Bx, Cc, Dr, Eg, *He*, *Hl*, La, Lm, Ln,
Lt, *N*, Ny, o, *Pl*, Pr, r, Ra, s, Se, Si, Ta, Tc, Ua, Ub,
Ul, w, Wo, Yo, ι

26 **Friday after Ash Wednesday** (Isa. 58: 1–9)   LV
contained in *Ar*, As, Ba, Bo, Bx, Cc, Dr, Eg, *He*, *Hl*, La, Lm, Ln,
Lt, *N*, Ny, o, *Pl*, Pr, r, Ra, s, Se, Si, Ta, Tc, Ua, Ub,
Ul, w, Wo, Yo, ι

27 **Saturday after Ash Wednesday** (Isa. 58: 9–14)   LV
contained in *Ar*, As, Ba, Bo, Bx, Cc, Dr, Eg, *He*, *Hl*, La, Lm, Ln,
Lt, *N*, Ny, o, *Pl*, Pr, r, Ra, s, Se, Si, Ta, Tc, Ua, Ub,
Ul, w, Wo, Yo, ι

28 **Monday in the first week of Lent** (Ezek. 34: 11–16)   LV
contained in *Ar*, As, Ba, Bo, Bx, Cc, Dr, Eg, *He*, *Hl*, La, Lm, Ln,
Lt, *N*, Ny, o, *Pl*, Pr, r, Ra, s, Se, Si, Ta, Tc, Ua, Ub,
Ul, w, Wo, Yo, ι

29 **Tuesday in the first week of Lent** (Isa. 55: 6–11)   LV
contained in *Ar*, As, Ba, Bo, Bx, Cc, Dr, Eg, *He*, *Hl*, La, Lm, Ln,
Lt, *N*, Ny, o, *Pl*, Pr, r, Ra, s, Se, Si, Ta, Tc, Ua, Ub,
Ul, w, Wo, Yo, ι

30 **Wednesday in the first week of Lent: First lesson** (Exod. 24: 12–   LV
18)
contained in *Ar*, As, Ba, Bo, Bx, Cc, Dr, Eg, *He*, *Hl*, La, Lm, Ln,
Lt, *N*, Ny, o, *Pl*, Pr, r, Ra, s, Se, Si, Ta, Tc, Ua, Ub,
Ul, w, Wo, Yo, ι

31 **Wednesday in the first week of Lent: Second lesson** (1 Kgs   LV
    19: 3–8)
    contained in *Ar*, As, Ba, Bo, Bx, Cc, Dr, Eg, *He*, *Hl*, La, Lm, Ln,
    Lt, *N*, Ny, o, *Pl*, Pr, r, Ra, s, Se, Si, Ta, Tc, Ua, Ub,
    Ul, w, Wo, Yo, ι

32 **Thursday in the first week of Lent** (Ezek. 18: 1–19)   LV
    contained in *Ar*, As, Ba, Bo, Bx, Cc, Dr, Eg, *He*, *Hl*, La, Lm, Ln,
    Lt, *N*, Ny, o, *Pl*, Pr, r, Ra, s, Se, Si, Ta, Tc, Ua, Ub,
    Ul, w, Wo, Yo, ι

33 **Friday in the first week of Lent** (Ezek. 18: 20–8)   LV
    contained in *Ar*, As, Ba, Bo, Bx, Cc, Dr, Eg, *He*, *Hl*, La, Lm, Ln,
    Lt, *N*, Ny, o, *Pl*, Pr, r, Ra, s, Se, Si, Ta, Tc, Ua, Ub,
    Ul, w, Wo, Yo
    atelous ι

34 **Saturday in the first week of Lent: First lesson** (Deut. 26: 15–   LV
    19)
    contained in *Ar*, As, Ba, Bo, Bx, Cc, Dr, Eg, *He*, *Hl*, La, Lm, Ln,
    Lt, *N*, Ny, o, *Pl*, Pr, r, Ra, s, Se, Si, Ta, Tc, Ua, Ub,
    Ul, w, Wo, Yo
    atelous ι

35 **Saturday in the first week of Lent: Second lesson** (Deut.   LV
    11: 22–5)
    contained in *Ar*, As, Ba, Bo, Bx, Cc, Dr, Eg, *He*, *Hl*, La, Lm, Ln,
    Lt, *N*, Ny, o, *Pl*, Pr, r, Ra, s, Se, Si, Ta, Tc, Ua, Ub,
    Ul, w, Wo, Yo
    atelous ι

36 **Saturday in the first week of Lent: Third lesson** (2 Macc. 1:   EV
    2–5)
    contained in *Ar*, As, Ba, Bo, Bx, Cc, Dr, Eg, *He*, *Hl*, La, Lm, Ln,
    Lt, *N*, Ny, o, *Pl*, Pr, r, Ra, s, Se, Si, Ta, Tc, Ua, Ub,
    Ul, w, Wo, Yo
    atelous ι

37 **Saturday in the first week of Lent: Fourth lesson** (Ecclus. 36:   LV
    1–10)
    contained in *Ar*, As, Ba, Bo, Bx, Cc, Dr, Eg, *He*, *Hl*, La, Lm, Ln,
    Lt, *N*, Ny, o, *Pl*, Pr, r, Ra, s, Se, Si, Ta, Tc, Ua, Ub,
    Ul, w, Wo, Yo
    atelous ι

38 **Saturday in the first week of Lent: Fifth lesson** (Dan. 3:   LV (CR)
    49–52)
    contained in *Ar*, As, Ba, Bo, Bx, Cc, Dr, Eg, *He*, *Hl*, La, Lm, Ln,

Lt, *N*, Ny, o, *Pl*, Pr, r, Ra, s, Se, Si, Ta, Tc, Ua, Ub,
Ul, w, Wo, Yo

atelous   *ι*

39   **Monday in the second week of Lent** (Dan. 9: 15–19)   LV
contained in   *Ar*, As, Ba, Bo, Bx, Cc, Dr, Eg, *He*, *Hl*, La, Lm, Ln,
Lt, *N*, Ny, o, *Pl*, Pr, r, Ra, s, Se, Si, Ta, Tc, Ua, Ub,
Ul, w, Wo, Yo

atelous   *ι*

40   **Tuesday in the second week of Lent** (1 Kgs 17: 8–16)   LV
contained in   *Ar*, As, Ba, Bo, Bx, Cc, Dr, Eg, *He*, *Hl*, La, Lm, Ln,
Lt, *N*, Ny, o, *Pl*, Pr, r, Ra, s, Se, Si, Ta, Tc, Ua, Ub,
Ul, w, Wo, Yo

atelous   *ι*

41   **Wednesday in the second week of Lent** (Esther 13: 9–17)   LV
contained in   *Ar*, As, Ba, Bo, Bx, Cc, Dr, Eg, *He*, *Hl*, La, Lm, Ln,
Lt, *N*, Ny, o, *Pl*, Pr, r, Ra, s, Se, Si, Ta, Tc, Ua, Ub,
Ul, w, Wo, Yo

atelous   *ι*

41   **Thursday in the second week of Lent** (Jer. 17: 5–10)   LV
contained in   *Ar*, As, Ba, Bo, Bx, Cc, Dr, Eg, *He*, *Hl*, La, Lm, Ln,
Lt, *N*, Ny, o, *Pl*, Pr, r, Ra, s, Se, Si, Ta, Tc, Ua, Ub,
Ul, w, Wo, Yo

atelous   *ι*

43   **Friday in the second week of Lent** (Gen. 37: 6–22)   LV
contained in   *Ar*, As, Ba, Bo, Bx, Cc, Dr, Eg, *He*, *Hl*, La, Lm, Ln,
Lt, *N*, Ny, o, *Pl*, Pr, r, Ra, s, Se, Si, Ta, Tc, Ua, Ub,
Ul, w, Wo, Yo

atelous   *ι*

44   **Saturday in the second week of Lent** (Gen. 27: 6–39)   LV
contained in   *Ar*, As, Ba, Bo, Bx, Cc, Dr, Eg, *He*, *Hl*, La, Lm, Ln,
Lt, *N*, Ny, o, *Pl*, Pr, r, Ra, s, Se, Si, Ta, Tc, Ua, Ub,
Ul, w, Wo, Yo

atelous   *ι*

45   **Monday in the third week of Lent** (2 Kgs 6: 1–15)   LV
contained in   *Ar*, As, Ba, Bo, Bx, Cc, Dr, Eg, *He*, *Hl*, La, Lm, Ln,
Lt, *N*, Ny, o, *Pl*, Pr, r, Ra, s, Se, Si, Ta, Tc, Ua, Ub,
Ul, w, Wo, Yo

atelous   *ι*

46   **Tuesday in the third week of Lent** (2 Kgs 4: 1–7)   LV
contained in   *Ar*, As, Ba, Bo, Bx, Cc, Dr, Eg, *He*, *Hl*, La, Lm, Ln,

Lt, *N*, Ny, o, *Pl*, Pr, r, Ra, s, Se, Si, Ta, Tc, Ua, Ub, Ul, w, Wo, Yo

atelous ι

47 **Wednesday in the third week of Lent** (Exod. 20: 12–24)   LV
contained in *Ar*, As, Ba, Bo, Bx, Cc, Dr, Eg, *He*, *Hl*, La, Lm, Ln, Lt, *N*, Ny, o, *Pl*, Pr, r, Ra, s, Se, Si, Ta, Tc, Ua, Ub, Ul, w, Wo, Yo

atelous ι

48 **Thursday in the third week of Lent** (Jer. 7: 1–7)   LV
contained in *Ar*, As, Ba, Bo, Bx, Cc, Dr, Eg, *He*, *Hl*, La, Lm, Ln, Lt, *N*, Ny, o, *Pl*, Pr, r, Ra, s, Se, Si, Ta, Tc, Ua, Ub, Ul, w, Wo, Yo

atelous ι

49 **Friday in the third week of Lent** (Num. 20: 1–13)   LV
contained in *Ar*, As, Ba, Bo, Bx, Cc, Dr, Eg, *He*, *Hl*, La, Lm, Ln, Lt, *N*, Ny, o, *Pl*, Pr, r, Ra, s, Se, Si, Ta, Tc, Ua, Ub, Ul, w, Wo, Yo

atelous ι

50 **Saturday in the third week of Lent** (Dan. 13: 1–62)   LV
contained in *Ar*, As, Ba, Bo, Bx, Cc, Dr, Eg, *He*, *Hl*, La, Lm, Ln, Lt, *N*, Ny, o, *Pl*, Pr, r, Ra, s, Se, Si, Ta, Tc, Ua, Ub, Ul, w, Wo, Yo

atelous ι

51 **Monday in the fourth week of Lent** (1 Kgs 3: 16–28)   LV
contained in *Ar*, As, Ba, Bo, Bx, Cc, Dr, Eg, *He*, *Hl*, La, Lm, Ln, Lt, *N*, Ny, o, *Pl*, Pr, r, Ra, s, Se, Si, Ta, Tc, Ua, Ub, Ul, w, Wo, Yo

atelous ι

52 **Tuesday in the fourth week of Lent** (Exod. 32: 7–14)   LV
contained in *Ar*, As, Ba, Bo, Bx, Cc, Dr, Eg, *He*, *Hl*, La, Lm, Ln, Lt, *N*, Ny, o, *Pl*, Pr, r, Ra, s, Se, Si, Ta, Tc, Ua, Ub, Ul, w, Wo, Yo

atelous ι

53 **Wednesday in the fourth week of Lent: First lesson** (Ezek.   LV
36: 23–8)
contained in *Ar*, As, Ba, Bo, Bx, Cc, Dr, Eg, *He*, *Hl*, La, Lm, Ln, Lt, *N*, Ny, o, *Pl*, Pr, r, Ra, s, Se, Si, Ta, Tc, Ua, Ub, Ul, w, Wo, Yo

atelous ι

70 **Good Friday: Second lesson** (Exod. 12: 1–12)   LV
    contained in *Ar*, As, Ba, Bo, Bx, Cc, Dr, Eg, *He*, *Hl*, La, Lm, Ln,
        Lt, *N*, Ny, o, *Pl*, Pr, r, Ra, s, Se, Si, Ta, Tc, Ua, Ub,
        Ul, w, Wo, Yo
    atelous   ι

71 **Easter Eve: First lesson** (Gen. 1: 1–2: 2)   LV
    contained in *Ar*, As, Ba, Bo, Bx, Cc, Dr, Eg, *He*, *Hl*, La, Lm, Ln,
        Lt, *N*, Ny, o, *Pl*, Pr, r, Ra, s, Se, Si, Ta, Tc, Ua, Ub,
        Ul, w, Wo, Yo
    atelous   ι

72 **Easter Eve: Second lesson** (Exod. 14: 24–15: 1)   LV
    contained in *Ar*, As, Ba, Bo, Bx, Cc, Dr, Eg, *He*, *Hl*, La, Lm, Ln,
        Lt, *N*, Ny, o, *Pl*, Pr, r, Ra, s, Se, Si, Ta, Tc, Ua, Ub,
        Ul, w, Wo, Yo
    atelous   ι

73 **Easter Eve: Third lesson** (Isa. 4: 1–6)   LV
    contained in *Ar*, As, Ba, Bo, Bx, Cc, Dr, Eg, *He*, *Hl*, La, Lm, Ln,
        Lt, *N*, Ny, o, *Pl*, Pr, r, Ra, s, se, Si, Ta, Tc, Ua, Ub,
        Ul, w, Wo, Yo
    atelous   ι

74 **Easter Eve: Fourth lesson** (Deut. 31: 22–30)   LV
    contained in *Ar*, As, Ba, Bo, Bx, Cc, Dr, Eg, *Hl*, La, Lm, Ln, Lt,
        N, Ny, o, *Pl*, Pr, r, Ra, s, Se, Si, Ta, Tc, Ua, Ub, Ul,
        w, Wo, Yo
    lacuna   *He*
    atelous   ι

75 **Pentecost Eve: First lesson** (Gen. 22: 1–19)   LV
    contained in *Ar*, As, Ba, Bo, Bx, Cc, Dr, Eg, *He*, *Hl*, La, Lm, Ln,
        Lt, *N*, Ny, o, *Pl*, Pr, r, Ra, s, Se, Si, Ta, Tc, Ua, Ub,
        Ul, w, Wo, Yo
    atelous   ι

76 **Pentecost Eve: Second lesson** (Deut. 31: 22–30)   LV (CR)
    contained in *Ar*, As, Ba, Bo, Bx, Cc, Dr, Eg, *He*, *Hl*, La, Lm, Ln,
        Lt, *N*, Ny, o, *Pl*, Pr, r, Ra, s, Se, Si, Ta, Tc, Ua, Ub,
        Ul, w, Wo, Yo
    atelous   ι
    omitted   Ta

77 **Pentecost Eve: Third lesson** (Isa. 4: 1–6)   LV (CR)
    contained in *Ar*, As, Ba, Bo, Bx, Cc, Dr, Eg, *He*, *Hl*, La, Lm, Ln,
        Lt, *N*, Ny, o, *Pl*, Pr, r, Ra, s, se, Si, Ta, Tc, Ua, Ub,
        Ul, w, Wo, Yo
    atelous   ι

omitted   Ta

78 **Pentecost Eve: Fourth lesson** (Baruch 3: 9–38)   LV
     contained in *Ar*, As, Ba, Bo, Bx, Cc, Dr, Eg, *He*, *Hl*, La, Lm, Ln,
                   Lt, *N*, Ny, o, *Pl*, Pr, r, Ra, s, Se, Si, Ta, Tc, Ua, Ub,
                   Ul, w, Wo, Yo
     atelous   ι

79 **Wednesday after Pentecost** (Wisd. 1: 1–7)   LV
     contained in *Ar*, As, Ba, Bo, Bx, Cc, Dr, Eg, *He*, *Hl*, La, Lm, Ln,
                   Lt, *N*, Ny, o, *Pl*, Pr, r, Ra, s, Se, Si, Ta, Tc, Ua, Ub,
                   Ul, w, Wo, Yo
     atelous   ι

80 **Saturday after Pentecost: First lesson** (Joel 3: 28–32)   LV
     contained in *Ar*, As, Ba, Bo, Bx, Cc, Dr, Eg, *He*, *Hl*, La, Lm, Ln,
                   Lt, *N*, Ny, o, *Pl*, Pr, r, Ra, s, Se, Si, Ta, Tc, Ua, Ub,
                   Ul, w, Wo, Yo
     atelous   ι

81 **Saturday after Pentecost: Second lesson** (Lev. 23: 9–21)   LV
     contained in *Ar*, As, Ba, Bo, Bx, Cc, Dr, Eg, *He*, *Hl*, La, Lm, Ln,
                   Lt, *N*, Ny, o, *Pl*, Pr, r, Ra, s, Se, Si, Ta, Tc, Ua, Ub,
                   Ul, w, Wo, Yo
     atelous   ι

82 **Saturday after Pentecost: Third lesson** (Deut. 26: 1–11)   LV
     contained in *Ar*, As, Ba, Bo, Bx, Cc, Dr, Eg, *He*, *Hl*, La, Lm, Ln,
                   Lt, *N*, Ny, o, *Pl*, Pr, r, Ra, s, Se, Si, Ta, Tc, Ua, Ub,
                   Ul, w, Wo, Yo
     atelous   ι

83 **Saturday after Pentecost: Fourth lesson** (Lev. 26: 1–12)   LV
     contained in *Ar*, As, Ba, Bo, Bx, Cc, Dr, Eg, *He*, *Hl*, La, Lm, Ln,
                   Lt, *N*, Ny, o, *Pl*, Pr, r, Ra, s, Se, Si, Ta, Tc, Ua, Ub,
                   Ul, w, Wo, Yo
     atelous   ι

84 **Saturday after Pentecost: Fifth lesson** (Dan. 3: 49–52)   LV (CR)
     contained in *Ar*, Ba, Bo, Bx, Cc, Dr, Eg, *He*, *Hl*, La, Lm, Ln, Lt,
                   N, Ny, o, *Pl*, Pr, Ra, s, Si, Ta, Tc, Ua, Ub, Ul, w, Wo,
                   Yo
     atelous   ι
     omitted   As, r, Se

85 **Wednesday in 17th week after Trinity: First lesson** (Amos   LV
     9: 13–15)
     contained in *Ar*, As, Ba, Bo, Bx, Cc, Dr, Eg, *He*, *Hl*, La, Lm, Ln,

Lt, *N*, Ny, o, *Pl*, Pr, r, Ra, s, Se, Si, Ta, Tc, Ua, Ub,
Ul, w, Wo, Yo

atelous   ɩ

86 **Wednesday in 17th week after Trinity: Second lesson** (2 Ezra   LV
8: 1–10)
contained in   *Ar*, As, Ba, Bo, Bx, Cc, Dr, Eg, *He*, *Hl*, La, Lm, Ln,
Lt, *N*, Ny, o, *Pl*, Pr, r, Ra, s, Se, Si, Ta, Tc, Ua, Ub,
Ul, w, Wo, Yo

atelous   ɩ

87 **Friday in 17th week after Trinity** (Hos. 14: 2–10)   LV
contained in   *Ar*, As, Ba, Bo, Bx, Cc, Dr, Eg, *He*, *Hl*, La, Lm, Ln,
Lt, *N*, Ny, o, *Pl*, Pr, r, Ra, s, Se, Si, Ta, Tc, Ua, Ub,
Ul, w, Wo, Yo

atelous   ɩ

88 **Saturday in 17th week after Trinity: First lesson** (Lev. 23: 26–   LV
32)
contained in   *Ar*, As, Ba, Bo, Bx, Cc, Dr, Eg, *He*, *Hl*, La, Lm, Ln,
Lt, *N*, Ny, o, *Pl*, Pr, r, Ra, s, Se, Si, Ta, Tc, Ua, Ub,
Ul, w, Wo, Yo

atelous   ɩ

89 **Saturday in 17th week after Trinity: Second lesson** (Lev.   LV
23: 33–43)
contained in   *Ar*, As, Ba, Bo, Bx, Cc, Dr, Eg, *He*, *Hl*, La, Lm, Ln,
Lt, *N*, Ny, o, *Pl*, Pr, r, Ra, s, Se, Si, Ta, Tc, Ua, Ub,
Ul, w, Wo, Yo

atelous   ɩ

90 **Saturday in 17th week after Trinity: Third lesson** (Mic. 7: 14–   LV
20)
contained in   *Ar*, As, Ba, Bo, Bx, Cc, Dr, Eg, *He*, *Hl*, La, Lm, Ln,
Lt, *N*, Ny, o, *Pl*, Pr, r, Ra, s, Se, Si, Ta, Tc, Ua, Ub,
Ul, w, Wo, Yo

atelous   ɩ

91 **Saturday in 17th week after Trinity: Fourth lesson** (Zech.   LV
8: 14–20)
contained in   *Ar*, As, Ba, Bo, Bx, Cc, Dr, Eg, *He*, *Hl*, La, Lm, Ln,
Lt, *N*, Ny, o, *Pl*, Pr, r, Ra, s, Se, Si, Ta, Tc, Ua, Ub,
Ul, w, Wo, Yo

atelous   ɩ

92 **Saturday in 17th week after Trinity: Fifth lesson** (Dan. 3:   LV (CR)
49–52)
contained in   *Ar*, As, Ba, Bo, Bx, Cc, Dr, Eg, *He*, *Hl*, La, Lm, Ln,

Lt, *N*, Ny, o, *Pl*, Pr, r, Ra, s, Se, Si, Ta, Tc, Ua, Ub,
Ul, w, Wo, Yo
atelous   ι
omitted   As, r, Se

93   **25th Sunday after Trinity** (Jer. 23: 5–8)   LV
     contained in   *Ar*, As, Ba, Bo, Bx, Cc, Dr, Eg, *He*, *Hl*, La, Lm, Ln,
                    Lt, *N*, Ny, o, *Pl*, Pr, r, Ra, s, Se, Si, Ta, Tc, Ua, Ub,
                    Ul, w, Wo, Yo
     atelous   ι

94   **Feast of relics** (Ecclus. 44: 10–15)   LV
     contained in   As, Ba, Bo, Bx, Cc, Dr, Eg, La, Lm, Ln, Lt, Ny, o, Pr,
                    r, Ra, s, Se, Si, Tc, Ua, Ub, Ul, w, Wo, Yo
     atelous   ι
     omitted   *Ar*, *He*, *Hl*, *N*, *Pl*, Ta

SANCTORALE

NOVEMBER

95   **St Andrew's Eve** (Prov. 10: 6; Ecclus. 44: 26–7; Ecclus. 45: 2–9):   IN
     Benedictio domini super caput iusti
     contained in   *Ar*, Ba, Bo, Bx, Cc, Dr, Eg, *He*, *Hl*, La, Lm, Ln, Lt,
                    Ny, o, *Pl*, Pr, r, Ra, s, Se, Si, Ta, Tc, Ua, Ub, Ul, w,
                    Wo, Yo
     atelous   ι
     lacuna   As
     omitted   *N*

DECEMBER

96   **St Nicholas** (given as St Silvester in some manuscripts) (Ecclus.   IN
     44: 16, 17, 20, 22, 25, 26, 27; 45: 3, 6, 8, 19, 20): Ecce sacerdos
     magnus qui in diebus suis
     contained in   *Ar*, Ba, Bo, Bx, Cc, Dr, Eg, *He*, *Hl*, La, Lm, Ln, Lt,
                    Ny, o, *Pl*, Pr, Ra, s, Si, Ua, Ub, Ul, w, Wo, Yo
     atelous   ι
     lacuna   As
     omitted   Tc, Ta, r, Se, *N*

97   **Conception of our Lady** (Ecclus. 24: 23–31)   LV (CR)
     contained in   Bx, Dr, Eg, La, Lm, Lt, o, r, Se, Tc, w, Wo
     atelous   ι
     lacuna   As
     omitted   *Ar*, Ba, Bo, Cc, *He*, *Hl*, Ln, *N*, Ny, *Pl*, Pr, s, Si,
                    Ua, Ub, Ul, Ta, Yo

98   **St Lucy** (Ecclus. 51: 13–17): Domine deus meus
     contained in   Bx, Dr, Eg, La, Lm, Lt, o, w, Wo
     atelous   ι
     lacuna   As
     omitted   Ar, Ba, Bo, Cc, He, Hl, Ln, N, Ny, Pl, Pr, r, Ra, s, Se,
                    Si, Ta, Tc, Ua, Ub, Ul, Yo

99   **Vigil of St Thomas** (Prov. 10: 6; Ecclus. 44: 26–7; 45: 2–9): Bene-
     dictio domini super caput iusti
     contained in   Bx, Dr, Eg, La, Lm, Lt, o, w, Wo
     atelous   ι
     lacuna   As
     omitted   Ar, Ba, Bo, Cc, He, Hl, Ln, N, Ny, Pl, Pr, r, Ra, s, Se,
                    Si, Ta, Tc, Ua, Ub, Ul, Yo

JANUARY

100 **St Maurus** (Ecclus. 39: 6–13): Iustus cor suum
     contained in   Bx, Dr, Eg, La, Lm, Lt, o, w, Wo
     atelous   ι
     lacuna   As
     omitted   Ar, Ba, Bo, Cc, He, Hl, Ln, N, Ny, Pl, Pr, r, Ra, s, Se,
                    Si, Ta, Tc, Ua, Ub, Ul, Yo

101 **St Sulpice** (Wisd. 10: 10–14): Iustum deduxit dominus
     contained in   Bx, Dr, Eg, La, Lm, Lt, o, w, Wo
     atelous   ι
     lacuna   As
     omitted   Ar, Ba, Bo, Cc, He, Hl, Ln, N, Ny, Pl, Pr, r, Ra, s, Se,
                    Si, Ta, Tc, Ua, Ub, Ul, Yo

102 **St Prisca** (Ecclus. 51: 13–17): Domine deus meus
     contained in   Bx, Dr, Eg, La, Lm, Lt, o, w, Wo
     atelous   ι
     lacuna   As
     omitted   Ar, Ba, Bo, Cc, He, Hl, Ln, N, Ny, Pl, Pr, r, Ra, s, Se,
                    Si, Ta, Tc, Ua, Ub, Ul, Yo

103 **St Wulfstan** (Ecclus. 44: 16, 17, 20, 22, 25, 26, 27; 45: 3, 6, 8, 19,
     20): Ecce sacerdos magnus qui in diebus suis
     contained in   Bx, Dr, Eg, La, Lm, Lt, o, w, Wo
     atelous   ι
     lacuna   As
     omitted   Ar, Ba, Bo, Cc, He, Hl, Ln, N, Ny, Pl, Pr, r, Ra, s, Se,
                    Si, Ta, Tc, Ua, Ub, Ul, Yo

104 **St Agnes** (Ecclus. 51: 1–12): Confitebor tibi domine rex
     contained in   Bx, Dr, Eg, La, Lm, Lt, o, w, Wo

atelous ι
lacuna As
omitted *Ar*, Ba, Bo, Cc, *He*, *Hl*, Ln, *N*, Ny, *Pl*, Pr, r, Ra, s, Se,
Si, Ta, Tc, Ua, Ub, Ul, Yo

105 **St Vincent** (Ecclus. 14: 22; 15: 3–4, 6): Beatus vir qui in sapientia
contained in Bx, Dr, Eg, La, Lm, Lt, o, w, Wo
atelous ι
lacuna As
omitted *Ar*, Ba, Bo, Cc, *He*, *Hl*, Ln, *N*, Ny, *Pl*, Pr, r, Ra, s, Se,
Si, Ta, Tc, Ua, Ub, Ul, Yo

106 **St Julian, bishop** (Ecclus. 47: 9–13; 24: 1–4): Dedit dominus
contained in Bx, Dr, Eg, La, Lm, Lt, o, w, Wo
atelous ι
lacuna As
omitted *Ar*, Ba, Bo, Cc, *He*, *Hl*, Ln, *N*, Ny, *Pl*, Pr, r, Ra, s, Se,
Si, Ta, Tc, Ua, Ub, Ul, Yo

107 **St Balthild** (Wisd. 7: 30; 8: 1–4): Sapientia vincit maliciam
contained in Bx, Dr, Eg, La, Lm, Lt, o, w, Wo
atelous ι
lacuna As
omitted *Ar*, Ba, Bo, Cc, *He*, *Hl*, Ln, *N*, Ny, *Pl*, Pr, r, Ra, s, Se,
Si, Ta, Tc, Ua, Ub, Ul, Yo

FEBRUARY

108 **Candlemas** (Mal. 3: 1–4)   LV
contained in *Ar*, Ba, Bo, Bx, Cc, Dr, Eg, *He*, *Hl*, La, Lm, Ln, Lt,
N, Ny, o, *Pl*, Pr, r, Ra, s, Se, Si, Ta, Tc, Ua, Ub, Ul,
w, Wo, Yo
atelous ι
lacuna As

109 **St Agatha** (Ecclus. 51: 1–12): Confitebor tibi domine rex
contained in Bx, Dr, Eg, La, Lm, Lt, o, w, Wo
atelous ι
lacuna As
omitted *Ar*, Ba, Bo, Cc, *He*, *Hl*, Ln, *N*, Ny, *Pl*, Pr, r, Ra, s, Se,
Si, Ta, Tc, Ua, Ub, Ul, Yo

110 **St Scholastica** (Wisd. 7: 30; 8: 1–4): Sapientia vincit maliciam
contained in Bx, Dr, Eg, La, Lm, Lt, o, w, Wo
atelous ι
lacuna As
omitted *Ar*, Ba, Bo, Cc, *He*, *Hl*, Ln, *N*, Ny, *Pl*, Pr, r, Ra, s, Se,
Si, Ta, Tc, Ua, Ub, Ul, Yo

111 **St Valentine** (Ecclus. 31: 8–11): Beatus vir qui inventus est
contained in   Bx, Dr, Eg, La, Lm, Lt, o, w, Wo
atelous   ι
lacuna   As
omitted   *Ar*, Ba, Bo, Cc, *He*, *Hl*, Ln, *N*, Ny, *Pl*, Pr, r, Ra, s, Se,
               Si, Ta, Tc, Ua, Ub, Ul, Yo

112 **St Juliana, virgin**
Ecclus. 47: 9–13; 24: 1–4 (Dedit dominus)
contained in   Bx, Lt
Ecclus. 51: 13–17 (Domine deus meus)
contained in   Dr, Eg, La, Lm, o, w, Wo
atelous   ι
lacuna   As
omitted   *Ar*, Ba, Bo, Cc, *He*, *Hl*, Ln, *N*, Ny, *Pl*, Pr, r, Ra, s, Se,
               Si, Ta, Tc, Ua, Ub, Ul, Yo

MARCH

113 **St Edward** (Ecclus. 31: 8–11): Beatus vir qui inventus est
contained in   Bx, Dr, Eg, La, Lm, Lt, o, w, Wo
atelous   ι
lacuna   As
omitted   *Ar*, Ba, Bo, Cc, *He*, *Hl*, Ln, *N*, Ny, *Pl*, Pr, r, Ra, s, Se,
               Si, Ta, Tc, Ua, Ub, Ul, Yo

114 **St Cuthbert** (Ecclus. 44: 16, 17, 20, 22, 25, 26, 27; 45: 3, 6, 8, 19,
20): Ecce sacerdos magnus qui in diebus suis
contained in   Bx, Dr, Eg, La, Lm, Lt, o, w, Wo
atelous   ι
lacuna   As
omitted   *Ar*, Ba, Bo, Cc, *He*, *Hl*, Ln, *N*, Ny, *Pl*, Pr, r, Ra, s, Se,
               Si, Ta, Tc, Ua, Ub, Ul, Yo

115 **St Benedict** (Ecclus. 39: 6–13): Iustus cor suum
contained in   Bx, Dr, Eg, La, Lm, Lt, o, w, Wo
atelous   ι
lacuna   As
omitted   *Ar*, Ba, Bo, Cc, *He*, *Hl*, Ln, *N*, Ny, *Pl*, Pr, r, Ra, s, Se,
               Si, Ta, Tc, Ua, Ub, Ul, Yo

116 **Annunciation** (Isa. 7: 10–15)   LV (CR)
contained in   *Ar*, Ba, Bo, Bx, Cc, Dr, Eg, *He*, *Hl*, La, Lm, Ln, Lt,
               Ny, o, *Pl*, Pr, Ra, s, Se, Si, Ua, Ub, Ul, w, Wo, Yo
atelous   ι
lacuna   As
omitted   *N*, r, Ta, Tc

APRIL

117 **St Richard** (Ecclus. 44: 16, 17, 20, 22, 25, 26, 27; 45: 3, 6, 8, 19, 20):
     Ecce sacerdos magnus qui in diebus suis
     contained in Bx, Dr, Eg, La, Lm, Lt, o, w, Wo
     atelous ι
     lacuna As
     omitted *Ar*, Ba, Bo, Cc, *He*, *Hl*, Ln, *N*, Ny, *Pl*, Pr, r, Ra, s, Se,
              Si, Ta, Tc, Ua, Ub, Ul, Yo

118 **St Ambrose** (Ecclus. 47: 9–13; 24: 1–4): Dedit dominus
     contained in Bx, Dr, Eg, La, Lm, Lt, o, w, Wo
     atelous ι
     lacuna As
     omitted *Ar*, Ba, Bo, Cc, *He*, *Hl*, Ln, *N*, Ny, *Pl*, Pr, r, Ra, s, Se,
              Si, Ta, Tc, Ua, Ub, Ul, Yo

119 **Sts Tiburtius and Valerian** (Prov. 15: 2–9): Lingua sapientium
     contained in Bx, Dr, Eg, La, Lm, Lt, o, w, Wo
     atelous ι
     lacuna As
     omitted *Ar*, Ba, Bo, Cc, *He*, *Hl*, Ln, *N*, Ny, *Pl*, Pr, r, Ra, s, Se,
              Si, Ta, Tc, Ua, Ub, Ul, Yo

MAY

120 **Sts Philip and James** (Wisd. 5: 1–5): Stabunt iusti   LV
     contained in *Ar*, Ba, Bo, Bx, Cc, Dr, Eg, *He*, *Hl*, La, Lm, Ln, Lt,
              N, Ny, o, *Pl*, Pr, r, Ra, s, Se, Si, Ta, Tc, Ua, Ub, Ul,
              w, Wo, Yo
     atelous ι
     lacuna As

121 **St John the Evangelist** (Ecclus. 15: 1–6): Qui timet deum
     contained in Bx, Dr, Eg, La, Lm, Lt, o, w, Wo
     atelous ι
     lacuna As
     omitted *Ar*, Ba, Bo, Cc, *He*, *Hl*, Ln, *N*, Ny, *Pl*, Pr, r, Ra, s, Se,
              Si, Ta, Tc, Ua, Ub, Ul, Yo

122 **Sts Gordianus and Epimachus** (Wisd. 3: 1–8): Iustorum animae
     contained in Bx, Dr, Eg, La, Lm, Lt, o, w, Wo
     atelous ι
     lacuna As
     omitted *Ar*, Ba, Bo, Cc, *He*, *Hl*, Ln, *N*, Ny, *Pl*, Pr, r, Ra, s, Se,
              Si, Ta, Tc, Ua, Ub, Ul, Yo

123 **Sts Nereus, Achilleus, Pancras** (Wisd. 5: 16–22): Iusti autem in
   perpetuum
   contained in Bx, Dr, Eg, La, Lm, Lt, o, w, Wo
   atelous   ι
   lacuna   As
   omitted   Ar, Ba, Bo, Cc, He, Hl, Ln, N, Ny, Pl, Pr, r, Ra, s, Se,
                  Si, Ta, Tc, Ua, Ub, Ul, Yo

124 **St Dunstan** (Ecclus. 44: 16, 17, 20, 22, 25, 26, 27; 45: 3, 6, 8, 19,
   20): Ecce sacerdos magnus qui in diebus suis
   contained in Bx, Dr, Eg, La, Lm, Lt, o, w, Wo
   atelous   ι
   lacuna   As
   omitted   Ar, Ba, Bo, Cc, He, Hl, Ln, N, Ny, Pl, Pr, r, Ra, s, Se,
                  Si, Ta, Tc, Ua, Ub, Ul, Yo

125 **Sts Urban and Aldhelm** (Wisd. 10: 10–14): Iustum deduxit
   dominus
   contained in Bx, Dr, Eg, La, Lm, Lt, o, w, Wo
   atelous   ι
   lacuna   As
   omitted   Ar, Ba, Bo, Cc, He, Hl, Ln, N, Ny, Pl, Pr, r, Ra, s, Se,
                  Si, Ta, Tc, Ua, Ub, Ul, Yo

126 **St Augustine** (Ecclus. 47: 9–13; 24: 1–4): Dedit dominus
   contained in Bx, Dr, Eg, La, Lm, Lt, o, w, Wo
   atelous   ι
   lacuna   As
   omitted   Ar, Ba, Bo, Cc, He, Hl, Ln, N, Ny, Pl, Pr, r, Ra, s, Se,
                  Si, Ta, Tc, Ua, Ub, Ul, Yo

127 **St Germanus** (Ecclus. 44: 16, 17, 20, 22, 25, 26, 27; 45: 3, 6, 8, 19,
   20): Ecce sacerdos magnus qui in diebus suis
   contained in Bx, Dr, Eg, La, Lm, Lt, o, w, Wo
   atelous   ι
   lacuna   As
   omitted   Ar, Ba, Bo, Cc, He, Hl, Ln, N, Ny, Pl, Pr, r, Ra, s, Se,
                  Si, Ta, Tc, Ua, Ub, Ul, Yo

JUNE

128 **St Nicomedes** (Ecclus. 14: 22; 15: 3–4, 6): Beatus vir qui in sapientia
   contained in Bx, Dr, Eg, La, Lm, Lt, o, w, Wo
   atelous   ι
   lacuna   As
   omitted   Ar, Ba, Bo, Cc, He, Hl, Ln, N, Ny, Pl, Pr, r, Ra, s, Se,
                  Si, Ta, Tc, Ua, Ub, Ul, Yo

129 **Translation of St Edmund** (Ecclus. 50: 4, 1, 5–13, 16, 17, 23–5):
 Ecce sacerdos magnus qui in vita sua
 contained in Bx, Dr, Eg, La, Lm, Lt, o, Ra, w, Wo
 atelous ι
 lacuna As
 omitted Ar, Ba, Bo, Cc, *He*, *Hl*, Ln, *N*, Ny, *Pl*, Pr, r, s, Se, Si,
 Ta, Tc, Ua, Ub, Ul, Yo

130 **Sts Basilides, Cyrinus, and Nabor** (Wisd. 3: 1–8): Iustorum
 animae
 contained in Bx, Dr, Eg, La, Lm, Lt, o, w, Wo
 atelous ι
 lacuna As
 omitted Ar, Ba, Bo, Cc, *He*, *Hl*, Ln, *N*, Ny, *Pl*, Pr, r, Ra, s, Se,
 Si, Ta, Tc, Ua, Ub, Ul, Yo

131 **St Basil** (Ecclus. 44: 16, 17, 20, 22, 25, 26, 27; 45: 3, 6, 8, 19, 20):
 Ecce sacerdos magnus qui in diebus suis
 contained in Bx, Dr, Eg, La, Lm, Lt, o, w, Wo
 atelous ι
 lacuna As
 omitted Ar, Ba, Bo, Cc, *He*, *Hl*, Ln, *N*, Ny, *Pl*, Pr, r, Ra, s, Se,
 Si, Ta, Tc, Ua, Ub, Ul, Yo

132 **Sts Vitus and Modestus** (Wisd. 5: 16–22): Iusti autem in perpetuum
 contained in Bx, Dr, Eg, La, Lm, Lt, o, w, Wo
 atelous ι
 lacuna As
 omitted Ar, Ba, Bo, Cc, *He*, *Hl*, Ln, *N*, Ny, *Pl*, Pr, r, Ra, s, Se,
 Si, Ta, Tc, Ua, Ub, Ul, Yo

133 **St Botulf** (Ecclus. 39: 6–13): Iustus cor suum
 contained in Bx, Dr, Eg, La, Lm, Lt, o, w, Wo
 atelous ι
 lacuna As
 omitted Ar, Ba, Bo, Cc, *He*, *Hl*, Ln, *N*, Ny, *Pl*, Pr, r, Ra, s, Se,
 Si, Ta, Tc, Ua, Ub, Ul, Yo

134 **Sts Mark and Marcellian** (Prov. 15: 2–9): Lingua sapientium
 contained in Bx, Dr, Eg, La, Lm, Lt, o, w, Wo
 atelous ι
 lacuna As
 omitted Ar, Ba, Bo, Cc, *He*, *Hl*, Ln, *N*, Ny, *Pl*, Pr, r, Ra, s, Se,
 Si, Ta, Tc, Ua, Ub, Ul, Yo

135 **St Edward** (Ecclus. 31: 8–11): Beatus vir qui inventus est
 contained in Bx, Dr, Eg, La, Lm, Lt, o, w, Wo

atelous   ι
lacuna   As
omitted   *Ar*, Ba, Bo, Cc, *He*, *Hl*, Ln, *N*, Ny, *Pl*, Pr, r, Ra, s, Se,
              Si, Ta, Tc, Ua, Ub, Ul, Yo

136 **St Alban**[36] (Wisd. 4: 7–15): Iustus si morte preoccupatus
     contained in Ba, Bx, Cc, Dr, Eg, La, Ln, Lm, Lt, o, Ua, Ub, Ul, w,
                   Wo
     atelous   ι
     lacuna   As
     omitted   *Ar*, Bo, *He*, *Hl*, *N*, Ny, *Pl*, Pr, r, Ra, s, Se, Si, Ta, Tc,
                   Yo

137 **Midsummer Eve/Eve of St John Baptist**[37] (Jer. 1: 4–10)   LV
     contained in *Ar*, Ba, Bo, Bx, Cc, Dr, Eg, *He*, *Hl*, La, Lm, Ln, Lt,
                   N, Ny, o, *Pl*, Pr, r, Ra, s, Se, Si, Ta, Tc, Ua, Ub, Ul,
                   w, Wo, Yo
     atelous   ι
     lacuna   As

138 **Midsummer Day/Nativity of St John Baptist**[38] (Isa. 49: 1–7)   LV
     contained in *Ar*, Ba, Bo, Bx, Cc, Dr, Eg, *He*, *Hl*, La, Lm, Ln, Lt,
                   N, Ny, o, *Pl*, Pr, r, Ra, s, Se, Si, Ta, Tc, Ua, Ub, Ul,
                   w, Wo, Yo
     atelous   ι
     lacuna   As

139 **Sts John and Paul**[39] (Ecclus. 44: 10–15): Hi sunt viri misericordiae
     contained in Ba, Bx, Cc, Dr, Eg, La, Ln, Lm, Lt, o, Tc, Ua, Ub,
                   Ul, w, Wo
     atelous   ι
     lacuna   As
     omitted   *Ar*, Bo, *He*, *Hl*, *N*, Ny, *Pl*, Pr, r, Ra, s, Se, Si, Ta, Yo

---

[36] This lection, along with the one for St Cyriacus and companions (no. 156), and for
St Hugh (no. 189), is frequently given in the Common rather than the Proper. Those cases are
included here, since those lections occur in the Common accompanied by a rubric explicitly
referring to the saint.

[37] Type II lectionaries use the term 'Midsummer eve', while Type I uses 'Eve of St John
Baptist'.

[38] Type II lectionaries use the term 'Midsummer day', while Type I uses 'Nativity of
St John Baptist'.

[39] There is some confusion in the lectionaries as to whether this is the feast of Sts John
and Paul or of Sts Peter and Paul, a feast which occurs a few days afterwards. The feast of Sts
Peter and Paul, however, commonly has a lection from Acts in the Sarum Missal (*The Sarum
Missal*, ed. Legg, 284).

JULY

140 **Octave of St John the Baptist** (Isa. 49: 1–7)   LV (CR)
     contained in Ba, Bo, Bx, Cc, Dr, Eg, La, Lm, Ln, Lt, Ny, o, Pr, Ra,
                   s, Si, Ua, Ub, Ul, w, Wo, Yo
     atelous   ι
     lacuna   As
     omitted   *Ar*, *He*, *Hl*, *N*, *Pl*, r, Se, Ta, Tc

141 **Translation of St Martin** (Ecclus. 44: 16, 17, 20, 22, 25, 26,   IN (CR)
     27; 45: 3, 6, 8, 19, 20): Ecce sacerdos magnus qui in diebus suis
     contained in *Ar*, Ba, Bo, Bx, Cc, Dr, Eg, *He*, *Hl*, La, Lm, Ln, Lt,
                   Ny, o, *Pl*, Pr, Ra, s, Si, Ua, Ub, Ul, w, Wo, Yo
     atelous   ι
     lacuna   As
     omitted   *N*, r, Se, Ta, Tc

142 **Octave of Sts Peter and Paul** (Ecclus. 44: 10–15): Hi sunt   LV (CR)
     viri misericordiae
     contained in *Ar*, Ba, Bo, Bx, Cc, Dr, Eg, *He*, *Hl*, La, Lm, Ln, Lt,
                   Ny, o, *Pl*, Pr, Ra, s, Si, Ua, Ub, Ul, w, Wo, Yo
     atelous   ι
     lacuna   As
     omitted   *N*, r, Se, Ta, Tc

143 **Translation of St Benedict** (Ecclus. 39: 6–13): Iustus cor suum
     contained in Bx, Dr, Eg, La, Lm, Lt, o, w, Wo
     atelous   ι
     lacuna   As
     omitted   *Ar*, Ba, Bo, Cc, *He*, *Hl*, Ln, *N*, Ny, *Pl*, Pr, r, Ra, s, Se,
                   Si, Ta, Tc, Ua, Ub, Ul, Yo

144 **St Kenelm** (Ecclus. 31: 8–11): Beatus vir qui inventus est
     contained in Bx, Dr, Eg, La, Lm, Lt, o, w, Wo
     atelous   ι
     lacuna   As
     omitted   *Ar*, Ba, Bo, Cc, *He*, *Hl*, Ln, *N*, Ny, *Pl*, Pr, r, Ra, s, Se,
                   Si, Ta, Tc, Ua, Ub, Ul, Yo

145 **St Arnulf** (Ecclus. 14: 22; 15: 3–4, 6): Beatus vir qui in sapientia
     contained in Bx, Dr, Eg, La, Lm, Lt, o, w, Wo
     atelous   ι
     lacuna   As
     omitted   *Ar*, Ba, Bo, Cc, *He*, *Hl*, Ln, *N*, Ny, *Pl*, Pr, r, Ra, s, Se,
                   Si, Ta, Tc, Ua, Ub, Ul, Yo

146 **St Margaret** (Ecclus. 51: 13–17): Domine deus meus
     contained in Bx, Dr, Eg, La, Lm, Lt, o, w, Wo
     atelous   ι

lacuna   As
omitted   *Ar*, Ba, Bo, Cc, *He*, *Hl*, Ln, *N*, Ny, *Pl*, Pr, r, Ra, s, Se,
            Si, Ta, Tc, Ua, Ub, Ul, Yo

147 **St Praxedes** (Wisd. 7: 30; 8: 1–4): Sapientia vincit maliciam
     contained in Bx, Dr, Eg, La, Lm, Lt, o, w, Wo
     atelous   *ι*
     lacuna   As
     omitted   *Ar*, Ba, Bo, Cc, *He*, *Hl*, Ln, *N*, Ny, *Pl*, Pr, r, Ra, s, Se,
                 Si, Ta, Tc, Ua, Ub, Ul, Yo

148 **St Mary Magdalene** (Prov. 31: 10–31)   LV
     contained in *Ar*, Ba, Bo, Bx, Cc, Dr, Eg, *He*, *Hl*, La, Lm, Ln, Lt,
                   N, Ny, o, *Pl*, Pr, r, Ra, s, Se, Si, Ta, Tc, Ua, Ub, Ul,
                   w, Wo, Yo
     atelous   *ι*
     lacuna   As

149 **St James Eve** (Prov. 10: 6; Ecclus. 44: 26–7; Ecclus. 45: 2–9):   IN (CR)
     Benedictio domini
     contained in *Ar*, Ba, Bo, Bx, Cc, Dr, Eg, *He*, *Hl*, La, Lm, Ln, Lt,
                   Ny, o, *Pl*, Pr, Ra, s, Si, Ua, Ub, Ul, w, Wo, Yo
     atelous   *ι*
     lacuna   As
     omitted   *N*, r, Se, Ta, Tc

150 **St Anne** (Prov. 31: 10–31)
     contained in Bx, Dr, Eg, La, Lm, Lt, o, w, Wo
     atelous   *ι*
     lacuna   As
     omitted   *Ar*, Ba, Bo, Cc, *He*, *Hl*, Ln, *N*, Ny, *Pl*, Pr, r, Ra, s, Se,
                 Si, Ta, Tc, Ua, Ub, Ul, Yo

151 **Seven Sleepers' Day** (Wisd. 3: 1–8): Iustorum animae
     contained in Bx, Dr, Eg, La, Lm, Lt, o, w, Wo
     atelous   *ι*
     lacuna   As
     omitted   *Ar*, Ba, Bo, Cc, *He*, *Hl*, Ln, *N*, Ny, *Pl*, Pr, r, Ra, s, Se,
                 Si, Ta, Tc, Ua, Ub, Ul, Yo

153 **St Samson**
     Ecclus. 44: 16, 17, 20, 22, 25, 26, 27; 45: 3, 6, 8, 19, 20 (Ecce sacerdos
         magnus qui in diebus suis)
     contained in Bx, Dr, Eg, La, Lm, o, w, Wo
     Ecclus. 50: 4, 1, 5–13, 16, 17, 23–5 (Ecce sacerdos magnus qui in vita
         sua)
     contained in Lt
     atelous   *ι*

lacuna   As
omitted   *Ar*, Ba, Bo, Cc, *He*, *Hl*, Ln, *N*, Ny, *Pl*, Pr, r, Ra, s, Se,
          Si, Ta, Tc, Ua, Ub, Ul, Yo

153 **Sts Felix, Simplicius, Faustinus** (Prov. 15: 2–9): Lingua sapien-
    tium
    contained in   Bx, Dr, Eg, La, Lm, Lt, o, w, Wo
    atelous   *ι*
    lacuna   As
    omitted   *Ar*, Ba, Bo, Cc, *He*, *Hl*, Ln, *N*, Ny, *Pl*, Pr, r, Ra, s, Se,
              Si, Ta, Tc, Ua, Ub, Ul, Yo

154 **St Germanus** (Wisd. 10: 10–14): Iustum deduxit dominus
    contained in   Bx, Dr, Eg, La, Lm, Lt, o, w, Wo
    atelous   *ι*
    lacuna   As
    omitted   *Ar*, Ba, Bo, Cc, *He*, *Hl*, Ln, *N*, Ny, *Pl*, Pr, r, Ra, s, Se,
              Si, Ta, Tc, Ua, Ub, Ul, Yo

AUGUST

155 **St Oswald** (Ecclus. 31: 8–11): Beatus vir qui inventus est
    contained in   Bx, Dr, Eg, La, Lm, Lt, o, w, Wo
    atelous   *ι*
    lacuna   As
    omitted   *Ar*, Ba, Bo, Cc, *He*, *Hl*, Ln, *N*, Ny, *Pl*, Pr, r, Ra, s, Se,
              Si, Ta, Tc, Ua, Ub, Ul, Yo

156 **St Cyriacus and companions** (Ecclus. 2: 7–11): Metuentes
    dominum
    contained in   *Ar*, Ba, Bx, Dr, Eg, *He*, *Hl*, La, Lm, Ln, Lt, o, *Pl*, Ra,
              Si, Ta, Ua, Ub, Ul, w, Wo, Yo
    atelous   *ι*
    lacuna   As
    omitted   *N*, r, Se, Tc

157 **St Lawrence Eve** (Ecclus. 51: 1–12): Confitebor tibi domine rex   LV
    contained in   *Ar*, Ba, Bx, Dr, Eg, *He*, *Hl*, La, Lm, Ln, Lt, o, *Pl*, Ra,
              Ua, Ub, Ul, w, Wo, Yo
    misnamed as St Cyriacus and companions[40] in
              Bo, Cc, Ny, Pr, s
    atelous   *ι*

[40] In several Type II B manuscripts there is some confusion between the lection for St Lawrence Eve and the lection for St Cyriacus. According to the Sarum Missal, Ecclus. 51 is the correct lection for St Lawrence Eve, but this lection is misnamed as St Cyriacus in some Type II B lectionaries. In Si the scribe realized the error and replaced Ecclus. 51 with the correct lection for St Cyriacus (Ecclus. 2). In the Common of these OTLs this lection is cross-referenced by its correct title, St Lawrence, which means that because of the misnaming of the lection this becomes in effect an empty cross-reference.

lacuna   As
omitted   Bo, Cc, *N*, Ny, Pr, r, s, Se, Si, Ta, Tc

158 **St Hippolytus and companions** (Wisd. 4: 7–15): Iustus si morte
     preoccupatus
     contained in Bx, Dr, Eg, La, Lm, Lt, o, w, Wo
     atelous   ι
     lacuna   As
     omitted   *Ar*, Ba, Bo, Cc, *He*, *Hl*, Ln, *N*, Ny, *Pl*, Pr, r, Ra, s, Se,
                   Si, Ta, Tc, Ua, Ub, Ul, Yo

159 **Assumption Eve** (Ecclus. 24: 14–16)   EV
     contained in *Ar*, Ba, Bo, Bx, Cc, Dr, Eg, *He*, *Hl*, La, Lm, Ln, Lt,
                   N, Ny, o, *Pl*, Pr, r, Ra, s, Se, Ta, Tc, Ua, Ub, Ul, w,
                   Wo, Yo
     atelous   ι
     lacuna   As
     omitted   Si

160 **Assumption Day** (Ecclus. 24: 11–20)   LV
     contained in *Ar*, Ba, Bo, Bx, Cc, Dr, Eg, *He*, *Hl*, La, Lm, Ln, Lt,
                   N, Ny, o, *Pl*, Pr, r, Ra, s, Se, Ta, Tc, Ua, Ub, Ul, w,
                   Wo, Yo
     atelous   ι
     lacuna   As
     omitted   Si

161 **Octave of Assumption** (S. of S. 3: 11; 4: 1, 7, 8, 10–16; 6: 9,   LV+IN
     10; 7: 6)
     contained in *Ar*, Ba, Bo, Bx, Cc, Dr, Eg, *He*, *Hl*, La, Lm, Ln, Lt,
                   N, Ny, o, *Pl*, Pr, r, Ra, s, Se, Ta, Tc, Ua, Ub, Ul, w,
                   Wo, Yo
     atelous   ι
     lacuna   As
     omitted   Si

162 **St Bartholomew Eve** (Prov. 3: 13–20): Beatus homo qui invenit
     contained in Bx, Dr, Eg, La, Lm, Lt, o, w, Wo
     atelous   ι
     lacuna   As
     omitted   *Ar*, Ba, Bo, Cc, *He*, *Hl*, Ln, *N*, Ny, *Pl*, Pr, r, Ra, s, Se,
                   Si, Ta, Tc, Ua, Ub, Ul, Yo

163 **St Rufus** (Ecclus. 14: 22; 15: 3–4, 6): Beatus vir qui in sapientia
     contained in Bx, Dr, Eg, La, Lm, Lt, o, w, Wo
     atelous   ι
     lacuna   As

        omitted   *Ar*, Ba, Bo, Cc, *He*, *Hl*, Ln, *N*, Ny, *Pl*, Pr, r, Ra, s, Se,
                    Si, Ta, Tc, Ua, Ub, Ul, Yo

164 **St Augustine** (Ecclus. 47: 9–13; 24: 1–4): Dedit dominus
     contained in Bx, Dr, Eg, La, Lm, Lt, o, w, Wo
     atelous   *ι*
     lacuna   As
     omitted   *Ar*, Ba, Bo, Cc, *He*, *Hl*, Ln, *N*, Ny, *Pl*, Pr, r, Ra, s, Se,
                  Si, Ta, Tc, Ua, Ub, Ul, Yo

165 **Decollation of St John Baptist/St John in harvest**[41] (Prov.   LV
     10: 28–11: 11)
     contained in *Ar*, As, Ba, Bo, Bx, Cc, Dr, Eg, *He*, *Hl*, La, Lm, Ln,
                   Lt, *N*, Ny, o, *Pl*, Pr, r, Ra, s, Se, Si, Ta, Tc, Ua, Ub,
                   Ul, w, Wo, Yo
     atelous   *ι*

166 **Sts Felix and Adauctus** (Wisd. 3: 1–8): Iustorum animae
     contained in Bx, Dr, Eg, La, Lm, Lt, o, w, Wo
     atelous   *ι*
     omitted   *Ar*, As, Ba, Bo, Cc, *He*, *Hl*, Ln, *N*, Ny, *Pl*, Pr, r, Ra,
                  s, Se, Si, Ta, Tc, Ua, Ub, Ul, Yo

SEPTEMBER

167 **Translation of St Cuthbert** (Ecclus. 44: 16, 17, 20, 22, 25, 26, 27;
     45: 3, 6, 8, 19, 20): Ecce sacerdos magnus qui in diebus suis
     contained in Bx, Dr, Eg, La, Lm, Lt, o, w, Wo
     atelous   *ι*
     omitted   *Ar*, As, Ba, Bo, Cc, *He*, *Hl*, Ln, *N*, Ny, *Pl*, Pr, r, Ra,
                  s, Se, Si, Ta, Tc, Ua, Ub, Ul, Yo

168 **Vigil of the Nativity of our Lady** (Ecclus. 24: 14–16)
     contained in Bx, Dr, Eg, La, Lm, Lt, o, w, Wo
     atelous   *ι*
     omitted   *Ar*, As, Ba, Bo, Cc, *He*, *Hl*, Ln, *N*, Ny, *Pl*, Pr, r, Ra,
                  s, Se, Si, Ta, Tc, Ua, Ub, Ul, Yo

169 **Nativity of our Lady** (Ecclus. 24: 23–31)   LV
     contained in *Ar*, Ba, Bo, Bx, Cc, Dr, Eg, *He*, *Hl*, La, Lm, Ln, Lt,
                   N, Ny, o, *Pl*, Pr, Ra, s, Si, Ta, Ua, Ub, Ul, w, Wo, Yo
     atelous   *ι*
     omitted   As, r, Se, Tc

170 **Octave of Nativity** (Wisd. 4: 1–7): O quam pulchra   LV
     contained in *Ar*, As, Ba, Bo, Bx, Cc, Dr, Eg, *He*, *Hl*, La, Lm, Ln,
                   Lt, *N*, Ny, o, Pr, r, Ra, s, Se, Si, Ta, Tc, Ua, Ub, Ul,
                   w, Wo, Yo

---

[41] The first term is used in Type II lectionaries, while the second is used in Type I.

atelous   ι
lacuna   Pl

171 **St Matthew Eve** (Prov. 3: 13–20): Beatus homo qui invenit   LV
    contained in *Ar*, Ba, Bo, Bx, Cc, Dr, Eg, *He*, *Hl*, La, Lm, Ln, Ny,
                o, Pr, Ra, s, Si, Ta, Ua, Ub, Ul, w, Wo, Yo
    atelous   Lt, ι
    lacuna   Pl
    omitted   As, *N*, r, Se, Tc

172 **St Matthew Day** (Ezra 1: 10–14): Similitudo vultus   LV
    contained in *Ar*, Ba, Bo, Bx, Cc, Dr, Eg, *He*, *Hl*, La, Lm, Ln, Ny,
                o, Pr, Ra, s, Si, Ta, Ua, Ub, Ul, w, Wo, Yo
    atelous   Lt, ι
    lacuna   Pl
    omitted   As, *N*, r, Se, Tc

173 **St Cyprian** (Wisd. 5: 16–22): Iusti autem in perpetuum
    contained in Bx, Dr, Eg, La, Lm, o, w, Wo
    atelous   *Ar*, Lt, ι
    lacuna   Pl
    omitted   As, Ba, Bo, Cc, *He*, *Hl*, Ln, *N*, Ny, *Pl*, Pr, r, Ra, s, Se,
                Si, Ta, Tc, Ua, Ub, Ul, Yo

174 **St Jerome** (Ecclus. 47: 9–13; 24: 1–4): Dedit dominus
    contained in Bx, Dr, Eg, La, Lm, o, w, Wo
    atelous   *Ar*, Lt, ι
    lacuna   Pl
    omitted   As, Ba, Bo, Cc, *He*, *Hl*, Ln, *N*, Ny, *Pl*, Pr, r, Ra, s, Se,
                Si, Ta, Tc, Ua, Ub, Ul, Yo

OCTOBER

175 **St Faith** (Ecclus. 51: 13–17): Domine deus meus
    contained in Bx, Dr, Eg, La, Lm, o, w, Wo
    atelous   *Ar*, Lt, ι
    lacuna   Pl
    omitted   As, Ba, Bo, Cc, *He*, *Hl*, Ln, *N*, Ny, *Pl*, Pr, r, Ra, s, Se,
                Si, Ta, Tc, Ua, Ub, Ul, Yo

176 **Translation of St Edward** (Ecclus. 39: 6–13): Iustus cor suum
    contained in Bx, Dr, Eg, La, Lm, o, w, Wo
    atelous   *Ar*, Lt, ι
    lacuna   Pl
    omitted   As, Ba, Bo, Cc, *He*, *Hl*, Ln, *N*, Ny, *Pl*, Pr, r, Ra, s, Se,
                Si, Ta, Tc, Ua, Ub, Ul, Yo

177 St Wolfram (Ecclus. 44: 16, 17, 20, 22, 25, 26, 27; 45: 3, 6, 8, 19,
    20): Ecce sacerdos magnus qui in diebus suis
    contained in Bx, Dr, Eg, La, Lm, o, w, Wo
    atelous   *Ar*, Lt, ι
    lacuna   *Pl*
    omitted   As, Ba, Bo, Cc, *He*, *Hl*, Ln, *N*, Ny, *Pl*, Pr, r, Ra, s, Se,
                 Si, Ta, Tc, Ua, Ub, Ul, Yo

178 St Luke (Ezek. 1: 10–14): Similitudo vultus   LV (CR)
    contained in Ba, Bo, Bx, Cc, Dr, Eg, *He*, La, Lm, Ln, Ny, o, Pr, Ra,
                 s, Si, Ua, Ub, Ul, w, Wo, Yo
    atelous   *Ar*, Lt, ι
    lacuna   *Pl*
    omitted   As, *Hl*, *N*, r, Se, Ta, Tc

179 11,000 virgins (Wisd. 4: 1–7): O quam pulchra
    contained in Bx, Dr, Eg, La, Lm, o, w, Wo
    atelous   *Ar*, Lt, ι
    lacuna   *Pl*
    omitted   As, Ba, Bo, Cc, *He*, *Hl*, Ln, *N*, Ny, *Pl*, Pr, r, Ra, s, Se,
                 Si, Ta, Tc, Ua, Ub, Ul, Yo

180 St Romanus (Wisd. 10: 10–14): Iustum deduxit dominus
    contained in Bx, Dr, Eg, La, Lm, o, w, Wo
    atelous   *Ar*, Lt, ι
    lacuna   *Pl*
    omitted   As, Ba, Bo, Cc, *He*, *Hl*, Ln, *N*, Ny, *Pl*, Pr, r, Ra, s, Se,
                 Si, Ta, Tc, Ua, Ub, Ul, Yo

181 Eve of Sts Simon and Jude (Wisd. 3: 1–8): Iustorum animae
    contained in Bx, Dr, Eg, La, Lm, o, w, Wo
    atelous   *Ar*, Lt, ι
    lacuna   *Pl*
    omitted   As, Ba, Bo, Cc, *He*, *Hl*, Ln, *N*, Ny, *Pl*, Pr, r, Ra, s, Se,
                 Si, Ta, Tc, Ua, Ub, Ul, Yo

NOVEMBER

182 St Leonard (Ecclus. 39: 6–13): Iustus cor suum
    contained in Bx, Dr, Eg, La, Lm, o, w, Wo
    atelous   *Ar*, Lt, ι
    lacuna   *Pl*
    omitted   As, Ba, Bo, Cc, *He*, *Hl*, Ln, *N*, Ny, *Pl*, Pr, r, Ra, s, Se,
                 Si, Ta, Tc, Ua, Ub, Ul, Yo

183 Four crowned martyrs (Wisd. 3: 1–8): Iustorum animae
    contained in Bx, Dr, Eg, La, Lm, o, w, Wo
    atelous   *Ar*, Lt, ι

III. LIST OF LECTIONS lxxix

lacuna *Pl*
omitted As, Ba, Bo, Cc, *He*, *Hl*, Ln, *N*, Ny, *Pl*, Pr, r, Ra, s, Se,
Si, Ta, Tc, Ua, Ub, Ul, Yo

184 **St Theodore** (Ecclus. 14: 22; 15: 3–4, 6): Beatus vir qui in sapientia
contained in Bx, Dr, Eg, La, Lm, o, w, Wo
atelous *Ar*, Lt, *ι*
lacuna *Pl*
omitted As, Ba, Bo, Cc, *He*, *Hl*, Ln, *N*, Ny, *Pl*, Pr, r, Ra, s, Se,
Si, Ta, Tc, Ua, Ub, Ul, Yo

185 **St Martin** (Ecclus. 44: 16, 17, 20, 22, 25, 26, 27; 45: 3, 6, 8, 19, 20):
Ecce sacerdos magnus qui in diebus suis
contained in Bx, Dr, Eg, La, Lm, o, w, Wo
atelous *Ar*, Lt, *ι*
lacuna *Pl*
omitted As, Ba, Bo, Cc, *He*, *Hl*, Ln, *N*, Ny, *Pl*, Pr, r, Ra, s, Se,
Si, Ta, Tc, Ua, Ub, Ul, Yo

186 **St Brice** (Wisd. 10: 10–14): Iustum deduxit dominus
contained in Bx, Dr, Eg, La, Lm, o, w, Wo
atelous *Ar*, Lt, *ι*
lacuna *Pl*
omitted As, Ba, Bo, Cc, *He*, *Hl*, Ln, *N*, Ny, *Pl*, Pr, r, Ra, s, Se,
Si, Ta, Tc, Ua, Ub, Ul, Yo

187 **St Malo** (Ecclus. 44: 16, 17, 20, 22, 25, 26, 27; 45: 3, 6, 8, 19, 20):
Ecce sacerdos magnus qui in diebus suis
contained in Bx, Dr, Eg, La, Lm, o, w, Wo
atelous *Ar*, Lt, *ι*
lacuna *Pl*
omitted As, Ba, Bo, Cc, *He*, *Hl*, Ln, *N*, Ny, *Pl*, Pr, r, Ra, s, Se,
Si, Ta, Tc, Ua, Ub, Ul, Yo

188 **St Edmund of Abingdon** (Ecclus. 50: 4, 1, 5–13, 16, 17, 23–5):
Ecce sacerdos magnus qui in vita sua
contained in Bx, Dr, Eg, La, Lm, o, w, Wo
atelous *Ar*, Lt, *ι*
lacuna *Pl*
omitted As, Ba, Bo, Cc, *He*, *Hl*, Ln, *N*, Ny, *Pl*, Pr, r, Ra, s, Se,
Si, Ta, Tc, Ua, Ub, Ul, Yo

189 **St Hugh** (Ecclus. 45: 1–6): Dilectus a deo
contained in Ba, Bo, Bx, Cc, Dr, Eg, La, Lm, Ln, o, Ra, s, Ua, Ub,
Ul, w, Wo, Yo
atelous *Ar*, Lt, *ι*
lacuna *Pl*
omitted As, *He*, *Hl*, *N*, Ny, Pr, Se, Si, r, Ta, Tc

190 **Octave of St Martin** (Ecclus. 44: 16, 17, 20, 22, 25, 26, 27; 45: 3, 6, 8, 19, 20): Ecce sacerdos magnus qui in diebus suis
contained in Bx, Dr, Eg, La, Lm, o, w, Wo
atelous *Ar*, Lt, ι
lacuna *Pl*
omitted As, Ba, Bo, Cc, *He*, *Hl*, Ln, *N*, Ny, *Pl*, Pr, r, Ra, s, Se, Si, Ta, Tc, Ua, Ub, Ul, Yo

191 **St Edmund, king** (Ecclus. 31: 8–11): Beatus vir qui inventus est
contained in Bx, Dr, Eg, La, Lm, o, w, Wo
atelous *Ar*, Lt, ι
lacuna *Pl*
omitted As, Ba, Bo, Cc, *He*, *Hl*, Ln, *N*, Ny, *Pl*, Pr, r, Ra, s, Se, Si, Ta, Tc, Ua, Ub, Ul, Yo

192 **St Cecilia** (Ecclus. 51: 13–17): Domine deus meus
contained in Bx, Dr, Eg, La, Lm, o, w, Wo
atelous *Ar*, Lt, ι
lacuna *Pl*
omitted As, Ba, Bo, Cc, *He*, *Hl*, Ln, *N*, Ny, *Pl*, Pr, r, Ra, s, Se, Si, Ta, Tc, Ua, Ub, Ul, Yo

193 **St Chrysogonus** (Prov. 3: 13–20): Beatus homo qui invenit
contained in Bx, Dr, Eg, La, Lm, o, w, Wo
atelous *Ar*, Lt, ι
lacuna *Pl*
omitted As, Ba, Bo, Cc, *He*, *Hl*, Ln, *N*, Ny, *Pl*, Pr, r, Ra, s, Se, Si, Ta, Tc, Ua, Ub, Ul, Yo

194 **St Catherine** (Ecclus. 51: 1–12): Confitebor tibi domine rex
contained in Bx, Dr, Eg, La, Lm, o, w, Wo
atelous *Ar*, Lt, ι
lacuna *Pl*
omitted As, Ba, Bo, Cc, *He*, *Hl*, Ln, *N*, Ny, *Pl*, Pr, r, Ra, s, Se, Si, Ta, Tc, Ua, Ub, Ul, Yo

C O M M O N[42] (including Type I Non-Sarum lections[43])

195 **Vigil of apostles 1** (Prov. 10: 6; Ecclus. 44: 26–7; 45: 2–9):   IN (CR)
Benedictio domini super caput iusti
contained in As, Ba, Bo, Cc, *He*, *Hl*, Ln, *N*, Ny, Pr, r, Ra, s, Se, Si, Tc, Ua, Ub, Ul, Yo

---

[42] Some of these lections, especially those which occur with only one feast, such as those of St Hugh and St Cyriacus, may be given in the Proper rather than the Common. Such lections are listed here as included.

[43] Type III texts do not contain a Common at all. Those lections contained in the Proper are listed above. Type I texts contain a short Common of non-Sarum lections, and these are included in the list below but clearly marked as belonging to Type I manuscripts.

atelous   *Ar*, Lt, ι
lacuna   *Pl*
omitted   Ta (Type I & III: Bx, Dr, Eg, La, Lm, o, w, Wo)

196 **Vigil of apostles 2** (Prov. 3: 13–20): Beatus homo qui invenit
contained in As, Ba, Bo, Cc, *He*, *Hl*, Ln, *N*, Ny, Pr, r, Ra, s, Se, Si,
Tc, Ua, Ub, Ul, Yo
atelous   *Ar*, Lt, ι
lacuna   *Pl*
omitted   Ta (Type I & III: Bx, Dr, Eg, La, Lm, o, w, Wo)

197 **One evangelist** (Ezek. 1: 10–14): Similitudo vultus   LV (CR)
contained in As, Ba, Bo, Cc, *He*, *Hl*, Ln, *N*, Ny, Pr, r, Ra, s, Se,
Si,Tc, Ua, Ub, Ul, Yo
atelous   *Ar*, Lt, ι
lacuna   *Pl*
omitted   Ta (Type I & III: Bx, Dr, Eg, La, Lm, o, w, Wo)

198 **One martyr 1** (Ecclus. 14: 22; 15: 3–4, 6): Beatus vir qui in sapientia   LV
contained in As, Ba, Bo, Cc, *He*, *Hl*, Ln, *N*, Ny, Pr, r, Ra, s, Se, Si,
Ta, Tc, Ua, Ub, Ul, Yo
atelous   *Ar*, Lt, ι
lacuna   *Pl*
omitted   (Type I & III: Bx, Dr, Eg, La, Lm, o, w, Wo)

199 **One martyr 2** (Ecclus. 31: 8–11): Beatus vir qui inventus est   LV
contained in As, Ba, Bo, Cc, *He*, *Hl*, Ln, *N*, Ny, Pr, r, Ra, s, Se, Si,
Ta, Tc, Ua, Ub, Ul, Yo
atelous   *Ar*, Lt, ι
lacuna   *Pl*
omitted   (Type I & III: Bx, Dr, Eg, La, Lm, o, w, Wo)

200 **One martyr 3** (Wisd. 4: 7–15): Iustus si morte preoccupatus   LV
contained in As, Ba, Bo, Cc, *He*, *Hl*, Ln, *N*, Ny, Pr, r, Ra, s, Se, Si,
Ta, Tc, Ua, Ub, Ul, Yo
atelous   *Ar*, Lt, ι
lacuna   *Pl*
omitted   (Type I & III: Bx, Dr, Eg, La, Lm, o, w, Wo)

201 **Many martyrs 1** (Wisd. 3: 1–8): Iustorum animae   LV
contained in As, Ba, Bo, Cc, *He*, *Hl*, Ln, *N*, Ny, Pr, r, Ra, s, Se, Si,
Ta, Tc, Ua, Ub, Ul, Yo
atelous   *Ar*, Lt, ι
lacuna   *Pl*
omitted   (Type I & III: Bx, Dr, Eg, La, Lm, o, w, Wo)

202 **Many martyrs 2** (Wisd. 5: 16–22): Iusti autem in perpetuum   LV
contained in As, Ba, Bo, Cc, *He*, *Hl*, Ln, *N*, Ny, Pr, r, Ra, s, Se, Si,
Ta, Tc, Ua, Ub, Ul, Yo

atelous   *Ar*, Lt, ι
lacuna   *Pl*
omitted   (Type I & III: Bx, Dr, Eg, La, Lm, o, w, Wo)

203 **Many martyrs 3** (Ecclus. 2: 7–11): Metuentes dominum   EV
     contained in As, Ba, Bo, Cc, *He*, *Hl*, Ln, *N*, Ny, *Pl*, Pr, r, Ra, s, Se,
                   Si, Ta, Tc, Ua, Ub, Ul, Yo
     atelous   *Ar*, Lt, ι
     omitted   (Type I & III: Bx, Dr, Eg, La, Lm, o, w, Wo)

204 **Many martyrs 4** (Wisd. 10: 17–20): Reddet deus mercedem   LV
     contained in Ba, Bo, Cc, *He*, *Hl*, *N*, Ny, *Pl*, Pr, s, Si, Ua, Yo (Type I:
                   Dr, Eg, La, Lm, o, w)
     atelous   *Ar*, Lt, ι
     omitted   As, Ln, r, Ra, Se, Ta, Tc, Ub, Ul (Type III: Bx, Wo)

205 **Many martyrs 5** (Prov. 15: 2–9): Lingua sapientium   LV
     contained in As, Ba, Bo, Cc, *He*, *Hl*, Ln, *N*, Ny, *Pl*, Pr, r, Ra, s, Se,
                   Si, Ta, Tc, Ua, Ub, Ul, Yo
     atelous   *Ar*, Lt, ι
     omitted   (Type I & III: Bx, Dr, Eg, La, Lm, o, w, Wo)

206 **Many martyrs 6** (Ecclus. 44: 10–15): Hi sunt viri misericordiae   LV (CR)
     contained in As, Ba, Bo, Cc, *He*, *Hl*, Ln, *N*, Ny, *Pl*, Pr, r, Ra, s, Se,
                   Si, Tc, Ua, Ub, Ul, Yo
     atelous   *Ar*, Lt, ι
     omitted   Ta (Type I & III: Bx, Dr, Eg, La, Lm, o, w, Wo)

207 **One confessor and bishop 1** (Ecclus. 44: 16, 17, 20, 22, 25, 26,   IN (CR)
     27; 45: 3, 6, 8, 19, 20): Ecce sacerdos magnus qui in diebus suis
     contained in As, Ba, Bo, Cc, *He*, *Hl*, Ln, *N*, Ny, *Pl*, Pr, r, Ra, s, Se,
                   Si, Tc, Ua, Ub, Yo
     atelous   *Ar*, Lt, ι
     omitted   Ta (Type I & III: Bx, Dr, Eg, La, Lm, o, w, Wo)

208 **One confessor and bishop 2** (Ecclus. 50: 4, 1, 5–13, 16, 17,   IN (CR)
     23–5): Ecce sacerdos magnus qui in vita sua
     contained in As, Ba, Bo, Cc, *He*, *Hl*, *N*, Ny, *Pl*, Pr, r, s, Se, Si, Tc,
                   Ua, Ul, Wo, Yo
     atelous   *Ar*, Lt, ι
     omitted   Ln, Ra, Ta, Ub (Type I & III: Bx, Dr, Eg, La, Lm, o,
                   w, Wo)

209 **One confessor and bishop 3** (Wisd. 10: 10–14): Iustum deduxit   LV
     dominus
     contained in As, Ba, Bo, Cc, *He*, *Hl*, Ln, *N*, Ny, *Pl*, Pr, r, Ra, s, Se,
                   Si, Ta, Tc, Ua, Ub, Ul, Yo
     atelous   *Ar*, Lt, ι
     omitted   (Type I & III: Bx, Dr, Eg, La, Lm, o, w, Wo)

210 **One confessor and bishop 4** (Ecclus. 45: 1–6): Dilectus a deo   LV
   contained in   As, Ba, Bo, Cc, *He, Hl*, Ln, *N*, Ny, *Pl*, Pr, r, Ra, s, Se,
             Si, Ta, Tc, Ua, Ub, Ul, Yo
   atelous   *Ar*, Lt, *ι*
   omitted   (Type I & III: Bx, Dr, Eg, La, Lm, o, w, Wo)

211 **One confessor and doctor 1** (Ecclus. 47: 9–13; 24: 1–4): Dedit LV+IN
   dominus
   contained in   As, Ba, Bo, Cc, *He, Hl*, Ln, *N*, Ny, *Pl*, Pr, r, Ra, s, Se,
             Si, Ta, Tc, Ua, Ub, Ul, Yo
   atelous   *Ar*, Lt, *ι*
   omitted   (Type I & III: Bx, Dr, Eg, La, Lm, o, w, Wo)

212 **One confessor and doctor 2** (Wisd. 7: 7–14): Optavi et datus est   LV
   mihi
   contained in   Ba, Bo, Cc, *He, Hl, N*, Ny, *Pl*, Pr, s, Si, Ua, Yo (Type I:
             Dr, Eg, La, Lm, o, w)
   atelous   *Ar*, Lt, *ι*
   omitted   As, Ln, r, Ra, Se, Ta, Tc, Ub, Ul (Type III: Bx, Wo)

213 **One confessor and abbot 1** (Ecclus. 39: 6–13): Iustus cor suum   LV
   contained in   As, Ba, Bo, Cc, *He, Hl*, Ln, *N*, Ny, *Pl*, Pr, r, Ra, s, Se,
             Si, Ta, Tc, Ua, Ub, Ul, Yo
   atelous   *Ar*, Lt, *ι*
   omitted   (Type I & III: Bx, Dr, Eg, La, Lm, o, w, Wo)

214 **One confessor and abbot 2** (Ecclus. 2: 18–21): Qui timent   SYN
   dominum[44]
   contained in   Ba, Bo, Cc, Ny, Pr, s, Si, Ua, Ul, Yo (Type I: Dr, Eg,
             La, o, w)
   atelous   *Ar*, Lt, *ι*
   omitted   As, *He, Hl, N*, Ln, r, Ra, Se, Ta, Tc, Ua, Ub, Yo
             (Type III: Bx, Wo)

215 **Many confessors** (Ecclus. 2: 18–21): Qui timent dominum
   contained in   *He, Hl, N, Pl*
   atelous   *Ar*, Lm, Lt, *ι*
   omitted   As, Ba, Bo, Cc, Ln, Ny, r, Ra, s, Se, Si, Ta, Tc, Ub,
             Ul, (Type I & III: Bx, Dr, Eg, La, o, w, Wo)

216 **One virgin and martyr 1** (Ecclus. 51: 13–17): Domine deus meus   LV
   contained in   As, Ba, Bo, Cc, *He, Hl*, Ln, *N*, Ny, *Pl*, Pr, r, Ra, s, Se,
             Si, Ta, Tc, Ua, Ub, Ul, Yo

---

[44] In some lectionaries there is confusion as to whether this lection is the same as Lection 203, which is given for feasts of many martyrs (Metuentes dominum, Ecclus. 2: 7–13). The confusion is easily explained, given the similarities between the Latin incipits and the fact that both lections are taken from Ecclus. 2. Neither *The Sarum Missal*, ed. Legg, nor *Missale*, ed. Dickinson, gives the lection 'Qui timent dominum' as an option for feasts of one confessor and abbot, but Legg lists it for feasts of many confessors.

atelous   *Ar*, Lm, Lt, ι
omitted   (Type I & III: Bx, Dr, Eg, La, o, w, Wo)

217 **One virgin and martyr 2** (Ecclus. 51: 1–12): Confitebor tibi
     domine rex)
     contained in   As, Ba, *He*, *Hl*, Ln, *N*, *Pl*, r, Ra, Se, Ta, Tc, Ua, Ub,
                     Ul, Yo
     empty cross-reference to St Lawrence Eve in Bo, Cc, Ny, Pr, s, Si
     atelous   *Ar*, Lm, Lt, ι
     omitted   (Type I & III: Bx, Dr, Eg, La, o, w, Wo)

218 **One virgin and martyr 3** (Ecclus. 24: 1–5; 21–2): Sapientia   EV+IN
     laudabit animam suam
     contained in   Ba, Bo, Cc, *He*, *Hl*, *N*, Ny, *Pl*, Pr, s, Si, Ua, Yo (Type I:
                     Dr, Eg, La, o, w)
     atelous   *Ar*, Lt, ι
     omitted   As, Ln, r, Ra, Se, Ta, Tc, Ub, Ul (Type III: Bx, Wo)

219 **One virgin not martyr 1** (Wisd. 7: 30; 8: 1–4): Sapientia vincit   LV
     maliciam
     contained in   As, Ba, Bo, Cc, *He*, *Hl*, Ln, *N*, Ny, *Pl*, Pr, r, Ra, s, Se,
                     Si, Ta, Tc, Ua, Ub, Ul, Yo
     atelous   *Ar*, Lm, Lt, ι
     omitted   (Type I & III: Bx, Dr, Eg, La, o, w, Wo)

220 **One virgin not martyr 2** (Isa. 61: 10–11; 62: 5): Gaudens gaudebo   LV
     contained in   Ba, Bo, Cc, *He*, *Hl*, *N*, Ny, *Pl*, Pr, s, Si, Ua, Ub, Yo
                     (Type I: Dr, Eg, La, o, w)
     atelous   *Ar*, Lm, Lt, ι
     omitted   As, Ln, r, Ra, Se, Ta, Tc, Ul (Type I & III: Bx, Wo)

221 **Many virgins** (Wisd. 4: 1–7): O quam pulchra   LV (CR)
     contained in   As, Ba, Bo, Cc, *He*, *Hl*, Ln, Ny, *Pl*, Pr, r, Ra, s, Se, Si,
                     Ua, Ub, Ul, Yo
     atelous   *Ar*, Lm, Lt, ι
     omitted   *N*, Ta, Tc (Type I & III: Bx, Dr, Eg, La, o, w, Wo)

COMMEMORATIONS

222 **Our Lady in Advent** (Isa. 7: 10–15)   LV
     contained in   Ba, Bo, Bx, Cc, Dr, Eg, *He*, *Hl*, La, Lm, Ln, Ny, o,
                     Pr, Ra, s, Si, Ua, Ub, Ul, w, Wo, Yo
     atelous   *Ar*, Lt, ι
     omitted   As, *N*, *Pl*, r, Se, Ta, Tc

223 **Our Lady from Candlemas to Easter** (Ecclus. 24: 14–16)   EV
     contained in   Ba, Bo, Bx, Cc, Dr, Eg, *He*, *Hl*, La, Lm, Ln, Ny, o,
                     Pr, Ra, s, Si, Ua, Ub, Ul, w, Wo, Yo
     atelous   *Ar*, Lt, ι

omitted As, *N*, *Pl*, r, Se, Ta, Tc

224 **Our Lady from Easter until Trinity Sunday** (Ecclus. 24: 14–16)   EV
   contained in As, Ba, Bo, Bx, Cc, Dr, Eg, *He*, *Hl*, La, Lm, Ln, Ny,
     o, Pr, r, Ra, s, Se, Si, Ta, Ua, Ub, Ul, w, Wo, Yo
   atelous *Ar*, Lt, ι
   omitted *N*, *Pl*, Tc

225 **For brothers and sisters** (Isa. 18: 7–19: 25)   IN
   contained in As, Ba, Bo, Bx, Cc, Dr, Eg *He*, *Hl*, La, Lm, Ln, Ny,
     o, Pr, r, Ra, s, Se, Si, Ta, Tc, Ua, Ub, Ul, w, Wo, Yo
   atelous *Ar*, Lt, ι
   omitted *N*, *Pl*

226 **For peace** (2 Macc. 1: 2–5)   EV
   contained in Ba, Bo, Bx, Cc, Dr, Eg, *He*, *Hl*, La, Lm, Ln, Ny, o,
     Pl, Pr, Ra, s, Si, Ua, Ub, Ul, w, Wo, Yo
   atelous *Ar*, Lt, ι
   omitted As, *N*, r, Se, Ta, Tc

227 **For clear weather** (Lam. 2: 19–58)   IN
   contained in As, Ba, Bo, Bx, Cc, Dr, Eg, *He*, *Hl*, La, Lm, Ln, *N*,
     Ny, o, *Pl*, Pr, r, Ra, s, Se, Si, Ta, Tc, Ua, Ub, Ul, w,
     Wo, Yo
   atelous *Ar*, Lt, ι

228 **For rain** (Jer. 14: 19–22)   LV
   contained in As, Ba, Bo, Bx, Cc, Dr, Eg, *He*, *Hl*, La, Lm, Ln, *N*,
     Ny, o, *Pl*, Pr, r, Ra, s, Se, Si, Ta, Tc, Ua, Ub, Ul, w,
     Wo, Yo
   atelous *Ar*, Lt, ι

229 **For battles** (Esther 13: 9–17)   EV
   contained in Bo, Bx, Cc, Dr, Eg, *He*, *Hl*, La, Lm, Ln, *N*, Ny, o, *Pl*,
     Pr, Ra, s, Si, Ua, Ub, Ul, w, Wo, Yo
   atelous *Ar*, Ba, Lt, ι
   lacuna As
   omitted r, Se, Ta, Tc

230 **For pestilence of beasts** (Jer. 14: 7–9)   EV
   contained in Bo, Bx, Cc, Dr, Eg, *He*, *Hl*, La, Lm, Ln, *N*, Ny, o, *Pl*,
     Pr, r, Ra, s, Se, Si, Ta, Tc, Ua, Ub, Ul, w, Wo, Yo
   atelous *Ar*, Ba, Lt, ι
   lacuna As

231 **For pilgrims** (Gen. 24: 7)   EV
   contained in Bo, Bx, Cc, Dr, Eg, *He*, *Hl*, La, Lm, Ln, *N*, Ny, o, *Pl*,
     Pr, r, Ra, s, Se, Si, Ta, Tc, Ua, Ub, Ul, w, Wo, Yo
   atelous *Ar*, Ba, Lt, ι

    lacuna   As

232 **Requiem Mass** (2 Macc. 12: 43–6)   EV
    contained in Bo, Bx, Cc, Dr, Eg, *He*, *Hl*, La, Lm, Ln, *N*, Ny, o, *Pl*,
                  Pr, r, Ra, s, Se, Si, Ta, Tc, Ua, Ub, Ul, w, Wo, Yo
    atelous   *Ar*, Ba, Lt, ι
    lacuna   As

233 **Salus populi** (Isa. 18: 7–19: 25)
    contained in Bx, *He*, *N*, *Pl*, r, Se, Tc
    atelous   *Ar*, Ba, Lt, ι
    lacuna   As
    omitted   Bo, Cc, Dr, Eg, *Hl*, La, Lm, Ln, Ny, o, Pr, Ra, s, Si,
                  Ta, Ua, Ub, Ul, w, Wo, Yo

IV. LANGUAGE

M. L. Samuels's observations on the dialect of Wycliffite manuscripts have had a major influence on the field. Samuels described Type I language, also called the Central Midland Standard, as 'the language of the majority of Wycliffite manuscripts' and saw it as 'a standard literary language based on the dialects of the Central Midland counties'.[45] He identified seven forms as typical for this language: *sich*, *mych*, *ony*, *silf*, *stide*, *3ouun*, and *si3*. In a later article he expanded this list to include spellings such as *poru*/*porou(3)* and the doubling of vowels in words such as *lijf* and *fijr*.[46] More recent publications have relativized Samuels's findings to some extent,[47] demonstrating the variability of spellings found in Wycliffite manuscripts. Most of the discussions of the language of Wycliffite manuscripts to date have focused on the language of the full biblical text, and very little has been said on the language of liturgical aids and paraliturgical materials.[48] The present analysis presents a linguistic profile for the base text Bo and the five

---

[45] M. L. Samuels, 'Some Applications of Middle English Dialectology', *English Studies*, 44 (1963), 81–94; repr. in A. McIntosh, M. L. Samuels, and M. Laing (eds.), *Middle English Dialectology: Essays on Some Principles and Problems* (Aberdeen, 1989), 64–80 at 67.

[46] M. L. Samuels, 'The Dialects of MS Bodley 959', in McIntosh, Samuels, and Laing (eds.), *Middle English Dialectology*, 136–49.

[47] See especially Matti Peikola, 'The Wycliffite Bible and "Central Midland Standard": Assessing the Manuscript Evidence', *Nordic Journal of English Studies*, 2 (2003), 29–51; Anne Hudson, 'Observations on the "Wycliffite Orthography"', in S. Horobin and A. Nafde (eds.), *Pursuing Middle English Manuscripts and their Texts: Essays in Honour of Ralph Hanna* (Turnhout, 2017), 77–98; and Elizabeth Solopova, 'Dialect', in Solopova (ed.), *The Wycliffite Bible*, 202–19.

[48] Elizabeth Solopova briefly discusses the Northern forms in the lectionaries in Harley 1710 and 1029, in 'Dialect', 215–16.

representative manuscripts which have been chosen for collation in this edition (Bx, La, Ny, Ra, Se). The questionnaire follows the one used by Elizabeth Solopova in her catalogue of Wycliffite manuscripts, which is in turn largely based on Samuels's forms characteristic of Type I language:[49]

any, each, fire, given, life, like, much, saw (singular), saw (plural), self, such, though, through; present indicative 3rd person singular, present indicative plural, present participle, 3rd person singular feminine pronoun in the nominative (she), 3rd person plural pronoun in the nominative (they), 3rd person plural pronoun in the oblique (them), 3rd person plural possessive (their)

As in Solopova's catalogue, a maximum of ten instances of each test item were recorded. For all manuscripts, it was exclusively the OTL that was examined, so that the resulting linguistic profiles can differ from profiles which take into account all the texts contained in these manuscripts.

Bo

ANY	ony (10)
EACH	eche (9)/ech (1)
FIRE	fire (9)/fyre (1)
GIVEN	ȝouun (7)/ȝoue (3)
LIFE	lijf (10)
LIKE	like (3)
MUCH	moche (6)/myche (1)
SAW *sg.*	say (10)
SAW *pl.*	sayen (4)/saien (4)
SELF	silf (10)
SUCH	suche (2)/such (1)
THOUGH	þouȝ (3)
THROUGH	þoruȝ (6)
pr ind. pl.	-en (10)
pr. p.	-ynge (8)/-inge (1)/-yng (1)
3 pl. pron., nom.	þei (10)
3 pl. pron., oblique	hem (10)
3 pl. pron., poss.	her (10)
3 sg. fem. pron., nom.	sche (10)
3 sg. pr. ind.	-iþ (9)/-eþ (1)

Bx

ANY	ony (10)
EACH	ech (5)/eche (5)

⁴⁹ Solopova, *MSS of WB*, 33.

FIRE	fier (10)
GIVEN	ȝouun (6)/ȝoue (2)
LIFE	lijf (10)
LIKE	lijc (2)/lijk (1)
MUCH	moche (3)/myche (1)
SAW *sg.*	sai (5)/saiȝ (4)/siȝ (1)
SAW *pl.*	saien (8)
SELF	silf (10)
SUCH	suche (1)/sich (1)
THOUGH	þowȝ (2)/þoȝ (1)
THROUGH	þourȝ (1)
pr. ind. pl.	-en (10)
pr. p.	-ynge (6)/-inge (4)
3 sg. fem. pron., nom.	she (6)/sche (4)
3 sg. pr. ind.	-iþ (6)/-eþ (4)
3 pl. pron., nom.	þei (10)
3 pl. pron., oblique	hem (10)
3 pl. pron., poss.	her (8)/hir (1)/here (1)

La

ANY	ony (10)
EACH	ech (10)
FIRE	fier (10)
GIVEN	ȝouen (9)/ȝoue (1)
LIFE	lijf (10)
LIKE	lijk (2)/lijknes(1)/lich (1)
MUCH	miche (3)/myche (3)
SAW *sg.*	siȝ (10)
SAW *pl.*	siȝen (10)
SELF	silf (10)
SUCH	sich (2)
THOUGH	þouȝ (3)
THROUGH	þoruȝ (6)
pr. ind. pl.	-en (10)
pr. p.	-ynge (6)/-inge (4)
3 sg. fem. pron., nom.	sche (10)
3 pl. pron., nom.	þei (10)
3 pl. pron., oblique	hem (10)
3 pl. pron., poss.	her (10)
3. sg. pr. ind.	-iþ (8)/-eþ (2)

Ny

ANY	ony (10)

EACH	ech (10)
FIRE	fier (10)
GIVEN	30uen (8)/30uun (2)
LIFE	lijf (6)/liyf (4)
LIKE	lijk (6)
MUCH	myche (4)/miche (1)
SAW *sg.*	saw (9)/si3 (1)
SAW *pl.*	sawen (9)/si3en (1)
SELF	silf (9)/self (1)
SUCH	sich (2)/siche (1)
THOUGH	þou3 (3)
THROUGH	þorou3 (6)/þorou (1)
pr. ind. pl.	-en (10)
pr. p.	-yng (4)/-ynge (5)/-ing (1)
3 sg. fem. pron., nom.	sche (10)
3 pl. pron., nom.	þei (9)/þey (1)
3 pl. pron., oblique	hem (10)
3 pl. pron., poss.	her (10)
3 sg. pr. ind.	-eþ (2)/-iþ (8)

Ra

ANY	eny (4)/ony (6)
EACH	eche (10)
FIRE	fijr (9)/fier (1)
GIVEN	30uen (10)
LIFE	lijf (9)/life (1)
LIKE	lijk (3), lijknes (2)/liknesse (2)/liche (1)/lyk (1)
MUCH	myche (3)/miche (1)
SAW *sg.*	say (4)/sai (6)
SAW *pl.*	saien (9)/sayen 1
SELF	self (6)/silf (4)
SUCH	sich (2)
THOUGH	þou3 (4)
THROUGH	þoru3 (3)/þorou3 (1)
pr. ind. pl.	-en (10)
pr. p.	-yng (6)/-ynge (3)/-ing (1)
3 sg. fem. pron., nom.	sche (10)
3 pl. pron., nom.	þei (10)
3 pl. pron., oblique	hem (10)
3 pl. pron., poss.	her (10)
3 sg. pr.	-eþ (9)/-iþ (1)

Se

ANY	ony (9)/eny (1)
EACH	ech (10)
FIRE	fier (10)
GIVEN	ʒouun (10)
LIFE	liʒf (5)/lyf (5)
LIKE	lijk (3)/liche (1)/liknesse (1)/licknesse (1)/lyk (1)
MUCH	myche (5)
SAW *sg.*	say (7)/saiʒ (2)/sayʒ (1)
SAW *pl.*	sayen (5)/saien (2)/syen (1)
SELF	silf (10)
SUCH	sich (2)
THOUGH	þouʒ (3)
THROUGH	þoruʒ (3)/þorouʒ (1)
pr. ind. pl.	-en (10)
pr. p.	-ynge (7)/-inge (3)
3 sg. fem. pron., nom.	sche (9)/she (1)
3 pl. pron., nom.	þei (8)/þey (1)/þei (1)
3 pl. pron., oblique	hem (10)
3 pl. pron., possessive	her (10)
3 sg. pr. ind.	-iþ (7)/-eþ (3)

Many of these linguistic profiles agree to some extent with Samuels's typical Type I forms: *sich*, *ony*, and *silf* are frequently the dominant forms, and doubling of vowels is evidenced by many instances of *liʒf*, although several manuscripts contain alternative forms such as *lyf* or *life*. There is little evidence of doubling of vowels in forms for FIRE, with most manuscripts containing *fier* or *fire* as the dominant form. Ra is the only manuscript which shows frequent instances of *fijr*. There is also much variation regarding forms for THROUGH, ranging from Type I spellings such as *þorouʒ* to other forms such as *þourʒ*. According to *LALME*, the dialect of all manuscripts is clearly Midland. This is, however, not an argument against the London production of Wycliffite books, as Irma Taavitsainen has shown.[50] There is little consistency between individual manuscripts, and although there is considerable overlap in the forms used overall, each text has its own distinct profile which is dissimilar to the others in various ways.

There is a great deal of consistency, however, in the spelling of each individual OTL. Only very rarely does an OTL show more than two to

---

[50] Irma Taavitsainen, 'Scientific Language and Spelling Standardisation 1375–1550', in L. Wright (ed.), *The Development of Standard English, 1300–1800: Theories, Descriptions, Conflicts* (Cambridge, 2006), 131–54.

three variants for a single test item, and many texts contain only one dominant form for a specific test item (e.g. *ony*, *lijf*, *like*, *say*, *silf*, *poruȝ* in Bo). Many variants are relatively minor, mostly relating to differences of *i/y* and word-final *-e*, as in the variants of the present participle in Ra (*-yng/ -ynge/-ing*) and La (*-ynge/-inge*), or the variants for EACH in Bx (*ech/eche*). Forms for GIVEN vary between *ȝouun/ȝoue* in most manuscripts, a reflection of the process of levelling of the final syllable to schwa, which was well under way at the time of the manuscripts' production. The ongoing levelling of vowels to schwa in unstressed syllables also explains the variation between the endings in the third-person singular present indicative (*-ip/-ep*) in most OTLs.

Interestingly, many of these linguistic profiles differ substantially from the profiles provided for the same manuscripts in Elizabeth Solopova's catalogue. Solopova's profiles refer to the language of entire manuscripts, while my analysis is restricted to OTLs only. There are frequent differences between the two: for instance, Solopova's catalogue records exclusively the form *eny* for ANY in Bo, while the only form that was found in OTL is *ony*. There are several similar cases of the OTL containing a spelling as the dominant form which is an infrequent variant in the manuscript overall, or which is not mentioned as one of the ten instances in the profile in the catalogue. Examples of this are FIRE, LIKE, SAW *sg.* in Bo; FIRE, GIVEN, SAW *sg.*; THROUGH in Ra; and ANY, FIRE, GIVEN, SAW *sg.* in Se. Keeping in mind that a profile based on ten instances cannot provide conclusive evidence, the overall picture nonetheless suggests that OTL and the other texts of these manuscripts were written by at least two different scribes. This is supported by the fact that the overwhelming majority of OTLs are codicologically separate in the manuscripts within which they appear, which means that they could easily have been written by a different scribe before being combined with the other texts and bound together.

In Bx there is a greater overlap between the two profiles than in Bo, which might be seen as an indication that in this manuscript the same scribe was responsible for both the OTL and the NT. This is supported by the fact that this is one of the few manuscripts in which OTL is not codicologically separate, with the prologue to Matthew's gospel starting immediately after the lectionary on f. 37ᵛ. In cases where the OTL starts on a new quire and where the language of the OTL is significantly different from that of the NT, involvement of different scribes is more likely.

V. TEXT AND CONTEXT OF THE
OLD TESTAMENT LECTIONARY

1. Tables of Lections

The table of lections (TOL) is the most frequent liturgical tool found in Wycliffite manuscripts. Approximately 40 per cent of all surviving manuscripts contain a TOL,[51] thus far outnumbering the manuscripts which contain OTLs. Nearly all manuscripts containing OTLs also contain TOLs, the exceptions being the full lectionaries in *He* and *Hl*, as well as Si, Ub, x, and *Pl* (some of which are incomplete manuscripts). The precise relationship between TOL and OTL is complex, and can vary from manuscript to manuscript.

In general terms, TOL is a liturgical aid which lists the feasts of the Use of Sarum and the OT and NT readings assigned to each occasion. In manuscripts containing NT and OTL, TOL would allow a reader to identify and locate the scriptural passages which were read on a particular day, and would thus be a crucial device for using NT and OTL together. TOLs contain finding aids to facilitate this process. Typically, TOLs in Wycliffite manuscripts follow a set pattern (see Plate 2 above). The entries for each feast give the liturgical occasion in red (sometimes with a blue initial), followed by a reference to the biblical book and chapter, an indexing letter (or referential letter)[52] in red, an incipit for the lection, the word 'ende' in red, and an explicit, which is often followed by double strokes in red or black. Many tables are ruled accordingly to ensure uniformity between the entries.

Elizabeth Solopova identifies two distinct groups of TOL, which she refers to as Type I and Type II.[53] The distinction between the two types is similar to that between Type I and Type II OTLs: Type I TOLs contain three distinct sections—the Temporale, the Sanctorale, and the Commemorations. In the Sanctorale, Proper and Common are combined into one section, which is indicated by a rubric: 'Now bigynneþ þe rule of þe sanctorum boþe of þe propre and comyn togidere' (La, f. 8ʳ). However, in some manuscripts the Sanctorale is not contained in the TOL but rather

---

[51] Matti Peikola, 'Tables of Lections in Manuscripts of the Wycliffite Bible', in Eyal Poleg and Laura Light (eds.), *Form and Function in the Late Medieval Bible* (Boston, 2013), 351–78. Peikola gives an analysis of the features of the TOLs and their likely purpose, but does not consider in detail the relationship between TOL and OTL. The TOL edited in F&M, iv. 683–97, is a conflated text of different TOLs based on a comparison of only eight manuscripts.

[52] See Solopova, *MSS of WB*, 7, and Peikola, 'Tables of Lections', 355, who uses the latter term.   [53] Solopova, *MSS of WB*, 6–17.

included in a separate calendar-lectionary, effectively creating a functional division between both liturgical aids.[54] The calendar-lectionary includes the incipits and explicits for lections on saints' feast days in a separate calendar, together with the relevant date. The selection of feasts in Type I is very uniform and transmitted with virtually no variation. By contrast, Type II TOLs contain four sections: Temporale, Commemorations, and Sanctorale subdivided into Proper and Common.[55] Here the selection of feasts is more variable, and is often much shorter than in Type I, including only widely venerated saints. Type II TOLs occur less frequently than Type I. They can also occur in conjunction with an EV text, which has been seen as an indication that Type II represents an earlier stage of Wycliffite TOLs.[56] This would certainly fit with the chronology of OTL as suggested in §II.2 above. As detailed above, this edition uses the term Type III to refer to TOLs into which the lections from the OT are inserted directly. This is a way of combining two distinct liturgical aids into one, and it is likely to have been developed for reasons of convenience (see Plate 3 above). Since none of the Type III OTLs uses EV exclusively, they are probably later than Type II, and, as has been suggested above, may have been an intermediary stage which led to the development of Type I OTLs.

2. Tables of Lections and the Old Testament Lectionary: Referencing Systems

TOLs are usually preceded by a rubric which explains how the table can be used to identify the relevant scriptural passages. This is a fixed rubric in Type I TOLs and is transmitted with very little variation. The rubric in Bo reads:

Here bigynneþ a reule þat telliþ in whiche chapitris of þe Bible ȝe may fynde þe lessouns, pistlis, and gospels þat ben redde in þe chirche at masse aftir þe vse of Salisbury markide wiþ lettris of þe a.b.c. at þe bigynnynge of þe chapitris toward þe myddil or ende aftir þe ordre as þe lettris stonden in þe abc. First ben set Sundaies and feriales togidir, and aftir þe sanctorum, comyn and propir togidir of al þe ȝeer. First writun a clause of þe bigynnynge þerof and of þe ending þerof also. (f. 1ʳ)

Rubrics in Type II TOLs tend to be shorter and less fixed: 'Here bigynneþ a reule þat telliþ in whiche chapitris of þe Byble, how ȝe moun fynde þe lessons, pistlis, and gospels þat ben rad by al þe ȝeer in hooli

---

[54] This is the case, for instance, in Lm.

[55] The order in which these sections appear can vary in both Type I and Type II; for further details see Peikola, 'Tables of Lections', 372–7.

[56] Solopova, *MSS of WB*, 7.

chirche' (ι, f. 31ʳ). The most striking difference between the two rubrics is that Type II does not attempt to explain the referencing system, even though the TOL in ι does contain indexing letters. Type I's more elaborate explanation of how the table is structured would have been highly useful to non-academic readers and laypeople as the practice of subdividing chapters of the Bible using letters of the alphabet, though widespread, would have been known mainly in an academic context in medieval England.[57] The system developed by the Parisian Dominicans at St-Jacques used the letters A–D for short chapters and A–G for longer chapters, but could be adapted to different texts as well.[58] WB appears to have been unique in further refining this system to an eleven-letter system A–L. Matti Peikola notes that the traditional A–G scheme is used in some manuscripts of EV,[59] but all of the TOLs in OTL manuscripts use the eleven-letter system.

In practical terms, the indexing system was a way in which TOL and OTL could be used together with minimal effort. Many OTLs give the appropriate indexing letter in the margin in addition to signalling the liturgical occasion and biblical verse and chapter for each lection. In the case of composite lections which consist of more than one section from different parts of the biblical text, several indexing letters are given in many OTLs. This is the case, for instance, in Lection 219 in Bo (Wisd. 7: 30; 8: 1–4), which gives the two indexing letters g and a. Since the liturgical occasion is always clearly signposted in OTL through the rubrics, indexing letters would not have been strictly necessary in the same way in which they are necessary for finding a specific passage in a continuous NT or a full Bible. The inclusion of this referencing system in OTL may reflect an academically minded desire for completeness and thoroughness which points towards the full biblical text rather than liturgical excerpts, as it would have enabled the reader to find any given passage from OTL in a full OT, Latin or otherwise. It might also be a way of increasing user-friendliness by providing as many finding aids as possible, which would enable even a non-academic reader to navigate back and forth between TOL and OTL. Very little, then, can be deduced from the referencing system as to the

---

[57] Ibid. 11.

[58] For a more detailed discussion, see Richard H. Rouse and Mary A. Rouse, 'The Verbal Concordance to the Scriptures', *Archivum Fratrum Praedicatorum*, 44 (1974), 5–30; Richard H. Rouse and Mary A. Rouse, *Preachers, Florilegia and Sermons: Studies on the Manipulus florum of Thomas of Ireland* (Toronto, 1979), 34; Mary J. Carruthers, *The Book of Memory: A Study of Memory in Medieval Culture* (Cambridge, 1990), 100; Peikola, 'Tables of Lections', 358–9; Solopova, *MSS of WB*, 10.

[59] Peikola, 'Tables of Lections', 359.

kind of reader TOL and OTL were aimed at, as it could have served academic, clerical, and lay readers alike. It may have been a convenient way of employing an academic referencing system in order to maximize the usefulness of the text for a wide and mixed audience.

However, in some manuscripts referring back and forth between TOL and OTL is difficult in spite of the referencing strategies discussed above. Perhaps surprisingly, Type II TOLs are not always combined with Type II OTLs. In fact, roughly 30 per cent of OTL manuscripts combine an OTL with a TOL of a different type. This means that frequently a TOL which does not list Proper and Common separately is combined with an OTL which does list them as separate sections. In this case, using TOL and OTL together would be difficult and would require some advanced liturgical knowledge. For instance, a reader looking at the entry for St Nicomedes in the TOL in Bo (f. 9^r) would be given the biblical book and chapter (Ecclus. xiiij), indexing letter (f), incipit ('Blessid is þe man'), and explicit ('him þe Lord oure God'), but would have to know that Nicomedes was a martyr in order to find the lection in the Common in OTL as one of the lections for feasts of one martyr. An additional difficulty is that the explicit here does not agree exactly between TOL and OTL, with the TOL giving the full explicit including the liturgical addition 'þe lord oure god', while the lection itself omits this and ends with 'schal enerite hym'. Other manuscripts show further examples of incipits and explicits in TOL not matching the lections in OTL. For instance, N has both a Type II TOL and a Type II OTL, possibly written by the same scribe. Nonetheless, the TOL gives the incipit for the lection for one martyr from Ecclus. 14 as 'Blessid is þe man þat in' and the explicit as 'schal heritagen him' (f. 5^r), while the lection in the OTL starts 'That man is blessid þe whiche' and ends 'schal enheriten him þe Lord oure God' (f. 234^r). Such inconsistencies may indicate that both liturgical aids were translated independently from each other.

The disagreement between TOLs and OTLs of different types is mainly a problem for the Sanctorale and would have made it challenging to locate the lections for certain feasts for readers who did not have a good knowledge of the liturgical calendar. This might be seen as evidence that these manuscripts were primarily aimed at those in possession of such knowledge, such as the clergy. The fact that even manuscripts which include the same type of TOL and OTL can show marked differences between incipits and explicits indicates that agreement between the two was not the primary focus, especially in early copies such as N. TOLs and OTLs are often codicologically separate, and this, together with the linguistic evidence discussed above (§IV), indicates that these parts of the manuscripts were written separately, in some cases by different scribes. Evidently, many copies were not carefully checked as to whether TOL and OTL agreed with each other, and this is especially the case for Type II OTLs, which are likely to be earlier than Type I.

There are some examples to the contrary, however. Elizabeth Solopova gives details of TOLs which were carefully adapted to reflect the range of biblical books included in a specific manuscript.[60] The most striking example among OTL manuscripts is o, which contains the gospel harmony *Oon of Foure* rather than the four gospels. The TOL in o is adapted to the nature of the text in this manuscript, containing a lengthy note following the traditional rubric which explains that the TOL refers to *Oon of Foure*:

But not wiþstondyng that in þe rubrisch here afore write is schewid in whiche chapter of þe bible ȝe may fynde þe lessoun and pistlis and gospels þat ben red in the chirche al þe ȝeere, ȝitt as in þis reule þe whiche here after sueþ ben marked oonli the gospels of þe ȝeere as þei ben write in ordre in þe stori called oon of foure, which stori biginneþ aftir þis kalender. (f. 1ʳ)

This creates problems for the gospel readings, since individual lections may not occur as continuous sections in *Oon of Foure* and sometimes have to be reconstructed from several separate chapters. Where such reconstruction is too difficult, the gospel pericopes are written out separately at the end of the text, after the Apocalypse. The TOL explains this practice: 'In þis gospel ben mo wordis and also stonden not in ordre after þe usse of Salisburi wherfore seke it in þe 9 leef after þe apocalips' (f. 5ʳ). Throughout o, the scribe is at pains to guide the reader through the text and make it possible to find specific lections, in spite of the problems caused by the nature of the manuscript. Considerable thought and effort must have gone into the design of this manuscript and the referencing system it employs.[61]

We also find examples of copies which use an alternative referencing system in addition to the traditional indexing letters discussed above. In three of the five Group II A manuscripts—As, Se, and Tc—the lectionary is divided up into different sections which are assigned a letter of the alphabet, A–E or A–D. Individual lections are then identified in the TOL and the OTL by this letter and a number, e.g. a1, a2, etc. It is interesting that this referencing system is given in addition to the indexing letters tra-

---

[60] Solopova, *MSS of WB*, 8.

[61] Such an adaptation of TOL to the nature of a specific manuscript is also found in manuscripts without OTL. For instance, part of the TOL in Windsor, St George's Chapel, MS 4 contains indexing letters only for NT lections. Indexing letters for OT lections were seen as superfluous since the manuscript contains only NT, and not an OT or OTL.

ditionally present, as if the aim was to make the relation between the TOL and the OTL unequivocally clear. In practical terms, this system would have increased the speed and ease with which individual lections could be found in the lectionary. In these manuscripts, as in o, a particular effort was made towards improving the referencing system of TOL and OTL. Among OTL manuscripts, such examples are certainly more the exception than the rule. It perhaps reflects a difference between manuscripts which were routinely produced and those which, like o, seem to have been bespoke copies. However, bespoke vs. routine production is not the only possible explanation, as a general trend is also noticeable. It is significant that o contains a Type I OTL, as opposed to Type II OTLs which frequently show inconsistencies between the TOL and the OTL as detailed above. Even in Type I OTL manuscripts with a TOL which shows no sign of being tailored to a specific manuscript, the tables agree very closely with the OTL. All Type I OTLs contain Type I TOLs and are in many ways more user-friendly than Type II OTLs. In general, then, later copies achieve much greater consistency between TOL and OTL, although even here there can be differences, as in Eg, where the order of Sanctorale and Commemorations is not identical in the TOL and the OTL. An OTL combined with a matching TOL which refers to it in a consistent and cohesive way seems to be the end product arising out of a period of experimenting with a range of different ways of presenting the information, and making a complex system of liturgical readings easily accessible. This period of experimentation is understandable given the lack of Latin antecedents; although some examples of Latin TOLs can be found which resemble the Wycliffite TOL relatively closely,[62] there are no close Latin equivalents of OTL, and so it might well have taken time to integrate both liturgical aids into a functional system.

There are no extant Type I OTLs which are accompanied by a Type II TOL, while there are Type II OTLs which are accompanied by a Type I TOL. Given the chronology suggested above, this means that Type I TOLs would have pre-dated Type I OTLs. As suggested above, Type I OTLs may have developed out of Type III, where the lections were integrated into a TOL which combines the Proper and the Common into a single section. The end point of this development was a well-thought-out and efficient referencing system between the TOL and the OTL, which would have enabled even a reader with limited knowledge of liturgical matters to locate a relevant reading.

---

[62] Peikola, 'Tables of Lections', 357; Solopova, *MSS of WB*, 9.

3. Methods of Cross-Referencing within the Old Testament Lectionary

In the different manuscripts there is much variation in the rubrics for each lection. The general pattern is the same—each rubric gives the liturgical occasion, biblical book, chapter, and (in many, though not all, OTLs) an indexing letter. Some manuscripts, especially of Group II D, also include a Latin incipit. However, rubrics vary in that some may refer to a lection as a 'pistil' and others as a 'lessoun',[63] and some may use roman or arabic numerals for the chapter number, while others spell out numbers in words. An occasion such as the third Friday in Advent (no. 6) can be referred to in other lectionaries as the Ember Friday in Advent instead. While Type I lectionaries achieve a great uniformity among references, Type II is more variable.

In general, Type I OTLs tend to contain more detailed rubrics, specifying the liturgical occasion at greater length than is the case for many Type II OTLs. For instance, where Bo refers to 'The iij Wednesday lessoun of Aduent' (no. 4), La has the rubric 'þe lessoun on þe þridde Wednesday þat is þe ymbir Wednesdai of Aduent'. Where several lessons are read on a specific day, Type I OTLs repeat the liturgical occasion in each rubric, while Type II tends to omit this. For instance, the second lesson on the Ember Wednesday in Advent (no. 5) is entitled merely 'Vpon þe same day anoþere lessoun' in Bo, while La has 'þe pistil on þe same ymbir Wednesdai of Aduent'. This would make it easier for a reader to identify the liturgical occasion for such a lection without having to turn back to the leaf on which the first lesson for this occasion is found. Such rubrics indicate that Type I OTLs strive to achieve the greatest possible clarity of reference, much more so than earlier Type II OTLs, which presuppose a reader who is reading the lectionary in a linear fashion and who is aware of the context of an individual lection. Such patterns can be observed throughout the lectionaries.

Most OTLs use a system of cross-references to save space and avoid repeating those lections which occur several times over the course of the liturgical year. The typical structure of such cross-references is a rubric in the usual format, followed by an incipit and a reference to a preceding or (more rarely) following lection which contains the reading. Thus, the fifth lesson on the first Saturday of Lent (no. 38) in Bo contains this cross-reference:

---

[63] Type I OTLs have a regular pattern here: 'pistil' is used for feasts which have only one epistle reading, while 'lessoun' is used for those feasts which have several readings.

The v lessoun on þe same day. Danyel iij.
An aungel of þe Lord and is in Ymbir Saturday bifore Cristmasse.

Broadly speaking, such cross-references can be divided into two categories: non-specific vs. specific references. The example given falls into the
former category: the cross-reference gives the liturgical occasion under
which the reading can be found in a non-specific way. This reference is
applicable to all lectionaries following the same liturgical use and is not
connected in any specific way to the manuscript at hand. Occasionally,
non-specific references may be even shorter and refer to the TOL rather
than another liturgical occasion. Thus, for the second and third lections
on the Eve of Pentecost, Se gives only the reference 'þe secunde and þe
þridde lessouns as þe kalender telliþ'.

By contrast, Type I lectionaries frequently contain specific cross-
references, which are specifically tailored to the manuscript within which
they appear. For instance, the cross-reference for the feast of St Nicholas
(no. 96) in La reads

The pistil on Seynt Nicholas dai bischop. Ecclesiastici xliiij capitulo.
Lo þe greet preest. This pistil ȝe schulen fynde writen tofore in þe viij leef,
and is red on Seint Siluester dai aftir Cristemas. (f. 141ʳ)

Here, a specific reference to the place in which the lection can be found—
the eighth leaf—is given, and leaves are numbered by the scribe throughout the OTL. Citation by leaf is highly unusual in manuscript culture. As
this reference applies only to this specific manuscript copy, it would have
required a scribe to take great care in counting the leaves and ensuring
such references were accurate. At the same time, such specific references
greatly enhance the user-friendliness of the lectionary, since they reduce
the time a reader has to spend on leafing through the book to find the relevant passages. This pattern is noticeable throughout Type I OTLs, which
go to some lengths in order to make references as clear and user-friendly
as possible. This could be taken as a sign that Type I is directed at an audience which is less liturgically proficient than that of Type II, or merely that
the problems and defects of Type II OTLs were recognized, and a better
system of reference was subsequently implemented in Type I. Additional
user-friendly improvements were made, such as the addition of months in
the Sanctorale of Type I OTLs, while most Type II lectionaries contain
the names of months only in the TOL and not in the OTL itself.

4. Underlining

Framing devices

The practice of underlining extra-biblical material to indicate that it is not part of the biblical text proper is well known from Wycliffite manuscripts. As Elizabeth Solopova has pointed out, such non-biblical material typically falls into one of the following categories: there are glosses, usually introduced by 'þat is', alternative translations, often preceded by 'or' or 'eþer', and additions of words which do not occur in the Latin but which are necessary in English for clarification or to conform to the requirements of English grammar, such as additions of forms of the verb 'to be'.[64] In OTL there is a further category of extra-biblical additions, which is by far the most frequent. These are liturgical framing devices, used to introduce and conclude a lection. In the Latin liturgical texts these occur as formulaic phrases for both epistle and gospel readings. The conventional introductions for OT readings are 'In diebus illis' for narrative passages and 'Haec dicit dominus' for readings from prophetic books. This may be expanded to include some context for the lection, such as the name of the prophet, as on Monday in the second week of Lent: 'In diebus illis oravit Daniel ad dominum dicens'.[65] As Walter Howard Frere has pointed out, closing formulae are chosen according to the nature of the preceding lection; 'dicit dominus deus noster' or 'vester', or 'dicit dominus omnipotens' frequently conclude prophetic lessons, while other lections close with a doxology or a phrase such as 'in saecula saeculorum. Amen.[66] In OTL these introductions are translated as 'The Lord seiþ þese þingis' and 'In þo daies', and the closing phrases as 'seiþ þe Lord almy3ti', 'seiþ oure Lord', 'fro þe world and til into þe world', and the like, following the Latin text closely.

These liturgical framing devices are underlined in most OTL manuscripts to indicate that they are additions and not part of the biblical text itself. How accurate and consistent these underlining practices are depends to a large extent on the diligence of a particular scribe (Bx is, on the whole, more accurate than Bo). However, as a rule Type I OTLs are more thorough and consistent in their underlining than Type II. For instance, the closing phrase 'þe Lord oure God' of the lection for St John's day in the Christmas Octave (no. 19) is correctly underlined in La, but in very few Type II manuscripts. On the other hand, La tends to be not only correct but hypercorrect in this regard. There are a number of lections

---

[64] Solopova, *MSS of WB*, 19–20.   [65] *The Sarum Missal*, ed. Legg, 67.
[66] Walter Howard Frere, *Studies in Early Roman Liturgy*, iii: *The Roman Epistle-Lectionary* (London, 1935), 91–2.

which include phrases such as 'seiþ þe Lord of oostis' —otherwise often used as liturgical framing devices—not as an addition but as a matter of course where they occur in the middle of a lection as part of the biblical text (e.g. second Wednesday in Advent, no. 2). Similarly, some lections start with what looks like a typical framing device, as 'The Lord God seiþ þese þingis', e.g. in the lection for the first Monday of Lent (no. 28), but these phrases actually occur in the biblical text itself and are not an addition. In such cases La usually underlines these phrases even though this is incorrect and marks them out as liturgical additions, which they are not. It would seem that the scribes of Type I manuscripts were so eager to be correct in formal terms and to underline all additions that they did so as soon as they recognized, or thought they recognized, a formulaic phrase, without checking such cases against the biblical text.

Type II D and Type III OTLs tend not to include such liturgical framing devices, while all other types do include them on a regular basis. In the case of Type III, this can be explained by the fact that OTL is incorporated in TOL. TOL contains incipits and explicits for each lection which do not include the framing devices (which would be less distinctive). When these incipits were expanded to include the full lections in Type III, the scribes followed the pattern already existing in TOL. In Group II D the reason why the framing devices were not included might be connected to the presence of Latin incipits. All Group II D OTLs contain these Latin incipits at the start of each lection. For instance, Lection 7 in *N* contains the Latin incipit 'Clamabunt ad', and the English translation starts 'Thei scholen crien', while many other OTLs include the framing device 'In þo daies' here. The Latin incipit may have prompted the scribes to start the lection in English immediately with a translation of the Latin phrase, rather than with the liturgical framing device.[67]

Composite lections

Apart from the addition of formulaic opening and closing phrases, the Sarum Use contains several lections in which the biblical text is edited and abbreviated in various significant ways. A note in the TOL in Hereford Cathedral, MS O. VII. 1 shows clearly that the translators were aware of these intricacies of the liturgical texts:

it is to undirstonde þat not ech lessone of þe oolde lawe is writen in þe Bible word bi word as it is red in chirche, but sum is taken a resoun of o chapitre and þe remenaunt

[67] This does not explain, however, why framing devices at the end of lections are not included in Group II D either, a question which is discussed in §V.5 below.

of anoþer, and summe ben taken of mo chapitris, and þat in diverse placis, and ȝit not accordinge fulli to þe text of þe Bible . . . and also in many lessouns þe chirche haþ set to boþe bigynnyngis and endingis þat ben not in þe Bible.[68]

The medieval note describes so-called 'composite lections', which do not follow the biblical text in a strict, linear way but modify and adapt it to the liturgical occasion. Frere describes these lections as follows:

The extent to which any adaptation within the lesson has been made varies greatly: sometimes only a verse or a phrase is omitted, or a single word is introduced or modified. On the other hand, there are a few lessons made up from many extracts drawn out and welded together either from one chapter or from several passages of the same context, or even from different books.[69]

The significance of the latter type of lection, which uses different chapters or books of the Bible, is discussed below (§V.6). The former type, which modifies one or several phrases or verses, is frequently the reason for those differences between the liturgical text and the biblical text which are marked by underlining in OTL. Additions to the biblical text in the Sarum Missal occur, for instance, in the second lection for the seventeenth Wednesday after Trinity (2 Ezra 8; Lection 86), which adds 'et steterunt juxta eum' at the end of verse 4. This is translated as 'and þei stoden bisidis hym' in OTL and marked as an addition by underlining in most manuscripts. The same is true for the addition 'and riȝtwisnesse' at the end of the lection on the first Monday of Lent (Ezra 34: 16; Lection 28)—here, however, Type I OTLs are more diligent in underlining the addition than Type II.

In the cases discussed so far, what the scribes mark out, or aim at marking out, are deviations from the biblical text for liturgical, linguistic, or interpretative reasons. However, underlining can also be used for the reverse situation. As indicated in the quotation from Frere, a number of lections abbreviate or omit parts of the biblical text. This is the case, for instance, in the lection on Thursday in the first week of Lent (Ezra 18: 1–19; Lection 32), where the Sarum lection omits a number of verses from the biblical text. Most of the OTLs follow the Sarum Missal rather than the Vulgate here and omit these verses in the translation. However, Type II B manuscripts follow the biblical text and include all verses. The same is true in all other cases of lections which omit certain parts of the biblical text.[70] In each case, Type II B follows the Vulgate rather

[68] Hereford, Hereford Cathedral Library, MS O. VII.1, f. 5ᵛ. I follow Mary Dove's transcription here (*The First English Bible*, 62).

[69] Frere, *Studies in Early Roman Liturgy*, iii: *The Roman Epistle-Lectionary*, 92.

[70] All of these cases are commented on in the Explanatory Notes.

than the Sarum Missal but shows that the scribes were aware of the differences between the two by underlining the verses which are omitted in the Sarum Missal. This is striking, since underlining is here used to indicate not a deviation from the Vulgate text, as is the typical practice in Wycliffite manuscripts, but rather a deviation from the liturgical text of the Sarum Use.

Thus, Type II B manuscripts use underlining for two opposite textual situations, without clearly differentiating between them on a visual level or explaining the differences to the reader. A reader of an OTL of this type would have to possess an advanced knowledge of the biblical and liturgical texts in order to make sense of this presentation of the text. Type II B seems to aim at a kind of textual completeness, which points out which parts of the lections are relevant for the liturgy while at the same time including the full biblical context of a lection. The situation is somewhat different in Type II A and C and Type I, which adhere more closely to the liturgical text. It is a tempting conclusion that Type II B is earlier than these other types, and that over time, the user-friendliness and visual clarity of OTL gradually increased, albeit at the expense of a certain amount of information about the textual relationship betweeen liturgical and biblical text. The evidence also suggests that Type II B, or earlier manuscripts in general, were intended to be used by an audience with a superior knowledge of liturgical matters, while later manuscripts may have been written with a wider audience in mind.

5. Codicological and Palaeographical Features

In many manuscripts, OTL is codicologically separate from the biblical text, although there are exceptions to this rule (e.g. Cc, *N*, Yo). The same is true for most TOLs. Elizabeth Solopova interprets the codicological separateness of the liturgical materials as a sign that 'they were copied and disseminated independently and were seen as optional add-ons appropriate for certain patrons'.[71] This is certainly a convincing hypothesis, and it would explain the fact that in many manuscripts the formats of TOL and OTL do not entirely agree with each other, as discussed above.[72] Further evidence pointing in this direction is the fact that the scribal hands of many OTLs have an aspect which is somewhat different from that of the biblical text.[73] In some other manuscripts, however, OTL is not codicologically separate and was designed to be an integral part of the manuscript from

---

[71] Solopova, *MSS of WB*, 22.   [72] See above, §V.2.

[73] See, for instance, Elizabeth Solopova's analysis of the hand in Egerton MS 1171 ('A Wycliffite Bible Made for a Nun of Barking', *Medium Ævum*, 85 (2016), 77–96 at 85).

the start. These cases, where the biblical text and OTL appear in the same quires, can be found in all three types of the text, albeit more frequently in Type II than in Type I. This could merely be due to chance survival, but the evidence fits with the fact that Type I manuscripts appear to be professional workshop productions of great uniformity, and the separate OTLs may reflect the division of labour to be expected of such workshops. In any case, it is apparent that OTL was produced for a range of different purposes and under different conditions.

This is also reflected in the variability of visual presentation. It is obvious from the overview of manuscript features in §I.2 that there is a great deal of convergence around typical manuscript features such as the use of textura and red and blue initials with red penwork, the arrangement of the text in two columns, the format of the rubrics preceding each lection which include the liturgical occasion, the biblical book, chapter and indexing letter, the running titles, and the underlining of extra-biblical material in red (see Plate 1 above). Most manuscripts have been carefully corrected, and corrections are often highlighted prominently in red. These features echo the typical layout familiar from other Wycliffite texts such as full Bibles, and they show that the production of OTL was closely aligned with the Wycliffite translation project of the biblical text proper. OTL was carefully and diligently produced, and although the degrees of formality of the handwriting can vary, the choice of textura indicates that the writing of the liturgical text would have required considerable time and effort. A significant number of manuscripts also contain one or several illuminated initials and coloured decoration, testifying to the expense involved in the making of these books.

However, there are a few manuscripts which deviate from this trend. Typically, variation as to the handwriting, design, and page layout occurs in Type II OTLs, especially early ones. In some rare cases, such as Ta and ι, manuscripts are written in a current script and give the impression of being less carefully produced. A few manuscripts prefer a single-column layout to two columns. This is the case for all Type III manuscripts due to their particular fusion of TOL and OTL, but it occurs in only three manuscripts of Type II (*He*, *Pl*, and Si). Both *He* and *Pl* are early, Type II D manuscripts, which explains the greater variability of their layout. In Si, the single-column layout may be connected to the small size of the manuscript and is likely to have been chosen in order to increase the readability of the text. While there is a certain amount of variability in earlier manuscripts, then, the presentation of Type I is characterized by a great uniformity and professionalism of both textual and visual features, mirroring the design of many LV manuscripts associated with professional London workshops. There was a certain amount of flexibility as to the inclusion of particular texts in a manuscript and room for adaptation to patrons' wishes, as the codicological separation of OTL and the evidence of adaptation of TOL in o (discussed above, §V.2) indicate.

6. Relation to the Sarum Missal and the Wycliffite Translations

Among biblical translations, OTL is distinctive in that it has two different sources: the biblical text proper and the lections used in the Sarum Missal, which, from lection to lection, can vary against the Vulgate. This relation is in some ways more complex than that between the Vulgate and EV/LV. The discussion above has shown different ways in which the translators mark out differences between Sarum and the Vulgate on a visual level, but these differences are also reflected in the translations which are chosen. An examination of the individual lections and their translations reveals that the overwhelming majority of lections in Bo use LV in a straightforward way. This is typically the case for lections which follow the biblical text in a linear manner. A number of lections, however, deviate from this pattern. These can be categorized into four groups: (1) lections which have been translated independently; (2) lections which use EV; (3) lections which use both EV and LV; (4) lections which use a synthesis of EV and LV.

Lections which have been translated independently

Lections which translate the text independently, without any obvious indebtedness to either EV or LV, are nos. 15, 20, 23, 95, 96, 225, and 227. All of these lections are composite lections, which use extracts from different verses or chapters from the Bible and modify them so as to create a lection fitting for a specific feast day. As the analysis in §II has shown, even Type II D OTLs translate such lections independently from the Sarum Missal. Since these lections do not follow the biblical text in a linear way, it is obvious that to translate such a lection using EV or LV would have taken considerable effort: the translator would have had to find the various relevant passages in the biblical text, understand in detail how they were used in the lection, and then find the appropriate passages in an EV and LV translation and use them in a way that would not obscure the sense. It is plausible to assume that it would have been easier and more time-efficient simply to translate these lections independently, and this is the solution that the OTLs adopt. Even the later, Type I OTLs take over these independent translations unchanged, with the single exception of

Lection 15 on Christmas morning sung by two voices, which replaces the independent translation of the verses from Isaiah with LV. Apart from the obvious practical benefits of saving time and labour, such independent translations also testify to the great respect which the translators had for the Use of Sarum: the lections are regarded as texts in their own right, worthy of a translation effort distinct from the translation of the biblical text proper.

Interestingly, there are three examples of composite lections which begin with EV or LV and then switch to an independent translation at some point during the lection. This is the case for Lection 161, which at first follows chapter 3 of the Song of Songs in a linear way, then switches to using various excerpts from different chapters and welding them together. This lection in Bo uses LV for the first part and translates the remainder of the lection independently because, it seems, it would have been more laborious to locate the relevant passages in LV. The scribes were clearly aware of the composite nature of this lection, which is signposted by the addition of various chapter numbers and indexing letters throughout the lection. The situation in Lection 211 is very similar. Predominantly the lection uses LV, but then it switches to an independent translation for the second part, which is taken from Ecclus. 24. As the analysis in §II shows, this entire lection is translated independently in the early Type II D manuscripts. Subsequently, the translators replaced the first part of the lection with LV in later manuscripts, but kept the second part of the lection in the independent translation since it would have required additional effort to find the rest of the lection in a different biblical chapter. Similarly, the first part of Lection 218 in Bo uses the biblical text in a linear way before switching to a verse later on in the same chapter; this is signalled by a different indexing letter. The translation used for the first half is EV, while the last section has been translated independently. Overall, it is evident that the translators were highly aware of the composite nature of some lections and worked around this problem by using independent translations where this was useful, in later manuscripts (i.e. Type I, Type II A–C, Type III) replacing these independent translations by LV where practical and appropriate.

It is an unresolved question whether the independent translations in OTL are contemporary with EV or pre-date it. There is some evidence to suggest that the translation method behind the independent translations is even more literal than what we find in EV. For instance, the lection on Christmas morning (no. 15), sung by two voices, directly translates a troped lesson from the *Missa in gallicantu* according to the Use of Sarum, which is based on the *Vetus Latina* instead of the Vulgate.[74] This accounts for differences between the Sarum text and the Vulgate, e.g. in Isa. 9: 2, where the Sarum Missal has 'populus gentium' whereas the Vulgate has simply 'populus'; hence the translation 'puple of folk' in Type II and Type III OTLs. However, the verse 'parvulus enim natus est nobis' (Isa. 9: 6) is the same in Sarum and in the Vulgate. Nonetheless, there are differences in translation. EV translates this verse as 'A litil child forsothe is born to vs', and LV has 'Forsothe a litil child is borun to vs', while OTL has 'Forsoþe þe litil is born to vs'. Both EV and LV supply 'child' to clarify the sense in English, but OTL shows an extremely literal translation of 'parvulus' as 'þe litil'.

Similar translation strategies can be found in Lection 161 from the Song of Songs. The verse 'veni in hortum meum soror mea sponsa messui murram meam cum aromatibus meis' (S. of S. 5: 1) is rendered in the different versions thus:

> EV: Cum in to my gardin, my sister, my spouse. I haue gedered my mirre, with my swoote spices
>
> LV: Mi sister spousesse, come thou in to my gardyn. Y haue rope my myrre, with my swete smellynge spices
>
> OTL: Come into my garden, sistir, my spousesse, I haue rope my myrre wiþ myn oynementis

OTL here interprets the possessive adjective 'mea' as referring only to 'sponsa' rather than both 'soror' and 'sponsa', as EV and LV do. Both interpretations are possible on grammatical grounds, but the latter seems more appropriate both contextually and idiomatically. OTL follows the Latin text in an extremely literal and linear way.

These independent translations, then, are marked by detailed attention to the Latin grammatical constructions and a very literal approach to translation. As I have discussed in greater detail elsewhere, this is especially noticeable not only with regard to word order but also in the use of the passive and the perfect tenses, which are consistently translated from Latin in a very literal way.[75] Such a level of literalness may be comparable to the cases of 'stencil' translation in the EV prologues which Anne Hud-

[74] See *The Sarum Missal*, ed. Legg, 26. See also Elizabeth Solopova, 'Manuscript Evidence for the Patronage, Ownership and Use of the Wycliffite Bible', in E. Poleg and L. Light (eds.), *Form and Function in the Late Medieval Bible* (Boston, 2013), 333–50, and Solopova, *MSS of WB*, 14.

[75] Cosima Clara Gillhammer, 'Neither EV nor LV: Independent Biblical Translation in the Wycliffite Old Testament Lectionary', in L. Edzard (ed.), *Bible Translations: Linguistic and Cultural Issues. Proceedings of the Erlangen Workshop on October 5 and 6, 2018*, Abhandlungen für die Kunde des Morgenlandes, 122 (Wiesbaden, 2021), 158–78.

son has observed,[76] and it indicates that these independent translations in OTL are very early—perhaps even earlier than EV. Nonetheless, the fact that the earliest OTLs use EV shows that EV was already in existence, or well under way, by the time OTL was written.

Lections which use EV

The lections in Bo which use EV exclusively are nos. 12, 17, 19, 36, 159, 203, 229, 230, 231, and 232. It is difficult to detect what prompted the translators to adhere to EV in these cases as there is no feature common to these lections to explain this policy. In this respect, however, it is noteworthy that Lections 229–32 are Commemorations. In general, the majority of the Commemorations tend to use either EV or an independent translation (for composite lections). For one reason or another, it was the preference of the translators not to replace these EV translations with LV translations in late OTLs even though LV was available to them. A hypothesis to explain this would be that the entire biblical text in LV was not available to the translators at all times, but this is very clearly not the case for the reading from the Book of Esther in Lection 229, which occurs a second time in the OTL (in the Temporale, Lection 41), where it uses LV rather than EV. Some other OTLs, such as Bx and Ny, merely have a cross-reference here and do not copy the lection in its EV translation. It is possible that the translators' focus was more on the Temporale and the Sanctorale, since these feasts were celebrated every year; the Commemorations, celebrated perhaps less regularly, may have been seen as a mere addition for purposes of completeness. In this case, to replace EV by the more recent LV might have been less of a priority to the translators. In other cases, such as Lections 12 and 17, the likely reason why EV was retained is the composite nature of the lections, and it would probably have been a matter of convenience. No obvious reason for the use of EV suggests itself for Lections 19, 36, 159, and 203, and it is unclear why EV was seen as preferable by the translators here.

Lections which use both EV and LV

There are four lections which use both EV and LV in Bo: nos. 4, 60, 67, and 68. In Lection 4 it is only the first sentence which uses EV, while the rest of the lection follows LV. In a similar manner, the first two verses of Lection 68 use EV, while the rest of the lection uses LV. The reasons for

---

[76] Anne Hudson, 'The Origin and Textual Tradition of the Wycliffite Bible', in Solopova (ed.), *The Wycliffite Bible*, 133–61 at 136–9.

this switch are difficult to determine; it is possible that the translators realized only after a few sentences that they had failed to replace EV by LV and simply switched from the former to the latter without going back to correct the error. Interestingly, Type III does not follow this practice and instead uses LV for the entire lection. In Lection 60 it is the first three verses which use LV, while the rest of the lection uses EV. This is a composite lection, but the switch from LV to EV does not coincide with a jump to a different biblical extract, so the reasons behind this shift are uncertain. Lection 67 is another composite lection, which uses LV for the first section from Isa. 62, but switches to EV for the section from Isa. 63. What seems to have happened here is similar to the approach used for the independent lections discussed above: at a point in the lection where the text jumps to a different biblical passage, the translators abandoned LV and reverted to EV. If a Type II D OTL was available to them at the time of copying, it would have been merely a matter of convenience to take over this section unchanged from the exemplar.

Lections which use a synthesis of EV and LV

The fourth category of lections comprises those which use a synthesis of both EV and LV. This means that the translation is not identifiable as either EV or LV, but is indebted to both to some extent. This is the case with nos. 14, 62, and 214. Lection 14 uses a synthesis for the first two verses of the lection, and reverts to EV after that. Lection 62 uses EV predominantly, but contains some variants which are more reminiscent of LV, especially in the last verse. Lection 214 follows LV overall in terms of syntax, but contains some variants which agree more closely with EV, and others which have no equivalent in either translation. The variability of translation in copies of EV or WB is, of course, well known,[77] but no version could be identified for the purposes of this study which shows the same textual variants as the ones found in these lections in OTL.

7. **Authorship, Ownership, Use**

Evidence as to the medieval ownership, patronage, and place of production of Wycliffite translations is notoriously scarce. It is hardly surprising, then, that the same is true for OTL. There are few notes by readers in OTL, and these are limited to infrequent small corrections, e.g. of indexing letters or individual aspects of the translations. It is impossible to draw a clear-cut picture of who was using OTL if we look at readers' notes in OTL

[77] Ibid.

in isolation. The manuscripts containing OTL reveal only occasional evidence of ownership. Elizabeth Solopova has argued convincingly, based on evidence from the calendar in Eg, that this manuscript was made for a nun of the Benedictine nunnery of Barking,[78] and that the calendars in Lm and Ra suggest ownership in London.[79] *Pl* has a medieval shelfmark belonging to Norwich Cathedral priory, *Hl* has a fifteenth-century inscription which identifies a chantry priest, Sir Roger Lyne of St Swithun, London Stone, as its owner,[80] and Bx contains a note which is signed 'by me Ryc(ardus) merton chanon'.[81] What little evidence we have therefore points towards the clergy as owners and patrons of books containing OTL. At first glance, this does not fit well with WB's General Prologue and symple creature's self-proclaimed aim of making 'Holy Write' widely available to 'lewide men' in English.[82] These polemical statements in the General Prologue have led to the modern assumptions that the audience of Wycliffite writings was a lay and unlearned one, but much recent scholarship in the field rather points towards the aristocracy and clergy as owners and patrons of WB.[83] OTL is no exception to this.

The textual features of OTL support such a view. As discussed above, early OTLs and TOLs require a great deal of knowledge of liturgical matters, and they could not easily be used by a lay audience. The standardized format of Type I OTLs seems to be aimed at a wider audience, as it is considerably more user-friendly; it is evidently intended to guide its readers through the complex material by means of precise cross-references and explanatory rubrics. These rubrics are strikingly elaborate and detailed, and presume a reader who is not closely familiar with academic tools of textual referencing. These textual tools were developed over a period of time,[84] reaching their most elaborate form in Type I. Although these strategies of structuring information in OTL would certainly have presented a challenge for anyone not familiar with academic referencing tools, it may have been possible for well-educated lay readers to follow these pointers with the help of the explanations given in the rubrics. Nonetheless, the most obvious audience of OTL is the religious and the clergy,

---

[78] Solopova, 'A Wycliffite Bible Made for a Nun of Barking'.

[79] Solopova, *MSS of WB*, 26.

[80] Elizabeth Solopova, 'The Manuscript Tradition', in Solopova (ed.), *The Wycliffite Bible*, 223–45.

[81] Solopova, 'Manuscript Evidence for the Patronage, Ownership and Use of the Wycliffite Bible', 345–6.

[82] F&M, i. 57.   [83] Solopova, 'The Manuscript Tradition'.

[84] The same trend is noticeable with TOL. Matti Peikola notes that tables without opening rubrics are often representative of the type of table designed to accompany EV manuscripts ('Tables of Lections', 365).

and direct evidence of manuscript ownership points exclusively towards this group.

The referencing tools employed in OTL show that its translators were extremely well trained academically and steeped in the Latin liturgical tradition. There is a great deal of innovation in the way in which indexing letters, rubrics, and cross-references are adapted to the requirements of the text, and these methods were refined over a period of time, as evidenced in the differences between Type II and Type I. It is difficult to imagine such innovative developments taking place outside a scholarly environment. Elizabeth Solopova has argued that the liturgical materials go back to a single early tradition around the time of the copying of EV, which would account for the limited scope of the Sanctorale in TOL and OTL.[85] The close connection between WB and OTL is obvious: OTL makes use of EV, or both EV and LV, and is very similar to WB in its presentation practices and scholarly approach. However, the exact relationship between the translators of OTL and the translators of WB is unclear. It remains a matter of speculation whether both texts were translated by the same group of scholars or whether OTL was a distinct initiative which used WB translations for a specific purpose.

It is a complex question whether OTLs originated in Lollard circles and are indicative of a Wycliffite agenda. Beyond the use of WB in OTL, there are three main pieces of evidence to suggest that OTL shows signs of the translators' possible Wycliffite objectives: first, the scope of the Sanctorale; second, adherence to the biblical rather than the liturgical text in early OTLs; and third, comments by the scribes or translators which are indicative of Lollard sentiments. The evidence for the first of these has been assessed in previous publications, some of which have seen the limited scope of the Sanctorale in early TOLs and OTLs as a sign of the translators' adherence to Wycliffite ideas.[86] Wyclif's writings display a dismissive attitude towards post-biblical saints, and this position is reflected in the stark reduction in the number of saints covered in the Wycliffite sermon cycles.[87] Most Type II OTLs include only a small number of saints, and that those are mostly biblical saints such as St Mary Magdalen, St John the Baptist, or Sts Philip and James. Perhaps most notably, all Type II D manuscripts exclude the feast of relics, while later OTLs do include it. However, even most of the earliest Type II texts include feasts of non-biblical saints such as St Cyriacus and St Lawrence. This evidence might seem at odds with Lollard attitudes towards saints who do not have a

[85] Solopova, forthcoming.   [86] Peikola, 'Tables of Lections', 371.
[87] Hudson, *The Premature Reformation*, 197.

scriptural basis. It is not completely unknown, however, for the Proprium Sanctorum in Wycliffite texts to include non-biblical saints, although in the surviving sets of Wycliffite sermons the number of these saints tends to be reduced even more drastically than in Type II OTLs.[88] If we look at OTL in isolation, the short Sanctorale of Type II OTLs might also be explained by the fact that most feasts of other, non-biblical saints, do not have their own Propers, but are usually taken from the pool of readings contained in the Common. The same is true for the feast of relics, which uses the same lection as no. 206, a feast of many martyrs in the Common. Therefore it would not have been strictly necessary to include these saints in the Proper. If we combine this with the evidence from TOL, which includes a small number of non-biblical saints in its early, Type II form, it is possible to interpret this as a sign of the tables going back to an early tradition which includes only widely venerated and especially important saints, which was then updated and expanded in Type I. This may, of course, reflect a clear Wycliffite agenda on the part of the translators, but this is not the only possible conclusion. At any rate, the short Sanctorale is likely to have appealed to readers with Lollard sympathies.

The second piece of evidence concerns the nature of the text of the lections. As pointed out above (§V.4), Type II B manuscripts tend to follow the Vulgate rather than the Sarum Missal in lections which omit certain parts of the biblical text. The same is true for the earliest OTLs in Group II D. In this group, as in II B, the lections translate the biblical rather than the liturgical text in cases where there are differences between the two. While such deviations from the liturgical text are usually marked by underlining in II B, no such underlining practice can be found in II D. What is more, II D almost never includes liturgical framing devices in the lections, while II B does include them and underlines them. It is evident, then, that the text of II D reflects a marked preference for the biblical text over the liturgical text. A similar impulse, though weaker, is noticeable in II B. By contrast, later OTLs, especially of Type I, are more accurate in liturgical terms and prioritize the liturgical over the biblical text. In view of the importance which the Wycliffites accorded to the biblical text, it is possible to see this adherence to the biblical text in early OTLs as reflective of the Wycliffite intentions behind the lectionary. Discussing the evidence of TOLs, Matti Peikola has raised the possibility that 'the practice of append-

---

[88] The Sanctorale of the English sermon cycle in *English Wycliffite Sermons*, ed. Pamela Gradon, ii (Oxford, 1988), contains only one feast of a non-biblical saint, St Martin (no. 108), while the (incomplete) Latin sermon cycle includes two non-biblical saints: St Nicholas and St Agnes (Christina von Nolcken, 'An Unremarked Group of Wycliffite Sermons in Latin', *Modern Philology*, 83 (1986), 233–49 at 248–9).

ing tables of lections to Bibles in English originated in Wycliffite circles', but that 'the Wycliffites relatively soon lost their ideological control over the transmission of the tables'.[89] The use of the liturgical vs. the biblical text in OTL would seem to support such a view, but the evidence is circumstantial rather than definite and can be interpreted in different ways. As the analysis of independent translations in Type II D has shown,[90] even the earliest OTLs show a great respect for the liturgical form of the text. In many composite lections where the liturgical text differs markedly from the biblical text, even the early OTLs regard the lection as a text in its own right and translate it independently. The preference for the biblical text over the liturgical text which we find in some lections in II D and II B could also be explained by a number of other factors, such as an academically minded desire for textual completeness, the lack of vernacular models for OTL, and the constant juggling of two source texts (the Vulgate and the Sarum Missal), so that the evidence is not necessarily indicative of heterodox purposes.

The third piece of evidence is similarly circumstantial. A rubric at the end of the TOL in MS Ashmole 1517 has been cited as evidence of the Wycliffite origin of the tables:

þe lokeris in þis kalender be riȝt wel war, for he shal not fynde alle þe bigynnyngis of þe lessuns of þe olde lawe acorde wiþ þe kalender. For bi ordy[n]aunce of þe chirche, þat is sett to þe bigynnyngis of many lessuns more and oþerwyse þan it is in þe bible, and þat is drawun vndir wiþ a styk of reed ynke, and it is not in þe kalender. For it is not so in þe text, and also it is in þe same maner of manye of þe endingis of þo lessuns.[91]

The rubric is concerned with pointing out the differences between the biblical text and the liturgical text in order to aid the user of the TOL and the OTL in finding the appropriate passages. Although some scholars have seen this rubric as overtly critical, it is not evident that this comment seeks to blame the 'ordynaunce of þe chirche' for making changes to the biblical text.[92] The note is descriptive in tone rather than critical and echoes the rubrics found at the start of most TOLs, which aim to describe the liturgical practice to make it accessible to those of lesser competence in these matters. Wycliffite attitudes overtly critical of church practices with regard to veneration of saints can indeed be found in a comment in a TOL

[89] Peikola, 'Tables of Lections', 371.   [90] See above, §§II.3 and V.6.
[91] As, f. 5ᵛ.
[92] Peikola ('Tables of Lections', 366–7) sees a clear criticism of church practices implied in this rubric.

in British Library, MS Egerton 618,[93] but the extant TOLs and OTLs suggest that this kind of material is very much the exception rather than the rule.

In summary, the evidence in OTL which may point to Wycliffite or Lollard intentions is somewhat ambiguous. Early OTLs may be more clearly reflective of a Wycliffite agenda than later ones, but the evidence can be interpreted in different ways. As pointed out in §V.2 above, early OTLs could have been used with ease only by a limited circle of academically and liturgically competent readers and do not seem to be aimed at 'lewide men'. The popularity of TOL and OTL in Wycliffite Bibles, the effort which must have been spent on improving its structure and developing sophisticated referencing tools over time, and the care with which the liturgical texts were written all testify to a great respect for the liturgy. The Lollards did, of course, attach great significance to readings from the Bible, but the manuscript evidence of OTL and its emphasis on liturgical practice are not reflective of what we might expect in the light of the polemic in Wycliffite sermons and the Lollards' widespread disregard for the Mass.[94]

At any rate, OTL manuscripts were circulated at least in part among unequivocally orthodox users.[95] The question of how the liturgical texts were used has been controversially debated in Wycliffite scholarship, and no consensus has emerged.[96] An obvious way in which clerics and laypeople alike could have used OTL was for private study and devout reflection on the liturgical readings, and, in the case of priests, as an aid to preparing homilies in the vernacular. Many OTL manuscripts are of a small, portable size (e.g. Bo, Bx, Ra) and are likely to have been designed for private use. Whether owners would have studied the scriptural passages for a liturgical occasion beforehand, or whether they would have brought their books to Mass with them to follow the readings in translation, is difficult to say, but that the latter practice existed is indicated by a section in *The Mirror of our Lady* which admonishes the Bridgettine sisters

[93] British Library, Egerton MS 618, f. 173ʳ–v; edited by Peikola, 'Tables of Lections', 377–8.

[94] On Wycliffite attitudes towards the Mass, see Hudson, *The Premature Reformation*, 149–52.

[95] Ta may be an exception to this rule, as it has traditionally been associated with Lollard owners, such as John Purvey and John Witton (who was accused of heresy in 1440). The association with Purvey is, however, contentious at best, and seems to stem from later Protestant readers; see J. Scattergood and G. Latré, 'Dublin, Trinity College Library MS 75: A Lollard Bible and Some Protestant Owners', in J. Scattergood, *Manuscripts and Ghosts: Essays on the Transmission of Medieval and Early Renaissance Literature* (Dublin, 2006), 163–80.

[96] For a summary of different views see Peikola, 'Tables of Lections', 367–71.

at Syon not to read scriptural passages in translation during the offices.[97] There is, however, a considerable number of larger-size manuscripts, such as As, Ln, and Ul, which are likely to have been intended for use on a lectern, whether in church or elsewhere. This brings us to the contested issue of whether lections were also read out at Mass in the vernacular. As Mary Dove has pointed out, those details of liturgical practice which are mentioned in OTL are focused on what the hearer can expect visually and aurally.[98] This is most obvious in the lection on Christmas morning (Lection 15) with its detailed rubric, explaining that the lection is sung in the pulpit by two voices, one of which gives the text from Isaiah, and the other a kind of gloss on the text. This rubric gives the impression of being written as an explanation for the hearer rather than as an instruction for someone performing an active role at Mass, especially given the fact that the lection can be sung only in Latin. A similar impression arises from Lection 11. This lection from Dan. 3 occurs a number of times in the course of the liturgical year during the Ember Days, but its length differs depending on the liturgical season. While many Type II OTLs include the text for different seasons, combined with markers such as 'In Lent rede but hidir to' etc., Type I OTLs do not include the text for different liturgical seasons and are thus incomplete in liturgical terms. It would be impossible to reconstruct the full lection for a specific season based on the text in a Type I OTL alone, which means that such lectionaries are unlikely to have been a basis for public reading in the vernacular.

In other places, the underlining practices in OTL mean that the text could feasibly be used only for private study rather than public reading. As pointed out above, there is a lack of distinction on a visual level between underlinings which mark passages that are not part of the biblical text and those marking passages that are part of the biblical text but not part of the lection after the Use of Sarum. This is particularly the case in Group II B, but occasionally also in other Type II groups and Type I. If a lection such as no. 16, which includes a lengthy underlined passage that is in the biblical text but not in the Sarum Missal, were used at Mass, it would be well-nigh impossible for the priest to know at a glance that the introductory section 'The lord seiþ þese þingis', which is underlined, is part of the lection and should be read aloud, while verses 3–5, which are also underlined, are not part of the lection and should not be read aloud. The diligent

---

[97] See Henry Hargreaves, 'The Mirror of Our Lady: Aberdeen University Library Ms. 134', *Aberdeen University Review*, 42 (1968), 267–80 at 278, who considers this section to be an addition. See also Dove, *The First English Bible*, 63.

[98] Dove, *The First English Bible*, 64.

reader could certainly make sense of these textual markers through private study, perhaps in comparison with the biblical text and the Latin lection. For a public reading of these lections, however, the underlining practices are unhelpful at best and error-inducing at worst. Although there is no definite proof that the lections were not used for public reading, on the whole the textual evidence points more towards a use of OTL for private study, scholarship, and devotion.

VI. EDITORIAL POLICY

The present edition is closely associated with the new edition of WB currently being produced at the English Faculty, Oxford.[99] For purposes of comparison, it was thought desirable to achieve a degree of consistency between the edition of WB and the present edition of the OTL, and this edition follows the editorial policy of the new edition of WB in many key points. Owing to the particular textual nature of OTL, some adjustments to this policy have been made.

As has become clear from the discussion above, the different types and groups of lectionaries show considerable variation in their inventories of lections and in the sources or combination of sources they use. It is not at all evident whether uniformity between the lectionaries was a goal from the outset (although it was achieved, to some extent, in Type I). As a result, there is great textual variation between different groups, while witnesses within each of these groups display relatively little variation. The body of witnesses thus presents a range of problems for the editor, and these problems mean that a conventional critical edition of this material would not be practicable. The solution which has been chosen is to use a manuscript of Group II B as a base text of this edition. As Type II shares features with both Type III and Type I OTLs, this choice is intended to capture the OTL at a specific stage in its development and in this way to highlight the adaptability and variability of the text. Group II B contains a number of texual features which are of special interest. From among the witnesses in this group, Oxford, Bodleian Library, Bodley 665 (Bo) has been chosen as the base text for the present edition. Bo is a suitable base text because of its comparatively long Common, with a full set of readings.

Variants have been collated from representative manuscripts from

[99] 'Towards a New Edition of the Wycliffite Bible', English Faculty, Oxford University. Researchers: Dr Elizabeth Solopova, Prof. Anne Hudson, Dr Daniel Sawyer. Parts of the edition can be found online at ⟨https://wycliffite-bible.english.ox.ac.uk/⟩.

all relevant textual groups. As pointed out on p. xx above, the method used in this edition aims at giving an accurate overview of the textual differences between various groups of the OTL, while remaining accessible for the reader. In view of the nature of the relationships between individual witnesses and groups of witnesses of the OTL, no attempt has been made to produce a traditional critical edition of witnesses within a single group. Given that there is relatively little variation between such witnesses, such an approach seemed less desirable than one which would help us understand the textual relationships between different groups. This edition, therefore, is intended as a 'working edition' which contains information on the textual features of all groups and similarities and differences between them. The collation includes all textual groups with the exception of Group II D. Subgroups A–C within Type II, along with Types I and III, show significant similarities in the translations used for the lections (predominantly LV, with some exceptions). Because of these similarities, a collation between these groups is feasible and reveals important information concerning the textual relationships between these witnesses. By contrast, the anomalous Group II D uses EV and independent translations exclusively, which means that a collation with other groups would not be possible. Group II D is therefore excluded from the collation, but as a test case five EV lections have been collated separately with other Group II D OTLs, and the results of this collation are reported above (see §II). Representative manuscripts have been selected for Type I, Type III, and subgroups A and C within Type II, and variants have been collated from these representative texts. The selected representative manuscripts for Type I and Type II are London, Lambeth Palace, 532 (La), Oxford, Bodleian Library, Rawlinson C. 259 (Ra), Oxford, Bodleian Library, Selden supra 51 (Se), and New York, New York Public Library, 64 (Ny). For Type III, Oxford, Bodleian Library, Bodley 531 (Bx) has been collated, apart from the lacuna which exists between the third lesson for Ember Saturday of Advent and Ash Wednesday. For this section, Warminster, Longleat House, 5 (Lt) has been used. There is some overlap between those two manuscripts with regard to the lection for the feast of St Silvester (Lection 20), since this lection occurs in the Sanctorale later on in Bx, and to account for the overlap this lection has been collated from both manuscripts.

In accordance with the aims of this edition, emendations have been introduced to correct the types of error described below. Editorial interventions are enclosed in square brackets. Where the manuscript text is illegible because of physical damage or imperfect scribal execution, a reading is conjectured on the basis of the evidence of other closely related manuscripts; such cases are marked by angle brackets. Mechanical errors by the scribe, such as cases of dittography or other obvious errors, have been emended. In cases where the base text offers acceptable Middle English but fails to translate the Vulgate or the Sarum Missal, emendation is made only if the evidence of other collated witnesses suggests that this acceptable Middle English variant is an error produced in the course of transmission. In such cases, details of the Vulgate text or words in question are given in the apparatus, followed by the siglum Vu. The Vulgate and the Sarum Missal do not always agree, and in some instances the latter is the obvious source. For these the Sarum Missal is used as the basis for the emendation and the Latin reading is marked by SM. In cases where the base text offers acceptable Middle English which varies from all or most of the other witnesses collated, but does not fail to translate the Vulgate or the Sarum Missal, the text has not been emended, but a note highlighting different variants is included in the Explanatory Notes.

Details of variant readings in the collated manuscripts Bx, La, Ny, Ra, Se, and part of Lt (for those lections which are missing in Bx) are noted in the critical apparatus. The apparatus records substantive variants, variants indicative of dialectal variation, lexical variants, and variations in word order. The apparatus does not record minor morphological variation (e.g. *without/withouten*, *parte/parten*, *told/teld*, plurals *day/days*, *thing/things*, and variation between *whiche/þe whiche*), variation between different ways of noting numerals (arabic or roman numerals, or spelling out the word), or variants which are obviously erroneous (dittography or misspellings). Throughout the apparatus, Explanatory Notes, and Glossary, superscript numbers are used to clarify references where the same word form occurs several times in a single line. For the purposes of these references, the superscript numbers follow the spelling regardless of capitalization: for example, *Hem* and *hem* count as two occurrences of the same word form, but *The* and *þe* do not. Because of the wide range of variants in the rubrics regarding the ways in which they refer to liturgical occasions and to chapter numbers, these variants are not recorded in the apparatus, but variants of particular interest and general trends are discussed in the Explanatory Notes. Similarly, differences in cross-references and incipits are not recorded in the apparatus, but general trends are discussed in the Explanatory Notes. The ordering of lections can vary significantly in different manuscripts. Those lections which could be collated have been collated, but the apparatus does not note differences in the order of lections, or whether these lections are given in full or as cross-references in the collated manuscripts.

The Explanatory Notes also contain further discussion of significant points regarding the textual features of OTL, as well as OTL's relation to WB and the Sarum Missal. In particular, the Explanatory Notes report on differences between OTL and the text of WB, based on a collation with Forshall and Madden's edited text (in default of a more recent comprehensive edition). Where necessary, the Explanatory Notes include an edition of some texts separately in cases where they occur only in the collated texts but not in the base text Bo.

To facilitate cross-referencing of lections with the lection list in §III, lection numbers have been supplied at the beginning of each lection. The lection list in §III is cumulative in nature, and Bo does not contain all the lections in this list. As a consequence, the numbering of lections in the text is not always continuous, skipping some numbers in accordance with the inventory of lections in Bo. Biblical verse numbers have been supplied in superscript at the beginning of each verse to facilitate comparison with modern editions of the biblical text. The Notes and Glossary are cued to the marginal numbering system. The Lectionary functions as continuous structured text with its own rubrics and system of cross-references. To reflect this textual whole, continuous lineation has been chosen for the marginal numbering system, even though individual lections also form distinctive units. The manuscripts consistently indicate the biblical source texts for individual lections in the rubrics. In cases where titles of biblical books or chapter numbers given in the manuscripts deviate from modern conventions, this information is supplied in square brackets in the edited text. Where the liturgical text is a composite lesson which uses material from different biblical chapters, chapter numbers are inserted in square brackets in the text in the appropriate places. In composite lessons where continuous numbering is not possible, relevant verse numbers are supplied in square brackets at the beginning of the lesson rather than as continuous numbers in the lection.

The spelling closely follows the practice of the manuscript. The form *þ* is used for thorn. The overall scribal practice in Bo is to use *Th* when the letter is capitalized, as evidenced in 'Theman', f. 253ra. In accordance with this practice, *Th* is used where word-initial *þ* has been capitalized by the editor. *3* and *ʒ* are used for yogh. *I/J* and *i/j*, as well as *u* and *v*, follow manuscript usage rather than modern practice. Word division, punctuation, and capitalization have been modernized. Abbreviations have been expanded silently. Where it is doubtful which value is indicated by a specific abbreviation, it has been expanded taking into account the specific context of a passage as well as the overall scribal practice. Rubrics in the manuscript are indicated by bold type in the edition. These are typically titles of individual lections, but can also contain comments on liturgical practice.

Quotation marks are not used to indicate speeches within the lections. One of the reasons for this decision is that some readings are taken from Hosea and the Song of Songs, where the identification of individual speakers and their speeches is highly debated even among experts; a solution to this debate is not attempted here. Another reason is that many OT lections are framed as God's speech in the liturgy ('The lord seiþ þese þingis'). This framing as a speech is usually a liturgical addition, but can occasionally be an echo of the rhetorical structure of the Vulgate text. To distinguish between those two cases on the level of punctuation is not always possible and would lead to inconsistencies. Therefore, it seemed more appropriate to forgo quotation marks in this edition so as to avoid confusion.

Manuscript usage concerning underlining of extra-biblical material such as liturgical additions, glosses, and alternative translations is not entirely consistent in Bo. Some other manuscripts are more consistent and careful in their underlining of extra-biblical material. The underlining practice in this edition mirrors the practice in carefully produced manuscripts. Where a section is underlined in Bo or three or more collated manuscripts, it is underlined in the edited text. To visualize the differences between the biblical and the liturgical text, the editorial decision has been made to italicize all extra-biblical material, including liturgical framing devices and 'þat is/or' glosses, regardless of whether this is marked by underlining in the manuscripts or not.

Where the manuscript contains running titles, these have been noted in the critical apparatus; this feature, however, is abandoned in the latter half of Bo. Scribal corrections have been noted in the apparatus. Changes of leaf and column are indicated in the margin, with a | in the text. Indexing letters, which are typically found in the margins of the manuscripts, are noted immediately after the heading of the lection to which they refer, separated by a comma. This edition deviates from the usual EETS policy of marking marginal and interlinear additions by forward and reverse primes. OTL manuscripts present almost all indexing letters in the margins (and occasionally as interlinear additions), and marking all of this material by primes in the edition would have hampered reading considerably; such markers are therefore not included.

The TOL in the Appendix is edited from Bo, following the same prin-

ciples as outlined above. In order to represent the features of this TOL
as they appear in Bo, no emendations have been made, even where the
TOL does not agree with the OTL in Bo. Because of the high level of variation between different versions of the TOL, no attempt has been made
to collate variants, but general tendencies in the TOLs are noted in the
discussion above (§V.1).

Editorial abbreviations

   add. added

  canc. cancelled, either by subpunction or by crossing through

 not in variant is not contained in

   om. omitted

  prec. preceded/preceding

BIBLIOGRAPHY

Abbott, T. K., *Catalogue of the Manuscripts in the Library of Trinity College, Dublin* (Dublin, 1900).

Antiphonale Sacrosanctae Romanae Ecclesiae pro diurnis horis, ed. Benedictines of Solesmes (Paris, 1949).

Bedingfield, M. Bradford, *The Dramatic Liturgy of Anglo-Saxon England* (Woodbridge, 2002).

Biblia Sacra iuxta Vulgatam versionem, ed. Robert Weber and Roger Gryson, 5th rev. edn., ed. Roger Gryson (Stuttgart, 2007).

Carruthers, Mary J., *The Book of Memory: A Study of Memory in Medieval Culture* (Cambridge, 1990).

A Catalogue of the Harleian Manuscripts in the British Museum, 4 vols. (London, 1808).

Catalogue of Manuscripts in the British Museum, NS, i: *The Arundel Manuscripts* (London, 1840).

A Catalogue of the Manuscripts Preserved in the Library of the University of Cambridge, Edited for the Syndics of the University Press, iii (Cambridge, 1858).

A Catalogue of the Manuscripts Preserved in the Library of the University of Cambridge, Edited for the Syndics of the University Library, iv (Cambridge, 1861).

Clemens, Raymond, Diane Ducharme, and Emily Ulrich, *A Gathering of Medieval English Manuscripts: The Takamiya Collection at the Beinecke Library* (New Haven, 2017).

Colker, Marvin L., *Trinity College Library: Descriptive Catalogue of the Mediaeval and Renaissance Latin Manuscripts*, i (Aldershot, 1991).

De Ricci, Seymour, with the assistance of W. J. Wilson, *Census of Medieval and Renaissance Manuscripts* (New York, 1937).

Dove, Mary, *The First English Bible: The Text and Context of the Wycliffite Versions*, Cambridge Studies in Medieval Literature, 66 (Cambridge, 2007).

The Earlier Version of the Wycliffite Bible, ed. C. Lindberg, 8 vols. (Stockholm, 1959–97).

Eldredge, L. M., *Index of Middle English Prose, Handlist IX* (Cambridge, 1992).

English Wycliffite Sermons, ed. Pamela Gradon, ii (Oxford, 1988).

Frere, Walter Howard, *Studies in Early Roman Liturgy*, iii: *The Roman Epistle-Lectionary* (London, 1935).

Gillhammer, Cosima Clara, 'Neither EV nor LV: Independent Biblical Translation in the Wycliffite Old Testament Lectionary', in L. Edzard (ed.), *Bible Translations: Linguistic and Cultural Issues. Proceedings of the Erlangen Workshop on October 5 and 6, 2018*, Abhandlungen für die Kunde des Morgenlandes, 122 (Wiesbaden, 2021) , 158–78.

Görlach, Manfred, *The Textual Tradition of the South English Legendary* (Leeds, 1974).

A Guide to the Exhibition of Some Part of the Egerton Collection of Manuscripts in the British Museum (London, 1929).

Hanna, Ralph, *The English Manuscripts of Richard Rolle: A Descriptive Catalogue* (Exeter, 2010).

—— 'The Palaeography of the Wycliffite Bibles in Oxford', in Solopova (ed.), *The Wycliffite Bible*, 246–65.

—— 'The Wycliffite Translators' Vulgate Manuscript: The Evidence from Mark', *Medium Ævum*, 86 (2017), 60–90.

—— and David Rundle, *A Descriptive Catalogue of the Western Manuscripts, to c. 1600, in Christ Church, Oxford* (*Using Materials Collected by Jeremy J. Griffiths*) (Oxford, 2017).

Hargreaves, Henry, 'The Mirror of Our Lady: Aberdeen University Library Ms. 134', *Aberdeen University Review*, 42 (1968), 267–80.

Hudson, Anne, 'Lollard Book Production', in J. Griffiths and D. A. Pearsall (eds.), *Book Production and Publishing in Britain 1375–1475* (Cambridge, 1989), 125–42.

—— 'Observations on the "Wycliffite Orthography"', in S. Horobin and A. Nafde (eds.), *Pursuing Middle English Manuscripts and their Texts: Essays in Honour of Ralph Hanna* (Turnhout, 2017), 77–98.

—— 'The Origin and Textual Tradition of the Wycliffite Bible', in Solopova (ed.), *The Wycliffite Bible*, 133–61.

—— *The Premature Reformation* (Oxford, 1988).

James, M. R., *A Descriptive Catalogue of the Manuscripts in the Library of Jesus College, Cambridge* (London, 1895).

—— *A Descriptive Catalogue of the Manuscripts in the Library of Lambeth Palace: The Mediaeval Manuscripts* (Cambridge, 1932).

—— *A Descriptive Catalogue of the Manuscripts in the Library of Sidney Sussex College, Cambridge* (Cambridge, 1895).

—— *The Western Manuscripts in the Library of Trinity College, Cambridge*, 3 vols. (Cambridge, 1900).

Ker, N. R., *Medieval Manuscripts in British Libraries*, i: *London* (Oxford, 1969).

—— *Medieval Manuscripts in British Libraries*, iii: *Lampeter–Oxford* (Oxford, 1983).

—— and A. J. Piper, *Medieval Manuscripts in British Libraries*, iv: *Paisley–York* (Oxford, 1992).

Lenker, Ursula, *Die westsächsische Evangelienversion und die Perikopenordnungen im angelsächsischen England* (Munich, 1997).

Lindberg, Conrad, 'The Manuscripts and Versions of the Wycliffite Bible', *Studia Neophilologica*, 42 (1970), 333–47.

McIntosh, A., M. L. Samuels, and M. Laing (eds.), *Middle English Dialectology: Essays on Some Principles and Problems* (Aberdeen: Aberdeen University Press, 1989).

McKitterick, Rosamond, and Richard Beadle, *Catalogue of the Pepys Library at Magdalene College, Cambridge*, v: *Manuscripts*, pt. i: *Medieval* (Cambridge, 1992).

Madan, Falconer, and H. H. E. Craster, *Summary Catalogue of Western Manuscripts in the Bodleian Library at Oxford*, ii, pt. 1: *Collections Received before 1660 and Miscellaneous MSS Acquired during the First Half of the 17th Century* (Oxford, 1922).

Manion, Margaret M., Vera F. Vines, and Christopher de Hamel, *Medieval and Renaissance Manuscripts in New Zealand Collections* (Melbourne, London, and New York, 1989).

Missale ad usum insignis et praeclarae ecclesiae Sarum, ed. Francis Henry Dickinson (Burntisland, 1861–83).

Nolcken, Christina von, 'An Unremarked Group of Wycliffite Sermons in Latin', *Modern Philology*, 83 (1986), 233–49.

Ogilvie-Thomson, S. J., *Index of Middle English Prose, Handlist VIII: A Handlist of Manuscripts Containing Middle English Prose in Oxford College Libraries* (Cambridge, 1991).

Peikola, Matti, 'Tables of Lections in Manuscripts of the Wycliffite Bible', in Eyal Poleg and Laura Light (eds.), *Form and Function in the Late Medieval Bible* (Boston, 2013), 351–78.

—— 'The Wycliffite Bible and "Central Midland Standard": Assessing the Manuscript Evidence', *Nordic Journal of English Studies*, 2 (2003), 29–51.

Pfaff, Richard W., *The Liturgy in Medieval England* (Cambridge, 2009).

Pickering, O. S., 'The Temporale Narratives of the South English Legendary', *Anglia*, 91 (1973), 425–55.

—— and V. M. O'Mara, *The Index of Middle English Prose, Handlist 13:*

Manuscripts in Lambeth Palace Library Including Those Formerly in Sion College Library (Woodbridge, 1999).

Ringrose, Jayne S., *Summary Catalogue of the Additional Medieval Manuscripts in Cambridge University Library Acquired before 1940* (Woodbridge, 2009).

Rouse, Richard H., and Mary A. Rouse, 'The Verbal Concordance to the Scriptures', *Archivum Fratrum Praedicatorum*, 44 (1974), 5–30.

——— *Preachers, Florilegia and Sermons: Studies on the* Manipulus florum *of Thomas of Ireland* (Toronto, 1979).

Samuels, M. L., 'The Dialects of MS Bodley 959', in McIntosh, Samuels, and Laing (eds.), *Middle English Dialectology*, 136–49.

——— 'Some Applications of Middle English Dialectology', *English Studies*, 44 (1963), 81–94; repr. in McIntosh, Samuels, and Laing (eds.), *Middle English Dialectology*, 64–80.

The Sarum Missal, Edited from Three Early Manuscripts, ed. J. Wickham Legg (Oxford, 1916).

Scattergood, John, and Guido Latré, 'Dublin, Trinity College Library MS 75: A Lollard Bible and Some Protestant Owners', in J. Scattergood, *Manuscripts and Ghosts: Essays on the Transmission of Medieval and Early Renaissance Literature* (Dublin, 2006), 163–80.

——— Niamh Pattwell, and Emma Williams, *Trinity College Library Dublin: A Descriptive Catalogue of Manuscripts Containing Middle English and Some Old English* (Dublin, 2021).

Schnorr von Carolsfeld, Franz, and Ludwig Schmidt, *Katalog der Handschriften der Sächsischen Landesbibliothek zu Dresden: Korrigierte und verbesserte, nach dem Exemplar der Landesbibliothek photomechanisch hergestellte Ausgabe des Kataloges der Handschriften der Königlichen Öffentlichen Bibliothek zu Dresden*, 4 vols. (Leipzig, 1882–1923; repr. Dresden, 1979–86).

Scott, Kathleen L. (gen. ed.), *An Index of Images in English Manuscripts from the Time of Chaucer to Henry VIII, c. 1380–c.1509: The Bodleian Library, Oxford*, 3 vols. (Turnhout, 2000).

Solopova, Elizabeth, 'Dialect', in Solopova (ed.), *The Wycliffite Bible*, 202–19.

——— 'Index of Manuscripts of the Wycliffite Bible', in Solopova (ed.), *The Wycliffite Bible*, 484–92.

——— 'Manuscript Evidence for the Patronage, Ownership and Use of the Wycliffite Bible', in E. Poleg and L. Light (eds.), *Form and Function in the Late Medieval Bible* (Boston, 2013), 333–50.

—— 'The Manuscript Tradition', in Solopova (ed.), *The Wycliffite Bible*, 223–45.

—— *Manuscripts of the Wycliffite Bible in the Bodleian and Oxford College Libraries*, Exeter Medieval Texts and Studies (Liverpool, 2016).

—— 'A Wycliffite Bible Made for a Nun of Barking', *Medium Ævum*, 85 (2016), 77–96.

—— (ed.), *The Wycliffite Bible: Origin, History and Interpretation*, Medieval and Renaissance Authors and Texts, 16 (Leiden, 2017).

Speculum Vitae: A Reading Edition, ed. Ralph Hanna, 2 vols., EETS os 331–2 (Oxford, 2008).

Taavitsainen, Irma, 'Scientific Language and Spelling Standardisation 1375–1550', in L. Wright (ed.), *The Development of Standard English, 1300–1800: Theories, Descriptions, Conflicts* (Cambridge, 2006), 131–54.

Thompson, Edward Maunde, *Wycliffe Exhibition in the King's Library* (London, 1884).

Thomson, Rodney M., *A Descriptive Catalogue of the Medieval Manuscripts in Worcester Cathedral Library* (Cambridge, 2001).

Tyndale, William, *The Newe Testament yet once agayne corrected by Willyam Tindale; where vnto is added a kalendar and a necessarye table wherin earlye and lightelye maye be founde any storye contayned in the foure Euangelistes and in the Actes of the Apostles*, STC 2830 (1534).

Tyson, Moses, Jr., *Hand-List of the Collection of English Manuscripts in the John Rylands Library, 1928* (Manchester, 1929).

Venema, G. J., *Reading Scripture in the Old Testament: Deuteronomy 9–10; 31; 2 Kings 22–23; Jeremiah 36; Nehemiah 8*, Oudtestamentische Studiën, 48 (Leiden, 2004).

THE OLD TESTAMENT LECTIONARY

And here bigynnen þe lessouns and pistlis of þe
olde lawe þat ben redde in þe chirche bi al þe ȝeeris.

[LECTION 1]

The first Friday lessoun in Aduent. Isaye li capitulo.

The Lord seiþ þese þingis: ¹Heriþ me, ȝe þat suen þat þat is iust, and seken
þe Lord. Take ȝe heede to þe stoon fro whennes ȝe ben falle doun, and to 5
þe caue of þe lake fro whiche ȝe ben kute doun. ²Take ȝe heede to Abraham, ȝoure fadir, and to Sare, þat childide ȝou, for I clepide hym oon, and
I blessid him, and I multipliede hym. ³Therfor þe Lord schal counforte
Sion, and he schal counforte alle þe fallyngis þerof, and he schal set þe
desert þerof as delicis, and þe wildernesse þerof as a gardyn | of þe Lord. f. 227ʳᵃ
Ioie and gladnesse schal be founden þerynne, þe doing of þankyngis and þe 11
voice of heriynge. ⁴My puple, take ȝe heed to me, and my lynage heer⟨e⟩ ȝe
me, forwhi a lawe schal go out fro me, and my doom schal reste into þe liȝt
of puplis. ⁵My iust man is nyȝ, my saueour is goon out, and myn armes
schulen deme puplis; ilis schulen abide me, and schuln suffre myn arm. 15
⁶Reisiþ ȝoure iȝen to heuene, and seeþ vndir erþe byneþe, forwhi heuenes
schuln mylte awey as smoke, and þe erþe schal be al tobrokun as a clooþ,
and þe dwellers þerof schulen perische as þes þingis, but myn helþe schal be
wiþouten ende, and my riȝtfulnesse schal not faile. ⁷ȝe puple þat knowun
þe iust man, heere me, my lawe is in þe herte of hem. Nyle ȝe drede þe 20
schenschipis of men, and drede ȝe not þe blasfemyes of hem. ⁸Forwhi a
worm schal ete hem so as a clooþ, and a mouȝþe schal deuoure hem so as
wolle, but myn heelþe schal be wiþouten ende, and myn riȝtfulnesse into
generaciouns of generaciouns.

[LECTION 2]

The secunde Wednesdai lessoun of 25
Aduent. Zacharie | þe eiȝtþe chapiter, b. f. 227ʳᵇ

³The Lord God of oostis seiþ þese þingis: I am turnede aȝen to Sion, and
I schal dwelle in þe myddil of Ierusalem, and Ierusalem schal be clepide

---

4 Lord] Lord God LaSeBx   Heriþ] Here Se, heer Bx   5 whennes] _prec. by_ w
canc. at end of prec. line Bo   8 I²] _om._ Ny   9 alle] _om._ Ny   10 f. 227ʳᵃ]
running title Aduent _continued until_ f. 230ʳ Bo   13 into] in Ra   14 My] and my
Ny   my] and my Ny   15 me] _om._ La   16 byneþe] bine Se   17 a] _om._ Ra
21 schenschipis] schenschip NySe, schenschipe La   23 wiþouten . . . riȝtfulnesse] _om._
LaBxRa   riȝtfulnesse] riȝtwisnesse Se

a citee of treuþe, and þe hille of þe Lord <u>schal be clepide</u> þe hille halo-
30 wide. ⁴The Lord of oostis seiþ þes þingis: 3it elde men and elde wommen
schulen dwelle in þe streetis of Ierusalem, and þe staf of man in his hond,
for þe multitude of 3eeris. ⁵And þe stretis of þe citee schulen be fillid wiþ
infauntis and maidens, pleiynge in þe stretis of it. ⁶The Lord of oostis seiþ
þes þingis: Thou3 it schal be seen hard bifor þe i3en of þe relifs of þis puple
35 in þo daies, seiþ þe Lord of oostis, wheþer bifor myn i3en it schal be seen
hard? seiþ þe Lord of oostis. ⁷The Lord of oostis seiþ þes þingis: Lo, I schal
saue my puple fro þe lond of þe eest and fro þe lond of goynge doun of þe
sunne, ⁸and I schal brynge hem, and þei schulen dwelle in þe myddil of
Ierusalem, and þei schulen be to me into a puple, and I schal be to hem
40 into a God, and in treuþe and in ri3twisnesse, <u>seiþ þe Lord Almy3ti</u>.

[LECTION 3]

The secunde Fridai lessoun of Aduent. Isaye lxij°, d. |

f. 227ᵛᵃ <u>The Lord seiþ þese þingis</u>: ⁶Vpon þi wallis, Ierusalem, I haue ordeynede
kepers; al day and al ny3t wiþouten ende þei schulen not be stille. 3e þat
þenken on þe Lord, be not stille, ⁷and 3eue 3e not scilence to hym, til he
45 stablische and til he sette Ierusalem preisynge in erþe. ⁸The Lord swoor
in his ri3t hond and in þe arm of his strengþe, I schal no more 3eue þi
wheete mete to þin enemyes, and aliene sones schulen not drynke þi wyne,
in whiche þou hast traueilid. ⁹For þei þat schuln gadere it togidir schuln ete
it, and schulen herie þe Lord, and þei þat beren it togidre schulen drynke
50 in myn holi for3erdis. ¹⁰Passe 3e, passe 3e bi þe 3atis; make 3e redi wei to þe
puple, make 3e a playn paþe, and chese 3e stoones, and reise 3e a signe to
puplis. ¹¹Lo, þe Lord made herd in þe laste partis of þe erþe: seie 3e to þe
dou3ter of Syon, lo, þi saueoure comeþ! Lo, his mede is wiþ hym, and his
werk is bifore hym. ¹²And þei schulen clepe hem þe holi puple, a3enbou3t
55 of þe Lord. Forsoþe þou schalt be clepide a citee sou3t, and not forsakun.

29 þe hille²] an hil NyLaSeBxRa   30 of oostis] *om.* Ra   31 and þe staf] and
(*abbr.*) and Bo   32 þe¹] *om.* Bx   40 ri3twisnesse] ri3tfulnes Ny   42 haue
ordeynede] ordeynede Ny   43 and] and and Bo   al²] *om.* Se   schulen] schul Ra
43–4 3e þat . . . stille] *om.* Ra   44 be] beþ Se   47 þi] þe Ny   48 it togidir]
om. Ny   49 and²] *om.* Bx   51 3e²] *add.* þe Ra   52 puplis] þe peplis Se   þe³]
om. LaSeBxRa   53 is] *om.* Se   54 is] *om.* Se

[LECTION 4]

The iij Wednesday lessoun of | Aduent. Isaye ij capitulo, a.   f. 227ᵛᵇ

In þo daies [Isaie], þe profete, seide: ²And þere schal be in þe laste daies bifor made redy þe mount of þe hous of þe Lord in þe cop of mountens, and it schal be rerid out upon hillis. And alle heþen men schulen flowe to hym, ³and many puplis schulen go, and schulen seie, Come ʒe, stie we to þe   60 hille of þe Lord, and to þe hous of God of Iacob, and he schal teche vs hise weies, and we schuln go in þe paþis of hym. Forwhi þe lawe schal go out of Sion, and þe word of þe Lord fro Ierusalem. ⁴And he schal deme heþen men, and he schal repreue many puplis, and þei schulen welle togidre her swerdis into scharis, and her speris into sikelis, *or siþis.* Folk schal no more   65 reise swerd aʒen folk, and þei schulen no more be hauntid to batel. ⁵Come ʒe, þe hous of Iacob, and go we in þe liʒt of þe Lord *oure God.*

[LECTION 5]

Vpon þe same day anoþere lessoun. Isaye vij capitulo.

In þo daies ¹⁰þe Lord spak to Achaz, ¹¹seiynge: Axe þou to þe a signe of þi Lord God, into | þe depþe of helle or into þe hiʒþe aboue. ¹²And Achaz   f. 228ʳᵃ seide: I schal not axe, and I schal not tempte þe Lord. ¹³And Isaye seide: 71 Therfor þe hous of Dauiþ, heere ʒe, wheþer it is litil to ʒou for to be diseseful to me[n], for ʒe ben deseseful to my God also? ¹⁴For þis þing þe Lord hymsilf schal ʒeue a signe to ʒou. Lo, a virgyn schal conseyue and schal bere a sone, and his name schal be clepide Emanuel. ¹⁵He schal ete botir   75 and hony, þat he kunne repreue yuel and chees good.

[LECTION 6]

The iij Fryday lessoun of Aduent. Isay xj capitulo, a.

The Lord God seiþ þese þingis: ¹A ʒerde schal go out of þe root of Iesse, and a floure schal stie on þe root of it. ²And þe spirit of þe Lord schal reste on

57 Isaie] NyLaSeBxRa, Isaac Bo   schal] schulen La   60 schulen go and] *om.*
Ra   to þe hille] to þe hille of þe hille Bo   61 to] *om.* Bx   62 in þe paþis] into
þe paþis NyRa   þe lawe] lawe Ny, and þe lawe Se   66 swerd] swerdis Ra   hauntid]
excercisid eiþer haunted SeBx   67 þe hous] to þe hous Ny   go we in þe liʒt] go we
out into þe liʒt Ny   þe Lord oure God] oure Lord God Ny   69 In þo daies] *om.* LaRa
70 into¹] in Ra   þe¹] *om.* Se   þe²] *om.* Se   73 to¹] of La   men] NyLaSeBxRa, me
Bo, hominibus Vu   also] *om.* Ny, *placed after* deseseful LaSeBxRa   75 He] and he Se

80 hym, þe spirit of wisdom and vndirstondynge, þe spirit of counceil and of strengþe, þe spirit of kunnynge and of pite, ³and þe spirit of þe drede of þe Lord schal fulfille hym. He schal not deme bi þe siȝte of iȝen, neþer he schal repreue, *eþer counuerte*, bi þe heerynge of eeris, ⁴but he schal deme in riȝtfulnesse pore men, and he schal repreue in equyte, for þe mylde men

f. 228ʳᵇ of erþe. And he schal smyte þe lond wiþ þe ȝerd | of his mouþ, and bi þe 86 spirit of hise lippis he schal sle þe wickid man. ⁵And riȝtfulnesse schal be þe girdil of hise leendis, and feiþ *schal be* þe girdil of hise reynes.

[LECTION 7]

The iij Saturday lessoun of Aduent. Isaye xix, f.

In þo daies ²⁰þei schulen crie to þe Lord fro þe face of þe troubler, and 90 he schal sende a sauyoure to hem, and a forefiȝter þat schal delyuer hem. ²¹And þe Lord schal be known of Egipt, and Egipcianes schuln knowe þe Lord in þat day, and þei schulen worschip hym in sacrificis and ȝiftis, and þei schulen make avowis to þe Lord, and þei schulen paye. ²²And þe Lord schal smyte Egipt wiþ a wounde, and schal make it hool. And Egipcianes 95 schulen turne aȝen to þe Lord, and he schal be plesid in hem, and he schal make hem hool, *þe Lord oure God*.

[LECTION 8]

The ij lessoun on þe same day. Isaye xxxv°, a.

The Lord God seiþ þes þingis: ¹The forsaken *Iudee* and wiþout wey schal be glad, and wildirnesse schal make ful out ioie, and schal floure as a lilie. ²It

f. 228ᵛᵃ buriownynge schal buriowne, | and it glad and preisynge schal make ful 101 out-ioie. The glorie of Liban is ȝouun to it, þe fairnesse of Carmel and of Saron; þei schulen se þe glorie of þe Lord, and þe fairnesse of oure God. ³Counforte ȝe clumside hondis, and make ȝe strong febil knees. ⁴Sey ȝe men of litil counfort, be ȝe counfortid and nyle ȝe drede. Lo, oure God 105 schal brynge þe veniaunce of ȝildynge, *þat is Crist*, God hymsilf schal come and schal saue vs. ⁵Thanne þe iȝen of blynde men schal be openede, and þe eeris of deef men schulen be open. ⁶Thanne a crokide man schal skippe as an herte, and þe tungen of doumbe men schal be openede, forwhi watris

---

83 þe] *om.* Se   92 þat] þe Ra   98 God] *om.* Bx   99 make] *om.*
Bx   101 Liban] þe liban LaSeRa   of³] *om.* Ra   104 men] to men Se
106 schal²] schulen LaSeBxRa   openede] opened for whi watris ben brokun out in desert
Ny   108 schal] schulen Ra

ben brokun out in desert, and streemes in wildirnesse. ⁷And þat þat was
drie *is made* into a ponde, and þe þirsti *is made* into wellis of watris, *seiþ*   110
oure Lord almy3ti.

[LECTION 9]

The iij lessoun on þe same day. Isaye xl°, c.

The Lord God seiþ þese þingis: ⁹Thou þat prechist to Sion, stie on an hi3e
hille. Thou þat prechist to Ierusalem, enhaunce þi voice in strengþe.
[Enhaunse þou]; nyle þou drede! Seye | þou to þe citees of Iuda: Lo, 3oure   f. 228ᵛᵇ
God! ¹⁰Lo, þe Lord God schal come in strengþe, and his arm schal holde   116
lordship. Lo, his mede is wiþ hym, and hise werk is bifor hym. ¹¹As a
scheperd he schal fede his flok, he schal gader lambren in his arm, and he
schal reise in his bosum, *þe Lord oure God*, *seiþ oure Lord*.

[LECTION 10]

The fourþe lessoun on þe same day. Isaye xlv°.   120

¹The Lord seiþ þese þingis to my crist, Cirus, whos ri3t hond I took, þat I
make suget folkis bifore his face, and turne þe backis of kyngis, and I schal
opene 3atis bifore hym, and þe 3atis schulen not be closide. ²I schal go
bifor þee, and I schal make lowe þi glorious men of erþe. I schal al tobreke
brasun 3atis, and I schal breke togidir yrun barris. ³And I schal 3eue hidde   125
tresouris to þee, and þe pryuy þingis of priuytees, þat þou wite þat I am þe
Lord þat clepiþ þi name, God of Israel, ⁴ for my seruaunt Iacob, and Israel
my chosun, and I clepide þee bi þi name, I liknede þee and þou knewe not
me. ⁵I am þe Lord, and þere is noon more. Wiþouten me is | no God. I   f. 229ʳᵃ
haue girde þee, and þou knewe not me. ⁶That þei þat *ben* at þe risynge of   130
þe sunne, þei þat *ben* at þe weste knowe þat wiþouten me is no God. ⁷I am
þe Lord, and noon oþere *God* is, foormynge li3t and makynge derknessis,
makynge pees and foormynge yuel. I am þe Lord, doinge alle þese þingis.

109 wildirnesse] *prec. by* w *canc. at end of prec. line* Bo   110 drie] dried Ny   is¹] *om.*
Se   113 on] vpon NySe   114 in] wiþ Ra   115 Enhaunse þou] NyLaSeRa,
om. Bo, exalta Vu   citees] citee Ny   3oure] oure NyRa   119 reise] *add.* hem Se
þe Lord oure God] *om.* NyLaSeLt   seiþ oure Lord] *om.* Ra   121 Lord] Lord god
LaSeRa   122 make suget] sogeite Ny   123 3atis¹] þe 3atis SeLtRa   124 þi]
þe LaSeRa   of] on Ra   125 I¹] and I Ra   126 þe¹] *om.* Ra   of priuytees]
om. Ra   127 clepiþ] clepe LaRa, clepide Se   128 clepide] clepe Ra   þi] *om.*
Lt   knewe] knewist SeRa   129 noon more] nomore La   130 girde] girdid Se
knewe] knewist LaSe   131 þei] and þei NyLaSeLtRa

⁸Heuenes sende ʒe out dewe fro aboue, and cloudis reyne a iust man; þe
135 erþe be openede and brynge forþ þe saueoure, *þat is Crist*, and riʒtfulnesse
be born to gidre, þe Lord haue made hym.

[LECTION 11]

The v lessoun on þe same day. Danyel iij, g.

In þo daies ⁴⁹þe aungel of þe Lord came doun wiþ Azarie and hise felowis
into þe furneise, and smoot out þe flawme of fire fro þe furneise, ⁵⁰and
140 made þe myddis of þe furneis as þe wiynd of dewe blowynge. And þe flawme
passide held out ouer þe furneise bi xlix cubitis and brak out and brente
whom of Caldeis it foond bisidis þe furneis. And vtterli þe fire touchide
f. 229ʳᵇ not hem, neþer made sorie, neþer dide ony þing of dissese. ⁵¹Thanne | þes
þre as of o mouþ herieden and glorifieden God, and blessiden God in þe
145 furneise, ⁵²seiynge:

In Aduent rede but hidir to.

Lord God of oure fadris, þou art blesside, and worþi to be preiside, and
glorious, and aboue enhauncid into worldis. Blesside is þe name of þi glorie,
whiche *name* is holi, and worþi to be heriede, and aboue enhauncid in all
150 worldis. ⁵³Thou art blessid in þe holi temple of þi glorie, and aboue preisable, and glorious into worldis. ⁵⁴Thou <u>art</u> blessid in þe troon of þi rewme,
and aboue preisable, and aboue enhauncid into worldis. ⁵⁵Thou art blessid
þat biholdist depþis of watris, and sittist on cherubyn, and *art* preisable,
and aboue enhauncid into worldis.

155 *In Lente rede but hidir to.*

⁵⁶Thou art blessid in þe firmament of heuene, and presable, and glorious
into worldis. ⁵⁷Alle werkis of þe <u>Lord, blesse ʒe þe Lord; herie ʒe and aboue</u>
enhaunce ʒe hym into worldis. ⁵⁸Aungelis of <u>þe Lord, blesse ʒe þe Lord;</u>

134 a iust] *prec. by* on *canc.* Bo   135 þat is Crist] þat *canc.* Ny   136 þe Lord]
prec. by and *canc.* Bo, I þe Lord NyLaSeRa   138 In þo daies] Forsoþe Lt   þe¹] an
LaLt   139 of fire] of þe fier LaRa   140 þe³] *om.* Lt   140–1 þe flawme . . .
out] al þe flawme was held Se, and al þeo flaume was hild out Lt   141 furneise] *add.*
and Lt   142 furneis] *add.* and þe mynystris of þe king whiche tendiden it Se   vtterli]
om. Lt   143 not hem] *add.* on al manere SeLt   sorie] sorwefol Lt   dide] broʒte in Lt
dissese] heuynesse SeLt   144 as] *om.* Ny   of] *om.* Ra   145 seiynge] and seiden
LaSe, *lection in* LaRa *ends here*   147 Lord . . . art blesside] blessed artow lord god of
oure fadres Lt   worþi] *prec. by* w *canc.* Bo   preiside] heryed Lt   148 worldis] *lection
in* Lt *ends here*   149 in¹] into Se   151 into] *add.* þe Se   worldis] *followed by* of
worldis *canc.* Bo   þe] *om.* Ny

herie ȝe and aboue enhaunce ȝe him into worldis. | ⁵⁹Heuenes, blesse ȝe   f. 229ᵛᵃ
þe Lord; herie ȝe and aboue enhaunce ȝe hym into worldis. ⁶⁰Alle þe watris   160
þat ben aboue heuenes, blesse ȝe þe Lord; heriee ȝe and aboue enhaunce
ȝe hym into worldis. ⁶¹Alle þe vertues of heuenes, blesse ȝe þe Lord; herie
ȝe and aboue enhaunce ȝe hym into worldis. ⁶²Sunne and moone, blesse
ȝe þe Lord; herie ȝe and aboue enhaunce ȝe hym into worldis. ⁶³Sterris
of heuene, blesse ȝe þe Lord; herie ȝe and aboue enhaunce ȝe hym into   165
worldis. ⁶⁴Reyn and dewe, blesse ȝe þe Lord; herie ȝe and aboue enhaunce
ȝe hym into worldis. ⁶⁵Eche spirit of God, blesse ȝe þe Lord; herie ȝe and
aboue enhaunce ȝe hym into worldis. ⁶⁶Fire and hete, blesse ȝe þe Lord;
herie ȝe and aboue enhaunce ȝe hym into worldis. ⁶⁷Coold and somer,
blesse ȝe þe Lorde; herie ȝe and aboue enhaunce ȝe hym into worldis.   170
⁶⁸Dewis and whiȝte frost, blesse ȝe þe Lord; herie ȝe and aboue enhaunce
ȝe hym into worldis. ⁶⁹Blak frost and coold, blesse ȝe þe Lord; herie ȝe and
aboue enhaunce ȝe hym into worldis. ⁷⁰Ysis and snowis, blesse ȝe þe Lord;
herie ȝe and aboue enhaunce ȝe hym into | worldis. ⁷¹Niȝtis and daies,   f. 229ᵛᵇ
blesse ȝe þe Lord; herie ȝe and aboue enhaunce ȝe hym into worldis. ⁷²Liȝt   175
and derknesse, blesse ȝe þe Lord; herie ȝe and aboue enhaunce ȝe hym
into worldis. ⁷³Leitis and cloudis, blesse ȝe þe Lord; herie ȝe and aboue
enhaunce ȝe hym into worldis. ⁷⁴The erþe blesse ȝe þe Lord; herie it and
aboue enhaunce it hym into worldis. ⁷⁵Mounteyns and litil hillis, blesse ȝe
þe Lord: herie ȝe and aboue enhaunce ȝe hym into worldis. ⁷⁶Alle buri-   180
ownynge þingis in erþe, blesse ȝe þe Lord; herie ȝe and aboue enhaunce ȝe
hym into worldis. ⁷⁷Wellis, blesse ȝe þe Lord; herie ȝe and aboue enhaunce
ȝe hym into worldis. ⁷⁸Sees and flodis, blesse ȝe þe Lord; herie ȝe and aboue
enhaunce ȝe hym into worldis. ⁷⁹Whallis and alle þingis þat ben moued in
watris, blesse ȝe þe Lord; herie ȝe and aboue enhaunce ȝe hym into worldis.   185
⁸⁰Alle briddis of þe eire, blesse ȝe þe Lord; herie ȝe and aboue enhaunce ȝe
hym into worldis. ⁸¹Alle wielde beestis and tame beestis, blesse ȝe þe Lord;
herie ȝe and aboue enhaunce ȝe hym into worldis. | ⁸²Sones of men, blesse   f. 230ʳᵃ
ȝe þe Lord; herie ȝe and aboue enhaunce ȝe hym into worldis. ⁸³Israel,
blesse þe Lord; herie it and aboue enhaunce it hym into worldis. ⁸⁴Prestis   190
of þe Lord, blesse ȝe þe Lord; herie ȝe and aboue enhaunce ȝe hym into
worldis. ⁸⁵Seruauntis of þe Lord, blesse ȝe þe Lord; herie ȝe and aboue
enhaunce ȝe hym into worldis. ⁸⁶Spiritis and soulis of iust men, blesse ȝe
þe Lord; herie ȝe and aboue enhaunce ȝe hym into worldis. ⁸⁷Holi men and
meke of herte, blesse ȝe þe Lord; herie ȝe and aboue enhaunce ȝe hym into   195

172 worldis] *prec. by* w *canc. at end of prec. line* Bo   177–8 Leitis . . . worldis] *om.* Ny
179 litil] *om.* Ny

worldis. [88]Ananye, Azarie, Misael, blesse ȝe þe Lord; herie ȝe and aboue enhaunce ȝe hym into worldis.

[LECTION 12]

The iiij Wednesday lessoun of Aduent. Ioel ij, g.

[23]Ioie, ȝe sones of Sion, and glade ȝe in þe Lord, ȝoure God, for he ȝaf
200 to ȝou a techer of riȝtwisnesse, and he schal make to come doun to ȝou morewe reyn and late reyn, as fro þe bigynnynge. [24]And feeldis schulen be fillid wiþ wheet, and pressouris schulen be plentyuous in wiyn and oyle.

Ioel iij, g.

f. 230rb [17]And ȝe schulen wite, for I þe Lord ȝoure God, dwellynge in | Sion, in
205 myn holi hille. And Ierusalem schal be holi, and alienes schuln no more passe þerbi. [18]And it schal be in þat day: mounteynes schulen droppe swetnesse and litil hillis schulen flowe wiþ mylke, and bi alle þe ryuers of Iuda watris schulen go. And a wel schal go out of þe hous of þe Lord, and schal moiste þe reyn streem of þornes. [19]Egipt schal be into desolacioun, and
210 Ydume into a desert of perdissioun, for þat þat þei diden wickidli into þe sones of Iuda, and schedden out innocent blood in her lond. [20]And wiþouten ende Iudee schal be enhabitid, and Ierusalem into generacioun and into generacioun. [21]And I schal clense þe blood of hem whiche I clensid not, and þe Lord schal dwelle in Sion *fro þe world and til into þe world*.

[LECTION 13]

215   #### The iiij Friday lessoun of Aduent. Zacharie ij[o], f.

The Lord seiþ þes þingis: [10]Douȝter of Syon, heere þou and glade, for lo, I come, and schal dwelle in þe myddil of þee, seiþ þe Lord. [11]Many folkis schulen be appliede to þe Lord in þat day. And þei schulen be to me into a
f. 230va pupil, and I schal dwelle in þe myddil | of þee. And þou schalt wite for þe
220 Lord of oostis sente me to þee. [12]And þe Lord schal weelde Iuda into his

196 Misael] *om.* Ny   197 worldis] *prec. by* w *canc. at end of prec. line* Bo
199 Ioie] *prec. by* The lord seiþ þese þingis LaSe, The lord God seiþ þese þingis Ra
in] into Se   202 fillid] ful fillid Ny   in] with NyRa   204 in[2]] *om.* Ny
206 in þat day] into dayes þat Lt   209 into] in Ra   210 a] *om.* NyLaSeLt
212 enhabitid] enhaunsid Ra   214 fro . . . into þe world] *om.* Lt   216 The
Lord . . . þingis] *om.* Lt   217 schal] I schal La   þe[1]] *om.* Se   218 into] in þat
day Se   219 f. 230va] *running title* Cristemasse day   for] þat SeLt

part in þe lond halowide, and schal [chese] ȝit Ierusalem. ¹³Be eche fleisch
stille fro þe face of þe Lord, for he roos fro his holy dwellynge place, _seiþ þe_
Lord almyȝti.

[LECTION 14]

The lessoun on Cristmasse Euen. Isaye lxijᵒ, a.

The Lord seiþ þese þingis: ¹[F]or Sion I schal not be stille, and for Ierusalem I   225
schal not reste, til þe tyme þat þe riȝtwisse go out of hym as schynynge, and
his saueour as a laumpe be tend. ²And heþen men schulen se þi riȝtwise
man and alle kyngis þi nobeley, and a newe name schal be clepide to þee
þat þe mouþ of þe Lord nempnede. ³And þou schalt be a coroun of glorie
in þe hond of þe Lord, and a deademe of þe rewme in þe hond of þi God.   230
⁴Thou schalt no more be clepide forsaken, and þi lond schal no more be
clepide desolat, but þou schalt be clepide my wille in it, and þi lond schal
be enhabitid, for it pleside to þe Lord in þee.

[LECTION 15]

On Cristemasse morewe þe firste lessoun at þe firste Masse,
þe whiche lesson is sungun in þe pulpit, þe | firste vers   f. 230ᵛᵇ
and þe laste of two togidre. But alle þe myddil vers oon   236
syngiþ oon, and anoþer syngiþ anoþer. The firste vers of
þo þat ben sungen bi hemsilf, is of þe tixte of Isaye þe
profete. And þe answere is as it were a glose of þe tixte.
And so it is bi and bi, þoruȝout þe lessoun, of whiche þis   240
is þe first vers þat is sungen of boþe togidre. Isaye ixᵒ.

I schal seie preisynges to God þoruȝ worldis, þe whiche haþ foormede me
wiþ his riȝt hond, and haþ raunsomed me in þe crosse wiþ þe blood of
his sone.

This is þe firste vers of þo þat ben sungen of oon bi hymsilf, whiche   245
is of þe tixte. b.

The lessoun of Isaye þe profete, in þe whiche þe schynynge birþe of Crist is

---

221 chese] NyLaSeLtRa, clensen Bo, eliget Vu   225 The lord . . . þingis] _abbr. add._
in margin Bo, _om._ Lt   For] Aor Bo   I shal not] _om._ Se   227 be] _om._ LtRa   þi] þe La
þi riȝtwisse man] hys riȝghtwesnesse Lt   229 a] _om._ Se   231–2 schal . . . desolat]
schal be clepid nomore desolat LaRa   233 to] _om._ Lt   247 þe²] _om._ La

profeciede. These þingis seiþ þe Lord, þe Fadir, þe Sone, and þe Holi Goost, in whom alle þingis ben made, boþe hiʒe þingis and lowe þingis. ²<u>The puple</u>
250 <u>of folk þat walkide in derknesses,</u> *whom þe enemye wiþ trecherous gile putte*
f. 231ʳᵃ *out of paradise, and ledde hem wiþ hym bi þraldom into helle,* <u>say a</u> | <u>greet</u>
<u>liʒt.</u> *There schoon greet liʒtis, boþe at mydnyʒt and vnto þe heerd-men.* <u>To hem</u>
<u>wonyinge in þe kyngdom of schadewe of deeþ: liʒt,</u> *liʒt euerlastynge and oure*
verri aʒenbiynge, <u>is sprungoun to hem.</u> *O þat wondirful birþe!* ⁶<u>Forsoþe, þe</u>
255 <u>litil is born to vs.</u> *But he schal be greet Jhesu, þe sone of God, and þe sone*
of þe hiʒe fadir <u>is ʒouun to vs</u> *fro þe souereyn hiʒþe, as it was seide bifore.*
<u>And his prinshede is made on þe schuldren of hym,</u> *for he schal gouerne*
heuenes and feeldis, <u>and his name schal be clepide:</u> *Messias, Sother, Emanuel,*
Sabaoth, Adonay, <u>wondirful</u> *root of Dauiþ,* <u>counceilour</u> *of God þe fadir þat*
260 *made alle þingis,* <u>strong God,</u> *brekynge þe strongist closuris of helle,* <u>fadir of þe</u>
<u>worlde þat is to come,</u> *kyng almyʒti, gouernynge alle þingis,* <u>prince of pees</u>
bi þe worldis euerlastynge. ⁷<u>His comaundynge schal be multipliede</u> *in Ieru-*
salem and in Iewrie and in Samarie. <u>And of his pees schal be noon ende, here</u>
and elliswhere. <u>And he schal sitte on þe seet of Dauiþ and on þe kingdom</u>
265 <u>of hym,</u> *and þere schal be no mark, neþer no teerme of his kyngdom.* <u>And he</u> |
f. 231ʳᵇ <u>schal make it stabil</u> *in þe wedde of bileeue.* <u>And he schal strengþe it in doom</u>
<u>and in riʒtwisnesse</u> *whanne he schal come domesman, to deme þe worlde.* <u>Fro</u>
<u>now forþ</u> *glorie, preisynge, and ioie be ʒolden vnto hym* <u>and</u> *into withouten*
ende. Worþi preisynge be sungen vnto þe creatoure of alle creaturis. Fro eest and
270 *weste, norþ and souþ, alle creaturis sey, so be it.*

[LECTION 16]

The secunde lessoun at þe same Masse. Isaye ixº, b.

The Lord seiþ þese þingis: ²The puple þat ʒede in derknessis say a greet liʒt.
Whanne men dwelliden in þe cuntreye of schadewe of deeþ, liʒt roos vp to
hem. ³Thou multipliedist folk, þou magnefiedist not gladnesse. Thei schu-

248 These . . . Lord] þe lord seiþ þes þingis Se   and] *om.* LaLt   249 þingis³] *om.* Se
250 derknesses] wyldurnesse Lt, *add.* which þou hast maad of noʒt Se   251 say a greet]
siʒ greet Ny   f. 231ʳᵃ] *running title* Cristmasse *contd. until f. 231ᵛ* Bo   252 liʒtis] liʒt
Lt, a gret liʒt Ra   boþe] *om.* Lt   253 wonyinge] dwellynge Se   of schadewe] of
þe schadowe Ny   liʒt²] *om.* Se   256 hiʒþe] liʒt Lt   seide bifore] byfore sayd Lt
257 on] vpon Ra   260 God] *placed after* fadir Lt   263 in Iewrie] in þe iewerie
Ny, Iude Ra   in²] *om.* Se   264 seet] citee Lt   267 þe] al þe Ra   268 now
forþ] hennes forþ Lt   vnto] to Lt   into] vnto NyLt, to Se   269 ende] *add.* þis vers
þat sueþ is sungen of boþe togidre as þe firste Se   vnto] to Se   272 The Lord . . .
þingis] These þingis seiþ þe Lord La, *om.* Lt   derknessis] derknes Ra   273 dwelliden]
dwellen Ra   of schadewe] of þe schadowe Ny   vp to] vpon Lt   274–80 Thou . . .
fire] *om.* LaSeRa. *Start and end marked in margin by* va *and* cat *in* Bo

len be glad bifor þee, as þei þat ben glad in heruest, as ouercomeris maken 275
ful out-ioie whanne þei han take a pry, whanne þei departen spoylis. ⁴For
þou hast ouercomen þe ʒok of hise briþeren, and þe ʒerde of his schuldre,
and þe septer of his wrongful axer, as in þe day of Madian. ⁵Forwhi al
violent raueyn with noyse, and a clooþ medelide with blood schal be into
brennynge, and schal be þe mete of fire. | ⁶Forsoþe, a litil child is borun   f. 231ᵛᵃ
to vs, and a sone is ʒouun to vs, and prinshede is made on his schuldre,   281
and his name schal be clepide: wondirful and counseilour, God strong, a
fadir of þe worlde to comynge, a prince of pees. ⁷His empire schal be multipliede, and noon ende schal be of _his_ pees. He schal sitte on þe seet of
Dauiþ and on þe rewme of hym, þat he conferme it and make strong in   285
doom and riʒtfulnesse, fro hennesforþ and til into withouten ende.

[LECTION 17]

The lessoun at þe secunde Masse
on Cristemasse day. Isaye lxjº, a.

The Lord seiþ þes þingis: ¹The spirit of þe Lord upon me, for þat he anoyntide me. He sente me to preche to pore men, to tel out to deboner men; he   290
sente me þat I schulde leche contrite men in herte, and preche to caitif men
forʒeuenesse, and to closide men openynge, ²and preche a ʒeer plesable to
þe Lord, and a day of veniaunce to oure God, þat I schulde counforte alle
weilynge men, ³þat I schulde putte counfort to þe weilynge men in Sion,
and ʒeue to hem a coroun for askis, oyle of ioie for weilynge, a mantel of   295
preisynge for þe spirit of moornynge. And þere schulen | be clepide in it   f. 231ᵛᵇ
strong men of riʒtwisnesse, plauntynge of þe Lord to glorifien.

Isaye lxijº, f.

¹¹Lo, þe Lord made herd in þe vtmest of erþe. Seye ʒe to þe douʒtir of
Syon: Lo, þi sauyoure comeþ! Lo, his mede wiþ hym, and his werk bifore   300
hym! ¹²And þei schulen clepe hym an holy puple, aʒenbouʒte of þe Lord.

282 and²] _om._ LtRa   strong] _add._ and Ra   285 and¹] _om._ Lt   make] _add._ it Ra
286 riʒtfulnesse] in riʒtfulnesse La   hennesforþ] hennes Lt   289 The Lord . . .
þingis] _om._ Lt   upon] on La   290 He sente . . . pore men] _om._ Lt   294 counfort]
weilynge Ny   299 made] herd made herd BoNy

[LECTION 18]

The lessoun at þe þridde Masse. Isaye lij°.

The Lord seiþ þese þingis: ⁶For þis þing my puple schal knowe my name in þat day. For lo, I mysilf þat spak, am presente. ⁷Ful faire ben þe feet of
305 hym þat telliþ and prechiþ pees on hillis, of hym þat telliþ good, of hym þat prechiþ heelþe and seiþ: Sion, þi God schal regne. ⁸The voice of þi biholders, þei reiseden þe voice, þei schulen herie togidre, for þei schulen se wiþ iȝe to iȝe whanne þe Lord haþ conuertid Sion. ⁹The desert þingis _eþer forsaken þingis_ of Ierusalem, make ȝe ioie and herie ȝe togidir! For þe
310 Lord haþ counfortid his puple; he haþ aȝenbouȝt Ierusalem. ¹⁰The Lord haþ made redy his holy arm in þe iȝen of alle folkis, and alle þe endis of erþe schulen se þe helþe of oure God.

[LECTION 19]

The pistil | on Seynt Ioones day
in Cristmas. Ecclesiasticus xv.

315 ¹Who drediþ God schal do good þingis, and who is wiþholdynge of riȝtwisnesse schal take it. ²And it schal mete to hym as a modir wor-shipide, and as a womman fro maydenhode it schal vndirtake him. ³It schal fede hym wiþ þe brede of lijf and vndirstondynge, and wiþ watir of holsum wisdom it schal ȝeue drynke to him. And it schal be fastnede
320 in hym, and not be bowide. ⁴And it schal wiþholden hym, and he schal not be confoundide. It schal enhaunce hym anentis hise neiȝboris. ⁵And in þe myddil of þe chirche it schal opene his mouþe, and þe Lord schal fulfille hym wiþ þe spirit of vndirstondynge and of wisdom, and wiþ þe stool of glorie it schal cloþe hym. ⁶Mirþe and ful out-ioiynge it schal
325 tresouren vpon hym, and in euerlastynge name it schal eritagen hym, _þe Lord oure God._

---

303 The Lord . . . þingis] _om._ Lt   Lord] _add._ God Ra   in] and Lt   304 mysilf] my silfe, e _canc._ Bo   305 pees] þe pees Ra   on] vpon Ra   310 counfortid] conuer-tid Se   313 f. 232ʳᵃ] _running title_ Iohun Bo   316 to] _om._ Se   317 and as a womman . . . vndirtake him] _om._ LaRa   fro] for Se   319 wisdom] techinge Se   be] _om._ Se   320 in hym] _om._ Lt   in] into Se   321 confoundide] _add._ and LaSeRa   323 vndirstondynge . . . wisdom] wijsdom and of vndirstondinge NyLaSeLtRa   vndirstondynge] _prec. by_ his _canc._ Bo   325 it] _om._ SeLtRa

[LECTION 20]

The lessoun on Seynt Siluestirs day.
Ecclesiastici l. [Ecclus. 4, 1, 5–13, 16, 17, 23–5]

Biholde, þis is þe greet prest þat kepte wel his flok in his lijf and þat dely-
uerid hem fro leesynge, þat held up þe hous and strengþide þe | temple f. 232rb
in hise daies, þat was my3ti at þe fulle to alargen þe citee, þat purchaside 331
hym glorie in þe conuersacioun of folk. As þe morwe sterre in þe myddil
of a cloude, and as þe ful moone, so schoon he in hise daies, and as þe
sunne ful schynynge, so schoon he in þe temple of God: As þe reynbowe
ful schynynge among þe cloudis of glorie, and as þe floure of roosis in 335
þe daies of cesonable somer, as þe lilies þat ben in þe passynge of watris
and as encense ful smellynge in þe daies of hottist somer, and as fire ful
schynynge, and as encense brennynge in fire, and as an hool vessel of gold
enuyrownede wiþ al maner preciouse stoon, as þe olyue buriownynge, and
as þe cipresse berynge itsilf vpon hi3. In takynge hym þe clooþ of glorie, 340
and in cloþinge hym wiþ þe endynge of vertu, in stiynge vp of þe holi auter,
he 3af hym glorie, þe cloþinge of holynesse, and also in takynge partis of
þe hond of prestis. And he, stondynge bisidis þe auter, putte forþ his hond
into sacrifiynge, and he sacrifiede þe godli odour vnto þe hi3e prince. And
he reherside his preier wilnynge | to schewe þe vertu of God, whiche haþ f. 232va
don wiþ vs aftir his merci, þat he 3eue to vs ioyfulnesse of herte and pees 346
to be made in oure daies in Israel bi daies euerlastynge.

[LECTION 21]

The lessoun on Twelfþe Day. Isaye lx°, a.

^{1}Rise þou, Ierusalem, and be þou li3tnede, for þi li3t is comen, and þe glorie
of þe Lord is sprungen vpon þee. ^{2}For lo, þe derknessis schulen hile þe erþe, 350
and myst _schal hile_ puplis. But þe Lord schal rise on þee, and his glorie schal
be seen in þee. ^{3}And heþen men schulen go in þi li3t, and kyngis _schulen go_

---

329 þat^2] om. Ra   330 f. 232rb] running title Siluestir Bo   331 purchaside] add.
to Se   333 þe^1] om. Se   so schoon he] schyneþ LaSeBx   and^2] om. Se   þe^2] om.
Se   334 As] and as Ra   335 floure] floures Lt   336 cesonable] couenable
Ny   watris] watir Ra   337 ful^1] om. LaSeBx   hottist] om. LaSeBx, estatis Vu   and^2]
om. LaSeLtBxRa   338 as^1] om. La   339 maner] add. of Ra   340 clooþ]
cloþinge LaSeBx   343 his] prec. by has canc. Bo   345 reherside] rehersynge La
232va] running title Twelfþe dai Bo   whiche] þe which LaSeBx   347 to] om. NyLt
349 þi] om. Lt   350 þe derknessis] derknessis Ny   hile] add. þe Se   352 þi]
þe Ra

in þe schinynge of þi risynge. ⁴Reise þin iȝen in cumpasse and se: alle þese
men ben gaderide togidir; þei ben comen to þee. Thi sones schulen come
355 fro fer, and þi douȝtris schulen rise fro þe side. ⁵Thanne þou schalt se, and
schalt flowe, and þin herte schal wondre and schal be alargide, whanne þe
multitude of þe see is conuertid to þee. The strengþe of þe heþen is come to
þee, þe flowynge of camels schal hile þe, þe leders of dromedis of Madian
and of Effa, alle men of Saba schulen come, bryngynge gold and ensence,
360 and tellynge heriynge to þe Lord.

[LECTION 22]

f. 232ᵛᵇ The lessoun on | þe Sunday wiþynne
þe vtas of þe Epiphanye. Isaye lx.

¹Rise þou, Ierusalem.

That is redde on þe Twelueþe Day bifor.

[LECTION 23]

365 In þe vtas of þe Twelueþe Day. Isay xxv, a. [Isa.
25: 1; 28: 5; 35: 1–2, 10; 41: 18; 52: 13; 12: 3–5]

Lord, my God, I schal worschip þee; I schal ȝeue preisynge to þi name,
whiche doist meruelous þingis; þin oold counceil be it made trewe.
Lord, þin arm is passynge hiȝe, God of oostis, coroun of hope, whiche is
370 enuyrownede wiþ glorie. The desert be it wel cheride, and þe wildirnesse
of Iordan be it wel cheride. And my puple schal be þe hiȝþe of þe Lord, and
þe maieste of God. And it schal be gaderide togidre and rounsomede bi
God, and Sion schal come wiþ preisynge and wiþ euerlastynge gladnesse
upon his heed, preisynge and glad cheer. And I schal opene floodis in
375 mounteyns, and I schal breste founteyns in þe myddil of feeldis, and I
schal ȝetun into þe erþe þristynge without watris. And my childe schal be
enhiȝede, and he schal be liftid vp and he schal be ful hiȝe.

353 þi] þe Ra   354 þei] *om.* Lt   355 þe] þi Ra   357 þe heþen] heþene
LaRa, heþene men SeLt   358 of Madian] and Madian Ny   361 f. 232ᵛᵇ] *running title* vtas Bo   369 þin arm] þi name Ny, brachium tuum SM   370 wel] *om.*
Ra   wildirnesse of Iordan be it] wildirnessis of Iordan be þei Ny, wildirnes of iordan be
þei LaRa, wildirnesse of Iordan be þei Se   375 and I schal breste founteyns] *om.* Ny
376 þe] *om.* Se   377 he schal be] *om.* Lt

Isaye xij, e.

ȝe schulen drawe watris in ioie fro þe founteyn of þe sauyoure, and ȝe |
schulen seie in þat day, be ȝe aknowun to þe Lord, and inclepe ȝe þe name   f. 233ra
of hym. Make ȝe þe vertues of hym knowun in puplis; synge ȝe to þe Lord,   381
for he haþ don meruelous þingis. Schewe ȝe þese þingis in alle erþe, *seiþ þe
Lord almyȝti.*

[LECTION 24]

The lessoun vpon Aischewednesday. Ioel ij°, d.

The Lord seiþ þese þingis: ¹²Be ȝe conuertid to me in al ȝoure herte, in   385
fastynge and wepynge and weilynge, ¹³and kerue ȝe ȝoure hertis, and not
ȝoure cloþis. And be ȝe conuertide to oure Lord God, for he is benygne and
merciful, patient, and of moche merci, and abidynge, *eþer forȝeuynge*, on
malice. ¹⁴Who woot if God be conuertid and forȝeue, and leue blessynge
aftir hym, and sacrifice and moiste sacrifice to oure Lord God? ¹⁵Synge ȝe   390
wiþ a trumpe in Sion, halowe ȝe fastynge, and clepe ȝe cumpenye, gadere
ȝe togidre þe puple, halowe ȝe þe chirche. ¹⁶Gadere ȝe togidre oold men,
gadere ȝe togidre litil children, and soukynge þe brestis. A spouse go out of
his bedde, and a spousesse of hir chaumbre. ¹⁷Prestis, þe mynystris | of þe   f. 233rb
Lord, schulen wepe bitwix þe porche and þe auter, and schulen seie: Lord,   395
spare þou, spare þi puple! And ȝeue þou not þin eritage into schenschip,
þat naciouns be lordis of hem. Whi seie þei among puplis: Where is þe God
of hem? ¹⁸The Lord louede gelousli his lond, and sparide his puple. ¹⁹And
þe Lord answeride and seide to his puple: Lo, I schal sende to ȝow wheete
and wijne and oyle, and ȝe schulen be fillid wiþ þo. And I schal no more   400
ȝeue ȝou schenschip among heþen men, *seiþ þe Lord almiȝti.*

[LECTION 25]

The nexte Thursday lessoun aftir
Aische Wedenesdai. Isaye xxxviij°, a.

¹In þo daies sikenede Ezechie til to þe deeþ. And Isaye þe profete, þe sone of
Amos, entride to him and seide to hym, The Lord seiþ þese þingis, Dispose   405

þin hous, for þou schalt die and schalt not lyue. ²And Ezechie turnede his
face to þe wal and preiede þe Lord, and seide, Lord, I biseche, ³haue þou
mynde, I biseche, hou I ȝede bifore þee in treuþe and perfiȝt herte. And
I dide þat þat was good bifore þin iȝen. And Ezechie wepte wiþ greet |

f. 233ᵛᵃ   wepynge. ⁴And þe word of þe Lord was made to Isaye, and seide, Go þou
411   and seye to Ezechie, The Lord God of Dauiþ, þi fadir, seiþ þese þingis,
          I haue herd þi preier and I say þi teeris. And lo, I schal adde on þi daies
          xv ȝeer, ⁶and I schal delyuere þee and þis citee fro þe hond of þe kyng of
          Assiriens, and I schal defende it, _seiþ þe Lord almyȝti._

[LECTION 26]

415   The nexte Friday aftir. Isaye lvijº. [Isa. 58]

The Lord God seiþ þes þingis: ¹Crie þou, ceesse þou not! As a trumpe,
enhaunce þi voice, and schewe þou to my puple her greet trispassis, and
to þe hous of Iacob her synnes. ²For þei seken me fro day into day, and þei
wolen knowe my weies, as a folk þat han don riȝtfulnesse and þat haþ not

420   forsake þe doom of her God. Thei preien me domes and riȝtfulnesse, and
        wolen nyȝhe to God. ³Whi fasten we, and þou biheldist not? We mekiden
        oure soulis, and þou knewist not? Lo, ȝoure wille is founden in þe day of
        ȝour fastynge, and ȝe axen alle ȝoure dettouris. ⁴Lo, ȝe fasten to chidingis

f. 233ᵛᵇ and stryuyngis, and smyten wiþ þe fiste wickidli. Nyle ȝe | faste as til to
425   þis day, þat ȝoure cry be herd an hiȝ. ⁵Wheþer suche is þe fastynge whiche
        I chees, a man to turmente his soule bi day? Wheþer to bynde his heed
        as a seercle and to make redi a sak and aisch? Wheþer þou schalt clepe
        þis a day of fastynge, and a day acceptable to þe Lord? ⁶Wheþer þis is not
        more þe fastynge whiche I chees? Vnbynde þou þe byndyngis of vnpite,

430   _eþer of cruelte_, releese þou birþuns pressynge doun, delyuer þou hem fre
        þat ben brokun, and breke þou eche birþun. ⁷Breke þi breed to an hungrie
        man and brynge into þin hous nedi men and herburles. Whanne þou seest
        a nakide man, hile þou hym and dispise not þi fleisch, _þat is broþer eþer
        sistir._ ⁸Thanne þe liȝt schal breke out as þe morwetide, and þin helþe schal

435   rise ful soon, and þi riȝtfulnesse schal go bifor þi face, and þe glorie of

406 schalt²] þou schalt LaSeBxRa   407 wal] _prec. by w canc. at end of prec. line_ Bo
408 perfiȝt] in perfiȝt LaBxRa   410 f. 233ᵛᵃ] _running title_ Fridai Bo   415 aftir]
_om._ Ny   419 han] haþ NyLaSeBxRa   420 and riȝtfulnesse] of riȝtwijsnes
Ny, of riȝtfulnesse LaSeBx, ofte riȝtfulnes Ra   421 fasten] fastiden NyLaSeBxRa
422 ȝoure] oure Ra   425 whiche] þat Ra   426 his] þe Ra   428 day of] _om._
LaSeBxRa   429 byndyngis] _add._ togider NyLaSeBxRa   433 dispise] _add._ þou
Ra   broþer] þi broþer Ra   434 þe¹] þi NyLaSeRa   435 þi¹] _om._ Ra

þe Lord schal gadere þee. ⁹Thanne þou schalt clepe to help, and þe Lord schal heer. Thou schalt crie and he schal seie, Lo, I am present, for I am merciful, þi Lord God.

[LECTION 27]

The Saturday lessoun. Isaye þe ei3te and fiftiþ chapitr, d. |

⁹If þou takist awey a chayne fro þe myddis of þee and ceessist to holde forþ   f. 234ʳᵃ
þe fyngir to speke þat þat profitiþ not, ¹⁰whanne þou schedist out þi soule to   441
an hungrie man, and fillist a soule turmentid, þi li3t schal rise in derknessis,
and þi derknessis schulen be as mydday. ¹¹And þe Lord þi God schal 3eue
euer reste to þee, and schal fille þi soule wiþ schynyngis, and schal delyuere þi boones. And þou schalt be as a watri garden and as a welle of watris,   445
whos watris schulen not faile. ¹²And þe forsaken þingis of worldis schulen
be bildide in þee, and þou schalt reise þe foundementis of generacioun and
generacioun, and þou schalt be clepide a bilder of heggis, turnynge awey
þe paþis of wickidnessis. ¹³If þou turnyst awei þi foot fro þe Saboth to do þi
wille in myn holiday, and clepist þe Saboth delicat and holi, þe gloriouse   450
of þe Lord, and glorifiest hym while þou doist not þi weies, and þi wille is
not founden þat þou speke a word, ¹⁴þanne þou schalt delite on þe Lord.
And I schal reise þee on þe hi3nesse of erþe, and I | schal fede þee wiþ þe   f. 234ʳᵇ
eritage of Iacob, þi fadir, forwhi þe mouþ of þe Lord spak.

[LECTION 28]

The firste Moneday lessoun of clene Lente. Ezechiel xxxiiij°, c.   455

¹¹The Lord God seiþ þese þingis: Lo, I mysilf schal seke my scheep, and
I schal visite hem. ¹²As a schepherd visitiþ his flok in þe dai whanne he is
in þe myddis of hise scheep scateride, so I schal visite my scheep. And I
schal delyuer hem fro alle placis in whiche þei werun scateride, in þe dai of
cloude and of derknesse. ¹³And I schal lede hem out of peplis, and I schal   460
gadere hem fro londis, and I schal brynge hem into her lond, and I schal
fede hem in þe hillis of Israel, and reueres and in alle seitis of þe erþe. ¹⁴I
schal fede hem in moost plentyuouse pasture, and þe lesewis of hem schulen be in þe hi3e hillis of Israel. There þei schulen reste in þe grene eerbis,

440 f. 234ʳᵃ] *running title* Firste woke of lente Bo   If] *prec. by* The lord god seiþ þese
þingis NyLaSeBxRa   ceessist] NyLaSeBxRa, ceessist not Bo, desieris Vu   441 þe]
þi Ra   to speke] and to speke NyLaSeBxRa   445 watri] watir LaRa   453 þee²]
om. Se   462 Israel] Ierusalem Se   þe²] *om.* LaSeBxRa   464 be] *om.* Ny   þe]
om. La   hi3e] *om.* SeBx   þe²] *om.* NyLaSeBxRa

465 and in fatte lesewis þei schulen be fed on þe hillis of Israel. ¹⁵I schal fede
my scheep and I schal make hem to ligge, seiþ þe Lord God. ¹⁶I schal seke
f. 234ᵛᵃ þat þat perischide, and I schal bringe aȝen þat þat was caste | awey, and I
schal bynde þat þat was brokun, and I schal make sad þat þat was sike, and
I schal kepe þat þat is fat and strong, and I schal fede hem in doom *and*
470 *riȝtwisnesse, seiþ þe Lord almiȝti.*

[LECTION 29]

The Tewisday lesson. Isaye lv°, c.

In þo daies, Isaye þe profete spak, seiynge: ⁶Seke ȝe þe Lord while he may be
founden, clepe ȝe hym to help while he is nyȝe. ⁷An vnfeiþful man forsake
his wey, and a wickid man *forsake* hise þouȝtis, and turne he aȝen to þe
475 Lord, and he schal haue merci on hym, and to oure God, for he is myche
to forȝeue. ⁸Forwhi my þouȝtis ben not ȝoure þouȝtis, and my weies ben
not youre weies, seiþ þe Lord. ⁹For as heuenes ben reisid fro erþe, so my
weies ben reisid fro ȝoure weies, and my þouȝtis fro ȝoure þouȝtis. ¹⁰And
as reyn and snowe comen doun fro heuene, and turneþ no more aȝen þidir,
480 but it filliþ þe erþe and bischediþ it, and makiþ it to buriowne, and ȝeueþ
seed to hym þat sowiþ, and breed to hym þat e[t]iþ, ¹¹so schal be my word
f. 234ᵛᵇ þat schal go out | fro my mouþ. It schal not turne aȝen voide to me, but
it schal do whateuer þingis I wolde, and it schal haue prosperite in þese
þingis to whiche I sente it, *seiþ þe Lord almyȝti.*

[LECTION 30]

485 The Wednesday lesson. Exodi xxiiij°.

In þo daies, ¹²þe Lord seide to Moyses : Stie þou to me in þe hille, and
be þou þere, and I schal ȝeue to þee tablis of stoon and þe lawe and
comaundementis, whiche I haue writun þat þou teche þe children of
Israel. ¹³Moyses and Iosue his mynystre risun, and Moyses stiede into þe
490 hil of God, ¹⁴and seide to þe elder men: Abide ȝe heere til we turnen aȝen
to ȝou. Ʒe han Aaron and Vr wiþ ȝou. If ony þing of questioun is made,
ȝe schuln telle to hem. ¹⁵And whanne Moyses had stiede, a cloude hilid

467 þat⁴] *om.* Bx   f. 234ᵛᵃ] *running title* I. w. lente Bo   472 ȝe] *om.* Se
473 founden] *add.* and Ra   476 and] neiþer Ra   ben not] *om.* Ra   477 fro]
add. þe NyRa   479 comen] comeþ Ny   no more aȝen] aȝen nomore NySeBx
481 etiþ] eriþ Bo, eeriþ Ny, comedenti Vu   482 fro] of LaSeBxRa   483 it¹] I Ra
486 in] into LaSeBxRa   489 mynystre] mynystres Ny   into] to Se

þe hil, and þe glorie of þe Lord dwellid on Synay, and keuered it wiþ a
cloude vj daies. Forsoþe, in þe seuenþe day þe Lord clepide hym fro þe
myddis of þe cloude. ¹⁷Forsoþe, þe liknesse of þe glorie of þe Lord was   495
as fire brennynge on þe coppe of þe hil in þe siȝt | of þe sones of Israel.   f. 235ʳᵃ
¹⁸And Moyses entride into þe myddis of þe cloude and stiede into þe hille,
and he was þere fourty daies and fourti nyȝtis.

[LECTION 31]

**Vpon þe same day anoþer lessoun
of þe iij Book of Kyngis xix cᵒ, b.**   500

In þo daies, ³Helie cam into Bersabe of Iuda, and he lefte þere his child,
⁴and ȝede into desert, þe wei of o day. And whanne he cam and saat vndir
a Iunypre tre, and he askide to his soule þat he schulde die. And he seide,
Lord, it sufficiþ to me, take my soule, for I am not bettir þanne my fadris.
⁵And he castide forþ himsilf and slept vndir þe schadewe of þe Iunypre tre.   505
And lo, þe aungel of þe Lord touchide him and seide to him: Rise þou, and
ete! ⁶And he bihelde, and lo, at his heed *was* a loof bakun vndir aischis, and
a vessel of watir. Therfor he eet and drank and slept eft. ⁷And þe aungel of
þe Lord turnede aȝen þe secunde tyme, and touchide him. And *þe aungel*
seide to hym: Rise þou and ete! For a greet wey is to þee. ⁸And whanne   510
he hadde rise, he eet and drank. And he ȝede in þe strengþe of þat mete xl
daies | and fourti nyȝtis, til to Oreb, þe hil of God.   f. 235ʳᵇ

[LECTION 32]

The Thursday lessoun. Ezechiel xviij cᵒ, a.

In þo daies, ¹þe word of þe Lord was made to me, ²and he seide: What
is it, þat ȝe turnen a parable among ȝou into þis prouerbe in þe lond of   515
Israel, and seien, Fadris eton a bittir grape and þe teeþ of sones ben an
egge *eþer astonyede*? ³I lyue, seiþ þe Lord God. This parable schal no more
be into a prouerbe to ȝou in Israel. ⁴Lo, alle soulis ben myne, as þe soule
of þe fadir, so and þe soule of þe sone is myn. Thilke soule þat doiþ synne,
schal die. ⁵And if a man is iust and doiþ doom and riȝtfulnesse, ⁶and etiþ   520

493 Synay] Syon Se   494 vj] vij Ra   495 þe²] *om*. Se   496 as] a Ra
on] in Ny   f. 235ʳᵃ] *running title* I. lente Bo   503 a] oo La   and] *om*. LaSeBxRa
505 castide] cast Ra   þe²] *om*. La   508 watir] *add*. and Se   514 he] *om*. Ra
516 sones] þe sones Se   518 in] into Ny   519 þe¹] *om*. Se   is myn] *om*. La
520 and³] *om*. SeBxRa

not in hillis, and reisiþ not hise iȝen to þe idolis of þe house of Israel, and
defouliþ not þe wijf of his neiȝbore, and neiȝeþ not to a womman defoulid
wiþ vnclene blood, ⁷and makiþ not a man sori, and ȝildiþ þe wedde to þe
dettour, rauyschiþ no þing bi violence, ȝeueþ his breed to þe hungrie, and
525 hiliþ a nakide man wiþ a clooþ, ⁸leeneþ not to vsure, and takiþ not more,
f. 235ᵛᵃ turneþ awei his hond fro wickidnesse, and | makiþ trewe doom bitwixe
man and man, ⁹and goeþ in my comaundementis, and kepiþ my domes,
þat he do treuþe, þis is a iust man; he schal lyue in lijf, seiþ þe Lord God.
¹⁰That if he gendriþ a sone, a þeef, schedynge out blood, ¹¹and doiþ oon of
530 þese þingis, and soþeli not <u>doynge alle þese þingis</u> but etynge in hillis and
defoulynge þe wijf of his neiȝbore, ¹²<u>makinge soruful a nedi man and pore,
raueischynge raueynes, not ȝildynge a wed, reisynge hise iȝen to ydolis,
doynge abhomynacioun, ȝeuynge to vsure, and takynge more,</u> ¹³<u>where he
schal lyue?</u> He schal not lyue whanne he haþ don alle þese abhomynable
535 þingis. He schal die bi deeþ; his blood schal be in hym. ¹⁴That if he gendriþ
a sone whiche seeþ alle þe synnes of his fadir, whiche he dide, <u>and drediþ
and doiþ noon like þo,</u> ¹⁵etiþ not on hillis, <u>and reisiþ not hise iȝen to idolis of
þe hous of Israel, and defouliþ not þe wijf of his neiȝbore,</u> ¹⁶<u>and makiþ not
sory a man, wiþholdiþ not a wedde, and rauyschiþ not raueyn, ȝeueþ his
540 breed to þe hungrie and hiliþ þe nakid wiþ a clooþ,</u> ¹⁷<u>turneþ awey his hond
f. 235ᵛᵇ fro þe wrong of a pore | man, takiþ not vsure and ouerabundaunce, *þat
is, noþing more þanne he lente*</u>, and haþ my domes, and goiþ in my comaundementis, þis <u>*sone*</u> schal not die in þe wickidnesse of his fadir, but he schal
lyue in lijf. ¹⁸For his fadir made false calenge, and dide violence to his
545 broþer, and wrouþte yuel in þe myddis of his puple. Lo, he is deed in his
wickidnesse. ¹⁹And ȝe seyn, whi beriþ not þe sone þe wickidnesse of þe
fad[ir]? That is to seie, for þe sone wrouȝte doom and riȝtfulnesse, he kept
alle my comaundementis and dide þo, he schal lyue in lijf, *seiþ þe Lord God
almyȝty*.

[LECTION 33]

550   **The Friday lessoun. Ezechiel xviij cᵒ, d.**

The Lord God seiþ þese þingis: ²⁰The soule þat doiþ synne schal die. The
sone schal not bere þe wickidnesse of þe fadir, and þe fadir schal not bere

521 þe¹] *om.* Se   523 and²] *om.* NyLaSeBxRa   525 a¹] þe Ra
529 gendriþ] gendre Ra   530–3 but etynge . . . takynge more] *om.* LaSeBxRa
534 He schal not lyue] *om.* LaSeBxRa   abhomynable þingis] þingis abhominable SeBx
536 and drediþ] and he drediþ Ny   537–42 etiþ not . . . he lente] *om.* LaSeBxRa   to]
to þe Ny   542 noþing more] not more Ny   haþ] doiþ LaSeBxRa   547 fadir] fad
Bo   riȝtfulnesse] riȝtwisnesse SeBx   548 God] *om.* NyRa   551 God] *om.* LaBx

þe wickidnesse of þe sone. The riȝtfulnesse o[f] a iuste man schal be on
hym, and þe wickidnesse of a wickid man schal be on hym. ²¹Forsoþe,
if a wickid man do penaunce of alle þe synnes whiche he wrouȝte, and   555
kepiþ alle myn heestis, and doiþ dome and | riȝtfulnesse, he schal lyue bi   f. 236ʳᵃ
life, and schal not die. ²²I schal not haue mynde of alle hise wickidnessis
whiche he wrouȝte. In his riȝtwisnesse whiche he wrouȝte he schal lyue.
²³Where þe deeþ of þe wickide man is of my wille, seiþ þe Lord God, and
not þat he be conuertide fro hise weies, and lyue? ²⁴Forsoþe, if a iust man   560
turneþ awey hymsilf fro his riȝtfulnesse and doiþ wickidnesse bi alle hise
abhomynaciouns, whiche a wickid man is wonte to worche, where he schal
lyue? Alle hise riȝtfulnessis whiche he dide schulen not be hadde in mynde;
in his trispassynge bi whiche he trispassyde, and in his synne whiche he
synned, he schal die in þo. ²⁵And ȝe seiden, þe weye of þe Lord is not   565
euen. Therfor, þe hous of Israel, heere ȝe, where my wey is not euen, and
not more ȝoure weies ben schrewide? ²⁶For whanne a riȝtful man turneþ
awey hymsilf fro his riȝtfulnesse and doiþ wickidnesse, he schal die in it; he
schal die in þe vnriȝtfulnesse whiche he [wr]ouȝte. ²⁷And whanne a wickid
man turneþ awei himsilf fro his wickidnesse whiche he wrouȝte, and [doiþ]   570
doom and | riȝtfulnesse, he schal quikene his soule. ²⁸For he, biholdynge   f. 236ʳᵇ
and turnynge awey hymsilf fro alle hise wickidnessis whiche he wrouȝte,
schal lyue in lijf and schal not die, *seiþ þe Lord almyȝty*.

[LECTION 34]

The Saturday lessoun. Deutronomye xxvjᵒ, e.

In þo daies, Moyses spak to þe Lord and seide: ¹⁵Biholde þou fro þi seyntuarie,   575
fro þe hiȝe dwellynge place of heuene, and blesse þou þi puple Israel, and
þe lond whiche þou hast ȝouun to vs, as þou hast sworun to oure fadris, þe
lond flowynge wiþ mylke and hony. *Here þou, Israel!* ¹⁶Today þi Lord God
comaundide to þee þat þou do þes comaundementis and domes, þat þou
kepe and fille of al þin herte and of al þe soule. ¹⁷Thou hast chose þe Lord   580
today, þat he be God to þee, and þou go in hise weies and þou kepe hise
cerymonyes and heestis and domes, and obeie to hise comaundementis.
¹⁸Lo, þe Lord chees þee today, þat þou be a special puple to hym, as he

553 of²] on Bo, of NyLaSeBxRa   555 do] doiþ LaSeBx   þe] hise LaSeBxRa   he]
sche, *first two letters canc.* Bo   558 riȝtwisnesse] riȝtfulnesse Se   whiche he wrouȝte]
om. Ra   559 of¹] *om.* Ra   God] *om.* Ny   563 riȝtfulnessis] riȝtwisnessis Ra
566 wey is] weies ben Ra   568 hymsilf] *om.* Ra   569 wrouȝte] wroouȝte, w
canc. Bo   570 doiþ] *om.* Bo, doiþ NyLaBx, doþ Se, dooþ Ra   572 wickidnessis]
wickednes Ra   573 schal] he schal Ra   580 þe] þi NyLaSeRa   581 þou²]
þat þou   583 a] *om.* SeBx

spak to þee, and þat þou kepe alle hise comaundementis. ¹⁹And he schal
585 make þee hiȝer þanne alle folkis whiche he made into his preisynge and
name and glorie, þat þou be an holi puple of þi Lord God, as he spak |
f. 236ᵛᵃ to þee.

[LECTION 35]

The secunde lessoun on þe same day. Deutronomi xj°, e.

In þo daies, Moyses seide to þe sones of Israel: ²²For if ȝe kepen þe heestis
590 whiche I comaunde to ȝou, and ȝe do þo, þat ȝe loue ȝoure Lord God and
go in alle hise weies and ²³cleue to hym, þe Lord schal distrie alle þese
heþen men bifor ȝoure face, and ȝe schuln weelde þe folkis þat ben gretter
and strenger þanne ȝe. ²⁴Ech place whiche ȝoure foot schal trede, schal be
ȝoure, fro þe desert and fro þe Liban and fro þe greet flood Eufrates til
595 to þe weste see schuln be ȝoure teermes. ²⁵Noon schal stonde aȝens ȝou.
Ȝoure Lord God schal ȝeue ȝoure outward drede and ȝoure ynward drede
on eche lond which ȝe schulen trede, as he spak to ȝou, *seiþ oure Lord*.

[LECTION 36]

The þridde lessoun of þe same
day. The secunde Machabeis j°, c.

600 *In þo daies þe prestis maden her preier while þei offriden sacrificis for þe puple of
Israel, Ionatha bigynnynge, and þe oþer answerynge, and seiȝnge*: ²God do wel
to ȝou, and haue mynde of his testament þat he spak to Abraham, Isaac, and
f. 236ᵛᵇ Iacob, hise trewe seruauntis. | ³And ȝeue herte to ȝou alle, þat ȝe worschip
hym and do þe wil of hym wiþ greet herte and wilful inwit. ⁴Opene *þe Lord*
605 ȝoure herte in his lawe and in hise heestis, and make he pees. ⁵Heere he
graciousli ȝoure preiers, and be recounceilide to ȝou, neþer forsake ȝou in
yuel tyme, *þe Lord oure God*.

585 preisynge and name] name preisynge LaRa   586 name and glorie] glorie and
name Ny   þi] þe Se   589 For] *om*. La   592 þe] þo NyLaSeRa   594 greet]
grettest Ra   596 ȝoure²] in ȝoure La   597 Lord] god Bx

[LECTION 37]

The iiij lessoun on þe same day.
Ecclesiastici xxxvj°, a. [Ecclus.]

¹God of alle þingis, haue merci on vs and biholde þou vs, and schewe þou   610
to vs þe liȝt of þi merciful doyngis. ²And sende þi drede on heþen men þat
souȝten not þee, þat þei knowun þat noon God is but þou, þat þei telle out
þi greet dedis. ³Reise þin hond on heþen men aliens, þat þei se þi power.
⁴For as þou were halowide in vs in þe siȝt of hem, so in oure siȝte þou schalt
be magnefiede in hem, ⁵þat þei knowe þee, as we han knowe þat noon oþer   615
God is outaken þee, Lord. ⁶Make þou newe signes and chaunge þou merueilis; ⁷[glorifie] þe hond and þe riȝt arm. ⁸Reise þou strong veniaunce
and schede out ire. ⁹Take awey þe aduersarie and turmente þe | enemye. f. 237ʳᵃ
¹⁰Haaste þou þe tyme, and haue þou mynde on þe ende, þat þei telle out þi
merueilis, *þe Lord oure God*.   620

[LECTION 38]

The v lessoun on þe same day. Danyel iij.

⁴⁹An aungel of þe Lord

and is in Ymbir Saturday bifore Cristmasse.

[LECTION 39]

The secunde Moneday lessoun of Lente. Danyel ix°, d.

In þo daies, Danyel preiede to þe Lord and seide: ¹⁵Oure Lord God þat led-   625
dist þi puple out of þe lond of Egipt in strong hond, and madist to þee a
name bi þis day, we han synnede, ¹⁶we han don wickidnesse, Lord, aȝens
þi riȝtfulnesse. I biseche þat þi wraþþe and þi strong veniaunce be turnede
awey fro þi citee Ierusalem and fro þin holi hille, forwhi for oure synnes
and for þe wickidnessis of oure fadris, Ierusalem and þi puple ben in schen- 630
schip to alle men, bi oure cumpas. ¹⁷But now, oure God, here þou þe preier
of þi seruaunt and þe bisechyngis of hym, and schewe þi face on þi seyntuarie, whiche is forsaken. ¹⁸My God, for þisilf bowe doun þin eere and

---

613 greet] *om.* Ny   615 as] *add.* and NyLaSeBx   616 God is] is God NyBx
signes] signes nes Bo   617 glorifie] glorified Ny, *om.* Bo, glorifica Vu   622 An]
prec. by In þo dayes SeBx   627 Lord] *add.* god Se   630 þe] oure Ra

f. 237rb heer; opene þin iȝen and se oure desolacioun, and þe citee on þe | whiche
635 þi name is clepide to help. For not in oure iustifiyngis we senten forþ teeris
mekeli bifore þi face, but in þi manye merciful doyngis. ¹⁹Lord, heere þou;
Lord, be þou plesid. Perseyue þou and do, my Lord God; tarie þou not
for þisilf, for þi name is clepide to help on þi citee and on þi puple, _Lord
oure God_.

[LECTION 40]

640   The Tewisdai lessoun. iij Book of Kyngis xvij°, c.

In þo daies, ⁸þe word of þe Lord was made to _Elie_, seiynge: ⁹Rise þou and
go into Sarepta of Sydonys, and þou schalt dwelle þere. For I comaundide
to a womman widewe þere þat sche fede þee. ¹⁰And he roos and ȝede into
Sarepta of Sydonys, and whanne he hadde come to þe ȝate of þe citee, a
645 womman widewe gaderynge stickis apperide to hym, and he clepide hir
and seide to hir: Ȝeue þou to me a litil of watir in a vessel, þat I drinke.
¹¹And whanne sche ȝede to brynge him, he criede bihynde hir bak and
seide: I biseche, bringe þou to me also a mossel of breed in þin hond. ¹²And
f. 237va sche answeride: Thi Lord God lyueþ! For I haue noon breed, no but | as
650 moche of mele in a pott as a fiste may take, and a litil of oyle in a vessel. Lo,
I gadere two stickis, þat I entre and make it to me and to my sone, þat we
ete and die. ¹³And Elie seide to hir: Nyle þou drede! But go and make as
þou seidist. Neþeles make þou firste to me of þat litil mele a litil loof, bake
vndir þe aischis, and brynge þou to me. Soþeli þou schalt make aftirward
655 to þee and to þi sone. ¹⁴Forsoþe, þe Lord God of Israel seiþ þese þingis, þe
pot of mele schal not faile, and þe vessel of oyle schal not be abatide, til to
þe dai in which þe Lord schal ȝeue reyne on þe face of þe erþe. ¹⁵And sche
ȝede and dide bi þe word of Elie, and he eet, and sche, and hir hous. ¹⁶And
fro þat day þe pot of mele failide not, and þe vessel of oyle was not abatide,
660 bi þe word of þe Lord, whiche hadde spoke in þe hond of Elie.

634 þe²] _om._ NyLa   635 teeris] _corr. to_ preiers _by different hand_ Bo, mekeli
preieris NyLaSeBxRa   638 þi²] þe NyLaSeBxRa   þi³] þe Ny   640 iij] þe iij
Ny   645 gaderynge] þat gaderid Ra   646 and seide to hir] _om._ Ny   of] _om._ Ra
647 him] _om._ NyLaSeBxRa   649 no] _om._ Ny   650 in a²] of Ny   654 þe]
_om._ NyRa   aischis] askis Ny   656 to] _om._ Ra   657 þe¹] _om._ La   658 and
dide] _om._ Bx   660 hadde] he hadde LaSeBxRa

[LECTION 41]

The Wednesday lessoun. Hester xiij°, c.

In þo daies, Hester preiede to þe Lord and seide: ⁹Lord God, kyng almy3ti, alle þingis ben set in þi lordschip, *eþer power*, and noon is þat may a3enstonde þi wille; if þou demest for to saue | Israel, we schulen be delyuered anoon. f. 237ᵛᵇ ¹⁰Thou madist heuene and erþe, and whateuer þing is conteynede in 665 þe cumpasse of heuene. ¹¹Thou art Lord of alle þingis, and noon is þat a3enstonde þi magiste. ¹²Thou knowist alle þingis and woost þat not for pride and dispite and ony coueitise of glorie I dide þis þing þat I worschip not Aman moost proude. ¹³For I was redy wilfuli to kisse, 3he, þe steppis of hise feet for þe heelþe of Israel, but I drede ¹⁴leste I schulde bere ouer 670 to a man þe onoure of my God, and leste I schulde worschipe ony man outaken my God. ¹⁵And now, Lord, king of kyngis, God of Abraham, haue merci on þi puple. For oure enemyes wolen leese vs and do awey þin eritage. ¹⁶Dispise not þi part, whiche þou a3enbou3tist fro Egipt. ¹⁷Here þou my preier and be þou merciful to þe lot and to þe part of þin eritage, 675 and turne þou oure moornynge into ioie, þat we lyuynge herie þi name, Lord, and close þou not þe mouþis of men heriynge þee, *Lord, oure God*.

[LECTION 42]

The Thursday lessoun, Ieremy xvij°, b.

In þo daies þe Lord God seide þese þingis: | ⁵Curside is þe man þat trustiþ in f. 238ʳᵃ man and settiþ fleische his arm, and his herte goiþ awey fro þe Lord. ⁶For 680 he schal be as bromes in desert, and he schal not se whanne God schal come, but he schal dwelle in drynesse in desert, in þe lond of saltnesse and vnabitable. ⁷Blessid is þe man þat trustiþ in þe Lord, and þe Lord schal be his trist. ⁸And he schal be as a tre whiche is plauntide ouer watris, which sendiþ hise rootis to moisture, and it schal not drede whanne heete schal 685 come, and þe leef þerof schal be greene, and it schal not be mouede in þe tyme of drynesse, neþer ony tyme schal faile to make fruyt. ⁹The herte of man is schrewide and vncercheable, *eþer may not be sou3t*. Who schal knowe

---

662 God] *om.* Ra   665 þing] þingis Ny   667 a3enstonde] a3enstondiþ LaSeBx
667–72 Thou knowist . . . outaken my God] *om.* LaSeBxRa   668 worschip] worschipide Ny   672 of²] *om.* Se   673 haue] haue þou LaSeRa   674 a3enbou3tist]
hast a3enbou3t Se   677 heriynge] preisinge Ny   679 seide] seiþ La
680 fro] *followed by* God *canc.* Bo   681 God] good Bx   684 ouer] *add.* of
Ny   which sendiþ] *prec. by* w *canc. at end of prec. line* Bo   685 rootis] rote Ny
686 þe²] *om.* Se   688 man] a man Ra

it? ¹⁰I am þe Lord sekynge þe herte and preuynge þe reynes, *eþer kidneiris,*
690 and I ȝeue to eche man aftir his wey and aftir þe fruyt of hise fyndyngis,
seiþ þe Lord almyȝti.

[LECTION 43]

The Fridai lessoun. Genesis xxxvij°, d.

In þo daies, ⁶Ioseph seide to hise briþeren: Heere ȝe þe sweuene whiche I
f. 238ʳᵇ say. ⁷I gesside þat we bounden | togidre hondfullis, and þat as myn hondful
695 roos and stood, and þat ȝoure hondfullis stoden aboute and worschipiden myn hondful. ⁸Hise briþeren answeriden: Where þou schalt be oure
kyng, eþer we schulen be mad suget to þi Lordschip? Therfor þis cause of
sweuenes and wordis mynystride þe nurisching of enuye and of haterede.
⁹Also Ioseph say anoþer sweuene, whiche he toold to þe briþeren and seide:
700 I say bi a sweuene þat as þe sunne and þe moone and xj sterris worschipiden
me. ¹⁰And whanne he hadde toolde þis sweuene to his fadir and briþeren,
his fadir blamede him and seide: What wole þis sweuene to itsilf whiche
þou hast seen? Wheþer I and þi modir and þi briþeren schulen worschip
þee on erþe? ¹¹For hise briþeren hadden enuye to hym. Forsoþe þe fadir
705 biheld priueli þis þing, ¹²and whanne hise briþeren dwelliden in Sychym
aboute flockis of þe fadir to be kept, ¹³Israel seide to Ioseph: Thi briþeren
kepen scheep in Sychymes; come þou, I schal sende þee to hem. ¹⁴And
f. 238ᵛᵃ whanne Iosep[h] answerid, I am redi, Israel | seide: Go þou and se wheþer
alle þingis ben redi anentis þi briþeren and scheep, and telle þou to me
710 what is don. He was sente fro þe valey of Ebron and came into Sychym.
¹⁵And a man foond hym errynge in þe feeld, and þe man askide what he
souȝte. ¹⁶And he answeride: I seke my briþeren. Schewe þou to me where
þei kepen flockis. ¹⁷And þe man seide to hym: Thei ȝeden awey fro þis
place. Forsoþe I herde hem seiynge: Go we into Dothaym. And Ioseph
715 ȝede aftir hise briþeren and fonde hem in Dothaym. ¹⁸And whanne þei
hadden seen hym afer, bifor þat he nyȝede to hem, ¹⁹þei þouȝten to sle
hym, and spaken togidre: Lo, þe dremer comeþ! Come ȝe, ²⁰sle we hym,
and sende we into an oold cesterne. And we schulen seie: A wielde beest
ful wickide haþ deuouride hym. And þanne schal appere what hise dremes

689 eþer] *add.* þe Ra   698 wordis] of wordis Ra   of²] *om.* Ra   699 þe]
hise SeRa   700 þe²] *om.* BxRa   702 whiche] þe whiche La   704 For]
þerfore LaSeBxRa   705 biheld] *placed after* priueli Ra   706 aboute] *add.* þe Ny
706–8 Thi briþeren . . . Israel seide] *om.* Ra   707 þou] ȝow La   708 Ioseph]
Iosep Bo   redi] esy LaSeBxRa   711 feeld] *add.* eiþir sekynge La   718 sende
we] *add.* him La   we¹] *add.* hym Ra   719 þanne] *add.* it NyLaSeBxRa

profiten to him. ²¹Soþeli Ruben herde þis and enforside to delyuere hym 720
fro her hondis, ²²and seide: Sle we not þe lijf of hym, neþer schede we
not his blood, but caste ȝe him into an oold cesterne, whiche is in wildir-
nesse, and kepe ȝe youre | hondis giltles. Forsoþe he seide þis wilnynge to f. 238ᵛᵇ
delyuere hem fro her hondis and to ȝilde to his fadir.

[LECTION 44]

The Saturday lessoun. Genesis xxvij, b.   725

In þo daies, ⁶Rebecca seide to hir sone Iacob, I herde þi fadir spekynge wiþ
Esau, þi broþer, and seiynge to hym: Brynge þou to me of þin huntynge,
⁷and make þou metis þat I ete, and þat I blesse þee bifore þe Lord bifor þat
I die. ⁸Now þerfor, my sone, assente to my counceilis, ⁹and go to þe flok
and brynge to me two þe beste kidis, þat I make metis of þo to þi fadir, 730
whiche he etiþ gladli, ¹⁰and þat whanne þou hast brouȝte yn þo metis and
he haþ ete, he blesse þee bifor þat I dye. ¹¹To whom Iacob answeride: Thou
knowist þat Esau, my broþer, is an heery man, also I am smoþe. If my fadir
touchiþ and feliþ me, ¹²I drede leste he gesse þat I wolde scorne hym, and
leste he brynge yn cursynge on me for blessynge. ¹³To whom þe modir 735
seide: My sone, þis cursynge be in me. Oonli heere þou my voice, and go
and brynge þat þat I seide. ¹⁴He ȝede and brouȝt and ȝaf to | his modir. f. 239ʳᵃ
Sche made redy metis, as sche knewe his fadir wolde, ¹⁵and sche cloþide
Iacob in ful good cloþis of Esau, whiche sche hadde at hoom anentis hirsilf.
¹⁶And sche cumpasside þe hondis wiþ litil skynnes of kidis and keuerid þe 740
nakide þingis of þe necke, ¹⁷and sche ȝaf seew and bitook þe looues whiche
sche hadde bake. ¹⁸And whanne þese were brouȝt yn, he seide: My fadir!
And he answeride: I heere! Who art þou, my sone? ¹⁹And Iacob seide: I
am Esau, þi firste gendride sone. I haue don to þee as þou comaundidist to
me. Rise þou, sitte and ete of myn huntynge, þat þi soule blesse me. ²⁰Efte 745
Isaac seide to his sone: My sone, hou myȝtist þou fynde so soone? Whiche
answeride: It was Goddis wille þat þis þat I wolde schulde come soone to
me. ²¹And Isaac seide: My sone, come þou hidir, þat I touche þee and þat
I preue wheþer þou art my sone Esaw, eþer nay. ²²He nyȝede to þe fadir,
and whanne he hadde felide hym, Isaac seide: Soþeli þe voice is þe voice of 750
Iacob, but þe hondis ben þe hondis of Esaw. ²³And Isaac knewe not Iacob

720 to¹] *om.* Ny   721 we not] not we Ny   722 not] *om.* Ny   ȝe] we SeBxRa
730 brynge] *add.* þou Ny   metis] mete Ra   732 blesse] schal blesse Ra   I] he
LaSeBxRa   734 gesse] *prec. by* wolde *canc.* Bo, *add.* wolde Ny   wolde] shulde Ny
740 of kidis] *om.* Ny   741 sche] *om.* Ra   742 þese] þei Se   744 to²] *om.*
BxRa   745 sitte] and sitte Ra   747 come soone] sone come Ra   749 eþer]
or Ny

f. 239ʳᵇ for þe heeri | hondis expressiden þe lickenesse of [þe] more sone. ²⁴Therfor
Isaac blesside him and seide: Art þou my sone Esau? And Iacob answeride:
I am. ²⁵And Isaac seide: My sone, brynge þou to me metis of þi huntynge,
755 þat my soule blesse þee. And whanne Isaac hadde ete þese metis brouȝt,
Iacob brouȝte also wiyn to Isaac. And whanne þis was drunken, ²⁶Isaac
seide to hym: My sone, come þou hidir, and ȝeue þou to me a cosse. ²⁷And
Iacob nyȝede and kissid hym, and anoon as Isaac felide þe odour of hise
cloþis, he blesside hym and seide: Lo, þe odour of my sone as þe odoure
760 of a feeld ful whiche þe Lord haþ blessid. ²⁸God ȝeue to þee of þe dewe of
heuene and of þe fatnesse of erþe, abundaunce of wheet and of wiyn and
of oyle, ²⁹and puplis serue þee, and lynagis worschip þee. Be þou Lord of
þi briþeren, and þe sones of þi modir be bowide bifor þee. Be he curside
þat cursiþ þee, and he þat blessiþ þee, be he fillide wiþ blessyngis. ³⁰Vneþe
765 Isaac hadde fillid þe word, and whanne Iacob was goen out, ³¹Esau cam and
brouȝte yn metis soden of þe huntynge to þe fadir, and seide: My fadir, |
f. 239ᵛᵃ rise þou and ete of þe huntynge of þi sone, þat þi soule blesse me. ³²And
Isaac seide: Who forsoþe art þou? Whiche answeride: I am Esau, þi firste
gendride sone. ³³Isaac dredde bi a greet stonyinge, and he wondride more
770 þanne it may be bileeuede, and seide: Who þerfor is he whiche a while ago
brouȝte to me huntynge taken, and I eet of alle þingis bifore þat þou camest,
and I blesside hym? And he schal be blessid. ³⁴Whanne þe wordis of þe fadir
werun herd, Esau rorid wiþ a greet cry and was astonyede and seide: My
fadir, blesse þou also me! ³⁵Which seide: Thi broþer came prudentli and
775 took þi blessynge. ³⁶And Esau addide: Iustli his name is clepide Iacob, for
lo, he supplauntid me anoþer tyme, bifore he took awey my firste gendride
þingis. And now þe secunde tyme he rauyschide pryueli my blessinge. And
efte he seide to þe fadir: Where þou hast not reseruede also a blessynge to
me? ³⁷Isaac answeride: I haue made hym þi Lord, and I haue made suget
780 alle hise briþeren to his seruage. I haue stablishid hym in wheet, wiyn, and
f. 239ᵛᵇ oyle. | And my sone, what schal I do to þee aftir þese þingis? ³⁸To whom
Esau seide: Fadir, where þou hast oonli o blessynge? I biseche þat also þou
blesse me. And whanne Esau wepte wiþ greet ȝellynge, ³⁹Isaac was stirid,
and seide to hym: Thi blessynge schal be in þe fatnesse of þe erþe and in
785 þe dewe of heuene fro aboue.

752 þe³] om. Bo, þe Ny   753 and] om. NyLaBxRa   754 me] marginal add. by
different hand Bo   755 þese] þo Se, þe Ra   757 and] om. NyLaRa   761 and²]
om. Ra   765 and¹] om. Ny   whanne] om. Ra   was] hadde Ny   769 bi a] with Ny
771 þat] om. Se   772 þe¹] þese Ra   777 rauyschide] rauischiþ Ny   778 not
reseruede also] not also reseruid Ny   784 fatnesse] swetnesse Bx   þe²] om. SeBx

[LECTION 45]

The iij Moneday lessoun of Lente. iiij Book of Kingis v°, a.

In þo daies, ¹Naaman, prince of þe cheuealrie of þe kyng of Sirie, was a greet man and worschipide anentis his Lord, for bi him þe Lord ȝaf heelþe to Sirie. Soþeli he was a strong man and riche, but leperous. ²Forsoþe, þeuis ȝeden out of Sirie and ledden prisoner fro þe lond of Israel, a litil   790 damysel þat was in þe seruyse of þe wijf of Naaman. ³Whiche damysel seide to hir ladi: I wolde þat my Lord hadde be at þe profete whiche is in Samarie! Soþeli þe profete schuld haue curid hym of þe lepre whiche he haþ. ⁴Therfor Naaman entride to his Lord, and toold to hym and seide: A damysel of þe lond of Israel spak so and so. ⁵Therfor þe kyng of Sirie   795 seide | to hym: Go þou! I schal sende lettris to þe kyng of Israel. And   f. 240ʳᵃ whanne he hadde go forþ and hadde take wiþ hym ten talentis of siluer and vj þousand golden platis, *eþer floreyns*, and ten chaungingis of cloþis, ⁶he brouȝte lettris to þe kyng of Israel bi þese wordis: Whanne þou hast take þis pistil, wite þou þat I haue sente to þee Naaman, my seruaunt, þat þou cure   800 him of his lepre. ⁷And whanne þe kyng of Israel hadde redde þe lettris, he to-rente hise cloþes and seide: Wheþer I am God þat may sle and quykene, for þis *king* sente to me þat I [cure] a man of his lepre? Perseyue and se þat he sekiþ occasiouns aȝens me. ⁸And whanne Elise, þe man of God, hadde herd þis, þat is, þat þe king of Israel hadde to-rente hise cloþis, he sente to   805 þe kyng and seide: Whi to-rentist þou þi cloþis? Come he to me, and wite he þat a profete is in Israel. ⁹Therfor Naaman cam wiþ hors and charis, and stood at þe dore of þe hous of Elise. ¹⁰And Elise sente to hym a messanger and seide: Go þou, and be þou waischun vij siþis in Iordan. And þi fleische schal resceyue heelþe, and þou schalt | be clenside. ¹¹Naaman was wrooþ,   f. 240ʳᵇ and ȝede awey and seide: I gesside þat he schulde come out to me, and   811 þat he schulde stonde and clepe þe name of his God, and þat he schulde touche wiþ his hond þe place of þe lepre, and schulde cure me. ¹²Where Abana and Pharfar, floodis of Damask, ben not bettir þanne alle þe wat- ris of Israel, þat I be waischun in þo, and be clenside? ¹³Therfor, whanne   815 he hadde turnede hymsilf and ȝede awei, hauynge indignacioun, hise ser- uauntis nyȝeden to hym and spaken to hym: Fadir, þouȝ þe profete hadde seide to þee a greet þing, certis þou ouȝtist to do hou moche more now, for

he seide to þee: Be þou waischen, and þou sch[a]lt be clenside. ¹⁴He ȝede
820 doun and waischide vij siþis in Iordan, bi þe word of þe man of God. And
his fleisch was restorid as þe fleische of a litil child, and he was clenside.
¹⁵And he turnyde aȝen wiþ al his feloushp to þe man of God, and cam, and
stood bifore hym and seide: Verili, I knowe þat noon oþer God is in al erþe,
no but oonli þe God of Israel.

[LECTION 46]

825   The Tewisday lessoun. iiij Book of Kyngis iiij cᵒ, a.

f. 240ᵛᵃ In þo daies, ¹a womman of þe wyues of profetis criede to Elise and seide:
Thi seruaunt, my husbond, is deed, and þou knowist þat þi seruant dredde
God. And lo, þe creauncer, *þat is he to whom þe dette is owide*, comeþ to take
my two sones to serue hym. ²To whom Elise seide: What wolte þou þat I do
830 to þee? Seie þou to me what þou hast in þin hous. And sche answeride: I,
þin hondmayde, haue not ony þing in myn hous but a litil of oyle, bi whiche
I schal be anoyntide. ³To whom he seide: Go þou and aske bi borowynge
of alle þi neiȝeboris voide vessels not fewe, ⁴and entre and close þi dore
whanne þou art wiþynne, þou and þi sones, putte þerof into alle þe vessels.
835 And whanne þo schulen be fillid, þou schalt take awey. ⁵Therfor þe womman ȝede and closide þe dore on hirsilf and on hir sones. Thei brouȝten
vessels and sche ȝotide yn. ⁶And whanne þe vessels werun ful, sche seide to
hir sone: Brynge þou ȝit a vessel to me. And he answeride, I haue not. And
þe oyle stood. ⁷Forsoþe, sche cam and schewide to þe man of God. And he
f. 240ᵛᵇ seide: | Go þou, sille þou þe oyle and ȝilde to þi creauncer. Forsoþe, þou
841 and þi children lyue of þe residewe.

[LECTION 47]

The Wednesday lesson. Exodi xxᵒ, c.

The Lord God seiþ þese þingis: ¹²Honoure þi fadir [and þi modir], þat þou be
long lyuynge vpon þe lond whiche þi Lord God schal ȝeue to þe. ¹³Thou
845 schalt not sle. ¹⁴Thou schalt do no leccherie. ¹⁵Thou schalt not do þefte.
¹⁶Thou schalt not speke false witnessynge aȝens þi neiȝbore. ¹⁷Thou schalt
not coueite þe hous of þi neiȝbore, neþer þou schalt desire his wijf, not

819 schalt] schlt Bo   822 he turnyde] þei turneden Ny   829 two] *om.* La
830 And] *om.* La   831 not ony] no LaRa   hous] *add.* no NyLaSeBxRa   834 þi]
om. La   837 ȝotide] ȝede Bx   840 þe] þin   þi] þe La   843 and þi modir]
NyLaSeBxRa, *om.* Bo, et matrem tuam Vu   844 þi] þe NyLaSeRa   845 do no]
not do LaSeBx   847 schalt] *add.* not Ra

seruaunt, not hondmaide, not oxe, not asse, neþer alle þingis þat ben hise.
¹⁸Forsoþe, al þe puple herden voicis and saien laumpis, *þat is schynynge*
liȝtis, and þe sown of a clarioun, and þe hille smokynge, and þei werun 850
afeerd and schaken with ynward drede, and stoden afer ¹⁹and seiden to
Moyses: Speke þou to vs, and we schulen here. The Lord speke not to vs,
lest perauenture we dien. ²⁰And Moyses seide to þe puple: Nyle ȝe drede!
For God cam to preue ȝou, and þat his drede schulde be in ȝou, and þat
ȝe schulden not do synne. ²¹And þe puple stood afer. Forsoþe, | Moyses f. 241ra
nyȝede to þe derknesse whereyn God was. ²²And þe Lord seide furþermore 856
to Moyses: Thou schalt seie þese þingis to þe sones of Israel: Ȝe saien þat
fro heuene I spak to ȝou. ²³Ȝe schulen not make goddis of siluer, neþer ȝe
schulen make to ȝou goddis of gold. ²⁴Ȝe schulen make an auter of erþe to
me, and ȝe schulen offre þereyn ȝoure brent sacrificis and pesible sacrifi- 860
cis, ȝour scheep and oxen, in eche place in whiche þe mynde of my name
schal be.

[LECTION 48]

The Thursday lessoun. Ieremy vij°, a.

In þo daies, ¹þe word þat was mad of þe Lord to Ieremye, ²and seide: Stonde
þou in þe ȝate of þe hous of þe Lord, and preche þere þis word, and seie: 865
Al Iuda þat entren bi þese ȝatis for to worschip þe Lord, heere ȝe þe word
of þe Lord. ³The Lord of oostis, God of Israel, seiþ þese þingis: Make ȝe
good ȝoure weies and ȝoure studyes, and I schal dwelle wiþ ȝou in þis place.
⁴Nyle ȝe truste in þe wordis of leesynge and seie: The temple of þe Lord,
þe temple of þe Lord, þe temple of þe Lord is. ⁵For if ȝe blessen ȝoure 870
weies and ȝoure studies, if ȝe don doom | bitwene a man and his neiȝbore, f. 241rb
⁶if ȝe maken not fals chalenge to a comelynge and to a faderles child and a
widewe, neþer scheden out ynnocent blood in þis place, and goen not aftir
aliene goddis into yuel to ȝousilf, ⁷I schal dwelle wiþ ȝou in þis place, in þe
lond whiche I ȝaf to ȝoure fadris, fro þe world and til into þe world, *seiþ þe* 875
Lord almyȝti.

850 liȝtis] *om.* Ny   856 þe¹] *om.* La   furþermore to Moyses] to moyses furþermore
Se   859 goddis of gold] golden goddis Ny   860 pesible] *prec. by þe canc.* Bo
864 þat was mad of þe Lord] of þe lord was maad LaSeBxRa   868 dwelle] *prec. by* d
canc. at end of prec. line Bo   872 and²] *add.* to NyLaSeBxRa   875 and] *om.* Se

[LECTION 49]

The Friday lessoun. Numery xx°, b.

In þo daies, ¹þe sones of Israel and al þe multitude camen ²aʒens Moyses and Aaron, and þei werun turnede into dissencioun and seiden: ᴣeue to vs
880 watir þat we drynke. ⁶And whanne þe puple was lefte, Moyses and Aaron entriden into þe tabernacle of boond of pees, and fillen lowe to þe erþe, and crieden to God, and seiden: Lord God, heere þe cry of þis puple and opene to hem þi tresoure, a welle of quicke watir, þat whanne þei be fil-lid, þe grucchynge of hem ceesse. And þe glorie of þe Lord apperide on
885 hem, ⁷and þe Lord spak to Moyses ⁸and seide: Take þe ʒerde and gadere
f. 241ᵛᵃ þe puple, þou and Aaron, þi broþer, and | speke ʒe to [þe] stoon bifor hem, and it schal ʒeue watir. And whanne þou hast ledde watir out of þe stoon, al þe multitude schal drinke, and þe beestis þerof *schulen drynke.* ⁹Therfor Moyses took þe ʒerde þat was in þe siʒt of þe Lord, as þe Lord comaundide
890 to hym. ¹⁰Whanne þe multitude was gaderide bifore þe stoon, and he seide to hem: Heere ʒe, rebel and vnbileueful, where we moun not brynge out to ʒou watir of þis stoon? ¹¹And whanne Moyses hadde reisid þe hond and hadde smyte þe flynte twies wiþ þe ʒerde, largist watris ʒeden out, so þat þe puple dranke, and þe beestis *drunken.* ¹²And þe Lord seide to Moyses
895 and to Aron: For ʒe bileueden not to me þat ʒe schulde halowe me bifore þe sones of Israel, ʒe schulen not lede þese puplis into þe lond whiche I schal ʒeue to hem. ¹³This is þe watir of aʒenseiynge, þere þe sones of Israel stryueden aʒens þe Lord, and he was halowide in hem.

[LECTION 50]

The Saturdai lesson. Daniel xiij°, a.

f. 241ᵛᵇ *In þo daies,* ¹a man was in Babuloyne, and his name | was Ioachym. ²And he
901 took a wijf, Sussan bi name, þe douʒtir of Helchie, a womman ful faire, and dredynge þe Lord. ³Forsoþe, hir fadir and hir modir, whanne þei werun riʒtful, tauʒte her douʒtir bi þe lawe of Moyses. ⁴Soþeli Ioachym was ful

---

880 puple] *corr. in different hand* multitude Bo, multitude NyLaSeBxRa   881 of boond] of þe boond Ny   to³] on Ra   882 and³] *om.* Bx   887 watir out] out watir Se   stoon] to stoon Bo, to *likely inserted by different hand,* þe stoon NyBxRa   890 to] *om.* NyLa   891 not] *om.* Se   892 to ʒou watir of þis stoon] of þis stoon watir to ʒou LaBxRa, watir of þis stoon to ʒou Se   hadde reisid þe hond] hadde reisid þe hond *copied twice, canc.* Bo   895 to¹] *om.* NyRa   þat ʒe schulde halowe me] *om.* Se   896 þese puplis] þis peple Ra   901 bi] *add.* her Ra   902 hir²] *om.* LaRa   903 Soþeli] *placed after* Ioachym Ra

riche, and he hadde a garden ny3 his hous. And þe Iewis camen to hym, for
he was þe moost worschipful of alle. ⁵And two oolde men werun ordeynede   905
iugis in þat 3eer, of whiche þe Lord spak þat wickidnesse 3ede out of Babu-
loyne, of þe elder iugis þat serueden to gouerne þe puple. ⁶These *iugis*
vseden ofte þe hous of Ioachym, and alle men þat hadden domes camen to
hem. ⁷Forsoþe, whanne þe puple hadde turnede a3en aftir mydday, Susan
entrid and walkide in þe garden of hir hosebonde. ⁸And þe elder men saien   910
hir entrynge eche day and walkinge, and þei brenneden out in þe coueitise
of hir. ⁹And þei turneden awey her witte and bowiden adoun her i3en, þat
þei sayen not heuene neþer biþou3ten on iust domes. ¹⁰Soþeli boþe were
woundide bi þe loue of hir, and þei schewiden not | her sorwe bi hem-   f. 242ʳᵃ
silf togidre, ¹¹ for þei were aschamede to schewe to hemsilf her coueitise,   915
willynge to ligge fleischli bi hir. ¹²And þei aspieden eche day more bisili to
aspien hir. ¹³And oon seide to þe toþer: Go we hoom, for þe hour of mete is.
And þei 3eden out and departiden fro hemsilf. ¹⁴And whanne þei hadden
turnede a3en, þei camen into o place, and þei axiden eche of oþere þe cause,
and þei knoulechiden her coueitise. And þanne in comyn þei ordeyneden   920
a tyme whanne þei my3ten fynde hir aloon. ¹⁵Forsoþe it was don. Whanne
þei aspieden a couenable day, sche entride sumtyme as 3istirday and þe
þridde day ago, with two damysels aloon, and wolde be waischun in þe
gardeyn, forwhi heete was. ¹⁶And ony man was not þere outaken two oold
men hid, biholdynge hir. ¹⁷Therfor sche seide to þe damysels: Bringe 3e to   925
me oyle and oynementis and close þe doris of þe garden, þat I be waischun.
¹⁸And þei deden as sche hadde comaundide, and þei closiden þe doris of þe
gardeyn and 3eden out bi a posterne to brynge þo þingis þat sche | hadde   f. 242ʳᵇ
comaundide. And þei wisten not þat þe oold men werun hidde þerynne.
¹⁹Soþeli whanne þe damysels werun goen out, two oold men risun and   930
runnen to hir and seiden: Lo, ²⁰þe dooris of þe gardeyn ben closide and
no man seeþ vs. And we ben in þe coueitise of þee, wherfor assente þou
to vs and be þou medelide wiþ vs. ²¹That if þou wolte not, we schulen seie
witnessynge a3ens þee, þat a 3onge man was wiþ þee, and for þis cause þou
sentist out þe damysels fro þee. ²²And Sussan ynwardli sorowide, and seide: 935
Angwischis ben to me on ech seide, for if I do þis, deeþ is to me. Forsoþe
if I do not, I schal not ascape 3oure hondis. ²³But it is bettir to me to falle
into 3oure hondis wiþout werk þanne to do synne in þe si3t of þe Lord.
²⁴And Sussan criede with greet voice, but also þe elder men crieden a3ens

904 þe Iewis] þei Ny   907 serueden] semeden NySe, videbantur Vu   910 and
walkide in] into Ra   911 brenneden] brenten Se   in] into NyLaSeBxRa   914 bi¹]
to La, in Se   924 two] the two La   925 3e] *om.* Se   926 close] *add.* 3e La
þe¹] *om.* Se   928 a] anoþir Ny   938 into] in SeRa   do] *om.* Ra   939 Sussan]
marginal note Sussan Bo

940 hir. ²⁵Forsoþe, oon ranne and openede þe dore of þe gardeyn. ²⁶Forsoþe
whanne þe seruauntis of þe hous hadde herde þe cry [in] þe gardeyn, þei
fillen yn bi þe posterne to se what it was. ²⁷But aftir þat þese oold men |

f. 242ᵛᵃ spaken, þe seruauntis werun aschamede greetli, for neuer was suche a word
seide of Susan. And þe morewe day was made. ²⁸Whanne þe puple was
945 come to Ioachym, hir husbonde, also þe two prestis ful of wickide þou3te
camen a3ens Susanne for to sle hir. ²⁹And þei seiden bifor al þe multitude: Sende 3e to Susan, þe dou3tir of Helchie, þe wijf of Ioachym. And
anoon þei senten. ³⁰And sche cam wiþ hir fadir and modir and children
and alle kynnesmen. ³¹Certis Susan was ful delicat, *eþer tendir*, and faire of
950 schap. ³²And þe wickide men comaundiden þat sche schuld be vnhilide,
for sche was keueride, þat nameli so þei schulden be fillid of hir fairnesse.
³³Therfor hir *kynsmen* wepten and alle þat knewen hir. ³⁴Forsoþe þe two
prestis reiseden togidre in þe myddis of þe puple and setten hire hondis
on þe heed of hir. ³⁵And sche wepte, and bihelde to heuene, and hir herte
955 hadde truste in þe Lord. ³⁶And þe prestis seiden: Whanne we walkiden

f. 242ᵛᵇ aloone in þe gardeyn, þis *Susanne* entride wiþ two damysels, | and sche
closide þe dore of þe gardeyn and lefte þe damysels. ³⁷And a 3unge man
þat was hid cam to hir and lay bi hir. ³⁸Certis whanne we werun in a corner
of þe gardeyn, we saien þe wickidnesse and runnen to hem, and we sayen
960 hem medelide togidre. ³⁹And soþeli we my3ten not take hym, for he was
stronger þanne we. And whanne he hadde openede þe doris, he skipt out.
⁴⁰But whanne we hadde take þis *womman*, we axiden who was þis 3unge
man, and sche wolde not schewe to vs. Of þis þing we ben witnessis. ⁴¹The
multitude bileeuede to hem, as to þe elder men and iugis of þe puple, and
965 condempneden hir to deeþ. ⁴²Forsoþe sche criede loude wiþ a greet voice
and seide: Lord God, wiþouten bigynnynge and ende, þou art knower of
hidde þingis; þou knowist alle þingis bifor þat þei ben don. ⁴³Thou woste
þat þei han born false witnessynge a3ens me. And lo, I die, whanne I haue
not don ony of þese þingis whiche þese men han made maliciousli a3ens

f. 243ʳᵃ me. ⁴⁴Forsoþe, þe Lord herd | þe voice of hir. ⁴⁵And whanne sche was led
971 to þe deeþ, þe Lord reiside þe holi spirit of a 3unge childe, whos name was
Danyel. ⁴⁶And he criede loude wiþ a greet voice: I am cleene of þe blood
of þis *womman*! ⁴⁷And al þe puple turnede a3en to hym and seide: What is

941 whanne] *prec. by* w *canc. at end of prec. line* Bo   in] NyBx, of Bo   944 seide]
herd Ny   Whanne] and whanne NySeBxRa   945 þe] *om.* Bx   ful of] wiþ Ra
946 multitude] peple NyLaSeBxRa   949 alle] *om.* Ra   951 nameli] nakidly Se
of] wiþ Ra   953 reiseden] risen Se   954 wepte] *prec. by* w *canc. at end of prec. line*
Bo   962 þis²] þe SeBxRa   964 þe¹] *om.* Ra   965 deeþ] þe deeþ Ny   sche]
Susanne LaSeBxRa   a] *om.* NyLaBxRa   þat] *om.* Ra   968 witnessynge] witnesse Se   969 whiche] þat
Ny   971 whos] to whom þe Ny

þis word whiche þou hast spoke? ⁴⁸And whanne he stood in þe myddis of
hem, he seide: So ȝe, fonned children of Israel, not demynge neþer know- 975
ynge þat þat is trewe, condempneden þe douȝtir of Israel. ⁴⁹Turne ȝe aȝen
to þe doom, for þei spaken false witnessynge aȝens hir. ⁵⁰Therfor þe puple
turnede aȝen wiþ haast, and þe elde men seiden to hym: Come þou and sitte
in þe myddis of vs and schewe to vs, for God haþ ȝoue to þee þe onoure
of elde. ⁵¹And Danyel seide to hem: Departe ȝe hem atwynny fer, and 980
I schal deme hem. ⁵²Therfor, whan þei werun departide þat oon fro þat
oþer, he clepide oon of hem and seide to hym: Thou elde man and of yuel
daies, new þi synnes ben comyn, whiche þou wrouȝtist bifor, ⁵³demynge
vniust domes, oppressynge ynnocentis and | delyuerynge gilti men, whan f. 243rb
þe Lord seiþ, þou schalt not sle an ynnocent and iust man. ⁵⁴But now, if þou 985
say hir, sey þou, vndir what tre þou saist hem spekynge togidre to hemsilf?
Whiche seide: Vndir an hawe tre. ⁵⁵Forsoþe Danyel seide: Riȝtli þou liest
in þin heed, for lo, þe aungel of þe Lord, bi a sentence takun of him, schal
kitte þee bi þe myddil. ⁵⁶And whanne he was stirid aweye, he comaundide
þat oþere to come, and seide to him: Thou seed of Canaan and not of Iuda, 990
fairnesse haþ disceyued þee, and coueitise haþ mysturnede þin herte; ⁵⁷þus
ȝe diden to þe doitris of Israel, and þei dredden and spaken to ȝou, but þe
douȝtir of Iuda suffride not ȝoure wickidnesse. ⁵⁸Now þerfor seye þou to
me, vndir what tre saiest þou hem spekynge togidre to hemsilf? ⁵⁹Whiche
seide: Vndir a blacke þorn. Forsoþe Danyel seide to hym: Riȝtli also þou 995
liest in þin heed, for þe aungel of þe Lord dwelliþ and haþ a swerd, þat
he kitte þee bi þe myddil and sle ȝou. ⁶⁰Therfor al þe puple criede loude
wiþ greet voice and | blessiden þe Lord þat saueþ hem þat hopen in hym. f. 243va
⁶¹And þei riseden togidre aȝens þe two prestis, for Danyel hadde conuictid
hem bi her mouþ, þat þei hadden bore false witnessynge. And þei diden to 1000
hem as þei hadden don yuel aȝens her neiȝboresse, ⁶²þat þei schulden do
bi þe lawe of Moyses, and þei killiden hem. And giltles blood was sauede
in þat day.

[LECTION 51]

The iiij Monedai lessoun of Lente. [iiij] Book of Kingis iij°, e.

¹⁶*In þo daies*, tweye wommen strumpetis camen to þe kyng and stoden 1005
bifor hym, ¹⁷of whiche oon seide, My Lord, I biseche: I and þis womman

975 he] and Se   976 condempneden] condempnynge   977 spaken] han
spoken La   980 fer] afer La   981 þat²] þe Bx   982 and²] *om.* NyLaSeBx
985 ynnocent] *followed by* man *canc.* Bo   iust] a iust NySeBx   986 to] bi Ny
988 in] into Ny   for] *om.* SeBx   þe] a   990 þat] þe SeBx   994 saiest þou] þou
sawist Ny   996 in] into Ny   a] *om.* Se   1001 her] þe LaSeBx   1004 iij¹]
iiij Bo, iij NyLaSeBxRa

dwelliden in oon hous, and I childide at hir in a couche. ¹⁸Soþeli in þe þridde day aftir þat I childide, also þis womman childide, and we werun togidre in þe hous, and noon oþer was with vs in þe hous, outaken vs tweine.

1010 ¹⁹Forsoþe, þe sone of þis womman was deed in þe ny3t, for sche slepte and oppresside hym, ²⁰and sche roos in þe fourþe part of þe ny3te in scilence and took my sone fro þe side of me, þin hondmayde slepynge, and settid

f. 243ᵛᵇ in hir bosum; forsoþe sche puttide in my bosum hir sone þat | was deed. ²¹And whanne I hadde rise eerly to 3eue mylke to my sone, he apperide

1015 deed, whom I biheld diligentlier bi cleer li3t, and I perseyuede þat he was not myn, whom I hadde gendride. ²²The oþer womman answeride: It is not so as þou seist, but þi sone is deed. Forsoþe my sone lyueþ. A3enward sche seide: Thou liest, for my sone lyueþ, and þi sone is deed! And bi þis maner þei stryueden bifor þe kyng. ²³Thanne þe kyng seide: This womman seiþ,

1020 My sone lyueþ and þi sone is deed, and þis womman answeriþ, Nay, but þi sone is deed, forsoþe my sone lyueþ! ²⁴Therfor þe kyng seide: Brynge 3e to me a swerd! And whanne þei hadden brou3te a swerd bifor þe kyng, he seide: ²⁵Departe 3e þe quicke 3ong child in two partis, and 3eue 3e þe half to þe oon and þe half part to þe toþir. ²⁶Forsoþe þe womman whos sone was

1025 quicke seide to þe kyng, for hir entrailis werun mouede on hir sone, Lord, I biseche, 3eue 3e to hir þe quicke childe, and nyle 3e sle hym. A3enward sche seide, Be he neþer to me, neþer to þee, but be he departide! ²⁷The

f. 244ʳᵃ kyng answeride | and seide: 3eue 3e to þis womman þe childe quicke, and be it not slayn. Forsoþe, þis is þe modir. ²⁸Therfor al Israel herd þe doom

1030 whiche þe kyng hadde demede, and þei dredden þe kyng, and saien þat þe wisdom of God was in hym to make doom.

[LECTION 52]

The Tewisday lessoun. Exodi xxxij°, b.

In þo daies, ⁷*þe Lord spak to Moyses and seide* : Go þou doun of þe hille, þi puple haþ synnede, whom þou leddist out of þe lond of Egipt. ⁸Thei 3eden

1035 awey soone fro þe wey whiche þou schewedist to hem, and þei maden to hem a 3otun calf, and worschipiden. And þei offriden sacrificis to it and seiden, Israel, þese ben þi goddis þat ledden þee out of þe lond of Egipt. ⁹And efte þe Lord seide to Moyses, I se þat þis puple is of hard nol. ¹⁰Suffre

1014 eerly] *om.* Ra   1016 myn] my sone Ny   1023 3ong] *om.* Ny   in] into NyLaBxRa   3e²] *om.* NyBxRa   half] *add.* part Se   1024 þe³] *om.* LaSeBx Ra   þe⁴] þis Ny   1028 childe quicke] quyk child Ny   1029 it] he LaSeBxRa 1030 saien] þei sawen Ny   1033 spak . . . seide] seide to Moises Ny   þi] þe Se 1034 out of þe lond] *copied twice, canc. once* Bo   1036 þei] *om.* Se   1037 lond] *prec. by* l *canc. at end of prec. line* Bo

þou me þat my wickidnesse, _þat is my strong veniaunce_, be wrooþ aȝens hem, and þat I do awey hem, and I schal make þee into a greet folk. ¹¹Forsoþe, 1040
Moyses preiede his Lord God and seide, Lord, whi is þi veniaunce wrooþ aȝens þi puple, whom þou leddist out of þe lond of Egipt in greet strengþe and in | strong hond? ¹²I biseche þat Egipcianes seyn not, He ledde hem f. 244ʳᵇ
out felli to sle in þe hillis, and to do awey fro þe erþe. Thin ire ceesse, and be þou queemful on þe wickidnesse of þi puple. ¹³Haue þou mynde of 1045
Abraham, of Isaac, and of Israel, þi seruauntis, to whiche þou hast swoor bi þisilf and seidist, I schal multiplie ȝoure seed as þe sterris of heuene, and I schal ȝeue to ȝoure seed al þis lond of whiche I spak, and ȝe schuln weeld it euer. ¹⁴And þe Lord was pleside, þat he dide not þe yuel whiche he spak aȝens his puple, _and he hadde merci of his puple, þe Lord oure God_. 1050

[LECTION 53]

The Wednesday lessoun. Ezechielis xxxv[j]º.

The Lord God seiþ þese þingis: ²³I schal halowe my greet name, whiche is defoulid among heþen men, whiche ȝe defouleden in þe myddis of hem, þat heþen men wite þat I am þe Lord, seiþ þe Lord of oostis, whanne I schal be halowide in ȝou bifor hem. ²⁴For I schal take awey ȝou fro heþen 1055
men, and I schal gadere ȝou fro alle londis, and I schal brynge ȝou into ȝoure lond. ²⁵And I schal schede out | clene watir on ȝou, and ȝe schulen f. 244ᵛᵃ
be clenside fro alle ȝoure filþis. And I schal clense ȝou fro alle ȝoure ydolis. ²⁶And I schal ȝeue to ȝou a newe herte, and I schal sette a newe spirit in þe myddis of ȝou. And I schal do awey an herte of stoon fro ȝoure fleisch, 1060
and I schal ȝeue to ȝou an herte of fleisch. ²⁷And I schal sette my spirit in þe myddis of ȝou. And I schal make þat ȝe go in my comaundementis, and kepe and worschip my domes. ²⁸And ȝe schulen dwelle in þe lond which I ȝaf to ȝoure fadris, and ȝe schulen be a puple to me, and I schal be into a God to ȝou. 1065

1039 my²] _om._ SeRa   wrooþ] _prec. by_ w _canc. at end of prec. line_ Bo   1040 and þat I do awey hem] _om._ La   1044 sle] _add._ hem Se   1050 of] _on_ NySeRa 1051 xxxvj] xxxv Bo, sixe and þritty Ny, xxxvj LaSeBxRa   1052–3 whiche is . . . myddis of hem] _om._ LaSeBxRa   1054 seiþ þe Lord of oostis] _om._ LaSeBxRa 1064 be¹] _add._ into Ny   a²] _om._ SeBxRa   1065 ȝou] _add._ seiþ þe lord almyȝty NyLaSeBxRa

[LECTION 54]

On þe same day anoþer lessoun. Isaye jº, d.

The Lord God seiþ þese þingis: ¹⁶Be ȝe waischun, be ȝe clene, do ȝe awey yuel of ȝoure þouȝtis fro myn iȝen, ceesse ȝe to do weywardli, lerne ȝe to do wel. ¹⁷Seke ȝe doom, helpe ȝe hym þat is oppressid, deme ȝe to þe fadirles and 1070 modirles child, and defende ȝe a widewe. ¹⁸And come ȝe and repreue ȝe me, *seiþ þe Lord.* Thouȝ ȝoure synnes be made as blood reed, þo schulen be f. 244ᵛᵇ made whiȝte as snowe. And þou⟨ȝ⟩ þo ben reed as vermyloun, | þei schuln be whiȝte as wolle. ¹⁹If ȝe wolen, and heere me, ȝe schulen ete þe goodis of erþe.

[LECTION 55]

1075   ### The Thursday lessoun. iiij Book of Kyngis iiijº, d.

In þo dayes, a womman of Sunamytis cam to Elise, þe profete, ²⁵into þe hil of Carmel. And whanne þe man of God hadde seen hir euen aȝens, he seide to Gisy, his child, Lo, þilke Sunamyte! Go þou þerfor into þe metynge of hir, ²⁶and seie þou to hir, Wheþer it is doon riȝtfulli aboute þee and aboute 1080 þi husbonde and aboute þi sone? And sche answeride, Riȝtli. ²⁷And whanne sche hadde come to þe man of God into þe hille, sche took hise feet, and Gysy nyȝede þat he schulde remoue hir. And þe man of God seide, Suffre þou hir, for hir soule is in bitternesse, and þe Lord held pryuy fro me and schewide not to me. ²⁸And sche seide to hym, Wheþer I askide my sone 1085 of my Lord? Where I seide not to þee, scorne þou not me? ²⁹And he seide to Gyezi, Girde þi lendis, and take my staffe in þin hond and go. If a man f. 245ʳᵃ metiþ þee, grete þou not hym, and if ony man gretiþ þe, | answere þou not to hym, and putte þou my staf on þe face of þe child. ³⁰Forsoþe, þe modir of þe child seide, The Lord lyueþ and þi soule lyueþ, I schal not leeue þee. 1090 Therfor he roos and suede hir. ³¹Soþeli Gyesy ȝede bifore hem and put-tide þe staf on þe face of þe child, and voice was not, neþer wit. And Gysy turnede aȝen into þe metinge of hym, and toold to hym and seide, The child roos not. ³²Therfor Elise entride into þe hous, and lo, þe deed child lay in his bedde. ³³And he entride and closide þe dore on hymsilf and on þe

1067 awey] *add.* þe LaSeBxRa   1070 and¹] *om.* LaSeBxRa   repreue] preue
Ra   1071 made] *om.* LaSeBxRa   1073 If] and if Ra   and] *om.* LaSeBxRa
1074 of] of þe La   erþe] *add.* seiþ þe lord almyȝty NyLaSeBxRa   1076 into] in Ny
1079 riȝtfulli] riȝtli NyBx   1080 Riȝtli] riȝtfully LaSeRa   1088 þou] *om.* Ny
1090 Therfor he roos and suede hir] *prec. by* þerfor he roos and suede hir *canc.* Bo

child, and preiede to þe Lord. [34]And he stiede, and lay on þe child, and he 1095
puttide his mouþe on þe moouþ of þe child, and hise iȝen on þe iȝen of þe
child, and hise hondis on þe hondis of þe child. And he bowide hymsilf on
þe child, and þe fleische of þe child was made hoot. [35]And he turnede aȝen
and walkide in þe hous oonys hidir and þidir. And Elise stiede, and lay on
þe child, and þe child ȝoxide seuen siþis, and openede þe iȝen. [36]And he 1100
clepide Gyesy and seyde to hym, Clepe þou | þis Sunamyte. And sche was f. 245rb
clepide and entride to hym. And he seide, Take þi sone! [37]And sche cam
and fil doun at hise feet, and worschipide on erþe. And sche took hir sone
and ȝede out. [38]And Elise turnede aȝen into Galgala.

[LECTION 56]

The Friday lessoun. iij Book of Kyngis xviiᵒ, c.   1105

In þo dayes, [17]þe sone of a womman hussewijf was sike, and þe sikenesse
was moost stro[n]g, so þat breeþ dwelte not in hym. [18]Therfor sche seide
to Elie, What to me and to þee, þou man of God? Entridist þou to me,
þat my wickidnesse schulde be remembride, and þat þou schuldist sle my
sone? [19]And Elie seide, Ȝeue þi sone to me. And he took þat sone fro hir 1110
bosum, and bare into þe soler where he dwelte, and he puttide hym on
his bed. [20]And he criede to þe Lord and seide, My Lord God, where þou
hast turmentide þe widewe, at whom I am susteynede in al maner, þat þou
killidist hir sone? [21]He spred abrood hymsilf and mette on þe child bi þre
tymes, and he criede to þe Lord and seide, My Lord God, I biseche, þe 1115
soule of þe child turne aȝen into þe | entraylis of hym. [22]The Lord herd f. 245va
þe voice of Elye, and þe soule of þe child turnede aȝen wiþyn hym, and he
lyued aȝen. [23]And Elie took þe child and puttide hym doun of þe soler into
þe lower hous, and bitook to his modir, and seide to hir, Lo, þi sone lyueþ!
[24]And þe womman seide to Elye, Now in þis I haue knowe þat þou art þe 1120
man of God, and þe word of God is sooþ in þi moouþ.

[LECTION 57]

The Saturday lessoun. Isay xlix, c.

The Lord God seiþ þes þingis: [8]In a plesaunt tyme I herd þee, and in þe day
of heelþe I helpide þee, and I kepte þee and ȝaf þee into a boond of pees of

1095–6 on þe child . . . his mouþe] *om.* Se   1095 and³] *om.* Ra   1096 puttide]
putte Ra   1097 child²] *prec. by* c *canc. at end of prec. line* Bo   1102 þi] þe
Bx   1107 strong] strog Bo   1112 where] *prec. by* w *canc. at end of prec. line*
Bo   1116 þe¹] þis NySeBxRa   1119 and²] *add.* he Ra   seide] he seide La

1125 þe puple, þat þou schuldist reise þe erþe and haue in possessioun eritage
distriede, ⁹þat þou schuldist seie to hem þat ben bounden, Go 3e out!, and
to hem þat ben in derknesses, Be 3e schewide! Thei schulen be fedde on
weies, and þe lesewis of hem *schulen be* in alle pleyn þingis. ¹⁰Thei schulen not hungir and þei schulen no more þurste, and heete and þe sunne
1130 schal not smyte hem, for þe merciful doer of hem schal gouerne hem, and
f. 245ᵛᵇ I schal 3eue drynke to hem at | þe wellis of watris. ¹¹And I schal sette alle
myn hillis into wey, and my paþis schulen be enhauncid. ¹²Lo, þese men
schulen come fro fer, and lo, þei *schulen come* fro þe norþ and fro þe see,
and þese fro þe souþ lond. ¹³Heuenes, herie 3e, and þe erþe make ful out-
1135 ioie! Hillis, synge 3e, hertli heriynge, for þe Lord counfortide his puple,
and schal haue mercy on hise pore men. ¹⁴And Sion seide, The Lord haþ
forsake and þe Lord haþ for3etun me. ¹⁵Wheþer a womman may for3ete
hir 3ung child, þat sche haue not merci on þe sone of hir wombe? Thou3
sche for3etiþ, naþeles I schal not for3ete, *seiþ þe Lord almi3ti*.

[LECTION 58]

1140   The lessoun of Passioun Moneday. Ionas iij°, d.

In þo daies, ¹þe word of þe Lord was made to Ionas þe secunde tyme, and
seide, Rise þou, ²and go into Nynyue, þe greet citee, and preche þou in it þe
prechynge whiche I speke to þee. ³And Ionas roos and wente into Nynyue,
bi þe word of þe Lord. And Nynyue was a greet citee, of þe iourney of þre
f. 246ʳᵃ daies. ⁴And Ionas bigan for to | entre into þe citee, bi þe iourney of oo day,
1146 and criede and seide, 3it fourty dayes, and Nynyue schal be vndirturnede
or distriede. ⁵And men of Nynyue bileueden to þe Lord, and prechiden
fastynge, and werun cloþide wiþ sackis, fro þe more til to þe lasse. ⁶And
þe word cam to þe kyng of Nynyue, and he roos fro his seete and castide
1150 awey his cloþinge fro hym, and was cloþide in sak and sat in aische. ⁷And
he criede and seide in Nynyue of þe mouþ of þe kyng and of hise prynces,
and seide, Men and werk beestis and oxen and scheep taast not ony þing,
neþer be fed, neþer drynke watir. ⁸And be men hilide wiþ sackis, and werk
beestis crye to þe Lord in strengþe, and be a man conuertide fro his yuel
1155 wey, and fro wickidnesse þat is in þe hondis of hem. ⁹Who woot if God be

1127 in] *om.* Ny   1129 þe] *om.* Ny   1130 not] nomore NySe
1131 schal¹] *prec. by* s *canc. at end of prec. line* Bo   And] *om.* Se   1133 and
fro þe] *om.* SeBx   fro þe²] *om.* LaRa   1134 herie] heere La   þe²] þou LaSe-
BxRa   1136 schal] he schal Ra   1137 Lord] *prec. by* l *canc. at end of prec. line* Bo
1141 and seide] *om.* La   1144 þre] *om.* Se   1145 for] *om.* Ny   1149 fro]
of LaBxRa   1150 cloþinge] cloþis La   in¹] wiþ LaSeBxRa   1151 in] *om.* Se

conuertid and for3eue, and be turnede a3en fro woodnesse of his wraþþe, and we schulen not perische? ¹⁰And God say þe werkis of hem, and þei werun conuertide fro her yuel wey. And God hadde mercy on þe malice whiche he spak, þat | he schulde do to hem, and dide not, *and oure Lord* f. 246ʳᵇ *God hadde mercy on his puple.*   1160

[LECTION 59]

The Tewisday lessoun. Danyel xiiij°, c.

In þo dayes, men of Babuloyne ²⁸*werun gaderide togidre to þe kyng, and seiden,* Bitake þou to vs Danyel, þat distriede Beel and killide þe dragoun, ellis we schulen sle þee and þin hous. ²⁹Therfor þe kyng say þat þei fillen yn on hym greetli, and he was compellide bi nede, and bitook Danyel to hem, 1165 ³⁰whiche senten hym into þe lake of liouns. And he was þere seuene dayes. ³¹And seuen liouns werun in þe lake, and two bodyes and two scheep werun 3ouun to hem eche day. And þanne þo werun not 3ouun to hem, þat þei schulden deuoure Danyel. ³²Forsoþe, Abacuk þe profete was in Iudee, and he hadde sode potage and hadde set in loues in a litil panyer, and he 3ede 1170 into þe feeld to bere to repers. ³³And þe aungel of þe Lord seide to Abacuk, Bere þou þe mete whiche þou hast, into Babuloyne to Danyel, whiche is in þe lake of lyouns. ³⁴And Abacuk seide, Lord, I say not Babuloyn, and I knewe not þe lake. | ³⁵And þe aungel of þe Lord took hym bi his top and f. 246ᵛᵃ bare him bi þe heer of his heed, and he settide þilke *Abacuk* in Babuloyne 1175 on þe lake, in þe feersnesse of his spirit. ³⁶And Abacuk criede and seide, Danyel, þe seruaunt of God, take þou þe mete þat God haþ sente to þee. ³⁷And Danyel seide, Lord God, þou hast mynde on me and hast not forsaken hem þat louen þee. ³⁸And Danyel roos and eet. Certis þe aungel of þe Lord restorid Abacuk anoon in his place. ³⁹Therfor þe kyng cam in þe 1180 seuenþe day to biweile Danyel, and he cam to þe lake and lokide yn, and lo, Danyel sittynge in þe myddis of liouns. ⁴⁰The kyng criede an hi3e wiþ greet voice and seide, Lord God of Danyel, þou art greet! And *þe kyng* drowe him out of þe lake. ⁴¹Soþeli he sente hem into þe lake þat werun cause of his perdiscioun, and þei werun deuourid in a moment bifore hym. ⁴²Thanne þe 1185

1157 þe werkis] þe *copied twice, then canc.* Bo   and²] þat SeBxRa   1158 wey] *prec. by* w *canc. at end of prec. line* Bo   1160 God] *om.* Ra   1165 on hym greetli] greetly on him NyLaRa   and¹] *om.* Ra   1168 And] *om.* Ny   1169 deuoure] distroye Se   1170 sode] soþe Bx   1172 whiche²] þe whiche La   1174 his] þe Ny   1175 þilke] *om.* Ny   1178 on] of Ny   hast²] þou hast Ra   1180 in¹] into SeBx   1182 wiþ greet] wiþ a greet Ny   1184 Soþeli] certis NyLaSeBxRa hem] *om.* LaSeBxRa   þat] hem þat LaSeBxRa

kyng seide, Thei þat dwellen in al erþe, drede þe God of Danyel, for he is God lyuynge into worldis. He is delyuerer and sauyour, doynge myraclis

f. 246vb and merueilis in heuene and in erþe, þat delyueride | Danyel fro þe lake of liouns.

[LECTION 60]

1190 The Wednesday lessoun. Leuiticus xix°, c.

¹The Lord spak to Moyses and seide: ²Speke þou to al þe cumpeny of þe sones of Israel, and þou schalt seye to hem: ¹¹Ȝe schulen not do þefte. Ȝe schuln not lie, and no man disceyue his neiȝbore. ¹²Thou schalt not forswere in my name, neþer þou schalt defoule þe name of þi God; I am 1195 þe Lord. ¹³Thou schalt not make false chalange to þi neiȝbore, neþer þou schalt oppresse hym bi violence. The werk of þin hyrid man, *þat is þe hyre of his werk*, schal not dwelle at þee til to þe morewetide. ¹⁴Thou schalt not curse a deef man, ne þou schalt putte þing of lettynge bifor a blynde man, but þou schalt drede þe Lord þi God, for I am Lord. ¹⁵Thou schalt 1200 not do þat þat is wickide, ne vnriȝtwisli þou schalt not deme. Thou schalt not biholde þe persone of þe pore, ne þou schalt not honoure þe cheer of þe myȝti. Riȝtwisli deme þou þi neiȝbore. ¹⁶Thou schalt not be a wrong-
f. 247ra ful accuser of greuouse synne, ne pryuy yuel speker | in puplis, ne þou schalt stonde aȝens þe blood of þi neiȝbore; I þe Lord. ¹⁷Hate þou not þi 1205 broþer in þin herte, but opynli vndirnyme þou hym, þat þou haue of hym no synne. ¹⁸Thou schalt not seke veniaunce, neþer þou schalt haue mynde on þe wrong of þi citesens. Thou schalt loue þi frend as þisilf; I þe Lord. My lawis kepe ȝe. *I forsoþe am youre Lord God.*

[LECTION 61]

The Thursday lessoun. Danyel iij°, h.

1210 *In þo daies*, Danyel preiede þe Lord: ³⁴Distrye not þi testament, ³⁵neþer do awei þi merci fro vs, for Abraham, þi derlynge, and Isaac, þi seruaunt, and Israel, þin holy, ³⁶to whiche þou spakist, biheetynge þat þou schuldist mul-

1186 drede] add. ȝe Ra   1191 Lord] add. god Ra   1194 schalt] add. not Ra
1195 to] aȝens Ny   1196 schalt] add. not Ra   1198 ne þou schalt] þou schalt
not Ny   1199 Lord²] alord Ny   1200 þat²] om. LaRa   not²] om. NyLaSeBx
1201 not²] om. NyLaSe   1202 þi] to þi LaSeRa   1204 I þe Lord] I am alord
Ny   1205 þou²] om. LaSeBxRa   1206 schalt²] add. not Se   1207 on] of
NyLaSeBxRa   I þe] I am þe NyLa   1208 I forsoþe] Forsoþe I Ny   1210 Danyel]
Azarie La   Lord] add. and seide La   þi] þe Ny   do] do þou La

tiplie her seed as þe sterris of heuene, and as þe grauel whiche is in þe
brynke of þe see. ³⁷Forwhi, Lord, we ben mad litil, more þanne alle folkis,
and we ben lowe in al erþe today, for oure synnes. ³⁸And in þis tyme is no   1215
prince and duyk and profete, neþer brent sacrifice, ne sacrifice, ne offrynge,
neþer encence, neþer place of firste fruytis bifore þee, ³⁹þat we mowe fynde
þi merci, but be we resceyuede in contrite soule | and in spirit of meke-   f. 247ʳᵇ
nesse. ⁴⁰As in brent sacrificis of rammes and of boolis, and as in þousandis
of fatte lambren, so oure sacrifice be made today in þi siȝte, þat it plese   1220
þee, for no schame is to hem þat tristen in þee. ⁴¹Now we suen þee in al
þe herte, and we dreden þee, and we seken þi face. ⁴²Schende þou not vs,
but do wiþ vs þi myldenesse, and bi þe multitude of þi merci, ⁴³and delyuere þou vs in þi merueilis, and ȝeue þou glorie to þi name, Lord. ⁴⁴And
alle men be schent þat schewen yuel to þi seruauntis, be þei schent in al   1225
þi myȝte, and þe strengþe of hem be al tobrokun. ⁴⁵And þei schulen wite
þat þou art þe Lord God aloone, and glorious on þe roundenesse of londis,
Lord oure God.

[LECTION 62]

The Fryday lessoun. Ieremye xvij°, d.

In þo daies, Ieremye seide: ¹³Lord, alle þat forsaken þee schulen be schent.   1230
Thei þat goen awey fro þee, in þe erþe schulen be writun, for þei forsoken þe
Lord, þe veyne of lyuynge watris. ¹⁴Heele me, Lord, and I schal be heelide;
saue me, and I schal be saaf, for my preisynge þou art. ¹⁵Lo, þei seien | to   f. 247ᵛᵃ
me, Where is þe word of þe Lord? Come it. ¹⁶And I am not disturblide,
folowynge þe schepherd, and þe day of man I desirid not, þou woost. That   1235
þat is goen out fro my lippis, riȝt was in þi siȝte. ¹⁷Be þou not to ferdful
to me, þou myn hope in þe day of turmentynge. ¹⁸Be þei confoundide þat
pursuen me, and be not I confoundide. Inwardli drede þei, and inwardli
drede not I. Brynge þou on hem a day of turment, and defoule hem bi
doubil defoulynge, *Lord oure God*.   1240

1213 þe²] *om.* LaSeBxRa   1216 neþer] ne Se   ne¹] neiþir LaSeBxRa   ne²]
neiþer NyLaSeBxRa   1219 sacrificis] sacrifice Bx   of²] *om.* Ra   1221 Now]
and now BxRa   al þe] oure Ny   1223 vs] *om.* Ny   1225 yuel] yuelis NyLa
1232 veyne] beme Bx   1233 saue me] saaf make me NyLaBx   for my preisynge þou
art] for þou art my preisinge SeBx   1236 fro] of La

[LECTION 63]

The Saturday lessoun. Ieremy xviij°, c.

In þo daies, þe wickide men of Iewis seiden togidre: [18]Come ȝe, and þenke we þouȝtis aȝens Ieremye, forwhi þe lawe schal not perische fro a prest, neþer counceil *schal perische* fro a *wise* man, neþer word *schal perische* fro a pro-
1245 fete. Come ȝe, and smyte we hym wiþ tunge, and take we noon heede to alle þe wordis of hym. [19]Lord, ȝeue þou tente to me, and heere þou þe voice of myn aduersaries. [20]Where yuel is ȝoldon for good, for þei han diggid a pitte to my soule, haue þou mynde þat I stood in þi siȝt to speke good for
f. 247vb hem, and to turne awey þin indignacioun fro hem. | [21]Therfor ȝeue þou
1250 þe sones of hem into hungir, and lede forþ hem into hondis of swerd. The wyues of hem be made wiþout children, and *be made* widewis, and þe hus-bondis of hem be slayn bi deeþ. The ȝonge men of hem be peerside togidre bi swerd in bateil. [22]Cri be herd of þe housis of hem, for þou schalt brynge sodeynli a þeef on hem. For þei diggiden a pitte to take me and hidden
1255 snaris to my feet. [23]But þou, Lord, knowist al þe counceil of hem aȝens me into deeþ; do not merci to þe wickidnesse of hem, and þe synne of hem be not doen awey fro þi face. Be þei made fallynge adoun in þi siȝt, in þe tyme of þi strong veniaunce, *Lord*, *my God*.

[LECTION 64]

The lessoun on Palme Soneday. Exody xv[j]°, a.

1260 *In þo daies*, [1]þe sones, forsoþe, of Israel camen into Elym, where werun twelue wellis of watris and lxx palme trees, and þei settiden tentis bisidis þe watris. And þei ȝeden forþ fro Helym, and al þe multitude of þe sones of Israel camen into desert of Syn, whiche is bitwixe Helym and Synay,
f. 248ra in | þe fiftenþe day of þe secunde moneþe aftir þat þei ȝeden out of þe lond
1265 of Egipt. [2]And al þe congregacioun of þe sones of Israel grucchiden aȝens Moyses and aȝens Aaron in wildirnesse. [3]And þe sones of Israel seiden to hem, We wolden þat we hadden be deed bi þe hond of þe Lord in þe lond of Egipt, whanne we saten on þe pottis of fleischis and eten looues in plentee. Whi ledden ȝe vs into þis desert, þat ȝe schulden sle al þe multitude wiþ

1242 of] of þe NyRa   1246 þou[1]] *om.* Ny   1247 aduersaries] aduersarie La
1249 to] *om.* Se   1250 into[1]] into þe Ny   1253 of[1]] in Ra   1256 do] *add.*
now LaSeBx, *add.* þou Ra   1257 þe] *om.* La   1258 þi] *om.* Se   1259 xvj]
xv BoNySeBxRa, xvj La   1260 þe sones forsoþe] forsoþe þe sones NySeBx
1266 aȝens] *om.* Ra

hungir? ⁴Forsoþe, þe Lord seide to Moyses, Lo, I schal rey[ne] on ȝou   1270
looues fro heuene. The puple go out þat it gadere þo þingis þat sufficiþ bi
eche day, þat I asay þe puple where it goiþ in my lawe, eþer nay. ⁵Soþeli, in
þe sixte day gadere þei þat þat þei schulen bere yn, and be it doubil ouer þat
þat þei werun wont to gadere bi eche day. ⁶And Moyses and Aaron seiden
to alle þe sones of Israel, At euentide ȝe schulen wite þat þe Lord ledde ȝou   1275
out of þe lond of Egipt, ⁷and in þe morewetide ȝe schulen se þe glorie of
þe Lord, for I herde ȝoure grucchinge aȝens þe Lord. Soþeli, | what ben   f. 248ʳᵇ
we, for ȝe grucchen aȝens vs? ⁸And Moyses seide, The Lord schal ȝeue
to ȝou at euentide fleischis to ete, and looues in þe morewetide in plente,
for he herde ȝoure grucchingis bi whiche ȝe grucchiden aȝens hym. For-   1280
whi, what ben we? Ȝoure grucchinge is not anentis vs but aȝens þe Lord.
⁹And Moyses seide to Aaron, Seye to alle þe congregaciouns of þe sones
of Israel: Nyȝe ȝe bifor þe Lord, for he herde ȝoure grucchynge. ¹⁰And
whanne Aaron spak to al þe cumpenye of þe sones of Israel, þei bihelden
into þe wildirnesse, and lo, þe glorie of þe Lord apperide in a cloude.   1285

[LECTION 65]

The Moneday lessoun. Isaye 1º, d.

In þo dayes, Isaye *seide*: ⁵The Lord God openede an eere to me. Forsoþe, I
aȝenseie not, I ȝede not abak. ⁶I ȝaf my body to smyters and my chekis to
pullers. I turnede not awei my face fro men blamynge and spetynge on me.
⁷The Lord God is myn helper, and þerfor I am not schent, þerfor I haue   1290
sette my face as a stoon moost hard, and I | woot þat I schal not be schent;   f. 248ᵛᵃ
⁸he is nyȝ þat iustifieþ me. Who aȝenseiþ me? Stonde we togidre. Who is
myn aduersarie? Nyȝe he to me. ⁹Lo, þe Lord God is myn helper, who
þerfor is he þat condempneþ me? Lo, alle schulen be defoulid as a clooþ,
and a mouȝþe schal ete hem. ¹⁰Who of ȝou drediþ þe Lord and heeriþ þe   1295
voice of his seruaunt? Who ȝede in derknesses and liȝt is not in him, hope
he in þe name of his Lord, and truste he on his God.

1270 reyne] rey Bo   1271 sufficiþ] suffisen Ny, sufficen LaBxRa   1272 Soþeli]
and soþeli Ny   1273 þat³] *om.* LaSeBxRa   1277 for] for so Ny   1278 gruc-
chen] grucchiden Ny   1280 grucchingis] *prec. by* g *canc. at end of prec. line* Bo
1281 anentis] aȝens NyLaSeBxRa   1282 Seye] *add.* þou LaSeBxRa   1287 God]
om. NySe   openede] opene Ra   1288 aȝenseie] aȝenstood Ra   1294 he] *om.* Bx
1295 a] *om.* Se   1297 his¹] þe NyLaSeBx

[LECTION 66]

The Tewisday lessoun. Ieremy xj°, e.

In þo daies, Ieremye seyde: ¹⁸Thou, Lord, forsoþe hast schewide to me, and
1300 I knewe; þou schewedist to me þe studies of hem. ¹⁹And I am as a mylde
lomb whiche is borun to slayn sacrifice, and I knewe not þat þei þouȝten
counceils of me and seiden, Sende we a tre into þe breed of hym, and reise
we hym awey fro þe lond of lyuers, and his name be no more hadde in
mynde. ²⁰But þou, Lord of oostis, þat demyst iustli and preuest reynes
1305 and hertis, se I þi veniaunce of hem, for to þee I schewide my cause, *Lord
my God.*

[LECTION 67]

The Wednesday lessoun. Isaye lxij°, g. |

f. 248ᵛᵇ *The Lord God seiþ þese þingis:* ¹¹Seye ȝe to þe douȝtir of Syon, Lo, þi sauyoure comeþ; lo, his mede is wiþ hym, and his werk is bifore hym. ¹²And
1310 þei schulen clepe hym an holy puple, aȝenbouȝt of þe Lord. Thou, forsoþe,
schalt be clepide a souȝt citee, and not forsaken.

lxiij°, a.

¹Who is þis þat cam fro Edom, wiþ steynede cloþis of Bozra? This schapli
in his stoole, goynge in þe multitude of his vertu? I þat speke riȝtwisnesse,
1315 and a forfiȝter am to sauen. ²Whi þanne is þi cloþinge reed, and þi cloþinge
as of men tredynge in þe presse? ³The presse I trad aloon, and of þe folk of
kynde þere is not a man wiþ me; I tradde hem in my woodnesse, and togidre
trad hem in my wraþþe, and þe blood of hem is spreynt on my cloþis, and
alle my cloþingis I defoulid. ⁴Forwhi a day of veniaunce is in myn herte,
1320 and þe ȝeer of myn ȝildynge cam. ⁵I biheeld aboute, and þere was not an
helper. I souȝte, and þere was not þat halp, and myn indignacioun sauede to
f. 249ʳᵃ me myn arm and it halp to me. | ⁶I al to-trad puplis in my woodnesse, and
I drunkenede hem in myn indignacioun, and drowe doun þe vertu of hem
into erþe. ⁷Of þe mercy doyngis of þe Lord I schal recorde, þe preysingis
1325 of þe Lord on alle þingis þat haþ ȝolden to vs þe Lord, *oure God.*

1299 and] þat Ny   1305 þi] þe Ny   1313 of] fro LaSeBxRa   1318 in] *om.*
Se   1322–4 I al . . . into erþe] *om.* LaBxRa   1324 erþe] þe erþe Ny   preysingis]
preisinge Se

[LECTION 68]

On þe same day anoþer lessoun. Isaye liij°, a.

In þo daies, Isaye seide: Lord, ¹who bileuede to oure heerynge? And þe arm
of þe Lord, to whom is it schewide? ²And it schal stye vp as a quicke hegge
bifore hym, and as a root fro þe þristynge erþe. There is not schap to hym,
neþer fairnesse, and we seyen hym, and he was not of siȝt, and we desiriden   1330
hym, ³dispisid and þe laste of men, a man of sorowis and knowynge sikenesse. And his cheer was as hid and dispiside, wherfor and we arettiden not
hym. ⁴Verrili he suffrid oure sikenessis, and he bare oure sorowis, and we
arettiden him as a myssel, and smytun of God, and made lowe. ⁵Forsoþe,
he was woundide for oure wickidnessis, he was defoulid for oure greet   1335
trispassis, þe lernynge of oure pees | was on hym, and we ben mad [hool]   f. 249ʳᵇ
bi his wannesse. ⁶Alle we erriden as scheep, eche man bowide into his owne
wey; þe Lord puttide in hym þe wickidnesse of vs alle. ⁷He was offride, for
he wolde, and he openede not his mouþ as a scheep he schal be ledde to
sleynge, and he schal be doumbe as a lomb bifore hym þat clippiþ it, and he   1340
schal not opene his mouþ. ⁸He is takun awey fro angwische and fro doom.
Who schal telle out þe generacioun of hym? For he was kitte doun fro þe
lond of lyuers. I smoot him for þe greet trispasse of my puple. ⁹And he
schal ȝeue vnfeiþful men for biriynge and riche men for his deeþ, for he
dide not wickidnesse, neþer gile was in his mouþ, ¹⁰and þe Lord wolde   1345
defoule hym in sikenesse. If he puttiþ his lijf for synne, he schal se seed
long durynge, and þe wille of þe Lord schal be dressid in his hond. ¹¹For
þat þat his soule traueilid, he schal se, and schal be fillid. Thilke my iust
seruaunt schal iustifie many men in his | comynge, and he schal bere þe   f. 249ᵛᵃ
wickidnesse of hem. ¹²Therfor I schal ȝilde, *eþer dele,* to hym ful many men, 1350
and he schal departe spuylis of þe strong *fendis,* for þat þat he ȝaf his lijf into
deeþ, and was arettide with felownesse men, and he dide awey þe synne of
many men, and he preiede for trispassouris, *þat it schulde not perische, seiþ*
þe Lord almiȝti.

1328 as a quicke hegge bifore hym] bifore him as a quyk hegge LaRa   1329 þe] *om.*
Se   1331 a] *om.* Bx   1336 hool] LaRa Vu, lowe Bo, lowȝ Ny   1337 Alle]
and Ny   1340 it] him La   1342 doun] awey Ny   1347–51 For þat . . .
strong fendis] *om.* LaBxRa   1349 comynge] kunnyng Se   1350 wickidnesse]
wickidnessis Ny   1351 þat¹] *om.* Ra   1353 it schulde] þei schulden LaSeBxRa
not] *om.* Ny

[LECTION 69]

1355   The firste lessoun on Good Fryday. Osee vj°, a.

¹In her tribulacioun, þei schulen rise erli to me. Come ʒe, and turne we
aʒen to þe Lord. ²For he took, and schal heele vs. He schal smyte and schal
make vs hool. ³He schal quykene vs aftir two daies, and in þe þridde day
he schal reise vs, and we schulen lyue in his siʒt. We schulen wite and sue
1360   þat we knowe þe Lord. His goynge out is made redy as þe morewetide,
and he schal come as a reyn to vs, which is tymful and lateful to þe erþe.
⁴Effrahym, what schal I do to þee? Iuda, what schal I do to þee? ʒoure merci
is as a cloude of þe morewetide and as dewe passynge forþ eerli. ⁵For þis
f. 249ᵛᵇ   þing I hewide in profetis, | I killide hem in þe wordis of my mouþ. ⁶And
1365   þi domes schulen go out as liʒt. For I wolde merci and not sacrifice, and þe
kunnynge of God more þanne brent sacrifice.

[LECTION 70]

The secunde lessoun of þe same dai. Exodi xij°, a.

¹The Lord seide to Moyses and Aaron in þe lond of Egipt: ²This moneþe,
þe bigynnynge of moneþis to ʒou, schal be þe firste in þe moneþis of þe
1370   ʒeer. ³Speke ʒe to al þe cumpenye of þe sones of Israel and seie ʒe to hem,
In þe tenþe day of þis moneþe, eche man take a lomb bi hise meynees and
housis. ⁴But if þe noumbre is lasse, þat it may not suffice to ete þe lomb,
he schal take his neiʒbore whiche is ioynede to his hous, bi þe noumbre of
soulis þat moun suffice to þe etynge of þe lomb. ⁵Forsoþe, þe lomb schal
1375   be a male of o ʒeer, withoute wemme, bi whiche custum ʒe schuln take also
a kyde. ⁶And ʒe schulen kepe hym til to þe fourtenþe day of þis moneþe,
and al þe multitude of þe sones of Israel, þat is eche hous, schal offre hym
f. 250ʳᵃ   at euentide. | ⁷And þei schulen take of his blood and schulen putte on
euer eiþer post and in þe hiʒer þreischfoldis of þe housis in whiche þei schu-
1380   len ete hym. ⁸And in þat nyʒte þei schulen ete fleischis, roostide wiþ fire,
and þerf looues wiþ letusis of þe feeld. ⁹ʒe schulen not ete þerof ony rawe
þing, neþer soden in watir, but roostide oonli bi fire. ʒe schulen deuouren
þe heed wiþ feet and entraylis þerof; ¹⁰neþer ony þing þerof schal abide
til to þe morwetide. If ony þing is residewe, ʒe schulen brenne in þe fire.

1356 erli] *om.* Ny   1360 þe²] *om.* Se   1361 a] *om.* Se   1363 as¹] *om.* Se
1364 I²] and I Ny   in²] in in Bo   1375 schuln] mowen Ra   1376 to] *om.* SeBxRa
1379 þe¹] *om.* LaSeBxRa   1382 schulen] *add.* not Ra   1383 wiþ] and La   feet]
þe feet Ny   and] wiþ La   1384 in] it in Ny   þe²] *om.* SeBx

¹¹Forsoþe, þus ȝe schulen ete hym: ȝe schulen girde ȝoure reynes and ȝe 1385
schulen haue schoon in þe feet, and ȝe schulen holde staues in hondis, and
ȝe schulen ete hastili, for it is phase, þat is, passynge of þe Lord.

[LECTION 71]

The firste lessoun on Estir Euen. Genesis j°, a.

¹In þe firste bigynnynge God made of nauȝt heuene and erþe. ²Forsoþe, þe
erþe was idil and voide, and derknessis werun on þe face of depþe. And þe 1390
spirit of þe Lord was born on watris. ³And God seide: Liȝt be made. And
liȝt was made. ⁴And God say þe liȝt, þat | it was good, and he departide þe f. 250ʳᵇ
liȝt fro derknessis, and he clepide þe liȝt, day, and derknessis, nyȝt. And
þe euentide and þe morewetide was made, oo day. ⁶And God seide: The
firmament be made in þe myddis of watris, and departe watris fro watris. 1395
⁷And God made þe firmament and departide þe watris þat werun vndir þe
firmament fro þese watris þat werun on þe firmament. And it was don so.
⁸And God clepide þe firmament, heuene. And þe euentide and þe morwetide was made on þe secunde day. ⁹Forsoþe, God seide: The watris þat
ben vndir heuene be gaderide into o place, and a drye place appere. And 1400
it was don so. ¹⁰And God clepide þe drye place, erþe, and he clepide þe
gaderyngis togidre of watris, þe sees. And God say þat it was good, ¹¹and
seide: The erþe brynge forþ greene erbe and makynge seed, and an appil
tre makynge fruyt bi his kynde, whos seed be in itsilf on erþe. And it was
don so. ¹²And þe erþe brouȝt forþ greene erbe and makynge seed bi his 1405
kynde, and a tre makynge fruyt, and eche hauynge seed bi his kynde. And
God say | þat it was good. ¹³And þe euentide and þe morewetide was mad, f. 250ᵛᵃ
þe þridde day. ¹⁴Forsoþe, God seide: Liȝtis be made in þe firmament of
heuene, and departe þo þe dai and þe nyȝte, and be þo into signes and
tymes and daies and ȝeeris, ¹⁵and schyne þo in þe firmament of heuene, 1410
and liȝtne þo erþe. And it was don so. ¹⁶And God made two greet liȝtis, þe
gretter liȝt þat it schulde be bifore to þe day, and þe lasse liȝte þat it schulde
be bifore to þe nyȝte. And God *made* sterris ¹⁷and settide þo in þe firmament of heuene, þat þo schulden schyne on erþe, ¹⁸and þat þo schulden be
bifore to þe day and nyȝt, and schulden departe liȝt and derknesse. And 1415

1389 firste] *om.* NyLaSeBxRa   1392 þe²] *om.* La   1393 day] þe day Ny
derknessis] þe derknessis Se   1394 þe²] *om.* NyLaSeBxRa   1398 þe²] *om.* Se
þe³] *om.* SeBxRa   1399 on] *om.* NyLaSeBxRa   1404 makynge] make Ra   be]
ben Se   in] *om.* Se   on erþe] on þe erþe Ny   1406 makynge] make Ra   1407 and]
þe morewetide] *om.* Se   þe²] *om.* LaBxRa   1409 þe] *om.* LaBxRa   1411 erþe] þe
erþe Ny   1412 to] *om.* Ny   1413 to] *om.* Ny   settide] stettide Se   1414 þo²]
þei Ra   1415 derknesse] derknessis Ny

God say þat it was good. ¹⁹And þe euentide and þe morewetide was made, þe fourþe day. ²⁰Also God seide: The watris brynge forþ a crepynge beest of soule lyuynge, and a brid fleynge aboue þe erþe vndir þe firmament of heuene. ²¹And God made of nauȝt greet whalis, and eche soule lyuynge and

1420 mouable, whiche þe watris brouȝten forþ into her kyndis. And God made

f. 250ᵛᵇ of nauȝte eche volatil bi his kynde. And | God say þat it was good, ²²and blesside hem, and seide: Wexe ȝe and be ȝe multipliede, and fille ȝe þe watris of þe see, and briddis be multipliede on erþe. ²³And þe euentide and þe morwetide was made, þe fifþe day. ²⁴And God seide: The erþe brynge forþ

1425 a lyuynge soule in his kynde, werk beestis and crepynge beestis and beestis of erþe bi her kyndis. And it was don so. ²⁵And God made [vn]resonable beestis of erþe bi her kyndis and werk beeste and eche crepynge beest of erþe in his kynde. And God say þat it was good and seide: ²⁶Make we man to oure ymage and lickenesse, and be he souereyn to þe fisschis of þe see

1430 and to þe volatils of heuene and to vnresonable beestis of erþe and to eche creature and to eche reptile whiche is mouede in þe erþe. ²⁷And God made of nauȝte a man to his ymage a[nd] liknesse; God made of nauȝte a man to þe ymage of God. God made of nauȝt hem, male and female. ²⁸And God blessid hem and seide: Encreese ȝe and be ȝe multiplied, and fille ȝe

1435 þe erþe, and make ȝe it suget, and be ȝe lordis to fisschis of þe see, and to

f. 251ʳᵃ volatils | of heuene, and to alle lyuynge beestis þat ben moued on þe erþe. ²⁹And God seide: Lo, I haue ȝouun to ȝou eche erbe berynge seed on erþe, and alle trees þat han in hemsilf seed of her kynde, þat þo ben into mete to ȝou, ³⁰and to alle liuynge beestis of þe erþe, and to eche bridde of heuene,

1440 and to alle þingis þat ben mouede on erþe, and in which is lyuynge soule, þat þo han to ete. And it was don so. ³¹And God say alle þingis whiche he made, and þo werun ful good. And þe euentide and þe morwetide was made, þe [sixte] day. [Gen. 2] ¹Therfor heuenes and erþe ben made perfiȝt, and al þe ournement of þo. ²And God fulfild in þe seuenþe day his werk

1445 whiche he made, and he restid in þe seuenþe day fro his werk whiche he hadde made.

1416 þe²] om. LaSeBxRa   1423 þe³] om. LaSeBxRa   1426 erþe] þe erþe NyLaSeRa   vnresonable] vnresonable LaSeBxRa, resonable BoNy, bestias terrae Vu   1427 erþe] þe erþe NyRa   beeste] beestis NyLaSeRa   eche] prec. by e canc. Bo   1428 erþe] þe erþe Ny   1429 to¹] on Ny   1430 vnresonable] þe vnresonable NySe   erþe] þe erþe Ny   1431 to] om. Ra   1432 and] and NyLaSeBxRa, a Bo   God made of nauȝte a man to þe ymage of God] om. Se   1435 lordis] lord Ra   fisschis] þe fisschis Ny   1436 volatils] þe volatilis Ny   1439 of þe] on La, of SeBxRa   1440 on] in SeBxRa   and²] om. Ny   1442 made] had made Ra   þe²] om. LaRa   1443 sixte] sixte LaSeBx, vj Ra, seuenþe Bo, sextus Vu   1445 made] hadde maad Ny   fro] of Ny

[LECTION 72]

The secunde lessoun. Exodi xiiij°, c.

²⁴And now was come þe morewtide, and now, lo, þe Lord biheld on þe castels of Egipcians bi a piler of fire and of cloude, and killid þe oost of hem.
And he distriede þe wheelis of charis, ²⁵and | þo werun borun into depþe.   f. 251ʳᵇ
Therfor Egipcianes seiden: Fle we Israel, for þe Lord fiȝtiþ for hem aȝens   1451
vs! ²⁶And þe Lord seide to Moyses: Holde forþ þin hond on þe see, þat þe
watris turne aȝen to Egipcianes, on þe charis and knyȝtis of hem. ²⁷And
whanne Moyses had holde forþ þe hond aȝens þe see, it turnede aȝen firste
in þe morwetide to þe former place. And whanne Egipcians fledden, þe   1455
watris camen aȝen, and þe Lord wlappide hem in þe myddis of þe floodis.
²⁸And þe watris turneden aȝen and hileden þe charis and knyȝtis of al þe
oost of Farao, whiche sueden and entriden into þe see, soþeli, not oon of
hem was alyue. ²⁹Forsoþe [þe] sones of Israel ȝeden þoruȝ þe myddis of þe
drie see, and þe watris werun to hem as a wal on þe riȝt side and lefte side.   1460
³⁰And in þat day, þe Lord delyuerid Israel fro þe hond of Egipcianes, and
þei sayen þe Egipcianes deed on þe brynke of þe see, ³¹and *þei sayen* the
greet hond whiche þe Lord hadde vside aȝens hem, and þe puple dredde
þe Lord, and þei bileueden to þe Lord and to Moyses his seruaunt. [Exod.
15] ¹Thanne | Moyses song, and þe sones of Israel, þis song to þe Lord,   f. 251ᵛᵃ
and seiden.   1466

[LECTION 73]

The iij lessoun. Isaye iiij°, a.

The Lord seiþ þes þingis: ¹Seuen wommen schulen cacche o man in þat day,
and schulen seie: We schulen ete oure breed, and we schulen be hilid wiþ
oure cloþis: oonli þi name be clepide on vs; do þou awey oure schenschip.   1470
²In þat day, þe burioynynge of þe Lord schal be in greet worschip and
glorie, and þe fruyt of erþe *schal* be hiȝe, and ful out-ioie *schal be* to hem
þat schulen be saued of Israel. ³And it schal be: eche þat is lefte in Syon
and is residue in Ierusalem schal be clepide holy, eche þat is writun in lijf
in Ierusalem, ⁴if þe Lord waischiþ awey þe filþis of þe douȝtris of Syon,   1475

1448 was] is Ny   now²] *om.* NyLaSeRa   biheld] *add.* wraþfulli La   1449 cloude]
a cloude Se   1450 depþe] þe depþe LaSeBx   1451 Egipcianes] þe egipcians
SeBx   1454 aȝens] on SeBx   1455 þe¹] *om.* Ra   Egipcians] þe egipcians
Se   1456 wlappide] wrappide Ny, involvit Vu   1459 þe sones] þe sones Ny,
sones BoLaSeBx   1460 þe¹] *om.* SeBx   as] *add.* for LaSeBxRa   1470 name]
add. Lord Se   1475 douȝtris] doȝtir Bx

and waischiþ þe blood of Ierusalem fro þe myddis þerof, in þe spirit of doom, and in þe spirit of heete. ⁵And þe Lord made on eche place of þe hil of Syon and where he was clepide to help, a cloude bi day, and smoke and briȝtnesse of fire flawmynge in þe nyȝte, forwhi hilinge, *or defendynge*, schal

f. 251ᵛᵇ be aboue al glorie. ⁶And a tabernacle schal be into a | schadewynge place
1481 of þe day of heete and into sikirnesse and into huydynge fro whirlewind and fro reyn.

[LECTION 74]

The iiij lessoun. Deuteronomy xxxjº, f.

In þo daies, ²²Moyses wroot þe song and tauȝte þe sones of Israel. ²³And
1485 þe Lord comaundide to Iosue, þe sone of Nun, and seide: Be þou counfortid and be þou strong, for þou schalt lede þe sones of Israel into þe lond which I bihiȝte, and I schal be wiþ þee. ²⁴Therfor aftir þat Moyses wroot þe wordis of þis lawe in a book and fillide, ²⁵he comaundide þe Leuytees þat baren þe ark of boond of pees of þe Lord, ²⁶and seide, Take ȝe þis book,
1490 and putte ȝe it in þe side of þe ark of boond of pees of [ȝ]oure Lord God, þat it be þere aȝens þee into witnessyng. ²⁷For I knowe þi stryuynge and þi hardist nolle, ȝit while I lyuede and entrid wiþ ȝou, ȝe diden euer stryuyngli aȝens þe Lord. How moche more whanne I schal be deed? ²⁸Gadere ȝe to me alle þe gretter men in birþe and techers bi [ȝ]oure lynagis, and I
1495 schal speke to hem heerynge þese wordis. I schal clepe aȝens hem heuen |
f. 252ʳᵃ and erþe. ²⁹For I knowe þat aftir my deeþ ȝe schulen do wickidli, and schulen bowe awey soone fro þe wey whiche I comaundide to ȝou, and yuelis schulen come to ȝou in þe laste tymes whanne ȝe han don yuel in þe siȝt of þe Lord, þat ȝe terre him to yre bi þe werkis of ȝoure hondis. ³⁰Therfor
1500 while al þe cumpenye of þe sones of Israel herde, Moyses spak þe wordis of þis song, and fillid til to þe ende.

[LECTION 75]

The firste lessoun on Witson Euen. Genesis xxijº, a.

¹God asaiede Abraham and seide to hym: Abraham, Abraham! He answeride: I am present. ²God seide to hym: Take þi sone oon gendride,

1481 of] fro NyLaSeBxRa   1487 which] þat La   bihiȝte] *add.* hem La
1490 ȝoure] ȝoure NyLaSeBxRa, oure Bo, vestri Vu   1492 hardist] hard Ra
1494 ȝe] *om.* Se   ȝoure] ȝoure NyLaSeBxRa, oure Bo, vestras Vu   1495 wordis] *add.*
and LaSeBxRa   1498 tymes] tyme Bx   1504 sone oone gendride] oon gendrid
sone Ny

whom þou louest, Isaac, and go into þe lond of visioun, and offre þou hym 1505
þere into brent sacrifice on oon of þe hillis whiche I schal schewe to þee.
³Therfor Abraham roos bi ny3te and sadelid his asse, and ladde wiþ hym
two 3unge men and Isaac, his sone. And whanne he hadde hewe trees
into brent sacrifice, he 3ede to þe place whiche God hadde comaundide to
hym. ⁴Forsoþe, in þe þridde day he reiside hise i3en and | say a place afer, f. 252ʳᵇ
⁵and he seide to hise children: Abide 3e heer wiþ þe asse, I and þe child 1511
schulen go þidir. And aftir þat we han worschipide, we schulen turne a3en
to 3ou. ⁶And he took þe trees of brente sacrifice and puttide on Isaac, his
sone. Forsoþe, he bare fire and a swerd in hise hondis. And whanne þo two
3eden togidre, Isaac seide to his fadir: My fadir! ⁷And he answerd: What 1515
wolte þou, sone? And he seide: Lo, fire and trees, where is þe beest of
brent sacrifice? ⁸Abraham seide: My sone, God schal purueie to hym þe
beest of brent sacrifice. ⁹Therfor þei 3eden togidre and camen to þe place
whiche God hadde schewide to hym, in whiche place Abraham bildide an
auter and dresside trees aboue. And whanne he hadde bounden togidre 1520
Isaac, his sone, he puttide Isaac in þe auter on þe heep of trees. ¹⁰And
he heeld forþ his hond and took þe swerd to sacrifice his sone. ¹¹And lo,
an aungel of þe Lord criede fro heuene and seide: Abraham, Abraham!
¹²Whiche answerid: I am present. And þe aungel seide to hym, Holde þou
not forþ þi hond on þe child, | neþer do þou ony þing to hym. Now I haue f. 252ᵛᵃ
knowe þat þou dredist God and sparist not þin oon gendride sone for me. 1526
¹³Abraham reiside hise i3en and say bihynde his bak a ram cleuynge bi
þe hornes among breris, whiche he took and offride brent sacrifice for þe
sone. ¹⁴And he clepi[de] þe name of þat place: þe Lord seeþ. Therfor it is
seide til to þis day, þe Lord schal se in þe hil. ¹⁵Forsoþe, þe aungel of þe 1530
Lord clepide Abraham þe secunde tyme fro heuene ¹⁶and seide: The Lord
seiþ, I haue swoor bi mysilf, for þou hast do þis þing and hast not sparide
þin oon gendride sone for me, ¹⁷I schal blesse þee and I schal multiplie
þi seed as þe sterris of heuene and as grauel whiche is in þe brynke of þe
see. Thi seed schal gete þe 3atis of þin enemyes, ¹⁸and alle þe folkis of erþe 1535
schulen be blessid in þi seed, for þou obeyedist to my voice. ¹⁹Abraham
turnede a3en to hise children, and þei 3eden to Bersabe togidre, and he
dwellide þere.

1509 to¹] into Ra   whiche] *prec. by* w *canc. at end of prec. line* Bo   1514 a]
om. Ra   1515 What] *prec. by* w *canc. at end of prec. line* Bo   1516 sone] my
sone Ny   And] *om.* SeBxRa   1519 hadde] haþ Ny   1521 trees] þe trees
Se   1524 þou] *om.* Ra   1525 þou] *add.* not Se   1527 and] *add.* he NyLaSeRa
1529 clepide] clepiþ BoSeRa, clepide NyLa, appellavitque Vu   1534 grauel] þe grauel
Ny   1536 Abraham] and abraham Ny

[LECTION 76]

The secunde lessoun on þe same day.

1540 Moyses wroot a song *et cetera.*

And is red bifore on Ester Euen. |

[LECTION 77]

f. 252ᵛᵇ   And þe þridde is þis.

And seuen wommen schulen cacch.

And is red on Ester Euen also.

[LECTION 78]

1545   The iiij lessoun on þe same day. Baruk iij, a.

⁹Israel, heere þou þe comaundementis of lijf, and perseyue þou with eeris, þat þou kunne prudence. ¹⁰Israel, what is it [þat] þou art in þe lond of enemyes? ¹¹And þou wexidist elde in an alien lond. Thou art defoulid wiþ deed men; þou art arettid with hem þat goen doun into helle. ¹²Thou hast 1550 forsake þe wel of wisdom, ¹³ forwhi if þou haddist go in þe weyes of God, soþeli þou haddist dwellide in pees on erþe. ¹⁴Lerne þou where is wisdom, where is prudence, where is vertu, where is vndirstondynge, þat þou wite togidre where is long durynge of lijf and lifelood, where is liȝt of iȝen and pees. ¹⁵Who foond þe place þerof, and who entride into þe tresouris þerof? 1555 ¹⁶Where ben þe pryncis of heþen men þat ben lordis ouer þe beestis þat ben on erþe? ¹⁷Whiche pleyen wiþ þe briddis of heuene, ¹⁸whiche tresouren | f. 253ʳᵃ siluer and gold, in whiche men tristen, and noon eend is of þe purcha-synge of hem? Whiche maken siluer and ben bisy, and no fyndynge is of her werkis? ¹⁹Thei ben distriede and ȝeden doun to hellis, and oþer men 1560 riseden in þe place of hem. ²⁰The ȝonge men of hem sayen liȝt and dwel-liden on erþe, but þei knewen not þe wey of wisdom, neþer vndirstoden þe paþis þerof, ²¹neþer þe sones of hem resceyueden it. It was made fer fro þe face of hem; ²²it is not herd in þe lond of Chanaan, neþer is seen in Theman. ²³Also þe sones of Agar þat souȝten out prudence which is of

1546 and] *om.* SeBx   1547 þat²] *om.* Bo, þat NyLaSeBx   1548 And] *om.*
NyLaSeBxRa   1550 haddist] hast Ra   in] *om.* Se   1551 haddist] hast Ra
1555 Where] *prec. by* w *canc. at end of prec. line* Bo   men] *add.* and SeBxRa   1564 þat]
whiche Ny

erþe, þe marchauntis of erþe and of Theman, and þe tale tellers, and þe 1565
sekers out of prudence and of vndirstondynge, but þei knewen not þe wey
of wisdom, neþer hadden mynde on þe paþis þerof. ²⁴A Israel, þe hous of
God is ful greet, and þe place of his possessioun is greet; ²⁵it is greet and
haþ noon ende, hi3 and greet withouten mesure. ²⁶Namyde giauntis werun
þere; þei þat werun of greet stature at þe | bigynnynge and knewen bateil. f. 253ʳᵇ
²⁷The Lord chees not þese, neþer þei founden þe wey of wisdom, þerfor 1571
þei perischeden. ²⁸And for þei hadden not wisdom, þei perischeden for her
vnwisdom. ²⁹Who stiede into heuene and took þat _wisdom_, and brou3te it
doun fro þe cloudis? ³⁰Who passide ouer þe see and foond it, and brou3te it
more þan chosun gold? ³¹And noon is þat may knowe þe weye þerof, neþer 1575
þat sekiþ þe paþis þerof, ³²but he þat can alle þingis knewe it, and foond it
bi his prudence. Which made redy þe erþe in euerlastynge tyme, and fillid
it wiþ two footid beestis and foure footide beestis, ³³which sendiþ out li3t,
and it goiþ, and clepide it, and it obeyede to hym in tremblynge. ³⁴Forsoþe,
sterris 3auen li3t in her kepyngis and werun glad; ³⁵þo werun clepide, and 1580
þo seiden, We ben present. And þo schyneden into hym wiþ greet myrþe,
þat made þo. ³⁶This is oure God, and noon oþer schal be gessid a3ens hym.
³⁷This foond ech wey of wisdum, and 3af it to Iacob, his child, and to Israel,
his derlynge. ³⁸Aftir þes þingis he | was seen in londis and lyuede wiþ men. f. 253ᵛᵃ

[LECTION 79]

The Wednesdai lessoun in Witsoun Woke. Sapience j°, c.   1585

In þo dayes, Salomon seide to þe sones of Israel: ¹Loue 3e ri3twisnesse þat
demen þe erþe, fele 3e of þe Lord in goodnesse, and seke 3e hym in symple-
nesse of herte. ²For he is founden of hem þat tempten not hym. Forsoþe, he
apperiþ to hem þat han feiþ into hym. ³Forwhi weyward þoou3tis departen
fro God, but preuede vertu repreuyþ vnwise men. ⁴Forwhi wisdom schal 1590
not entre into an yuel soule, neþer schal dwelle in a body suget to synnes.
⁵Forsoþe, þe Holi Goost of wisdom schal fle awei fro a feynede man, and
he schal take awey hymsilf fro þou3tis þat ben wiþout vndirstondynge, and
þe man schal be punyschid of wickidnesse comynge aboue. ⁶For þe spirit
of wisdom is benygne, and he schal not delyuer a curside man fro hise lip- 1595
pis, forwhi God is witnesse fro hise reynes, and þe sercher of his herte is

1565 erþe²] þe erþe Ny   1568 greet³] _om._ Ny   1574 Who] and who Se
1575 And] _om._ LaSeBxRa   1576 þingis] þing Ra   1578 which] _prec. by_ w _canc._
at end of prec. line Bo   1579 clepide] clepiþ Ra   in] _om._ Se   1581 greet]
_om._ LaSeBxRa   1587 of] _om._ Se   in²] _add._ þe LaSeBxRa   1589 to] into
Ra   1591 yuel] yuel willid NyLaSeRa   1596 fro] of La   þe] _om._ Se

trewe, and þe heerer of his tunge. ⁷Forwhi þe spirit of þe Lord haþ fillid þe
f. 253ᵛᵇ worlde, þat þis | þing þat conteyneþ alle þingis haþ þe kunynge of voice.

[LECTION 80]

On Trynyte Euen þe first lessoun. Ioel iijᵒ, a. [Joel 2]

1600 The Lord God seiþ þes þingis: ²⁸I schal schede out my spirit on ech man,
and ȝoure sones and ȝoure douȝtris schulen profecie; ȝoure elde men schulen dreme dremes, and ȝoure ȝunge men schulen se visiouns *eþer reuela-
ciouns*. ²⁹But also I schal schede out my spirit on my seruauntis and handmaydens in þo daies, ³⁰and I schal ȝeue greet wondris in heuene and in
1605 erþe, blood and fire and þe heete of smoke. ³¹The sunne schal be turnede
into derknessis and þe moone into blood, bifor þat þe grete day and orible
of þe Lord schal come. ³²And it schal be: eche þat schal clepe to help þe
name of þe Lord, schal be saaf.

[LECTION 81]

The secunde lessoun on þe same day. Leuiticus xxiijᵒ, c.

1610 *In þo daies*, ⁹þe Lord spak to Moyses and seide: ¹⁰Speke þou to þe sones of
Israel, and þou schalt seye to hem, Whanne ȝe han entride into þe lond
whiche I schal ȝeue to ȝou, and han repe corn, ȝe schulen bere hond-
f. 254ʳᵃ fullis of eeris of corn, þe firste fruytis | of ȝoure ripe corn, to þe prest,
¹¹and þe prest schal reise a bundel bifore þe Lord, þat it be acceptable for
1615 ȝou, in þe toþer day of Saboth, *þat is of pask*, and þe preest schal halowe
þat bundel. ¹⁵Therfor ȝe schulen noumbre fro þat oþer day of Saboth, in
which ȝe offriden hondfullis of firste fruytis, ¹⁶seuen ful wookis til to þe
toþer day of fillynge of þe seuenþe woke, *þat is fifti daies*. And so ȝe schulen
¹⁷offre newe sacrifice to þe Lord of alle ȝoure dwellynge placis, two loues
1620 of þe firste fruytis of þe two tenþe partis, *whiche þe preest schal reise bifore
þe Lord*, of floure diȝte wiþ sourdouȝ, which loues ȝe schulen bake into þe
firste fruytis to þe Lord. ¹⁸And ȝe schulen offre wiþ looues seuen lambren
of o ȝeer wiþoute wemme, and o calf of þe droue, and two rammes, and
þese schulen be wiþ brent sacrifice, wiþ her fletynge offryngis into swettist

1598 þat] and La   1599 iij] þe secunde chapiter Ny   1605 þe] *om.* La
1607 schal¹] *om.* LaSeBxRa   to help] *om.* LaSeBxRa   1611 seye] *prec. by* s *canc.
at end of prec. line* Bo   1615 in] into NySe   of²] *om.* SeBx   1616 þat²] þe LaSe
BxRa   1617 to] *om.* La   1618 þat is fifti daies] *om.* LaSeBxRa   1620 þe²]
om. BxRa   tenþe] ten La   1621–8 of floure diȝte . . . into vse] *om.* LaSeBxRa

odoure to þe Lord. ¹⁹3e schulen make also a bucke of geet for synne, and 1625
two lambren of o 3eer, sacrificis and pesible þingis. ²⁰And whanne þe preest
haþ reisid | þo wiþ þe looues of firste fruytis bifor þe Lord, þo schulen f. 254ʳᵇ
falle into vse. ²¹And 3e schulen clepe þis day moost solempne and moost
holy; 3e schulen not do þerynne ony seruyle werk. It schal be a lawful þing
euerlastynge in alle 3oure dwellyngis and generaciouns, _seiþ þe Lord almy3ti_. 1630

[LECTION 82]

The iij lessoun on þe same day. Deutronomy xxvj, a.

In þo daies, Moyses seide to þe sones of Israel: Heere, Israel, what I seye to
þee today! ¹Whanne þou hast entride into þe lond whiche þi Lord God
schal 3eue to þee to weeld, and þou hast gete it, and hast dwellide þeryn,
²þou schalt take þe firste fruytis of alle þi fruytis, and þou schalt putte in 1635
a panyer, and þou schalt go to þe place whiche þe Lord God chees, þat his
name be ynwardli clepide þere. ³And þou schalt go to þe preest þat schal
be in þo daies, and þou schalt seie to hym, I knouleche today bifore þi Lord
God, ⁷which herd vs and biheeld oure mekenesse and trauel and angwi-
schis, ⁸and he ledde vs out of Egipt in my3ti hond and arm holden forþ, | 1640
in greet drede, in myraclis and greet wondris, ⁹and ledden into þis place, f. 254ᵛᵃ
and 3af to vs a lond flowynge wiþ mylke and hony. ¹⁰And þerfor I offre now
to þee þe firste fruytis of þe fruytis of þe lond whiche þe Lord 3af to me.
And þou schalt leue þo in þe si3te of þi Lord God. And whanne þi Lord
God is worschipide, ¹¹þou schalt ete in alle þe goodis whiche þi Lord God 1645
schal 3eue to þee.

[LECTION 83]

The iiij lessoun on þe same day. Leuiticus xxvjº, b.

In þo daies, [Lev. 25] ¹þe Lord spak to Moyses: ²Speke to þe sones of Israel,
and þou schalt seye to hem: [Lev. 26] ³If 3e goen in myn heestis and kepen
my comaundementis and don þo, I schal 3eue to 3ou reynes in her tymes, 1650
⁴and þe erþe schal brynge forþ his fruyt, and trees schulen be fillid wiþ
applis. ⁵The þreischynge of ripe cornes schal take vendage, and vyndage

1628 vse] his vss Ny   1633 þi] þe Ra   1634 dwellide] weeldid Ra
1636 þe²] þi LaSeBxRa   1638 þi] þe Se   1640 he] _om._ Ny   Egipt] þe
lond of egipt Se   holden] holdynge Ny   1643 of þe fruytis] _om._ Ny   1644 þi
Lord God] þe lord SeBx   1645 worschipide] _prec. by_ w _canc. at end of prec. line_ Bo
þe] _om._ Ra   God] _om._ Ny   1646 schal 3eue] 3af LaSeBxRa   1652 vendage]
prec. by þe _canc._ Bo

schal ocupie seed, and 3e schulen ete 3oure breed in fulnesse, and 3e schulen dwelle in 3oure lond wiþouten drede. ⁶I schal 3eue pees in 3oure coostis;

f. 254ᵛᵇ 3e schulen slepe, and noon schal be þat schal make 3ou aferd. I schal | do
1656 awey yuel beestis fro 3ou, and a swerd schal not passe bi 3oure termes. ⁷3e
schulen pursue 3oure enemyes, and þei schulen falle bifore 3ou; ⁸ fyue of
3oure men schulen pursue an hundrid aliens, and an hundride of 3ou *schulen* pursue ten þousand; 3oure enemyes schulen falle bi sweerd in 3oure
1660 si3t. ⁹And I schal bihold 3ou, and I schal make to encrees; 3e schulen be
multipliede, and I schal make stidfast my couenaunt wiþ 3ou. ¹⁰3e schulen
ete eldist of elde þingis, and 3e schulen caste forþ elde þingis whanne newe
þingis schulen come aboue. ¹¹I schal sette my tabernacle in þe myddis of
3ou, and my soule schal not caste 3ou awey. ¹²I schal go among 3ou, and I
1665 schal be 3oure God, and 3e schulen be a puple to me, *seiþ þe Lord almy3ti*.

[LECTION 84]

The v lessoun on þe same day. [Dan. 3]

The aungel of þe Lord cam doun wiþ Azarie.

And is red on þe þridde Saturday of Aduent.

[LECTION 85]

The xvij Wednesdai aftir þe Trinite. Amos ix°, f.

f. 255ʳᵃ *The Lord seiþ þes þingis*: ¹³Lo, daies comen, seiþ þe Lord, and þe erer | schal
1671 take þe reper, and þe treder, *or stamper*, of grape *schal take* þe man sendynge seed, and mounteyns schulen droppe swetnesse, and alle smale hillis
schulen be tilid. ¹⁴And I schal conuerte þe caytifte of my puple Israel, and
þei schulen bilde forsaken citees, and schulen dwelle, and schuln plaunte
1675 vyners, and þei schulen drinke wiyn of hem, and schulen make gardens,
and schulen ete fruytis of hem. ¹⁵And I schal plaunte hem on her lond,
and I schal no more drawe out hem of her lond, whiche I 3af to hem, *seiþ*
þe Lord almy3ti.

1654 coostis] oostis Ra, finibus Vu   1659 þousand] þousandis Ny   1669 xvij] xxvij
Bo, seuentenþe BxNy, xvij LaRa, ymbir wodnesday in septembre Se   1674 schuln]
þei schulen Ny   1677 hem¹] *om.* Ny

[LECTION 86]

The secunde lessoun on þe same day. ij Esdre viijº.

¹Al þe puple was gaderide togidre as o man, to þe street whiche is bifore þe   1680
ȝate of watris. And þei seiden to Esdras, þe scribe, þat he schulde brynge
þe book of þe lawe of Moyses, whiche þe Lord hadde comaundide to Israel.
²Therfor Esdras, þe preest, brouȝte þe lawe bifor þe multitude of men and
of wommen, and bifore alle þat myȝten vndirstonde, in þe firste day of þe
seuenþe moneþ. | ³And he radde in it opynli in þe street þat was bifor   f. 255ʳᵇ
þe ȝate of watris, fro þe morwetide til to mydday, in þe siȝt of men and   1686
wommen and of wise men, and þe eeris of al þe puple werun reisid to þe
book. ⁴Forsoþe, Esdras þe writer stood on þe grees of þe greet tre, whiche
he hadde made to speke þeron, _and þei stoden bisidis hym_. ⁵And Esdras
openede þe book bifore al þe puple, for he apperide ouer al þe puple, and   1690
whanne he hadde openede þe book, al þe puple stood. ⁶And Esdras blessid
þe Lord God wiþ greet voice, and al þe puple answerid, Amen, reisynge
her hondis. And þei werun bowide, and þei worschipiden God loweli on
þe erþe. ⁷Forsoþe, Iosue and Baany and Serebie and Iamyn, Acub, Septay,
Odia, Maasie, Selitha, Azarie, Iosabeth, Anan, Fallaye, dekenes, maden   1695
scilence in þe puple for to heere þe lawe. Soþeli þe puple stood in her
degre, ⁸and þei redden in þe book of Goddis lawe distynctli, _eþer atreet_, and
opynli to vndirstonde, and þei vndirstoden whanne it was red. ⁹Forsoþe, |
Neemye seide, he is Athersata, and Esdras, þe prest and writer, and þe   f. 255ᵛᵃ
dekenes expownynge to al þe puple: It is a day halowide to oure Lord God.   1700
Nyle ȝe moorne and nyle ȝe wepe! For al þe puple wepte whanne it herd
þe wordis of þe lawe. ¹⁰And he seide to hem, Go ȝe and ete ȝe fatte þingis,
and drynke ȝe wiyn made swete wiþ hony, and sende ȝe partis to hem þat
maden not redi to hemsilf, for it is an holiday of þe Lord. Nyle ȝe be sory,
for þe ioye of þe Lord is ȝoure strengþe.   1705

[LECTION 87]

The Fryday lessoun. Osee xiiij, b.

The Lord seiþ þese þingis: ²Israel, be þou conuertid to þi Lord God, for þou
fildist doun in þi wickidnesse. ³Take ȝe wordis wiþ ȝou and be ȝe conuertid

1684 of²] _om._ Ra   1687 wommen] of wymmen La   1694-5 Iosue . . . Fallaye]
_om._ LaSeBxRa   1694 Baany] Bany Ny   1695 Maasie] Masie Ny   1699 he
is Athersata] _om._ LaSeBxRa   1700 expownynge] expowneden Ra   1701-2 For
al þe puple . . . þe lawe] _om._ LaSeBx   1703 ȝe¹] Se   1704 not] _om._ Ny
1706 Osee xiiij] Osee xiij La   1707-8 þi Lord . . . conuertid to] _om._ Ny

to þe Lord, and seye ȝe to hym: Do þou awey al wickidnesse, and take þou
1710 good, and we schulen ȝilde þe calues of oure lippis. ⁴Assur schal not saue
vs; we schulen not stie on hors, and we schulen no more seye, Oure Goddis ben werkis of oure hondis. For þou schalt haue merci on þat modirles
f. 255ᵛᵇ child which is in þe. ⁵I schal make hool þe sorowis | of hem, I schal loue
hem wilfuli, for my strong veniaunce is turnede awey fro hem. ⁶I schal be
1715 as dewe, and Israel schal burioyne as a lilie. And þe root þerof schal breke
out as þe Liban; ⁷þe braunchis þerof schulen go, and þe glorie þerof schal
be as an olyue tre, and þe odour þerof _schal be_ as of þe Liban. ⁸Thei schulen
be conuertid and sitte in þe schadewe of hym; þei schulen lyue bi wheete
and schulen burioyne as a vyne. The memorial þerof _schal be_ as þe wiyn
1720 of þe Lyban. ⁹Effrahym, what _schulen_ ydolis do͟ more to me? I schal heere
hym, and I schal dresse hym as a greet fir tre. Thi fruyt is founden of me.
¹⁰Who is wijs and schal vndirstonde þese þingis? Who is vndirstondynge
and schal kunne þese þingis? For þe weyes of þe Lord ben riȝtful, and iust
men schulen go in þo.

[LECTION 88]

1725   The Saturday lessoun, Leuiticus xxiij, e.

In þo daies, ²⁶þe Lord spak to Moyses and seide: In þe tenþe day of þis
seuenþe mooneþ, ²⁷þe day of clensingis schal be moost solempne, and it
f. 256ʳᵃ schal be clepide holy. | ȝe schulen turmente ȝoure soulis to God, and ȝe
schulen offre brent sacrifice to þe Lord; ²⁸ȝe schuln not do ony werk in þe
1730 tyme of þis dai, for it is þe day of clensynge, þat ȝoure Lord God be mercy-
ful to ȝou. ²⁹Ech man which is not turmentid in þis day, schal perische fro
hise puplis, ³⁰and I schal do awey fro his puple þat man þat doiþ ony þing
of werk _in þat day_. ³¹Therfor ȝe schulen not do ony þing of werk in þat day.
It schal be a lawful þing euerlastynge to ȝou in alle ȝoure generaciouns and
1735 habitaciouns; ³²it is þe Sabat of restynge. ȝe schulen turmente ȝoure soulis
fro þe nynþe day of þe moneþ; fro euentide to euentide ȝe schulen halowe
ȝoure Sabotis, _seiþ þe Lord almyȝti_.

1715 schal¹] _om._ Se   1717 as¹] _add._ of SeBx   1718 þei] and þei Se
1720 þe] _om._ SeBxRa   1721 a greet] a grene NySeBx, a greene La, _virentem_ Vu
1728 ȝe] and ȝe NyLaSeBxRa   1733 ȝe] _om._ Se   werk] _prec. by_ w _canc. at end of prec._
line Bo   1735 Sabat] Saboth NyLa

[LECTION 89]

The secunde lesson on þe same day. Leuiticus xxiij°.

In þo daies, ³³þe Lord spak to Moyses ³⁴and seide: Speke þou to þe sones
of Israel, Fro þe fiftenþe day of þis seuenþe moneþ schulen be þe feries   1740
of tabernaclis, in seuen dayes to þe Lord. ³⁵The firste day schal be clepide
moost solempne and moost holy; 3e schulen not do ony seruyle werk þeryn.
³⁶And in seuen daies 3e schulen offre brent sacrificis to þe Lord and | þe   f. 256ʳᵇ
ei3tþe day schal be moost solempne and moost holy, and 3e schulen offre
brent sacrifice to þe Lord, for it is þe day of cumpanye and of gaderynge.   1745
3e schulen not do ony seruyle werk þerynne. ³⁷These ben þe feries of þe
Lord, whiche 3e schulen clepe moost solempne and moost holy. And in þo
3e schulen offre offryngis to þe Lord, brent sacrifice and fletynge offryngis,
bi þe custum of eche day, ³⁸outaken þe Sabotis of þe Lord, and 3oure 3iftis
and whiche 3e offren bi avow, eþer which 3e 3euen bi fre wil to þe Lord.   1750
³⁹Therfor fro þe xv day of þe seuenþe moneþ, whan 3e han gaderide alle þe
fruytis of 3oure lond, 3e schulen halowe þe feries of þe Lord seuen dayes; in
þe firste day and in þe ei3tþe schal be Sabat, þat is, reste. ⁴⁰And 3e schulen
take to 3ou in þe first day fruytis of þe fairist tre, and braunchis of palm
trees, and braunchis of a tre of þicke bowis, and salewis of þe rennynge   1755
streem, and 3e schulen be glad bifor 3oure Lord God, ⁴¹and 3e schulen
halowe his solempnyte vij dayes bi þe 3eer. It schal be a lawful þing euer-
lastynge in 3oure generaciouns. | In þe vij moneþ 3e schulen halowe feestis   f. 256ᵛᵃ
⁴²and 3e schulen dwelle in schadowynge placis vij daies; eche man þat is of
þe kyn of Israel schal dwelle in tabirnaclis, þat 3oure aftircomers lerne ⁴³þat   1760
I made þe sones of Israel to dwelle in tabernaclis whanne I ledde hem out
of þe lond of Egipt; I am 3oure Lord God.

[LECTION 90]

The iij lesson on þe same day. Mychee vij°, f.

Lord oure God, ¹⁴ fede þou [þi] puple in þi 3erde, þe flok of þin eriatage,
þat dwellen aloone in wielde wood *bi oold daies,* in þe myddil of Carmel þei   1765
schulen be fed of Basan and of Galaad, ¹⁵bi elde dayes, bi daies of þi goinge
out of þe lond of Egipt. I schal schewe to hym wondirful þingis; ¹⁶heþen

1740 þis] þe LaSeRa   seuenþe] *om.* Bx   1740–51 schulen be . . . þe seuenþe moneþ]
om. LaSeBxRa   1747 Lord] *prec. by* l *canc. at end of prec. line* Bo   1752 þe¹] *om.* Se
1753 in] *om.* NyLaSeBxRa   Sabat] Saboth La   1764 þi¹] my Bo, þi NyLaSeBxRa,
tuum Vu   1765 in¹] *add.* þe Ra   1765–7 in þe myddil . . . wondirful þingis] *om.*
LaSeBxRa

men schulen se and þei schulen be confoundide on al her strengþe. Thei
schulen putte hondis on her mouþe, þe eeris of hem schulen be deef; [17]þei
1770 schulen lik dust as a serpent, as crepynge þingis of erþe þei schulen be
disturblide of her housis; þei schulen not desire oure Lord God, and þei
f. 256vb schulen drede þee. [18]God, who is like þee, þat doist awey wickidnesse | and
berist ouer þe synne of relifis of þin eritage? He schal no more sende yn his
strong veniaunce, for he is willynge merci; he schal turne aȝen, [19]and schal
1775 haue merci on vs. He schal putte doun oure wickidnessis and schal caste
fer into depnesse of þe see alle oure synnes. [20]Thou schalt ȝeue treuþe to
Iacob, merci to Abraham, which þou sworist to oure fadris fro elde daies,
Lord oure God.

[LECTION 91]

The iiij lessoun on þe same day. Zacharie viij°, e.

1780 *In þo daies, þe word of þe Lord is don to me, seiynge*: [14]For þe Lord of oostis
seiþ þes þingis, As I þouȝte for to turmente ȝou whanne ȝoure fadris hadden
terrid me to wraþþe, seiþ þe Lord, and I hadde not merci, [15]so I conuertid
þouȝt in þese daies for to do wel to þe hous of Iuda and to Ierusalem; nyle ȝe
drede. [16]Therfor þes ben þe wordis whiche ȝe schulen do. Speke ȝe treuþe,
1785 eche man wiþ his neiȝbore; deme ȝe treuþe and doom of pees in ȝoure ȝatis,
[17]and þenke ȝe not in ȝoure hertis ony man yuel aȝens his freend, and loue
f. 257ra ȝe not a false ooþ, for alle þes þingis it ben which I hate, seiþ | þe Lord.
[18]And þe word of þe Lord of oostis was made to me, [19]and seide, The Lord
of oostis seiþ þese þingis: Fastynge of þe fourþe *moneþ*, and fastynge of þe
1790 fifþe, and fastinge of þe seuenþe, and fastynge of þe tenþe schal be to þe
hous of Iuda and to ioye and gladnesse, into solempnytees ful cleer; loue
ȝe oonli treuþe and pees; [20]þe Lord of oostis seiþ þes þingis.

[LECTION 92]

The v lessoun on þe same dai. Danyel iij°, k.

The aungel of þe Lord cam doun.

1795 *And seke it on þe þridde Saturday of Aduent.*

1768–72 Thei schulen putte . . . schulen drede þee] *om.* LaSeBxRa   1772 like] *add.*
to SeBx   1774 schal] *om.* NyLaBxRa   1776 depnesse] depþe Ra   1777 þou]
om. La   1781 for] *om.* Ny   1792 þe Lord . . . þes þingis] seiþ þe lord of oostis
LaSeBxRa

[LECTION 93]

A lessoun on þe xxv Sunday aftir þe Trynyte. Ieremy xxiij°, b.

⁵Lo, daies comen, seiþ þe Lord, and I schal reise a iust burioynynge, *eþer seed*, to Dauiþ, and he schal regne kyng and he schal be wijs, and he schal make doom and rijtfulnesse in erþe. ⁶In þo daies Iuda schal be sauede, and Israel schal dwelle tristeli. This is þe name whiche þei schulen clepe hym,   1800 þe Lord oure riȝtful. ⁷For þis þing, lo, dayes comen, seiþ þe Lord, and þei schulen no more seye, þe Lord lyueþ þat ledde þe sones of Israel out of þe lond of Egipt, ⁸but þe Lord lyueþ þat ledde out and brouȝt þe seed | of þe   f. 257ʳᵇ hous of Israel fro þe lond of þe norþ and fro alle londis to whiche I hadde caste hem out þidir, and þei schuln dwelle in her lond, *seiþ þe Lord almyȝti*.   1805

[LECTION 94]

A pistil in þe feest of relikis. Ecclesiasticus xliiij°, c.

¹⁰Tho men of mercy ben, whos pitees faileden not, ¹¹and good eritage dwellide wiþ þe seed of hem contynueli, ¹²and þe seed of her sones stood in testament, ¹³and þe eritage of her sones dwellide bifore hem, into wiþouten ende. The seed of hem and þe glorie of hem schal not be forsaken. ¹⁴The   1810 bodies of hem ben biriede in pees, and þe name of hem schal lyue into generaciouns and generaciouns. ¹⁵Puplis tellen þe wisdom of hem, and þe chirche telliþ þe preisynge of hem.

Here endiþ þe reule of Sundayes and feriales, and bigynneþ þe rule of þe Propre Sanctorum.   1815

[LECTION 95]

Vpon Seint Andrewis Euen a lessoun. Ecclesiastici xliiij°, g. [Prov. 10: 6; Ecclus. 44: 26–7; Ecclus. 45: 2–9]

The blessynge of þe Lord is on þe heed of a riȝtwise man, and þerfor he haþ ȝoue eritage vnto hym, and he haþ deuydide a part vnto hym among

---

1797 Lo] *om.* Bx   1798 he³] *om.* Se   1799 rijtfulnesse] riȝtwisnesse Ny 1800 This] and þis NySeBxRa   þei] ȝe Se   1805 caste] hadde cast Ny   1807 men of mercy ben] ben men of mersy SeBx   1808 dwellide . . . contynueli] dwellide con-tynuely with þe seed of hem LaSeBx, dwelliþ contynueli wiþ þe seed of hem Ra   in] *add.* þe Ra   1809 dwellide] dwelliþ NyLaBxRa   1817 xliiij] xiiij Se   1818 þe heed of] *om.* Ny   riȝtwise] iust La   1819 vnto¹] to Se

f. 257va þe twelue kynredis, and he haþ founden grace in þe siȝt of al fleisch, | and
1821 he haþ magnefiede hym in drede of enemyes, and in hise wordis he haþ
made wondris plesynge. He haþ glorifiede hym in siȝt of kyngis, and he
haþ schewide his glorie vnto hym. In bileue and softnesse of hym he haþ
made hym holy. And he haþ chosun hym of al fleisch; he haþ ȝoue vnto
1825 hym [h]eestis and þe lawe of lijf and of lernynge, and he haþ made hym ful
hiȝ; he sette to hym an euerlastynge testament. He haþ gird hym aboute
wiþ a girdil of riȝtwisnesse, and þe Lord haþ cloþide hym wiþ þe coroun
of glorie.

[LECTION 96]

The lessoun on S. Nicholas dai. Ecclesiasticus xliiij°, d.

1830   [Ecclus. 44: 16, 17, 20, 22, 25, 26, 27; Ecclus. 45: 3, 6, 8, 19, 20]

Lo, þe greet preest which pleside to God in hise dayes, and was founden
riȝtwise, and in þe tyme of wraþfulnesse, he was made recounceilinge.
There is noon founden like to hym, þat kepte þe lawe of þe hiȝe God. Therfor þe Lord, þoruȝ his greet ooþ, haþ made hym to waxe vp into his puple.
1835 He haþ ȝouun to hym þe blessynge of alle folkis, and he haþ confermede his
testament on his heed. He haþ knowen hym in hise blessyngis; he haþ kept
f. 257vb his | mercy to hym, and he haþ founden grace bifore þe iȝen of þe Lord.
And he haþ made hym greet in þe biholdynge of kyngis, and he haþ ȝouun
to hym þe coroun of glorie. He haþ ordeyned to hym þe euerlastynge testa-
1840 ment, and he haþ ȝouun to hym greet presthode, and haþ made him blisful
in glorie to vse presthode in fredom, and to haue preising in þe name of
hym, and to offre to hym þe worþi encense into þe smelle of swetnesse.

[LECTION 108]

The lessoun on Candilmasse Day. Malachie iij°, b.

The Lord God seiþ þese þingis: ¹Lo, I sende myn aungel, and he schal make
1845 redy wey bifore my face, and anoon þe lordschiper, whom ȝe seken, schal
come to his holy temple, and þe aungel of þe testament, whom ȝe wolen.
Lo, he comeþ, seiþ þe Lord of oostis. ²And who schal mowe þenke þe day

---

1821 drede] þe drede NyLa   1822 siȝt] þe siȝt LaRa   1825 heestis] beestis
BoNy, heestis LaSeBxRa, precepta SM   ful] silf Se   1826 to] vnto SeBxRa   He]
and he SeRa   aboute] aboue SeBx   1831 to] *om.* NyRa   1836 on] upon Ra
1837 to] *prec. by* vn *canc.* Bo   1840 greet] þe greet NyRa   1840–1 and haþ . . .
to vse presthode] *om.* Ra   1846 þe²] *om.* LaRa

of his comynge? And who schal stonde for to se him? For he <u>schal be</u> as fyre wellynge togidre, and as erbe of fulleris, <u>eþer toukers</u>, ³and he schal sitte wellynge togidre and clensynge siluer, and he schal purge þe sones 1850 of Leuy. And he schal purge hem as gold and as siluer, and þei | schulen f. 258ʳᵃ be offrynge to þe Lord sacrificis in riȝtfulnesse. ⁴And þe sacrifice of Iuda and of Ierusalem schal plese to þe Lord, as þe daies of þe world and as oold ȝeeris, <u>seiþ þe Lord almyȝti</u>.

[LECTION 116]

The pistle in þe Anunciacioun of oure Ladi.   1855

The Lord spak to Achaz, c.

And is in Ymbir Wednesday bifore Cristemasse.

[LECTION 120]

The lessoun vpon Seynt Philip day and Iacob. Sapiens vᵒ, a.

¹Iuste men schulen stonde in greet stidfastnesse aȝens hem þat angwi-schen *iust men*, and which token awey her trauels. ²Thei schulen se and 1860 schulen be disturblide with orible drede, and þei schulen wondre in þe sodeynte of heelþe vnhopide, and þei schulen weile for angwische of spirit, ³and þei schulen seie, doynge penaunce wiþ[in] hemsilf and weilinge for þe angwische of spirit: These men it ben whiche we hadden sum tyme into scorne and into likenesse of vpbreidynge. ⁴We wode men gessiden her lijf 1865 woodenesse, and þe ende of hem wiþouten ony onour. ⁵Hou þerfor ben þei rikenede among þe sones of God, and her part is among seyntis?

[LECTION 137]

The lessoun on Mydsomer Euen. Ieremy primo, a. |

In þo daies, ⁴þe word of þe Lord was made to me, seiynge: Bifore þat I f. 258ʳᵇ fourmede þee in wombe, I knewe þee, and bifor þat þou ȝedist out of þe 1870 wombe, I halowide þee, and I ȝaf þee a profete among folkis. ⁶And I seide: A! A! A! Lord God, lo, I can not speke, for I am a child. ²And þe Lord

1849 erbe] þe erþe NyLa, herba Vu   eþer] *add.* of Se   1850 sitte] sette
La   1852 sacrificis] sacrifise Ny   riȝtfulnesse] riȝtwisnesse NyLaSeBxRa
1853 world] *prec. by* w *canc. at end of prec. line* Bo   1859 angwischen] anguisschiden
La   1863 wiþin] wiþ men Bo   þe] *om.* Ra   1870 þat] *om.* Se

seide to me: Nyle þou seie þat I am a child, for þou schalt go to alle þingis
to whiche I schal sende þee, and þou schalt speke alle þingis, whateuer *þingis*
1875 I schal comaunde to þee. ⁸Drede þou not of þe face of hem, for I am wiþ
þee to delyuer þee, seiþ þe Lord. ⁹And þe Lord sente his hond and touchid
my mouþ, and þe Lord seide to me: Lo, I haue ȝoue my wordis in þi mouþ.
Lo, ¹⁰I haue ordeynede þee today on folkis and on rewmes, þat þou drawe
vp, and distrye, and leese, and scater, and bilde, and plaunte.

[LECTION 138]

1880   The lessoun on Mydsomer Day. Isaye xlix°, a.

The Lord seiþ þese þingis: ¹Ylis, heere ȝe, and peplis afer, perseyue ȝe! The
Lord clepide me fro þe wombe; he þouȝte on my name fro þe wombe of my
f. 258va modir. ²And he haþ sette my | mouþ as a scharp sword; he defendid me
in þe schadewe of his hond, and sette me as a chosun arowe; he hidde me
1885 in his arowe caas ³and seide to me, Israel, þou art my seruaunt, for I schal
haue glorie in þee. ⁴And I seide, I trauailide in veyn, I wastide my strengþe
wiþout cause, and veynli, þerfor my doom is wiþ þe Lord, and my werk
is wiþ my God. ⁵And now þe Lord, foormynge me a seruaunt to hymsilf
fro þe wombe, seiþ þese þingis, þat I brynge aȝen Iacob to hym. And Israel
1890 schal not be gaderide togidre, and I am glorifiede in þe iȝen of þe Lord, and
my God is mad my strengþe. ⁶And he seide, It is litil þat þou be a seruaunt
to me to reise þe lynagis of Iacob and to conuerte þe drastis of Israel. I
ȝaf þee into liȝt of heþen men, þat þou be my helþe til to þe laste part of
erþe. ⁷The Lord, þe aȝenbier of Israel, þe holy þerof, seiþ þese þingis to a
1895 dispisable soule and to a folk had into abhomynacioun, to þe seruaunt of
lordes: Kyngis schulen see, and princis schulen rise togidre, and schulen
worschip, for þe Lord *þi God*, for he is feiþful, and *for* þe holy of Israel þat
f. 258vb chees | þee.

1879 scater] *followed by* abrood *canc.* Bo   plaunte] *add.* seiþ þe lord almiȝty
LaSeRa   1881 The Lord seiþ þese þingis] *om.* SeBx   1883 sette] settide
NySeBx   1886–8 And I seide . . . my God] *om.* LaSeBxRa   1888 foormynge]
formed Ra   1889–92 þat I bringe . . . drastis of Israel] *om.* LaSeBxRa   1892 to²]
into Bx   1894 erþe] þe erþe Ny   1894–6 The Lord . . . of lordes] *om.*
LaSeBxRa   1894 þe¹] *om.* Ny   1897 for¹] *om.* LaSeBxRa   þe¹] þee
Bx   for he is feiþful] *om.* LaSeBxRa   and] *om.* LaRa   for³] *om.* LaSeBxRa

[LECTION 140]

The lessoun in þe vtas of S. Ioon Baptist. Isaye xlix°, a.

The Lord seiþ þes þinges.   1900

[LECTION 141]

The lessoun in þe translacioun of S. Martyn.
Ecclesiasticus j° and S. Nicholas day.

Lo, a greet prest.

[LECTION 142]

The lessoun in þe vtas of S. Petir and
Poul. Ecclesiastici xliij, c. [Ecclus.]   1905

Tho men of merci ben.

Seke in þe feest of relikis.

[LECTION 148]

The lessoun on Mary Mawdeleyn day. Prouerbiorum xxxj°, c.

¹⁰Who schal fynde a strong womman? The prise of her is fer, fro þe laste
endis. ¹¹The herte of her husbonde tristiþ in hir and sche schal not haue   1910
nede to spoylis. ¹²Sche schal ȝilde to hym good and not yuel in alle þe daies
of hir lijf. ¹³Sche souȝte wolle and flexe, and wroouȝte bi þe counceil of hir
hondis. ¹⁴Sche is made as þe schip of a marchaunt þat beriþ his breed fro
fer. ¹⁵And sche roos bi nyȝte and ȝaf pray to her meynealis, and metis to her
meydens. ¹⁶Sche biheeld a feld and bouȝte it; of þe fruyt of hir hondis sche   1915
plauntid a vyner. ¹⁷Sche girde hir lendis wiþ strengþe and made strong her
arm. ¹⁸Sche tastide and say þat hir marchaundise was good. | Hir lanterne   f. 259ʳᵃ
schal not quenche in þe nyȝte. ¹⁹Sche puttide hir hondis to strong þingis,
and hir fyngris token þe spyndil. ²⁰Sche openede hir hond to a nedy man,
and strecchid forþ hir hondis to a pore man. ²¹Sche schal not drede for hir   1920
hous of þe cooldis of snowe, for alle hire meynealis ben cloþide wiþ doubil

1909 fer] *add.* and SeBxRa   1910 sche] *om.* Ra   1912 hir¹] his Ny   þe] *om.*
Ny   1913 a] *om.* Ra   1914 to²] *om.* Se   1918 puttide] putte Se   hondis]
hond Bx   1920 hir¹] hise Bx   1921 of] for Ny

cloþis. ²²Sche made to hir aray clooþ; biys, *eþer whiȝte silk*, and purpur is þe clooþ of hir. ²³Hir husbond is nobil in þe ȝatis whanne he sittiþ wiþ þe senatouris of erþe. ²⁴Sche made lynnyn clooþ and seeld, and ȝaf a girdil of
1925 a Chananey. ²⁵Strengþe and fairnesse is þe cloþinge of hir, and sche schal leiȝhe in þe laste day. ²⁶Sche openede hir mouþe to wisdom, and þe lawe of merci is in hir tunge. ²⁷Sche bihelde þe paþis of hir hous, and sche eet not breed idili. ²⁸Hire sones riseden and prechiden hir moost blessid; hir husbonde roos and preisid hir. ²⁹Many douȝtris gaderiden ricchessis; þou
1930 passidist alle. ³⁰Fairnesse is disceyuable grace and veyn; þilke womman þat
f. 259ʳᵇ drediþ þe Lord schal be preisid. ³¹Ȝeue ȝe to hir of | þe fruyt of hir hondis, and hir werkis preise hir in þe ȝatis.

[LECTION 149]

The lessoun on Seynt Iames euen. Ecclesiasticus xliiij, g.

The blessynge of þe Lord.

1935 *Seke it in Seynt Andrews euen.*

[LECTION 157]

The lessoun on S. Siriak and hise
felowis. Eccleciastici ljᵒ. [Ecclus.]

¹Lord kyng, I schal knoweleche to þee, and I schal togidre herie þe, my sauyour. ²I schal knouleche to þi name, for þou art an helper and a defender
1940 to me, ³and þou hast delyuerid my bodi fro perdissioun, fro þe snare of a wickide tunge, and fro þe lippis of hem þat worchen a leesynge, and in þe siȝt of hem þat stonden nyȝ þou art made an helper to me. ⁴And þou hast delyuerid me bi þe multitude of mercy of þi name, fro rorers made redi to mete, ⁵ fro þe hondis of hem þat souȝten my soule, and fro many tribula-
1945 ciouns þat cumpassiden me, ⁶and in þe myddis of fire I was not brent, ⁷ fro þe depþe of þe wombe of helle, and fro a tunge defoulid, and fro a word of leesynge, fro a wickid kyng, and fro a tung vniust. ⁸Til to deeþ my soule
f. 259ᵛᵃ schal preise þe Lord, | ⁹and my lijf was nyȝynge to helle byneþe. ¹⁰Thei cumpassiden me on eche side, and noon was þat helpide; I was biholdynge
1950 to þe help of men, and noon was. ¹¹Lord, I hadde mynde of þi merci, and

1923 þe²] *om.* Bx   1924 seeld] solde it Ny   of²] to La   1926 wisdom] *prec. by* w *canc. at end of prec. line* Bo   1939 art] *add.* maad NyLaSeBxRa   1943 made] and Ny   1944 fro þe] fro þe fro þe Bo   1946 þe²] *om.* Se   1947 deeþ] þe deeþ NyLaSeBx   1949 helpide] *add.* me Se   1950 of²] on LaSeBxRa

on þi worchinge togidre þat ben fro þe world, ¹²for þou delyuerist hem
þat abiden þee, and delyuerist hem fro þe hond of men hatynge þee, *Lord*
my God.

[LECTION 159]

The lessoun on Assumpcioun
euen. Ecclesiastici xxiiij°. [Ecclus.]

¹⁴Fro þe bigynnynge and bifore worldis I am foormyd, and into þe world
to come I schal not ceesse to be, and in holy wonyinge bifore hym I ser-
uede. ¹⁵And so in Sion I am fastnede, and in an halowide citee like maner
I restide, and in Ierusalem my power. ¹⁶And I hadde root in a puple worschipide, and into þe partis of my God þe eritage of hym, and in þe plente
of halowis my wiþholdynge.

1955

1960

[LECTION 160]

þe lesson on Assumpcioun day. Ecclesiastici xxiiij°, b. [Ecclus.]

¹¹In alle þes *men* I souȝte reste, and I schal dwelle in þe eritage of þe Lord.
¹²Thanne þe creatoure of alle comaundide | and seide to me, and he þat
formede me restide in my tabernacle, and he seide to me: ¹³Dwelle þou in
Iacob, and take þou eritage in Israel, and sende þou rootis in my chosun
men. ¹⁴I was gendride fro þe bigynnynge and bifore worldis, and I schal
not faile til to þe world to comynge, and I mynystrid in an holy dwellynge
bifore hym. ¹⁵And so I was made stidfast in Sion, and in like maner I restide
in a citee halowide, and my power was in Ierusalem. ¹⁶And I rootide in
a puple honourid, and þe eritage þerof into partis of my God, and myn
wiþholdynge in þe fulnesse of seyntis. ¹⁷I was enhauncid as a cedre in
Liban, as a cipresse tre in þe hil of Syon. ¹⁸I was enhauncid as a palm
tre in Cades, and as þe plauntinge of rose in Ierico. ¹⁹As a faire olyue tre in
feeldis, I was enhauncid as a palm tre bisidis watir in stretis. ²⁰As canel and
bawme ȝeuynge greet smel, I ȝaf odour; as chosun myrre I ȝaf þe swetnesse
of odour.

f. 259vb

1965

1970

1975

1951 delyuerist] delyueridist La   1952 and] *add.* þou Ra   1956 þe²] *om.*
Ra   1958 an] *om.* Se   1959 and] *om.* Se   1964 alle] *followed by* þingis
canc. Bo   1967–9 I was gendride ... bifore hym] *om.* LaSeBxRa   1970 was] *add.*
maad Se   1971 partis] þe partis NyLaSeBxRa   1973 Liban] *add.* and SeBxRa
1974 As] and as SeRa   in²] *add.* þe Se   1975 feeldis] *add.* and LaSeBx   1976 I²]
and Se

[LECTION 161]

The lessoun in þe vtas of Assumpcioun. |

f. 260ʳᵃ   **The Book of Songis iijᵒ, g.**

1980   ¹¹Tho douȝtris of Syon, goiþ out and se kynge Salomon, in þe deademe
bi þe which his modir corownede hym, in þe day of his spousynge, and in
þe day of þe gladnesse of his herte. [S. of s. 4] ¹My frendesse, þou art ful
faire; þou art ful faire and semely. Thin iȝen ben of culueris, wiþout þat
þat is withynne. ⁷My frendesse, þou art ful faire; þou art ful faire and no
1985   wemme is in þee. ⁸Come, my spousesse, come þou fro þe Liban, come þou!
Thou schalt be crownede fro þe heed of Ammona, fro þe toppe of Sanyr
and Hermon, fro þe dennes of liouns, fro þe hillis of perdis. ⁹My sistir, my
spousesse, þou hast woundide myn herte; þou hast woundide myn herte in
oon of þin iȝen, and in oon heer of þi necke. ¹⁰My sistir spousesse, þi teetis
1990   ben ful faire; þi teetis ben fairer þanne wyne, and þe odoure of þi cloþis is
aboue alle swete smellynge oynementis. ¹¹Spousesse, þi lippis ben an hony-
coomb droppynge; hony and mylk ben vndir þi tunge, and þe odoure of þi
f. 260ʳᵇ   cloþis is as þe smelle of encense. ¹²Garden | encloside, sistir my spousesse,
garden encloside, wel enseelide. ¹³Thi buriownynge braunchis, paradise of
1995   pomegarnadis, with þe fruyt of appil trees.

g.

¹⁵Welle of gardens, pitte of watris liuynge, þe whiche smertli stirten out of
þe Liban.

vᵒ, b. [S. of S. 5]

2000   ¹Come into my garden, sistir, my spousesse; I haue rope my myrre wiþ
myn oynementis.

vjᵒ, d. [S. of S. 6]

⁸Oon is my perfiȝt and my culuer; oon is þe chosun of his modir, þe geter.
The douȝtris of Syon han seen hir and han prechide *hir* þe moost blessid,
2005   and þe qweenes of þe concubyns han preisid hir. ⁹What is sche þis þat
passiþ forþ as þe morwe risynge togidre, ¹⁰ faire as þe moone, chosun as þe

---

1980 Tho] ȝe LaSeBx   þe] *om.* LaBxRa   1981 þe¹] *om.* Se   1982 þe²] *om.*
Ra   1984 withynne] hid wiþinne NyLaSeBxRa   ful¹] al LaRa   þou art ful faire²] *om.*
NyLaSeBxRa   1985 Come] *add.* fro þe liban LaSeBxRa   1986–9 Thou schalt . . .
þi necke] *om.* LaSeBxRa   1991 aboue] *prec. by* as *canc.* Bo   1995 þe] *om.* Se

sunne, ferdful as þe ordeynede scheltrun of castels? [S. of S. 7] ⁶How faire art þou, and hou semely, my derist, in delytis, and þi state is lickenede to þe palme, and þi brestis to clustris of grapis.

[LECTION 165]

The lessoun in þe decolacioun of
S. Ioon Baptist. Prouerbiorum x°.

2010

²⁸ᵗThe abidynge of iust men is gladnesse, but þe hope of wickide men schal perische. ²⁹The strengþe of a symple man is þe wey of þe Lord, | and drede   f. 260ᵛᵃ to hem þat worchen yuel. ³⁰A iust man schal not be mouede wiþouten ende, but wickide men schulen not dwellen on erþe. ³¹ᵗThe mouþ of a   2015 iust man schal brynge forþ wisdom; þe tunge of schrewis schal perische. ³²ᵗThe lippis of a iust man biholden plesaunt þingis, and þe mouþe of wickid men *biholdeþ* weyward þingis. [Prov. 11] ¹A gileful balaunce is abhomyn- able anentis God, and an euen wei3te is his wille. ²Where pride is, þere also dispisynge schal be, but where mekenesse is, þere also wisdom is.   2020 ³The symplenesse of iust men schal dresse hem, and þe disceyuynge of weyward men schal distrie hem. ⁴Richessis schulen not profite in þe day of veniaunce, but ri3tfulnesse schal delyuer fro deeþ. ⁵The ri3tfulnesse of a symple man schal dresse his wey, and a wickide man schal falle in his wickidnesse. ⁶The ri3tfulnesse of ri3tful men schal delyuer hem, and   2025 wickide men schulen be takun in her aspiyngis. ⁷Whanne a wickid man is deed, noon hope schal be furþer, and abidynge of bisy men schal perische. ⁸A iust | man is delyueride fro angwische, and a wickide man schal be   f. 260ᵛᵇ 3ouun for hym. ⁹A feyner bi mouþ disceyueþ his frende, but iust men schu- len be delyueride bi kunnynge. ¹⁰A citee schal be enhauncid in þe goodis   2030 of iust men, and preisynge schal be in þe perdiscioun of wickide men. ¹¹A citee schal be enhauncid bi blessynge of iust men.

2008 and²] *om.* Se   state] stature BxRa   2009 þe palme] a palme tree La
2013 is] *add.* in Se   2015 on] *add.* þe SeBxRa   2018–20 A gileful . . . wisdom
is] *om.* LaSeBxRa   2018–19 abhomynable] abhomynacioun Ny   2020 wisdom
is] is wijdom Ny   2021 iust] *om.* Se   2022–5 Richessis schulen . . . his wickid-
nesse] *om.* LaSeBxRa   2025 and] *add.* þe Se   2026–7 Whanne a wickid . . . schal
perische] *om.* LaSeBxRa   2028 is] schal be La   2032 enhauncid] *add.* wiþinne
Se

[LECTION 169]

The lessoun in þe Natyuyte of
oure Lady. Ecclesiasticus xxiiij, b.

2035   ²³I as a vyne made fruyt þe swetnesse of odoure, and my flouris ben þe
fruytis of honoure and honeste. ²⁴I am modir of faire loue, and of drede,
and of knowynge, and of holy hope. ²⁵In me is al grace of wey and of treuþe;
in me is al hope of lijf and of vertu. ²⁶Alle 3e þat coueiten me, passe to
me, and be 3e fillid of my generaciouns. ²⁷Forwhi my spirit is swete aboue
2040   hony, and honycomb. ²⁸My mynde is in þe generacioun of worldis. ²⁹Thei
þat eten me, schulen hungir 3it, and þei þat drynken me, schulen þirste 3it.
³⁰He þat heeriþ me, schal not be schent, and þei þat worchen in me, schu-
f. 261ʳᵃ   len not do synne, and þei þat declaren | me, ³¹schulen haue euerlastynge
lijf.

[LECTION 170]

2045   ### The lessoun in þe utas of þe Natyuyte
of oure Lady. Sapiens iiij°, a.

¹How fair is chaast generacioun wit[h] cleernesse, for þe mynde þerof is
vndedely, for it is knowun boþe anentis God and anentis men. ²Whanne
it is present, þei suen it; þei desiren it, whanne it haþ ledde out itsilf,
2050   and it ouercomynge getiþ bi victorie þe mede of batels vndefoulide, and
is corownede withouten ende. ³But þe manyfoold gendride multitude of
wickid men schal not be profitable, and plauntyngis of avoutrie schulen not
3eue depe rootis, neþer schulen sette stabil stidfastnesse. ⁴Thou3 þei buriowne in bowis in tyme, þei sette vnstidfastli schulen be mouede of þe wynde
2055   and schulen be drawe out bi þe root of gretnes of wyndis. ⁵Forwhi bowis
vnperfi3t schulen be brokun togidre, and þe fruytis of hem ben vnprofit-
able and sour to ete, and couenable to no þing. ⁶Forwhi alle sones þat ben
borun of wickide men ben witnessis of wickidnesse a3ens fadris and mode-
f. 261ʳᵇ   ris in her axyng. ⁷But | a iust man, þou3 he be bifor ocupiede bi deeþ, schal
2060   be in refreischynge.

2036 and¹] add. of SeBxRa   2037 of⁴] om. Bx   2039 of] add. alle Se
2047 is¹] add. a LaSe, add. þe Ra   with] wit Bo   2052 plauntyngis] plauntinge Bx
schulen] schal SeBx   2059 axyng] corr. from axyngis Bo   be] om. Ra

[LECTION 171]

The lessoun on S. Mathu euen. Prouerbiorum iij°, c.

¹³Blessid is þe man þat fyndiþ wisdom, and which [flowiþ] wiþ prudence. ¹⁴The getynge þerof is bettir þanne þe marchaundise of gold and of siluer; þe fruytis þerof ben þe firste and þe clenneste. ¹⁵It is preciouser þanne alle ricchessis, and alle þingis þat ben desirid moun not be comperisownede to 2065 þis. ¹⁶Lengþe of daies is in þe riȝt half þerof; ricchessis and glorie ben in þe left half þerof. ¹⁷The weies þerof ben faire weies, and alle þe paþis þerof ben pesible. ¹⁸It is a tre of lijf to hem þat taken it, and he þat holdiþ it, is blesside. ¹⁹The Lord foundide þe erþe bi wisdom; he stablischide heuenes bi prudence. ²⁰The depþis of watris braken out bi his wisdom, and cloudis 2070 woxen togidre bi dewe.

[LECTION 172]

The lessoun on S. Mathu day. Ezechiel j°, c.

¹⁰The lickenesse of þe cheer, *eþer face, of foure beestis*, was þe face of a man and þe face of a lioun at þe riȝt half of þo foure. Forsoþe, þe face of an oxe was | at þe left half of þo foure, and a face of an egle was aboue þo foure. f. 261ᵛᵃ ¹¹And þe facis of þo and þe wyngis of þo werun strecchid forþ aboue. Two 2076 wyngis on eche werun ioynede togidir, and two hiliden þe bodies of þo. ¹²And ech of þo ȝeden bifore his face. Where þe fersnesse of þe wynde was, þidir þo ȝeden, and turneden not aȝen whanne þo ȝeden. ¹³And þe licke- nesse of þo beestis and þe biholdynge of þo was as of brennynge coolis of 2080 fire, and as þe biholdynge of laumpis. This was þe siȝte rennynge aboute in þe myddis of þo beestis, þe schynynge of fire, and leit goynge out of þe fire. ¹⁴And þe beestis ȝeden and turneden aȝen at þe liknesse of leit schynynge.

[LECTION 178]

The lessoun on Seint Lukis day. Ezechiel j°, c.

The liknesse of þe cheer.   2085

Here endiþ þe Proþre Sanctorum and bigynneþ þe Comoun Sanc- torum.

2062 flowiþ] NyLaSeBxRa, *om.* Bo   2063 þerof] *add.* and LaSeBx   of²] *om.* Ra 2066 þerof] *add.* and Ra   2067 þe¹] *om.* Se   2075 a face of an egle] þe face of an egle Ny   2080 of²] *om.* Ra   2081 as] *om.* Bx   siȝte] siȝt of Ny   2082 þo] *om.* NyLaSeBxRa   þe fire] fire Ra   2083 aȝen] not *marginal add.* aȝen Ny

[LECTION 195]

In þe vigil of oon apostil a lessoun.
Ecclesiastici xliiij°, g. b. [Ecclus.]
2090 The blessynge of þe Lord.
Seke on S. Andrewe euen.

[LECTION 196]

Vpon þe same a lessoun. Prouerbiorum iij°, c.
Blessid is þe man.

[LECTION 197]

In feestis of oon euaungelist. A lessoun Ezechiel j°, f.
2095 The liknesse. |

[LECTION 198]

f. 261ᵛᵇ   In þe feestis of oon martir. Ecclesiasticus xiiij°, f.

²²Blessid is þe man þat schal dwelle in wisdom, and þat schal biþenke in
riȝtfulnesse, and þat schal biþenke in þe biholdynge of God in wit. [Ecclus.
15] ³It schal fede him wiþ þe breed of lijf and vndirstondynge, and of þe
2100 watir of helþful wisdom it schal ȝeue hym drynke, and it schal be fastnede
in hym, and he schal not be bowide. ⁴And it schal wiþholde hym, and he
schal not be confoundide, and it schal enhiȝe him anentis hise neiȝboris,
⁶and with þe euerlastynge name he schal enerite hym.

[LECTION 199]

The lessoun on þe same. Ecclesiasticus xxxj°, b.

2105 ⁸Blessid is a riche man which is founden withouten wemme, and þat ȝede
not aftir gold, neþer hopide in money and tresouris. ⁹Who is þis, and we

2098 riȝtfulnesse] riȝtwisnesse Se   2102 enhiȝe] enhaunse Ny   2103 and] om.
Se   enerite hym] add. þe lord oure god LaSeBxRa   2105 a] þe NySe   riche] om.
LaSeBxRa

schulen preise hym? For he dide merueilis in his lijf, ¹⁰whiche is preuede
þerynne and is founden perfiȝt, and euerlastynge glorie schal be to hym,
whiche myȝte trispasse and trispassid not, and do yuel, and dide not.
¹¹Therfor hise goodis ben | stablischide in þe Lord, and al þe chirche of f. 262ʳᵃ
seyntis schal tel out hise almesdedis.   2111

[LECTION 200]

Anoþer lessoun on þe same. Sapience iiij°, c.

⁷A iust man, þouȝ he be bifore ocupiede bi deeþ, schal be in refreischinge.
⁸Forwhi worschipful elde is not of long tyme, neþer is rikened bi þe
noumbre of ȝeeris. The wittis of a man ben hoore, ⁹and þe age of eeld is 2115
lijf wiþouten wemme. ¹⁰He pleside God and was made derworþe, and he
lyuynge among synners was borun ouer. He was rauyschid, ¹¹lest malice
schulde chaunge his vndirstondynge, eþer lest feynynge schulde disceyue
his soule. ¹²Forwhi disceyuynge of trifelynge makiþ derk good þingis,
and contynuaunce of couetise turneþ ouer þe wit withouten malice. ¹³He 2120
was endide in schort tyme, and fillide many tymes, ¹⁴forwhi his soule was
plesaunt to God; for þis þing *God* haastide to lede hym out fro þe myddis
of wickidnesses, but puplis sayen and vndirstoden not, neþer settiden
such þingis in þe entraylis. ¹⁵Forwhi þe grace and mercy of God is on hise
seyntis, and biholdynge of | *Goddis comfort* is on hise chosun.   f. 262ʳᵇ

[LECTION 201]

In þe feestis of many martris a lessoun. Sapience iij°, a.   2126

¹The soulis of iust men ben in þe hondis of God, and þe turnement of
deeþ schal not touche hem. ²Thei semeden to þe iȝen of vnwise men to
dien, and turment was demede þe outgoynge of hem. ³And fro iust wey,
þei ȝeden into distryinge, and þat is of vs þe wey of distryinge, but þei ben 2130
in pees. ⁴Thouȝ þei suffriden turmentis bifore men, þe hope of men is ful
of vndedelynesse. ⁵Thei werun traueilide in a fewe þingis, *and þei* schulen
be disposide wel in many þingis, forwhi God asayede hem and foond hem
worþi to hemsilf. ⁶He preuede hem as gold in a furneise, and he took hem

2109 yuel] yuelis Ra   2119–20 Forwhi . . . withouten malice] *om.* LaSeBxRa
2123–4 but puplis . . . entraylis] *om.* LaSeBxRa   2125 chosun] chosun men NyBxRa
2127 hondis] hond NyLaSeBx   turnement] turment Bx   2128–9 Thei semeden . . .
outgoynge of hem] *om.* Ra   2129 wey] weies Ra   2131 men²] men BoSeBxRa,
hem NyLa, illorum Vu   2132 and] *om.* Se

2135 as þe offrynge of brent sacrifice, and þe biholdynge of hem schal be in tyme
of ʒildynge. ⁷Iust men schulen schyne and schulen renne aboute as sparklis in a place of rehed. ⁸Thei schulen deme naciouns, and þei schulen be
Lordis of puplis, and þe Lord of hem schal regne withouten ende.

[LECTION 202]

Anoþer lessoun vpon þe same. Sapience vᵒ, b.

f. 262ᵛᵃ ¹⁶Iust men schulen lyue wiþouten ende, and þe mede | of hem is anentis
2141 þe Lord, and þe þouʒte of hem is anentis þe hiʒeste. ¹⁷Therfor þei schulen take of þe hond of þe Lord þe rewme of fairnesse and þe diademe of
comelynesse, for he schal gouerne hem wiþ his riʒt hond, and he schal
defende hem wiþ his holi arm. ¹⁸And his feruent loue schal take armure,
2145 and he schal arme þe creature to þe veniaunce of enemyes. ¹⁹He schal cloþe
riʒtfulnesse for an haburiown, and he schal take certeyn doom for a basenet;
²⁰he schal take a scheeld þat may not be ouercomen, equyte, *or euennesse.*
²¹Forsoþe, he schal whette hard wraþþe into a spere, and þe world schal
fiʒte wiþ hym aʒens vnwitti men. ²²Streite sendingis out of leitis schulen
2150 go, and *oure Lord God* schal lede hem to a certeyn place.

[LECTION 203]

S. Ciriaci and hise felowis. Ecclesiastici ijᵒ, c. [Ecclus.]

⁷Ʒe dredynge þe Lord, susteyneþ þe mercies, and bowiþ not doun fro hym,
leste ʒe fallen. ⁸Ʒe þat dreden þe Lord, ʒeueþ feiþ to him, and ʒoure mede
schal not be voidide awey. ⁹Ʒe þat dreden þe Lord, hopiþ into hym, and
f. 262ᵛᵇ into likynge schal come to ʒou mercy. | ¹⁰Ʒe þat dreden þe Lord, loueþ
2156 hym, and ʒoure hertes schal be liʒtnede. ¹¹Biholdiþ, ʒe sones, þe naciouns
of men, and witiþ, no man hopiþ in þe Lord and is schent, ¹²or abood stille
in hise heestis, and is forsaken. Who ynwardli clepide hym, and he dispisid
hym? ¹³For piteuous and merciful is *þe Lord.*

2137 þei] *om.* LaSeBxRa   2142 þe hond of] *om.* Se   2145 þe²] *om.* Ra
2146 riʒtfulnesse] riʒtwijsnes Ra   he]*om.* SeBx   2148–9 and þe world ... vnwitti men]
om. LaSeBxRa   2150 God] *om.* Bx   to] into Se   2152 ʒe] The Ny   susteyneþ]
susteyne Se   mercies] merci of him Ny, mercies of him SeBxRa   2154 voidide]
avoidid Ny   and into likynge schal come to ʒou mercy] and merci schal come to ʒou into
likinge LaSeBx   2155 into] in Ra   þat] *om.* Ny   2156 schal] schulen NySeBx
Biholdiþ ʒe sones] Sones biholdiþ ʒe La   ʒe] þe NyRa   þe] of Ra   2157 witiþ] *add.*
þat Se

[LECTION 204]

In þe birþe of many martris a lessoun. Sapience x°, c.   2160

[17]*God* ȝildide to iust men þe mede of her trauelis, and ledde hem forþ in a wondirful wey, and it was to hem in hilynge of þe day, and in þe liȝt of sterris bi nyȝt. [18]And it translatide, *eþer ledde ouer*, hem þoruȝ þe rede see, and bare hem ouer þoruȝ ful moche watir. [19]But it drenchide doun þe enemyes of hem into þe see, and ledde hem out fro þe depþis of hellis. Therfor iuste   2165 men token awey þe spuylis of wickide men, [20]and, Lord, þei magnefieden in song þin holi name and preiseden þin hond ouercomer.

[LECTION 205]

Vpon þe same a lessoun. Prouerbiorum xv, a.

[2]The tunge of wise men ourneþ kunnynge; þe mouþ of foolis buyliþ out foly. [3]In eche place þe iȝen | of þe Lord biholden good men and yuel   f. 263ra men. [4]A plesaunt tunge is þe tre of lijf, but þe tunge which is vnmesurable 2171 schal defoule þe spirit. [5]A fool scorneþ þe techynge of his fadir, but he þat kepiþ blamyngis schal be mad wiser. Moost vertu schal be in plentyuous riȝtwisnesse, but þe þouȝtis of wickide men schulen ben drawen vp bi þe root. [6]The hous of a iust man is moost strengþe, and þe disturblynge is in   2175 þe fruytis of a wickide man. [7]The lippis of wise men schulen sowe abrood kunnynge; þe herte of foolis schal be vnlike. [8]The sacrificis of wickide men ben abhomynable to þe Lord, and þe vowis of iust men ben plesaunt. [9]The lijf of þe vnpiteuous man is abhomynacioun to þe Lord; he þat sueþ riȝtfulnesse schal be loued of þe Lord.   2180

[LECTION 206]

Anoþer on þe same. [Ecclesiastici] xliiij°, c. [Ecclus.]

These ben men of mercy.

Seke þis in þe vtas of Petir and Poul.

2167 ouercomer] *add.* þe lord oure god La   2172–5 A fool ... þe root] *om.* LaSeBxRa
2179 The lijf ... abhomynacioun to þe Lord] *om.* LaSeBxRa   2181 Ecclesiastici] *om.*
Bo, Ecclesiastici Ny

[LECTION 207]

In þe birþe of o confessour and
bisshop. Ecclesiastici xliiij, d. [Ecclus.]

2185

Lo, þe greet prest.

Seke þis on S. Nicholas day.

[LECTION 208]

Anoþer of þe same. Ecclestiastici 1°, a. [Ecclus.]

Biholde, þis is þe greet prest.

2190 *Seke it on S. Siluestir day.* |

[LECTION 209]

f. 263ʳᵇ

Anoþer lessoun on þe same. Sapience x°, d.

¹⁰*The Lord* ledde forþ a iust man bi riȝtful weies, þat fledde fro þe ire of his broþer; it schewide to hym þe rewme of God, and ȝaf to hym þe kunnynge of seyntis; it made hym oneste in traueilis and fillide hise trauels. ¹¹It
2195 helpide hym in þe fraude of disceyuers, and made hym onest. ¹²It kepte hym fro enemyes and defendide hym fro disceyuers, and it ȝaf to hym a strong bateil, þat he schulde ouercome and wite þat wisdom is myȝtiest of alle. ¹³This *wisdom* forsoke not a iust man seeld, but delyuerid hym fro synners, ¹⁴and ȝede doun wiþ him into a diche, and it forsoke not
2200 hym in boondis, til it brouȝte to hym þe septere, *eþer kyngis ȝerd*, of þe rewme, and power aȝens hem þat oppressen hym, and it schewide hem liers þat defouleden hym, and it ȝaf to hym euerlastynge cleernesse, *þe Lord oure God.*

2192–3 þat fledde . . . his broþer] *om.* LaSeBxRa   2193 it] and it NyLaSeBxRa
2195 hym¹] *om.* NySe   þe fraude] defraude La   2198 hym] *om.* Ra   2199 ȝede]
it ȝede LaSeBxRa   2201 oppressen] oppressiden LaSeBx   2202 þe Lord] *add.*
is Bx

[LECTION 210]

In þe feest of o confessoure and bisschop
S. Hwe. Ecclesiastici xlv, a. [Ecclus.]   2205

¹Loued of God and of men, whos mynde is in blessynge. ²He made | hym f. 263ᵛᵃ
like in þe glorie of seyntis, and he magnefiede him in þe drede of enemyes,
and in hise wordis he made pesible þe wondris aȝens kynde. ³He glorifiede
hym in þe siȝt of kyngis, and he comaundide to hym bifore his puple, and
schewide his glorie to hym. ⁴In þe feiþ and myldenesse of hym *God* made 2210
him holy, and chees hym of alle men. ⁵For he herde hym and his voice, and
led in him in a cloude. ⁶And ȝaf in hym an herte to þe comaundementis,
and to þe lawe of lijf and of techynge.

[LECTION 211]

In þe feest of o confessoure and doctour
a lessoun. Ecclesiastici xlvij, c. [Ecclus.]   2215

⁹*The Lord* haþ ȝoue knoulechinge to his holi *God*, and hiȝe in þe word
of glorie. ¹⁰Of al his herte he heriede God, and he louede þe Lord þat
made hym and ȝaf to hym power aȝens enemyes. ¹¹And he made syngers to
stonde aȝens þe auter, and he made swete motetis in þe soun of hem. ¹²And
he ȝaf fairnesse in halowyngis, and he ournede tymes til to þe endynge of 2220
lijf, þat þei schulden preise þe holy name of þe Lord, and make large eerli
þe holynesse of God. ¹³Crist purgide þe synnes of hym, and enhauncide |
his horn wiþouten ende, and he ȝaf to hym þe testament of kyngis, and þe f. 263ᵛᵇ
seet of glorie in Israel.

Ecclesiastici xxiiij⁰, a.   2225

¹Wisdom schal preise his soule, and he schal be ournede in *oure Lord*, and
he schal be glorifiede in þe myddis of his puple. ²And he schal opene his
mouþ in þe chirchis of moost hiȝe, and in þe biholdynge of þe vertu of him
he schal be glorifiede. ³In þe myddis of his puple he schal be hiȝede, and
in holy fulhede he schal be merueilid. ⁴In þe multitude of chosun he schal 2230
haue preisynge, and among þe blesside he schal [be] blesside.

2213 techynge] *om.* La   2216 God] *om.* La   2218 to¹] *om.* La
2220 halowyngis] *preceded by* þe *canc.* Bo   2221 lijf] *add.* and Se   þat] and
Bx   2223 his horn] þe horn of him Ra   to] *om.* La   2231 and] *om.* Se   be] *om.*
Bo, be NySeRa

[LECTION 212]

Vpon þe same anoþer lessoun. Sapience vijº, b.

⁷I desiride, and wit was ȝouun to me, and I ynwardli clepide, and þe spirit of wisdom cam into me. ⁸And I settide wisdom bifore rewmes and seetis,
2235 and I seide þat riȝcchessis ben nouȝt in comperisoun of it. ⁹And I comperisownede not a preciouse stoon to it, forwhi al gold in comperisoun þerof is a litil grauel, and siluer schal be arettid as cley in þe siȝt þerof. ¹⁰I louede wisdom more þanne heelþe and fairnesse, and I purposide to haue it for |
f. 264ʳᵃ liȝt, for þe liȝt þerof may not be quenchide. ¹¹Forsoþe, alle goodis camen
2240 togidre to me wiþ it, and vnnoumbirable honeste is bi þe werkis þerof. ¹²And I was glad in alle þingis, for þis wisdom ȝede bifor me, and I knewe not, for it is þe modir of alle goodis. ¹³Which *wisdom* I lernede wiþouten feynynge, and I comoun wiþout enuye, and I huyde not þe oneste þerof. ¹⁴For it is tresour wiþout noumbre to men, and þei þat vseden þat tresoure
2245 werun made perteneris of Goddis frendschip.

[LECTION 213]

In þe feest of o confessoure and abbot. Ecclesiastici xxxixº, c. [Ecclus.]

⁶*The riȝtwis man* schal ȝeue his herte to wake eerli to þe Lord þat made him, and he schal biseche in þe siȝte of þe hiȝest. ⁷He schal opene his mouþ in
2250 preier, and he schal biseche for hise trispassis. ⁸For if þe gret Lord wole, he schal fille hym with þe spirit of vndirstondynge. ⁹And he schal sende þe wordis of his wisdom as reynes, and in preier he schal knouleche to þe Lord. ¹⁰And he schal dresse his counceil and techynge, and schal counceile
f. 264ʳᵇ in hise hidde | þingis. ¹¹And he schal make opyn þe wisdom of his techinge,
2255 and he schal haue glorie in þe lawe of þe testament of þe Lord. ¹²Many men schulen preise his wisdom, and it schal not be don awey til into þe world. ¹³His mynde schal not go awei, and his name schal be souȝt fro generacioun and into generacioun.

[LECTION 214]

Vpon þe same anoþer lessoun. Ecclesiastici ij. [Ecclus.]

¹⁸Tho þat dreden þe Lord schulen not be vnbileful to his word, and þei þat 2260
louen hym schulen kepe þe wey of hym. ¹⁹Tho þat dreden þe Lord schulen
seke þo þingis þat ben wel plesynge to hym, and þei þat louen hym schuln
be fillid bi þe lawe of hym. ²⁰And þei þat dreden þe Lord schulen make redy
her hertis, and schulen halowe her soulis in her spirit. ²¹Tho þat dreden þe
Lord kepen þe comaundementis of hym, and þei schulen haue pacience til 2265
to þe biholdynge of hym.

[LECTION 216]

In þe feest of o virgyn and marter. Ecclesiastici lj°, c. [Ecclus.]

¹³*My Lord God*, þou enhaunsidist my dwellynge on erþe, and I bisouȝte for
deeþ fletynge doun. ¹⁴I clepide to help þe Lord, fadir of my Lord, þat he |
forsake not me in þe day of my tribulacioun, and *forsake not me* wiþouten f. 264ᵛᵃ
help, in þe tyme of hem þat ben proude. ¹⁵I schal preise þi name contynueli, 2271
and I schal herie it togidre in knoulechynge, and my preier is herd. ¹⁶And
þou hast delyuerid me fro perdiscioun, and þou hast delyuerid me fro þe
wickid tyme. ¹⁷Therfor I schal knowleche, and I schal seye heeriynge to
þee, and I schal blesse þe name of þe, Lord, *þou art my God.* 2275

[LECTION 217]

Vpon þe same a pistil. Ecclesiastici lj. [Ecclus.]

Lord kyng, I schal knoweleche.

Seke on S. Laurence euen.

[LECTION 218]

Vpon þe same a lessoun. Ecclesiastici xxiiij, a. [Ecclus.]

¹Wisdom schal preise his soule, and in þe Lord he schal be worschipide, 2280
and in þe myddil of his puple he schal glorien. ²And in þe chirchis of

þe hiȝest he schal opene his mouþ, and in þe siȝt of þe vertu of hym he schal glorifien. ³And in þe myddis of his puple he schal be enhaunsid, and in þe holy plentee he schal moche wondre. ⁴And in þe multitude of
f. 264ᵛᵇ chosun men he schal haue preisynge, and among blessid men he schal | be
2286 blesside, seiynge, ⁵I of þe mouþ of þe hiȝest cam forþ, firste getun bifore eche creature.

d.

²¹I haue ȝoue moisture, *eþer moistid*, myn habitacioun as a liban þat is not
2290 kute, and my smelle is as bawme not medelide. ²²And I haue strecchide my bowis as þe therebynte, and my bowis ben of onour and grace.

[LECTION 219]

In þe feest of o virgin and not marter
a lessoun. Sapience vij° and viij°, g. a.

³⁰Wisdom ouercomeþ malice. [Wisd. 8] ¹Therfor wisdom strecchiþ forþ
2295 fro þe ende til to þe ende strongli, and disposiþ alle þingis sweteli. ²I louede þis *wisdom mad*, and I souȝte it out fro my ȝougþe, and I souȝte to take it a spousesse to me, and I am made a louyer of þe fairnesse þerof. ³He þat haþ þe felouschip of God glorifieþ þe gentilnesse þerof, but also þe Lord of alle þingis louede it. ⁴For it is þe techeresse of þe lernynge of God, and
2300 cheseresse of hise werkis.

[LECTION 220]

Vpon þe same anoþer lessoun. Isaye xlj° and xlvj°. [Isa. 61]

¹⁰I ioiynge schal haue ioie in þe Lord, and my soule schal make ful out-
f. 265ʳᵃ ioye in my God. For he haþ cloþide | me wiþ a clooþ of heelþe, and he haþ cloþide me wiþ a clooþ of riȝtfulnesse, as a spouse made faire wiþ a coroun,
2305 and as a spousesse ournede wiþ her brochis. ¹¹For as þe erþe bryngiþ forþ his fruyt, and as a garden buriowneþ his seed, so þe Lord God schal make to growe riȝtfulnesse and preisynge bifore alle folkis. [Isa. 62] ⁵For a ȝong man schal dwelle with a virgyn, and þi sones schulen dwelle in þee, and þe

2289 eþer] or La   2295 sweteli] *preceded by* s *canc. at end of prec. line* Bo
2296 and¹] *om.* Se   take] perfourme Bx   2298 God] *add.* and Bx   2299 and]
add. þe Se   2302 out-ioye] out ioiynge Ny   2306 his²] wiþ Ny   God] *om.* La

spouse schal haue ioie on þe spousesse, and þi God schal haue ioie on þee,
seiþ þe Lord almy3ti.   2310

[LECTION 221]

In þe feeste of many virgyns. Sap. iiij°, a.

How faire is a chast generacioun.

Seke þis in þe vtas of þe Natyuyte of oure Ladi.

*Here endiþ þe Comoun Sanctorum and bigynneþ þe comemoracioun
of oure Ladi in Aduent.*   2315

[LECTION 222]

Isaye vij°, c.

The Lord spak to Achaz.

Seke in þe iiij Wednesday of Aduent.

[LECTION 223]

In þe comemoracioun of oure Ladi fro
Candilmasse til Eestir. Sapience xxiiij, c.   2320

Fro þe biynnynge and bifor worldis.

[LECTION 224]

In þe comemoracioun of oure Lady fro
Estir til Trynyte Sunday. Sapience xxiiij, c.

Fro þe bigynnynge. |

[LECTION 225]

For briþeren and sistren a lessoun. Isaye xviij and xix, g.   f. 265rb

⁷In þat day, 3ifte schal be born to þe Lord of oostis   2326

2309 on²] in La   2325 xviij] xvij Se

c. [Isa. 19]

⁴and þe strong kyng schal haue lordschip on hem;

f.

2330   ¹⁹in þat dai schal be an auter to þe Lord in þe myddis of erþe

g.

²¹and oure Lord schal be knowun fro Egipt, and þei schulen worschip hym in sacrificis and ʒiftis, and þei schulen make biheestis to þe Lord and ʒilden hem. ²²And þei schulen be turnede to oure Lord, and he schal be pleside 2335 in hem, and he schal saue hem in þat day.

j.

²⁴Blessynge schal be in þe myddis of erþe, ²⁵to whiche þe Lord of oostis haþ blessid, seiynge: Blessid be my puple and þe werkis of myn hondis, Israel myn eritage, *seiþ þe Lord almyʒti.*

[LECTION 226]

2340   **For þe pees a lessoun. Machabeus j°, e.**

The prestis maden her preier.

Seke it on þe firste Saturday of Lente.

[LECTION 227]

        For cleer wedir a lessoun. Trenorum ij°, g. [Lam.]

¹⁹Rise up togidre, preise in þe nyʒt, and in þe bigynnynge of þi wakyn-
f. 265ᵛᵃ gis, and schede out þin herte as watir bifore | þe siʒte of þe Lord, *þi God*;
2346   lifte vp þin hondis to hym for þi children soulis, þe whiche han failide for hungir in þe heed of alle feterid men. ²⁰Se, Lord, and bihold, for þus þou hast rerid vp oure vyneʒerdis; þerfor lete not wommen ete her fruyt, her smale children at þe mesure of an hound. And þe prest and þe profete ben 2350 killid in þe sentuarie of þe Lord.

2328 on] of LaSeBx   2335 hem²] *add.* and Ra   2339 seiþ þe Lord almyʒti]
om. LaSeBxRa   2344 and] *om.* NySeBxRa   þi] þe SeBx   2345 and] *om.* Se
2346 þe whiche] whiche Ny   failide] defailid SeBxRa   2347 Lord] þe Lord Ny
2349 And] if NyLaSeBxRa

iij, f. [Lam. 3]

⁵⁴Watris han goen aboute myn heed; I haue seide þat I perischide. ⁵⁵I haue clepide þi name, Lord, fro þe laste lake. ⁵⁶Thou hast herd my voice; fro þe snobbingis and my criyngis turne not awey þi face! ⁵⁷Thou hast come ny3 in þat day þat I haue inclepide þee; þou hast seide: Drede þee no þing. ⁵⁸Thou hast demyd þe cause of my soule; þou art raunsomer of my soule, *my Lord and my God.*   2355

[LECTION 228]

For reyn a lessoun. Ieremy xiiij°, g.

¹⁹Wheþir þou castynge awey hast cast awey Iuda, eþer þi soule haþ wlatid Syon? Whi þerfor hast þou smetun vs, so þat noon helþe is? We abideden   2360
pees, and noon good is; we *abideden* tyme, and lo, disturblynge is. | ²⁰Lord,   f. 265ᵛᵇ
we han knowun oure vnfeiþfulnessis, and þe wickidnessis of oure fadris, for we han synnede to þee. ²¹3eue þou not vs into schenschip for þi name, neþer do þou dispite to vs; haue þou mynde on þe seet of þi glorie, make þou not voide þi boond of pees wiþ vs. ²²Wheþer in grauun ymagis of heþen men   2365
ben þei þat reynen, eþer heuenes moun 3eue reynes? Wheþer þou art not oure Lord God, whom we abiden? For þou madist alle þes þingis.

[LECTION 229]

For batels a pistil. Ecclesiastici xiij°, f. [Esther 13]

⁹Lord, kyng almy3ti, in þi power alle þingis ben sette, and þere is not þat may wiþstonde þi wil; if þou demest to saue Israel, anoon we schulen be   2370
delyuerid. ¹⁰Thou, *Lord*, forsoþe madist heuen and erþe, and alle þingis þat ben conteynede in þe cumpasse of heuene. ¹¹Lord of alle þingis þou art, ne þer is þat wiþstondiþ þi magiste. ¹⁵And now, Lord Kyng, God of Abra-ham, haue merci on þi puple, for oure enemyes wolen leese vs, and don awey oure eritage, ¹⁶ne dispise þou þi part þat þou a3enbou3t fro Egipt.   2375
¹⁷Heer my | preier; be þou merciful to þe lot and litil coord of þin eritage,   f. 266ʳᵃ
and turne oure weilynge into ioie, Lord, þat we lyuynge preise þi name, and ne close þou þe mouþis of men preisynge þee.

2352 perischide] perische Ra   2353 fro þe snobbingis . . . awey þi face] turne not
awey þi face fro þe snobbingis and my criyngis SeBx   2354 þe] my Ny   my] *om.* NyRa
2360 abideden] aboden Ny, abiden Ra   2361 we] and we SeRa   abideden] aboden
Ny, abiden Ra   tyme] *add.* of heelinge SeBx   2367 þes] *om.* Se

[LECTION 230]

For pestilence of beestis a lessoun. Ieremy xiij°, c. [Jer. 14]

2380   ⁷If oure wickidnessis schulen answere to vs, Lord, do for þi name, for many
ben oure turnyngis awey; to þee we han synnede. ⁸Thou bidynge of Israel,
his sauyoure in tyme of tribulacioun, whi as a comelynge tilier þou art to
me in þe lond, and as a weigoer bowynge doun to dwellynge? ⁹Whi art þou
to me as a man vagaunt and as a strong man þat may not saueren? Forsoþe,
2385   þou art, Lord, in vs, and þin holy name is clepide on vs.

[LECTION 231]

For weifaringe men a lessoun. Genesis xxiiij°, b.

⁷The Lord of heuene þat took me fro þe hous of my fadir, and fro þe [l]ond
of my birþe, þe whiche haþ spokun to me an[d] swore, seiynge: To þi seed
I schal ȝeue þis lond; h[e] schal sende his aungel bifore þee.

[LECTION 232]

f. 266ʳᵇ   ### Vpon þe masse of requiem a lesson. | ij Machabeis xij°, h.

2391   *In þo daies*, ⁴³collacioun, *or spekynge togidre* made Iudas, *þe man moost strong*,
sente twelue þousand dragmes of siluer to Ierusalem to be offride sacrifice
for deed men, wel and religiousli biþenkynge of aȝenrisynge, ⁴⁴(soþeli, if
he hopide not hem þat fillen to rise aȝen, it was seen superflu and veyn to
2395   preien for deed men,) ⁴⁵and for he biheld þat þei token slepynge, *or diynge*,
wiþ pite, hadden best grace kept. ⁴⁶Therfor helþful and holi þenkinge is to
preie for deed men, þat þei be vnbounden fro synnes.

Here enden þe lessouns and pistlis of al þe ȝeer.

2382 his sauyoure] þe sauiour þerof La   tyme of] *om.* Ra   2384 me] come
NyLaSeBx, futurus es Vu   and] *om.* SeRa   2387 lond] hond Bo   2388 þe]
om. Ny   and] an Bo   swore] *add.* to me Ra   2389 he] h Bo   2391 In þo daies]
om. Ny   2395 þei] *add.* þat LaSe   slepynge or diynge] deiynge or slepynge Ra

APPENDIX

TABLE OF LECTIONS

The following Table of Lections is edited from Bo (ff. 1ʳ–12ᵛ), using the conventions outlined in the editorial policy (Introduction, §VI). The TOL edited by Forshall and Madden (F&M, iv. 683–98) is a conflation of different versions, and therefore less than ideal for analysis. This is exemplified by the insertion of the feast of St Giles at the end of August in F&M, which occurs in only one of the collated manuscripts and is atypical for TOL. By contrast, the present edition aims to present the text of this Type I TOL as it appears in one specific manuscript. Owing to the specific textual features of the TOL, no collation with other manuscripts has been attempted.

f. 1ʳ Here bigynneþ a reule þat telliþ in whiche chapitris of þe Bible ȝe may fynde þe lessouns, pistlis, and gospels þat ben redde in þe chirche at masse aftir þe vse of Salisbury markide wiþ lettris of þe a.b.c. at þe bigynnynge of þe chapitris toward þe myddil or ende aftir þe ordre as þe lettris stonden in þe abc. First ben set Sundaies and feriales togidir, and aftir þe sanctorum, comyn and propir togidir of al þe ȝeer. First writun a clause of þe bigynnynge þerof and of þe ending þerof also.

þe first Sundai in Aduent	Romayns xiijᵒ	d We knowun þis tym	ende in þe Lord Ihesus Crist
	Mathu xxj	a Whanne Ihesus cam nyȝ	ende Osanna in hie þingis
Wednesday	James v	b Be ȝe pacient til to	ende in þe name of þe Lord
	Mark jᵒ	a þe bigynnynge of þe	ende ȝou in þe Holy Goost
Fryday	Isaye lj	a Heere ȝe me þat su	ende of generaciouns
	Mathu iij	a In þo daies Iohn bap	ende knoulechiden her synnes
Secunde Sunday in Aduent	Romayns xv cᵒ	b What euer þingis	ende and vertu of þe Holy Goost
	Luyk xxj cᵒ	e Tokenes schulen be	ende schulen not passe

Wednesday	Sach viij c°	b I am turnede aȝen in	ende	in riȝtwisnesse
	Math xj c°	c Treuli I seye to ȝou	ende	of heeringe, heere he
Friday	Isaye lxij c°	d Ierusalem I haue ordey	ende	and not forsaken
	John j c°	b Ioon beriþ witnessing	ende	haþ teld out
Thridde Sunday	j Corinth iiij	a So a man gesse vs	ende	to ech man of god
	Mt xj	b Whanne Ioon in boondis	ende	þi weye bifore þee
Ymbir Wednesday	Isaye ij° c°	a In þe laste daies þe	ende	þe Lord oure God
	Isaye vij	c þe Lord spak to Achas	ende	yuel and chees good
	Luk j	d þe aungel Gabriel	ende	to me aftir þi word
Fryday	Isaye vj	a A ȝerd schal go out	ende	girdil of hise reynes
	Luk j	e Marie roos up in þo	ende	in God myn heelþe
Satirday				
j lessoun	Isaye xix	f þei schulen crie to	ende	þe Lord oure God
ij lessoun	Isaye xxxv	a þe forsaken Iudee and	ende	oure Lord almyȝti
iij lessoun	Isay xl	c þou þat prechist to	ende	hem seiþ oure Lord
iiij lessoun	Isaye xlv	a þe Lord seiþ þes þingis	ende	I þe Lord haue mad hym
v lessoun	Danyel iij	g Forsoþe an aungel	ende	enhauncid into worldis
pistil	ij Tessal ij	a We preien ȝou bi	ende	of his comynge
gospel	Luk iij	a In þe fiftenþe ȝeer of	ende	þe heelþe of God
Fourþe Sunday	Filipenses	b Ioie ȝe in þe	ende	vndirstonding in
pistil	iij	Lord euer		Crist Ihesu |
gospel	Iohun j° c°	c Whanne Iewis senten	ende	schal dwelle in Syon

f. 1ᵛ (before gospel row)

Wednesday	Ioel ijº cº	**g** Ioie ȝe sones of Syon	ende	schal dwelle in Syon
	Luk vij cº	**c** And þis word wente	ende	is more þanne he
Fryday	Sach ij cº	**f** Douȝtir of Syon he	ende	seiþ þe Lord almyȝti
	Mark viij cº	**c** Se ȝe and be ȝe war	ende	seie to no man
Cristmasse euen	Isaye lxij cº	**a** For Syon I schal not	ende	pleside to þe Lord in þe
	Romans j cº	**a** Poul þe seruaunt	ende	clepide of Ihesus Crist
	Mathu j cº	**d** Whanne Marie þe	ende	saaf fro her synnes
In nyȝt at Laud	Mathu j cº	**a** þe book of þe genera	ende	þat is clepide Crist
Cristmas nyȝt at þe first masse	Isaye ix cº	**b** þe puple þat wenten	ende	into wiþouten ende
	Tite ij c	**c** þe grace of God oure	ende	þes þingis and moneste
	Luk ij cº	**a** Amaundement wen	ende	men of good wille
To þe ij masse	Isaye lxj cº	**a** þe spirit of þe Lord	ende	Aȝenbouȝt of þe Lord
	Tite iij cº	**b** þe benygnete and þe	ende	of euerlastynge lijf
	Luk ij	**c** þe schepherdis spa	ende	it was seide to hem
To þe hiȝe masse	Isaye lij	**c** For þis þing my pu	ende	heelþe of oure god
	Ebrews jº	**a** God þat spak sum	ende	schulen not faile
	Iohun j	**a** In þe bigynnynge	ende	ful of grace and of truþe
S Steuene	Actus vj cº	**d** Steuen ful	ende	þat spak
	vij	and þei hide	ende	he diede
	Mathu xxiij	**f** Lo I sende to ȝou pro	ende	name of the Lord

S Iohun	Ecclesiasti- ci xv	a Who drediþ God	ende	hym þe Lord oure God
	Iohun	f He seiþ to him sue þou	ende	witnessynge is trewe
Childirmas day	Apoc xiiij	a I siȝe and lo þe lomb	ende	þe troon of God
	Mathu ij	c Lo þe aungel of þe	ende	for þei ben not
S Thomas martir	Ebrews v	a Eche bishop takun	ende	of Mechisedech
	Luk xix	b A worþi man wente	ende	ȝede vp to Ierusalem
þe sixte day	Galathis iiij	a As long tyme as þe	ende	he is an eir bi God
	Luk ij	f And his fadir and h	ende	of God was in him
S Siluestir	Ecc xliiij	d Lo þe greet preest þat	ende	smel of swetnesse
	Mathu xxv	b A man þat goeþ in pilg	ende	into þe ioie of þi lord
Newe ȝeris day	Tite ij	e þe grace of God oure	ende	þes þingis and moneste
	Luk ij	d And aftir þat eiȝte dai	ende	conseyuede in wombe
Twelueþe euen	Tite iij	b þe benygnyte and	ende	of euerlastynge lijf
	Mathu ij	d Whanne Heroude	ende	clepide Anazarie |
Twelfþe nyȝt	Luk iij c°	e It was don whan	ende	aȝen fro Iordan
On twelfþe dai	Isaye lx c°	a Rise þou Ierusalem be	ende	heriynge to þe Lord
	Mathu ij c°	a Whanne Ihesus was	ende	into her cuntre
Sundai withyn vtas	Isaye lx c°	a Rise þou Ieru- salem and be	ende	heriynge to þe Lord
	Iohn j c°	d Iohun siȝ Ihesus comyng	ende	þe sone of God

f. 2ʳ

Vtas on twelfeþe day	Isaye xxv	a Lord my God I schal	ende	þe Lord almyȝti
	Mathu iij cº	d Ihesus cam fro Galile	ende	I haue pleside to me
First Sundai aftir vtas	Romans xij cº	a Briþeren I biseche	ende	membris oon of anoþer
	Luk ij cº	g Whanne Ihesus was	ende	anentis God and men
Wednesday	Romans x cº	a þe wil of myn herte	ende	man þat bileueþ
	Mt iiij cº	c Whanne Ihesus hadde	ende	heuenes schal come nyȝ
Fryday	Romans xiij cº	a Eueri soule be su	ende	for þe same þing
	Luk iiij cº	c Ihesus turnede aȝen in	ende	forþ of his mouþ
ij Sunday	Romans xij cº	b We þat han ȝiftis	ende	to meke þingis
	Ioon ij cº	a Weddingis werun	ende	bileeueden in hym
Wednesday	j Tymothe jº	f A trewe word and	ende	worldis amen
	Mark vj cº	a And he ȝede out	ende	vnbileue of hem
Fryday	Romans xiiij cº	d I woot and truste	ende	of feiþ is synne
	Luk iiij cº	e Ihesus cam doun into ca	ende	place of þe cuntre
iij Sunday	Romans xij cº	f Nile ȝe be prudent	ende	þou yuel bi good
	Mt viij cº	a Whanne Ihesus was	ende	heelid fro þat oour
Wednesday	Romans xv cº	f I biseche ȝou bi our	ende	with ȝou alle. Amen
	Mark iij cº	a He entride eftsone	ende	restorid to hym
Fryday	j Corinthis iij	e Witen ȝe not þat ȝe	ende	and crist of God
	Mt iij cº	f Ihesus ȝede about al ga	ende	hym moche puple

iiij Sunday	Romans xiij c°	c To no man oute ȝe	ende	fulfillynge of þe lawe
	Mt viij c°	e Whanne he was	ende	obeischen to hym
Wednesday	j Corinthis vij	a It is good to a man	ende	for ȝoure incontynence
	Luk ix c°	k It was don whan	ende	to þe rewme of God
Fryday	j Corinthis vij	d Eche man in what	ende	in þis anentis God
	Mark x c°	c þei brouȝten to him	ende	on hem and blessid hem
v Sunday	Colocensis iij	c ȝe as þe chosun of	ende	to þe fadir bi hym
	Mt xiij c°	e þe kyngdom of heuene	ende	into my berne
Wednesday pistil	j Tymothe ij c°	a I biseche firste of	ende	in feiþ and treuþe |
f. 2ᵛ gospel	Mt xxj	f A man hadde twey	ende	bileueden to hym
Sundai in Septuagesme	j Corinth ix	g Witen ȝe not þat	ende	þe stoon was Crist
	Mt xx	a þe kingdom of heue	ende	but fewe ben chosun
Wednesday	ij Corinth iiij	b For if also oure gos	ende	but lijf in ȝou
	Mark ix	f And þei ȝeden fro þens	ende	him þat sente me
Friday	ij Corinth iiij	d And we han þe sam	ende	ben euerlasynge
	Mt xij	e He þat is not with me	ende	þou schalt be dampnede
Sexagesme	ij Corin xj and xij	d ȝe suffren gladli	ende	vertu of Crist dwelle in my
	Luk viij	b Whanne moche pu	ende	forþ fruyt in pacience
Wednesday	ij Corinthis j°	g I clepe God to wit	ende	knowen hise þouȝtis
	Mark iij	a And eft Ihesus bigan	ende	of heerynge heer he

Friday	ij Corinth v	c We witynge þe dre	ende	for hem and roos aȝen
	Luk xvij	e And he was axide	ende	togidre also þe eglis
Quinquagesme	j Corinth xiij	a If I speke wiþ tun	ende	moost of þes is charite
	Luk xviij	f Ihesus took hise twel	ende	herynge to God
Aisch Wednesdai	Ioel ij	d Be 3e conuertide	ende	þe Lord almy3ty
	Mt vj	d Whanne 3e fasten	ende	also þin herte is
þursday	Isay xxxviij	a In þo daies sikened	ende	I schal defende it
	Mathu viij	b And whanne he had	ende	heelid fro þat cour
Fryday	Isaye lviij	a Crie þou ceese þou not	ende	I am þi Lord God
	Mt v and vj	g 3e han herd þat it	ende	schal quyte to þee
Saturday	Isaye lviij	d If þou takist awey	ende	mouþ of þe Lord spak
	Mark vj	h And whanne it was	ende	werun made said
First Sunday	ij Corinth vj	a We helpynge mo	ende	weeldyng alle þingis
	Mt iiij	a Ihesus was ledde into	ende	and serueden to him
Moneday	Ezechi xxxiiij	c Lo I my silf schal a	ende	fede hem in doom
	Mt xxv	e Whanne mannes	ende	euerlastynge lijf
Tewisdai	Isaye lv	c Sekiþ þe Lord þe w	ende	to whiche I sente it
	Mt xxj	c Whanne Ihesus hadde	ende	of þe kingdom of God
Wednesday	Exodi xxiiij	e Stie vp to me into	ende	fourti daies and xl ny3tis
	iijᵒ Regum xix	b Elye cam into ber	ende	to Oreb þe hil of God

þursday	Mt xij	**f** þe scribis and þe faresi	**ende**	broþer, sistir and modir
	Ezech xviij	**a** þe word of þe Lord	**ende**	seiþ þe Lord almiȝti
	Iohun viij	**f** Ihesus seide to þe Iewis	**ende**	heeriþ þe word of God |
f. 3ʳ Friday	Ezech xviij	**d** þe soule þat schal	**ende**	in lijf and schal not die
	Iohun v	**a** þere was a feest day	**ende**	þat made hym hool
Saturdai	Deuterono-mi xxvj	**e** Biholde þou fro þin	**ende**	as he spak to þee
	Deuterono-mi xj	**e** If forsoþe ȝe kepen	**ende**	as he spak to ȝou
	ij Machabes j	**a** þe prestis maden her preier	**ende**	ȝou in yuel tyme
	Eccl xxxvj	**a** Haue mercy of vs	**ende**	out þi merueilis
	Danyel iij	**g** An aungel of þe Lor	**ende**	enhauncid into worldis
	j Tessal v	**c** We preien ȝou rep	**ende**	of oure Lord Ihesus Crist
	Mathu xvij	**a** Ihesus took petir and Ia	**ende**	aȝen fro deed men
ij Sunday	j Tessal iiij	**a** We preien ȝou and	**ende**	and into holynesse
	Mathu xv	**d** Ihesus goen out fro þens	**ende**	heelide fro þat oour
Moneday	Danyel ix	**d** Oure Lord God þat led	**ende**	citee and on þi puple
	Iohun viij	**d** Lo I go and ȝe schulen	**ende**	þat ben plesaunt to him
Tewisday	iij Regum xvij	**c** þe word of þe Lord	**ende**	in þe hond of Elye
	Mt xxij	**a** Ihesus spak to þe tun	**ende**	schal ben enhauncid
Wednesdai	Hester xiij	**e** Lord God kyng al	**ende**	of men preisynge þe
	Mt xx	**d** Ihesus stiynge vp to	**ende**	redempcioun for many

þursdai	Ieremy xvij	**b** Cursid is þe man	**ende** fruyt of his
		þat	fyndingis
	Iohun v	**g** I may not of my	**ende** bileeuen to my
			wordis
Friday	Genesis xxxiiij	**b** Ioseph seide to hise	**ende** to ȝilde to his fadir
	Mt xxj	**g** þere was an husbond	**ende** hym as a profete
Saturday	Genesis xxvij	**b** Rebecca seide to hir	**ende** heuene fro aboue
	Luk xv	**c** A man hadde twey	**ende** and is founden
Sunday	Effec v	**a** Be ȝe folowers of God	**ende** riȝtwisnesse and treuþe
	Luk xj	**d** Ihesus was castynge	**ende** þe word of God and kepen it
Moneday	iiij Regum v	**a** Naaman prynce of	**ende** oonli þe God of Israel
	Luk iiij	**d** þe faresies seiden to	**ende** myddil of hem
Tewisday	iiij Regum iiij	**a** A womman of þe wi	**ende** lyue of þe residewe
	Mathu xviij	**d** If þi broþer synneþ	**ende** siþis seuen siþis
Wednesday	Exodi xx	**c** Honoure þi fadir and	**ende** mynde of my name
	Mt xv	**a** Scribis and faresies	**ende** defouliþ a man
þursday	Ieremy vij	**a** þe word of þe Lord	**ende** til into þe world
	Iohun vj	**e** Worche ȝe not mete	**ende** schal neuer þirste
Fridai pistil	Numery xx	**b** þe sones þei ȝeden togi	**ende** sauȝoure of þe world |
gospel	Iohun iiij	**b** Ihesus cam into a cite	**ende** was halowide in hem
Saturday	Danyel xiij	**a** A man was in babu	**ende** was sauede in þat day
	Iohun viij	**a** It is writun þat a	**ende** nyle þou synne more

f. 3ᵛ

iiij Sunday	Galath iij	d It is writun þat a	ende haþ made vs fre
	Iohun vj	a Ihesus wente ouer þe	ende come into þe world
Moneday	iijᵒ Regum iijᵒ	e In þo daies twei w	ende in hym to make doom
	Iohun ijᵒ	c þe pask of Iewis	ende what was in man
Tewisday	Exodi xxxij	b þe Lord spak to m	ende aȝens his puple
	Iohun vij	c Whanne þe myd	ende bileeuede in hym
Wednesday	Ezechiel xxxvj	e I schal halowe	ende be to ȝou in God
	Isaye j	d Be ȝe waischun	ende good is of erþe
	Iohun ix	a Ihesus passynge siȝ a	ende and worschip him
þursday	iiijᵒ Regum iiijᵒ	d A womman of suna	ende aȝen into Galgale
	Iohun v	d Mi fadir worschip	ende aȝenrising of doom
Friday	iijᵒ Regum xvij	e þe sone of a womman	ende in þi mouþ is sooþ
	Iohun xj	a þere was a sike man	ende bileueden in hym
Saturday	Isaye l	c þe Lord God seide þes	ende I schal not forȝete þe
	Iohun viij	c I am þe liȝt of þe	ende cam not ȝit
Passioun Sunday	Ebrews ix	c Crist beynge abis	ende euerlastinge eritage
	Iohun viij	h Who of ȝou schal	ende wente out of þe temple
Moneday	Ionas iij	a þe word of þe Lord	ende do to hem and dide not
	Iohun vij	f þe princes and þe fare	ende in hym schulden take
Tewisday	Danyl xiiij	e Ȝeue to vs Danyel	ende fro þe lake of lions
	Iohun vij	a Ihesus walkide into Ga	ende for drede of þe Iewis

Wednesday	Leuytici xix	c þe Lord spak to M	ende my lawis kepe 3e
	Iohun vij	e Festis of halowing	ende and I in þe fadir
þursday	Danyel iij	h Danyel preiede to þe	ende roundnesse of londis
	Iohun vij	g þerfor of þat cum	ende into his house
Friday	Ieremy xvij	d Lord alle þat forsaken	ende treding to trede hem
	Iohun xj	g þerfor þe bisschopis	ende wiþ hise disciplis
Saturday	Ieremi xviij	e Come 3e and þenke	ende þi strong veniaunce
	Iohun vj	k Treuli treuli I seye	ende oon of þe twelue
Palm Sunday			
lessoun	Exodi xv	a þe sones forsoþe of	ende apperide in a cloude
gospel	Iohun xij	c A moche puple þat	ende wente aftir hym |
pistil	Filipenses ij	b Fele 3e þis þing in	ende of God þe fadir f. 4ʳ
passioun	Mt xxvi	a 3e witen þat aftir	and contyneþ ij capitlis
Moneday	Isaye l	d Lord God opene to me	ende and truste he on his God
	Iohun xij	a Ihesus cam bifore sixe	ende and bileeueden in Ihesum
Tewisday			
pistil	Ieremy xj	e þou Lord forsoþe ha	ende I schewide my cause
passioun	Mark xiiij	a Pask and þe feest day	and contyneþ ij capitlis
Wednesday			
lessoun	Isaye lvij	g Seye 3e to þe dou3tir	ende þe Lord 3ildide to vs
pistil	Isaye liij	a Who bileeuede to oure	ende for trispassouris

passioun	Luk xxij	a þe haly day of þerf	and contyneþ almoost ij capitlis
Scheer þursday	j Corinth xj	d Whanne ȝe comen	ende wiþ þis worlde
	Iohun xiij	a Bifor þe feest day	ende to ȝou, so do ȝe
Good Friday			
j lessoun	Osee vj	a In her tribulacioun	ende þanne brent sacrificis
ij lessoun	Exodi xij	a þe Lord forsoþe seide	ende passinge forþ of þe Lord
passioun	Iohun xviij	a He wente out wiþ	and contyneþ twei capitlis
Eestir euen			
j lessoun	Genesis j	a In þe firste God mad	ende he hadde fulfild
ij lessoun	Exodi xiiij	e And now þe morw	ende to þe Lord and seiden
iij lessoun	Isaye iiij	a And seuen wommen	ende whirlwind and fro reyn
iiij lessoun	Deuterono- mi xxxj	f Moyses wroot a song	ende fulfillid vnto þe ende
pistil	Colocenses iij	a If ȝe han risun togi	ende appere wiþ him in glorie
passioun	Mt xxviij	a In þe euentide of þe	ende bifore seide to ȝou
Eester day	j Corinth v	c Clense ȝe out þe oold	ende cleernesse and of treuþe
	Mark xv	a Mary Maudeleyn	ende as he seide to ȝou
Moneday	Actus x	h ȝe witen þe word þat	ende synnes bi his name
	Luk xxiiij	c Lo tweyne of hem wen	ende in brekynge of breed
Tewisday	Actus xiij	f Briþeren and sones of	ende and aȝenreysid Ihesus
	Luk xxiiij	f Ihesus stood in þe myd	ende name to alle folkis

Wednesday	Actus iij	c Petir siȝ and answe	ende ȝoure synnes ben don awey	
	Iohun xxj	a Ihesus eftsone schewid	ende aȝen fro deeþ	
þursday	Actus viij	e An aungel of þe Lord	ende came to Cesarie	
	Iohun xx	c Marie stood at þe g	ende he seide to me	
Friday	j Petre iij	f Crist oonys diede for	ende riȝthalf of God	
	Mt xxviij	f Enleuen disciplis	ende endinge of þe world	
Saturday	j Petre ij	a Putte ȝe awey al	ende now ȝe han merci	
	Iohun xx	a In o day of þe woke	ende rise aȝen fro deeþ |	
Firste Sunday after Eestir	j Iohun v	b Al þing þat is borun	ende witnessynge of God in him	f. 4ᵛ
	Iohun xx	d Whanne it was euen	ende lijf in his name	
Wednesday	j Corinth xv	c If Crist is prechid	ende ech man in his ordre	
	Mark xvj	d Ihesus roos eerli þe fir	ende and telden to oþer	
Friday	Ebrews xiij	e Obeye ȝe to ȝoure souer	ende of worldis. Amen	
	Mt xxviij	b Mary Mawdeleyn	ende til into þis day	
ij Sunday aftir	j Petre ij	f Crist suffrid for vs	ende of oure soulis	
	Iohun x	c I am a good scheperd	ende and o schepherd	
Wednesday	j Petre j	e Witynge þat not bi	ende withouten ende	
	Luk xxiiij	a In o day of þe woke	ende on þat þat was don	
Fryday	Romayns v	d If þoruȝ þe gilt of	ende bi Ihesus Crist oure Lord	
	Mt ix	d þe disciplis of Iohun	ende and boþe ben kept	

iij Sunday	j Petre ij	d I biseche ȝou as co	ende	also to tyrauntis
	Iohun xvj	d A litil and þan ȝe	ende	fro ȝow ȝoure ioie
Wednesday	j Iohun ij	a My litil sones I wu	ende	liȝt schyneþ now
	Iohun iij	f A questioun was mad	ende	dwelliþ in hym
Fryday	j Tessal v	b For alle ȝe ben þe so	ende	edifie ȝe eche oþer
	Iohun xij	h I liȝt cam into þe	ende	seide to me, so I speke
iiij Sunday	Iames j	d Eche good ȝifte and ech	ende	saue ȝoure soulis
	Iohun xvj	b I go to hym þat sent	ende	schal telle to ȝou
Wednesday	Iames ij	a Nile ȝe haue þe feiþ	ende	aboue reisiþ doom
	Iohun xvij	c Holi fadir kepe hem	ende	kepe hem from yuel
Friday	Iames ij	f ȝe seen þat a man	ende	good workis is deed
	Iohun xiij	f litil sones ȝit a li	ende	sue aftirward
v Sunday	Iames j	f Be ȝe doers of þe	ende	vndefoulid fro þis world
	Iohun xvj	f Treuli treuli I seye	ende	wentist out fro God
Prosessioun Moneday	Iames v	f Knouleche ȝe ech to	ende	þe multitude of synnes
	Luk xj	b Who of ȝou schal ha	ende	to men þat axen hym
Ascencion euen	Actus iiij	f Of þe multitude of	ende	nede to eche man
	Iohun xvij	a Whanne he hadde ca	ende	and I come to þee
Ascencioun dai	Actus j	a Teofile first I made	ende	goynge into heuenes
	Mark xvj	f Whanne þe enle	ende	signes folowynge

Sundai wiþyn vtas	j Petre iiij	c Be ʒe prudent and	ende	bi Ihesus Crist oure Lord	
	Iohun xv	g Whanne þe counfor	ende	þat I tolde to ʒou |	
Vtas on Ascencioun	j Petre j	d þat also ʒe silf be ho	ende	into withouten ende	f. 5ʳ
	Luk xxiiij	h I schal sende þe bi	ende	and blessynge God	
Witsoun euen					
j lesson	Genesis xxij	a God temptid Abra	ende	and he dwelt þere	
ij lesson	Deuterono- mi xxxj	f Moyses wroot a song	ende	to þe ende fulfild it	
iij lesson	Isaye iiij	a And seuen wommen	ende	into sikirnesse and hiding	
iiij lesson	Baruch iij	a Heere þou Israel þe	ende	and lyuede wiþ men	
pistil	Actus xix	a It bifil whanne apo	ende	of þe kyngdom of God	
gospel	Iohun xiiij	c If ʒe louen me, kepe	ende	schewe to him mysilf	
Witsonday	Actus ij	a Whanne þe daies of	ende	þe greet þingis of God	
	Iohun xiiij	d If ony man loueþ	ende	comaundement to me, so I do	
Witmoneday	Actus x	g Petre openede his	ende	of þe Lord Ihesus Crist	
	Iohun iij	d God loued so þe wo	ende	þei ben don in God	
Wittewisday	Actus viij	c Whanne þe apostlis	ende	resceyueden þe Holi Goost	
	Iohun x	a Treuli, treuli, I seie	ende	more plentyuousli	
Witwednesdai	Sapiens j	a Loue ʒe riʒtwisnesse	ende	kunnynge haþ of voice	
	Actus ij	c Petir stood wiþ þe	ende	of þe Lord schal be saf	
	Iohun vj	j No man may come	ende	þe lijf of þe world	

þursday	Actus viij	b Filip came doun into	ende	made in þat citee
	Luk ix	a Twelue appostlis we	ende	heelynge euerywhere
Friday	Actus ij	e Men of Israel heere	ende	in myrþe with þi face
	Luk v	e It was don in oon of	ende	merueilous þingis todai
Satirday				
j lesson	Ioel iij	a I schal heeld out my	ende	þe Lord schal be saf
ij lesson	Leuit xxiij	c þe Lord spak to M	ende	in generaciouns
iij lesson	Deuterono-mi xxvj	a Whanne þou hast en	ende	haþ 3ouun to þee
iiij lesson	Leuitici xxvj	b If 3e goon in myn he	ende	be to me a puple
v lesson	Danyel iij	k þe aungel of þe Lord	ende	hym into þe worldis
pistil	Actus xiij	j Al þe citee cam togi	ende	ioie in þe Holy Goost
gospel	Luk iiij	f Ihesus roos up fro þe	ende	þe kyngdom of God
Trynyte day	Apoc iiij	a I si3 and lo, a dore was	ende	into worldis of worldis
	Iohun iij	a þere was a man of	ende	euerlastynge lijf
Corpus Christi day	j Corinth xj	e For I haue takun	ende	of þe blood of þe Lord
	Iohun vj	l My fleisch is verili	ende	schal lyue withouten ende
First Sunday aftir Trinite	j Iohun iiij	c God is charite in þe	ende	loue also his broþer
	Luk xvj	e þere was a riche man	ende	schulen bileue to him	
f. 5ᵛ Wednesday	ij Petr j	e We not suynge vn	ende	springe in 3our hertis
	Mt v	c Nile 3e deme þat I	ende	kyngdom of heuenes

ij Sunday	j Iohun iij	d Nile ʒe wondre if	ende	but in werk and truþe
	Luk xiiij	d A man made a greet	ende	schal taste my soper
Wednesday	Effecies iiij	e þerfor I seie and wit	ende	and holynesse of truþe
	Mark xj	f and whanne he wal	ende	power I do þes þingis
iiij Sunday	j Petre v	d Be ʒe mekide vndir	ende	and schal make sad
	Luk xv	a Pupplicans and synful	ende	doynge penaunce
Wednesday	ij Tymoth iiij	f þe Lord helpide me	ende	into worldis of worldis. Amen
	Mathu v	e Be þou consentynge	ende	þi bodi go into helle
iiij Sunday	Romayns viij	d I deme þat þe passi	ende	aʒenbiynge of oure bodi
	Luk vj	h Be ʒe merciful as youre	ende	of þi broþeris iʒe
Wednesday	j Iohun ij	b In þis þing we wi	ende	walke as he walkide
	Mathu xvij	c Hise disciplis axiden	ende	was heelid fro þat oour
v Sunday	j Petre iij	c In feiþ al of oon wil	ende	þe Lord Crist in ʒour hertis
	Luk v	a Whanne þe puple cam	ende	þingis and þei sueden him
Wednesday	j Tymoth ij	a I biseche firste of	ende	men in feiþ and in treuþe
	Luk viij	e It was don in oon of	ende	see and þei obeyen to him
vj Sunday	Romayns vj	b Whiche euer we ben	ende	in Ihesus Crist oure Lord
	Mathu v	d But ʒoure riʒtful	ende	and schalt offre þi ʒifte
Wednesday	j Iohun ij	e I wroot not to ʒou	ende	to vs euerlastynge lif
	Mark x	d Whanne Ihesus was goon	ende	but not anentis God

vij Sunday	Romans vj	**e** I seie þat þing þat	**ende**	in Crist Ihesus oure Lord
	Mark viij	**a** Whanne moche pu	**ende**	of men and he lefte hem
Wednesday	Romans viij	**a** Now no þing of damp	**ende**	spirit is lijf and pees
	Mathu xij	**a** Ihesus wente bi cornes	**ende**	condempnede innocentis
viij Sunday	Romayns viij	**c** Briþeren we ben dettouris	**ende**	eiris togidre with Crist
	Mathu vij	**d** Be 3e ware of false	**ende**	kingdom of heuenes
Wednesday	Romanys v	**b** God comendiþ his ch	**ende**	bi oure Lord Ihesus Crist
	Mark ix	**g** Maistir we sien oon cas	**ende**	fire is not quenched
ix Sunday	j Corynth x	**b** þat we be not couei	**ende**	þat 3e mown suffre
	Luk xvj	**a** þere was a riche man	**ende**	euerlastynge tabernaclis
Wednesday	Romayns vj	**d** Witen 3e not þat to	**ende**	of ri3tfulnesse
	Luk xvj	**c** He þat is trewe in þe	**ende**	abhominacion bifor God |
f. 6ʳ **x Sunday**	j Corinth xij°	**a** 3e witen þat whan	**ende**	bi hem silf as he wole
	Luk xix	**g** He si3 þe citee and w	**ende**	euery dai in þe temple
Wednesday	j Corinth xv	**e** Not ech fleisch is	**ende**	þat þat is spiritual
	Luk xxj	**f** Take 3e hede to 3ou	**ende**	bifore mannys sone
xj Sunday	j Corinth xv	**a** Briþeren I make þe	**ende**	was not voide in me
	Luk xviij	**b** He seide also to sum men	**ende**	schal be enhancid
Wednesday	j Corinth vj	**f** Witen 3e not þat 3oure	**ende**	bere 3e God in 3oure body
	Luk xviij	**a** He seide also to hem	**ende**	his chosun criynge to him

xij Sunday	j Corinth iij	**b** We han suche trust	**ende** is plentyuous in glorie
	Mark vij	**f** Ihesus ȝede out fro þe	**ende** and doumbe men speke
Wednesday	ij Corinth iiij	**c** We prechen not vs	**ende** schewide in ȝoure bodies
	Mathu xj	**e** þan Ihesus bigan to	**ende** þe day of dome þan to ȝou
xiij Sunday	Galath iij	**d** Biheestis werun seide	**ende** to hem þat bileeuen
	Luk x	**f** Blessid ben þe iȝen þat	**ende** and do þou on like maner
Wednesday	j Tessal ij	**d** Briþeren be ȝe mynde	**ende** in ȝou þat han bileued
	Mathu xij	**d** þe faresies wenten	**ende** schulen hope in his name
xiiij Sunday	Galath v	**d** Walke ȝe in spirit	**ende** vicis and coueityngis
	Luk xvij	**d** Ihesus wente into Ierusalem	**ende** haþ made þe saaf
Wednesday	ij Corinth vj	**f** Nile ȝe bere ȝocke	**ende** in þe drede of God
	Luk xij	**d** Oon of þe puple sei	**ende** and God fediþ hem
xv Sunday	Galath v	**g** If we lyuen bi spirit	**ende** homelich of þe feiþ
	Mt vj	**f** No man may serue	**ende** schulen be caste to ȝou
Wednesday	j Tymoth j	**c** We witen þat þe la	**ende** and loue þat as in Crist Ihesu
	Luk xx	**a** It was don in oon of	**ende** I schal do þes þingis
xvj Sunday	Effec iij	**e** I axe þat ȝe failen	**ende** wordlis of worldis
	Luk vij	**b** Ihesus wente into a ci	**ende** visitid his puple
Wednesday	Colocensis	**c** Se ȝe þat no man	**ende** to ȝou alle giltis
	Mark viij	**e** þei camen to Beth	**ende** streete seie to no man

Sunday	Ester iiij	**a** I bounden for þe Lord	**ende**	alle þingis and in vs alle
	Luk xiiij	**a** Whanne he hadde	**ende**	his schal be hiȝede
Ymbir Wednesday	Amos ix	**f** Lo daies come seiþ	**ende**	hem seiþ þe Lord þi God
	ij Esdre viij	**a** Al þe puple is gade	**ende**	is ȝoure strengþe
	Mark ix	**d** Oon of þe companye	**ende**	in preier and fastinge
Ymbir Friday pistil	Osee xiiij	**b** Israel be þou conuertid	**ende**	walke in hem |
f. 6ᵛ	Luk vij	**f** Oon of þe faresies	**ende**	go þou in pees
Saturday				
j lessoun	Leuit xxiij	**e** þe Lord God spak to	**ende**	ȝoure halidaies
ij lessoun	Leuit xxiij	**f** þe Lord God spak to	**ende**	I þe Lord ȝoure God
iij lessoun	Mychee vij	**f** Lord oure God fede	**ende**	fadris fro oold daies
iiij lessoun	Sach viij	**e** þe word of þe Lord	**ende**	seiþ þe Lord of oostis
v lessoun	Danyel iij	**k** þe aungel of þe Lord	**ende**	hym into worldis
pistil	Ebrews ix	**a** þe tabernacle was	**ende**	euerlastynge redempcioun
gospel	Luk xiij	**b** A man hadde a fige	**ende**	gloriousli don of him
xviij Sunday aftir Trinite	j Corinth j	**b** I do þankyngis to my	**ende**	oure Lord Ihesus Crist
	Mathu xxij	**f** Faresies heerynge	**ende**	to axe hym more
Wednesday	Romayns xv	**f** I biseche ȝou bi oure	**ende**	be wiþ ȝou alle. Amen
	Mathu xiij	**f** þe kyngdom of heuenes	**ende**	makinge of þe world

xix Sunday	Effec iiij	f Be 3e renewid in þe spi	ende 3eue to þe nedy
	Mathu ix	a Ihesus wente vp into	ende suche power to men
Wednesday	ij Tessal ij	g Briþeren stonde 3e	ende and in þe pacience of Crist
	Mathu xiij	g Disciplis camen to	ende of heerynge heer he
xx Sunday	Effec v	d Se 3e how warli 3e	ende in þe drede of Crist
	Mathu xxij	a Ihesus answerid and spak	ende but fewe chosun
Wednesday	ij Tymothe ij	a Be counfortid in grace	ende in alle þingis
	Luk xiiij	c He seide to hym þat	ende in þe rewme of God
xxj Sunday	Effecies vj	c Be 3e counfortid in	ende þat is þe word of God
	Iohun iiij	f A litil kyng was	ende he bileeuede and al his hous
Wednesday	j Tessal j	c 3e loued briþeren of	ende fro deeþ þe Lord Ihesus
	Luk vj	c It was don in anoþer	ende schulden do of Ihesu
xxij Sunday	Philipenses j	b Tristnynge þis ilke	ende heriynge of God
	Mathu xviij	f þe kyngdom of he	ende of 3oure hertis
Wednesday	Romans iij	d We witen þat whan	ende feiþ of Ihesus Crist
	Mark xj	e Treuli I seye to 3ou	ende 3ou 3oure synnes
xxiij Sunday	Philipen iij	f Briþeren be 3e my fo	ende suget to hym
	Mathu xxij	d þanne faresies 3eden	ende þingis þat ben of God
Wednesday	Romans v	d If þoru3 þe gilt of oo	ende Ihesus Crist oure Lord
	Mathu xvij	f Whanne þei camen tr	ende for þee and for me

xxiiij Sunday	Colocensis j	c þerfor we fro þe day	**ende**	remyssioun of synnes
	Mathu ix	e While þat Ihesus spak	**ende**	and þe damysel roos |
f. 7ʳ **Wednesday**	j Corinth x	e I nyle þat ȝe be made	**ende**	þe glorie of God
	Mathu xxj	f A man hadde twey so	**ende**	þat ȝe bileeueden to him
xxv Sunday aftir Trinite	Ieremi xxiij	b Lo daies comen seiþ þe	**ende**	In þer owne lond
	Iohun vj	b Whanne Ihesus hadde lift	**ende**	into þe worlde
In feest of relikis	Eccl xliiij	c þo men of merci ben	**ende**	telliþ þe preisinge of hem
	Mathu v	a Ihesus seynge þe puple	**ende**	plentyuous in heuenes
Dedicacioun day	Luk xix	a Ihesus turnede aȝen and	**ende**	þing þat perischide
Sunday withyn vtas	Luk vj	k Eche þat comeþ to	**ende**	was mad greet
Vtas of Dedicacioun	Iohun x	e But þe feestis of ha	**ende**	in me and I in þe fadir
In recounciling of chirche	Luk vj	j It is not a good tre	**ende**	was made greet
þe pistil to alle þes dayes	Apoc xxj	a I Iohun siȝe þe holi citee	**ende**	alle þingis newe

Here enden dominicalis and feriales and bigynnen comemoraciouns in þis ordre:

Comemoracioun of oure Ladi in Aduent: Isaye vij and Luk j as on þe þridde Wednesdai in Aduent.

Also fro Cristmas to Candilmas: Tite iij, Luk j as on Cristemasse nyȝt at þe secunde masse.

Also in Estir tyme	Eccl xxiiij	c Fro þe bigynnynge and	**ende**	myn wiþholdynge
	Iohun xix	e Bisidis þe crosse of	**ende**	hir into his modir

Comemoracioun of oure Ladi in alle oþer tymes of þe ȝeer: Eccl xxiiij and Luk xj as on Assumpcioun euen

Comemoracioun of þe Trinite	ij Corinth xiij	g þe grace of oure Lord	ende	in Crist Ihesus oure Lord
	Romans xj	g A þe hiȝnessis of rit	ende	be glorie into worldis
	Iohun xv	g Whanne þe counfortour	ende	þat I toold to ȝou
Of þe Holi Goost	Actus viij	c Whanne þe apostlis	ende	resceyue þe Holi Goost
	Iohun xiiij	d If ony man loueþ me	ende	to me so I do
Of þe crosse	Philipenses ij	c He mekide hymsilf	ende	of God þe fadir
	Mathu xx	d Ihesus wente vp to Ie	ende	rise aȝen to lijf
Of aungelis	Apoc xix	c He seide to me, write	ende	worschip þou God
	Iohun v	a Aftir þes þingis was	ende	sikenesse he was holdun
For briþeren and sistirs and salus populi	Isaye xviij	g In þat tyme ȝifte schal	ende	seiþ þe Lord almiȝti
	Mark xij	j Ihesus sittynge aȝens þe	ende	Al hir lifelode
For þe pees	ij Mach j	a þe prestis maden her	ende	ȝou in yuel tyme
	Iohun xvj	g Lo þe oour comeþ	ende	ouercome þe world
For cler wedir a pistil	Trenorum ij	g Rise vp togidre preise	ende	Lord and my God |
gospel	Luk viij	e And it was don	ende	þei obeyen to hym
For reyn	Ieremy xiiij	g Wheþer þou castynge	ende	madist alle þes þingis
	Mathu vj	g Nile ȝe be bisye sei	ende	caste to ȝou
In tyme of batel	Hester xiij	f Lord kyng almiȝti	ende	men preisynge þe
	Mark xj	e Truli I seie to ȝou	ende	to ȝou ȝoure synnes

f. 7ᵛ

A man for himsilf	Romanys vij	f I delite togidir to þe	ende	Ihesus Crist oure Lord
	Iohun xv	c If ȝe dwellen in me	ende	ben don to ȝou
For pestilens of beests	Ieremi xiiij	c If oure wickidnes	ende	ne forsake þou vs
	Mathu vij	c Axe ȝe and it schal be	ende	to men þat axen him
For pilgryms	Gen xxiiij	b þe Lord of heuene	ende	his aungel bifor þe
	Mathu x	b Go ȝe and preche	ende	þanne to þilke cite
For weddingis	j Corinth vj	f Witen ȝe not þat	ende	God in ȝoure bodi
	Mathu xix	b Faresies camen	ende	God haþ ioynede
For synners	Romayns v	b God comendiþ his	ende	in þe lijf of hym
	Luk v	f Ihesus wente out and	ende	men to penaunce
For sike	Iames v	e If ony of ȝou is so	ende	þat ȝe be sauede
	Luk iiij	f Ihesus roos fro þe sy	ende	and heelid hem
pistlis	j Thessalo iiij	f We wolen not þat ȝe	ende	in þes wordis
For dede	ij Mach xij	h Spekynge togidre	ende	be relesid fro synnes
Sunday	Apocal xiiij	e I herd a voice fro he	ende	of hem suen hem
Monday	j Corynth xv	c If Crist is prechid	ende	man in his ordre
Tewisdai	Iohun xj	c Martha seide to	ende	into þis world
Wednesdai	Iohun vj	h Al þing þat þe fadir	ende	it in þe laste day
þursdai	Iohun v	f Treuli, treuli, I seye	ende	aȝenrisyng of doom
Friday	Iohun v	e For as þe fadir rei	ende	fro deeþ into lijf
Saturdai	Iohun vj	g I am breed of lijf	ende	it in þe laste day
	Iohun vj	f Truli, Treuli, I seye	ende	it in þe laste day

Here endiþ þe rule of þe temporal and bigynneþ þe rule of þe sanctorum boþe of þe propre and þe comun

Of Nouembir

S Andreus euen	Eccl xliiij	g þe blessynge of þe	ende	crowne of glorie
	Iohun j	e Iohun stood and tweyne	ende	on mannys sone
Seynt Andrewis day	Romayns x	d Bi herte me bileeu	ende	endis of þe world
	Mathu iiij	e Ihesus walkide bisidis	ende	and sueden hym

In Decembir

Seynt Nicholas day	Eccl xliiij	d Lo þe greet prest	ende	of swetnesse
	Mathu xxv	b A man þat goiþ in	ende	ioye of þi Lord |
Vtas of Andrew	Romayns x	d Bi herte me bileeueþ	ende	þe endis of þe world f. 8ʳ
	Mark j	c Aftir þat Iohun was	ende	þei sueden hym
Concepcioun of oure Lady	Eccl xxiiij	d I as a vyne fruytid	ende	euerlastynge lijf
	Mathu j	a þe book of þe genera	ende	þat is clepide Crist
S Luce, virgyn	Eccl lj	c Mi Lord God þou en	ende	Lord þou art my God
	Mathu xiij	h þe kyngdom of heue	ende	newe þingis and oold
Vigil of Thomas, apostil	Eccl xliiij and xlv, b	g þe blessinge	ende	þe crowne of glorie
	Iohun xv	a I am a verry vyne	ende	schal be don to 3ou
S Thomas day, apostil	Effecies ij	f Now 3e ben not ges	ende	in þe Holi Goost
	Iohun xx	e Thomas oon of þe t	ende	and han bileeuede

Ianeuer

S Felice	ij Tymo iiij	a I witnesse bifor God	ende	louen his comynge
	Mathu xiij	h þe kyngdom of heuenes	ende	newe þingis and oold

S Mauri, abbot	Eccl xxxix	c þe riȝtwise he schal	ende	fro generacioun into generacioun
	Luk xj	f No man tendiþ a	ende	ȝeue liȝt to þee
S Marcellus, pope and martir	Ebrews v	a Eche bisschop takun	ende	of Melchisedech
	Mark xiij	f Se ȝe wake ȝe and preie	ende	to alle wake ȝe
S Sulfice, bisschop and confessour	Sapiens x	d þe Lord ledde forþ a	ende	euerlastinge cleernesse
	Mathu xxv	b A man þat goiþ in	ende	into þe ioie of þi Lord
S Prisse, virgin and martir	Eccl lj	c Mi Lord God þou en	ende	Lord þou art my God
	Mathu xiij	h þe kyngdom of heue	ende	newe þingis and oolde
St Wolston, bisschop and confessour	Eccl xliiij	d Lo þe greet prest	ende	smelle of swetnesse
	Mathu xxv	b As a man þat goiþ in	ende	þe ioie of þi Lord
S Fabian and Sebastian	Ebrews xj	f Whiche bi feiþ ouer	ende	witnessynge of feiþ
	Luk vj	e Ihesus cam doun fro	ende	is moche in heuene
S Agneys, virgin martir	Eccl lj	a Lord kyng I schal	ende	Lord my God newe
	Mathu xiij	h þe kyngdom of he	ende	newe þingis and oold
S Vincent, martir	Eccli xiiij and xv	f Blessid is þe b it schal	ende ende	of God Lord oure God
	Iohun xij	d But a corn of whe	ende	schal worschip him
Conuersioun of S Poul	Actus ix	a Saul ȝit a blower	ende	þat þis is Crist
	Mathu xix	g Petir answerid and	ende	euerlastynge lijf
S Iuhan, bisschop and confessour	Ecclu xlvij	c þe Lord haþ ȝoue	ende	he schal be blessid
	Mark xiij	f Se ȝe wake ȝe and	ende	to alle wake ȝe
S Agneis ij	ij Corinth x	g He þat glorieþ	ende	virgyn to Crist
	Mt xxv	a þe rewme of heuenes	ende	þe day ne þe oour |

S Batilde, queen	Sapiens vij	**g** Wisdom ouercomeþ	**ende** viij **a** of hise werkis	f. 8ᵛ
	Mathu xiij	**h** þe kingdom of heue	**ende** newe þingis and oolde	
Feuerer				
S Bride	ij Corinth x	**g** He þat glorieþ haue	**ende** virgyn to Crist	
	Mathu xxj	**a** þe kyngdom of heuenes	**ende** þe day ne þe oour	
Candilmas day	Malachie iij	**b** þe Lord God seiþ þes	**ende** seiþ þe Lord almiʒti	
	Luk ij	**e** And aftir þat þat þe dai	**ende** of þi puple Israel	
S Blaise, bish.	Ebrews v	**a** Eche bisschop takun	**ende** of Melchisedech	
	Mathu x	**e** No þing is hid þat	**ende** þat is in heuene	
S Agas, virgin	Eccl lj	**a** Lord kyng I schal k	**ende** þe Lord my God	
	Mathu xiij	**h** þe kyngdom of heuenes	**ende** newe þingis and oold	
S Vedast and Amand, confessours	Ebrews viij	**f** þe oþer werun made	**ende** offrynge hymsilf	
	Luk xij	**f** Be ʒoure leendis gird	**ende** mannys sone schal come	
S Scolastic, virgin	Sapiens vij	**g** Wisdom ouercomeþ ma	**ende** of hise werkis	
	Mathu xxv	**a** þe kyngdom of heue	**ende** þe day ne þe oour	
S Valentyn, martir	Eccl xxxj	**b** Blessid is a man w	**ende** hise almesdedis	
	Mathu xvj	**f** If ony man wole co	**ende** in his kyngdom	
S Iulian, virgin and martir	Eccl lj	**c** My Lord God þou en	**ende** Lord þou art my God	
	Mathu xiij	**h** þe kingdom of heue	**ende** newe þingis and elde	

Chayryng of S Petir	j Petre j	**a** Petir apostle of Ihesus	**ende** of Ihesus Crist
	Mathu xvj	**c** Ihesus cam into þe par	**ende** also in heuenes
S Mathi, apostle	Actus j	**d** Petir roos vp in þe	**ende** enleuene apostlis
	Mathu xj	**f** I knouleche to þee	**ende** my charge liȝt
March			
S Perpetue, virgin martir	j Corynth vij	**e** Of virgyns I haue no	**ende** in body and spirit
	Math xxv	**a** þe kyngdom of he	**ende** þe day ne þe oour
S Gregor, pope	Iames j	**b** Briþeren deme ȝe al	**ende** to men þat louen hym
	Mark xiij	**f** Se ȝe wake ȝe and prei	**ende** I seie to all wake ȝe
S Edward, kyng and martir	Eccl xxxj	**b** Blessid is a man w	**ende** hise almesdedis
	Luk xiiij	**f** If ony man comeþ	**ende** not be my disciple
S Cuthbert, bis. and confessour	Eccl xliiij	**d** Lo þe greet prest	**ende** smel of swetnesse
	Mathu xxv	**b** A man þat goiþ in pil	**ende** ioie of þe Lord
S Benet, abbot	Eccl xxxix	**c** þe riȝtwise man schal	**ende** ioie of þe Lord
	Luk xj	**f** No man tendiþ a lau	**ende** into generacioun
Annunciacioun of oure Lady	Isaye vij	**c** In þo dayes þe Lord	**ende** yuel and chees good
	Luk j	**d** þe aungel Gabriel	**ende** to me aftir þi word |
f. 9ʳ **April**			
S Richard, bish. and confessour	Eccl xliiij	**d** Lo þe greet prest	**ende** of swetnesse
	Mathu xxv	**b** a man þat goiþ in pil	**ende** ioie of þi Lord
S Ambrose, bissh. and confessour	Eccli xlvij	**f** þe Lord haþ ȝoue kno	**ende** he schal be blessid
	Mathu v	**b** ȝe ben salt of þe erþ	**ende** þat is in heuenes

S Tiburse and Valerian	Parables xv	**a** þe tunge of wise men	**ende** loued of þe Lord
	Ihoun xv	**b** I am a vyne ȝe þe	**ende** schal be don to ȝou
S Alfey, bish. and marter	Ebrews xiij	**c** Nile ȝe be led awey	**ende** God is discernede
	Iohun xv	**a** I am a verri vyne	**ende** schal be don to ȝou
S George, martir	Iames j	**b** Briþeren deme ȝe al	**ende** þat louen hym
	Iohun xv	**a** I am a verry vyne	**ende** schal be don to ȝou
Mark, euangelist	Effecies iiij	**b** To ech of vs grace	**ende** of þe plente of Crist
	Iohun xv	**a** I am a verry vyne	**ende** schal be don to ȝou
May Philip and Iacob	Sapiens v	**a** Iust men schulen stonde	**ende** is among seyntis
	Iohun xiiij	**a** Be not ȝoure herte	**ende** schal do þis þing
Fyndyng of þe crosse	Galath v	**c** I trist on ȝou	**end** ȝou in Crist
	vj	**d** For who euer	**ende** þe worlde
	Iohun iij	**a** þere was a man of	**ende** euerlastynge lijf
S Iohun Portlatyn	Eccl xv	**a** Who drediþ God	**ende** þe Lord oure God
	Iohun xxj	**f** He seiþ to hym sue	**ende** witnessynge is trewe
S Gordian and Epymach	Sapiens iij	**a** þe soulis of iust men	**ende** wiþouten ende
	Iohun xv	**b** I am a vyne ȝe þe	**ende** schal be don to ȝou
S Nerey and Achillei and Pancras	Sapiens v	**d** Iust men schulen li	**ende** a certeyn place
	Iohun xxj	**b** I am a vyne ȝe þe	**ende** schal be don to ȝou
S Dunston, bish.	Eccl xliiij	**d** Lo a greet prest	**ende** smelle of swetnesse
	Iohun xv	**a** I am a verri vyne	**ende** schal be don to ȝou
S Vrban and Aldelyn	Sapiens x	**d** þe Lord led forþ a	**ende** þe Lord is oure God
	Iohun xv	**a** I am a verri vyne	**ende** schal be don to ȝou

S Austyn of Engelond	Eccl xlvij	f þe Lord haþ ȝoue	ende	he schal be blessid
	Iohun xv	a I am a verry	ende	schal be don to ȝou
S German, bish. and confessour	Eccl xliiij	d Lo þe greet prest	ende	smal of swetnesse
	Mathu xxv	b As a man þat goiþ	ende	þe ioie of þi Lord
S Purnel, virgin	ij Corinth x	g He þat glorieþ ha	ende	a chast virgyn to Crist
	Mt xxv	a þe rewme of heuenes	ende	þe day ne þe oour
Juyn				
S Nicomede	Eccl xiiij	f Blessid is þe man	ende	him þe Lord oure God
	Mathu xvj	f If ony man wole co	ende	in his kyngdom |
f. 9ᵛ **S Marcel and Pete**	Apoc vij	d Oon of þe senyouris	ende	fro þe iȝen of hem
	Luk xxj	c Whanne ȝe schuln he	ende	into witnessynge
S Boneface, bish. and marter	j Corinth iiij	d We ben made a spec	ende	derworþe sones
	Mathu x	d Whanne þei pursue	ende	drede ȝe not hem
S Medard and Gildard	Ebrews vij	f þe oþer werun mad	ende	in offrynge hym silf
	Luk xij	f Be ȝoure leendis	ende	mannys sone schal come
Translacioun of S Edmund and Prime and Filiciane	Eccl l	a Biholde þis is þe gret	ende	bi daies euerlastynge
	Mathu xxv	b As a man þat goiþ	ende	into þe ioie of þi Lord
S Barnabe, apostle	Effec ij	f Now ȝe ben not ges	ende	in þe Holy Goost
	Iohun xv	d þis is my comaunde	ende	he ȝeueþ to ȝou
S Basilidis, Cyrini and Nabor	Sapiens iij	a þe soulis of iust men	ende	regne wiþouten ende
	Mathu x	c Lo, I sende ȝou as sche	ende	ende schal be saaf

S Basile, confessour	Eccl xliiij	**d** Lo, þe greet preest	**ende** smel of swetnesse
	Mathu xxv	**b** As a man þat goiþs	**ende** into þe ioie of þi Lord
S Vite and Modeste	Sapiens v	**d** Iust men schulen ly	**ende** into a certeyn place
	Luk xj	**h** Wo to ʒou þat bilden	**ende** mouþ to accuse him
S Botulf, abbot	Eccl xxxix	**c** þe riʒtwise man schal	**ende** generacioun into generacioun
	Luk xj	**f** No man tendiþ a	**ende** ʒe liʒt to þee
S Mark and Marcellian	Parab xv	**a** þe tunge of wise	**ende** be loued of þe Lord
	Mark xiij	**b** Loke ʒe þat no man	**ende** ende schal be saf
S Geruaise and Protaise	Romayns viij	**f** We witen þat to men	**ende** in Crist Ihesus oure Lord
	Mathu xxiiij	**a** Ihesus wente out of	**ende** ende schal be saf
Translacioun of S Edward king	Eccl xxxj	**b** Blessid is a man	**ende** hise almesdedis
	Luk xiiij	**f** If ony man comeþ	**ende** not be my disciple
S Albon, martir of Yngelond	Sapiens iiij	**c** A iust man þouʒ he	**ende** hise chosun men
	Mathu xvj	**f** If ony man wole	**ende** in his kyngdom
Vigil of Baptist	Ieremy j	**b** In þo daies þe word	**ende** seiþ þe Lord almiʒti
	Luk j	**a** þer was a preest and	**ende** puple to þe Lord
Natyuyte of Baptist	Isaye ij	**a** Ilis heere ʒe and puplis	**ende** Israel þat chees þe
	Luk j	**g** þe tyme of bering	**ende** of his puple
Ioon and Paul martirs	Eccl xliiij	**c** þo ben men of merci	**ende** telliþ þe preisynge of hem
	Luk xij	**a** Be ʒe ware of þe	**ende** aungelis of God
Vigil of Petir and Poul	Actus iij	**a** Petir and Iohun wen	**ende** bifilde to hym
	Iohun xxj	**e** Ihesus seiþ to Symound	**ende** glorifie God	

f. 10ʳ **Feest of Petir and** Actus xij a Heroude þe   ende þe puple of Iewis
    Poul   kyng sent

                          Mathu xvj c Ihesus came into ende also in heuenes
                                        þe

Comemoracioun of Galath j c Briþeren I make ende þei glorifien God
  Poul   k

                          Mathu xix g Petir answerid ende euerlastynge lijf
                                        and

Iuyl

Vtas of Baptist Isaye jl a Ilis heere ȝe and ende þat chees þee
                                    pu

                          Luk j c Zacharie seide to ende repreef among men

S Swithin, Proses Ebrews xj f Whiche bi feiþ ende witnessynge of feiþ
  and Martinus   ouer

                          Iohun xv e þes þingis I ende wiþouten cause
                                    coma

Translacion of S Eccl xliiij d Lo þe greet prest ende smel of swetnesse
  Martyn   Luk xij e Nile ȝe litil floc ende sone schal come
                                    dred

Vtas of Petir and Eccl xliiij c þo ben men of ende preisynge of hem
  Poul   merci

                          Mathu xliij e Ihesus compellid ende art Goddis sone
                                      þe dis

Translacion of S Ebrews v a Eche bisschop ende of Melchisedech
  Thomas   takun

                          Luk xix b A worþi man ende and ȝede vp to
                                    went   Ierusalem

Of vij briþeren Ebrews x f Haue ȝe mynde ende lyueþ of feiþ
                                  on

                        Mathu xij g ȝit while he spak ende and sistir and
                                            modir

Translacioun of S Eccl xxxix c þe riȝtwise schal ende into generacioun
  Benet   Luk xj f No man tendiþ a ende ȝeueþ liȝt to þee

Translacion of S Ebrews xij f þe oþer werun ende offrynge hymsilf
  Swithun   mad

                        Luk xij f Be ȝoure leendis ende sone schal come

S Kenelm, king and Eccl xxxj b Blessid is a man ende hise almesdedis
  martir   Luk xiiij f If ony man com ende not be my disciple

S Arnulf, king and marter	Eccl xiiij	f Blessid is	ende his wit
	xv	b and it schal	ende Lord oure God
	Mathu xvj	f If ony man wole	ende in his kyngdom
S Margerite, v.	Eccl lj	c My Lord God þou	ende þou art my God
	Mathu xiij	h þe kyngdom of he	ende newe þingis and oold
S Praxede, virgin	Sapiens vij	g Wisdom ouercomeþ	ende of hise werkis
	Mathu xxv	a þe rewme of heuenes	ende þe day ne þe oour
Mari Maudelyn	Prouerb xxxj	c Who schal fynde a	ende hir in þe ȝatis
	Luk vij	f Oon of þe faresies	ende go þou in pees
S Appolinar, martir	ij Tymo iiij	a I witnesse bifore God	ende louen his comynge
	Luk xxij	d Strijf was made a	ende kynredis of Israel
Vigil of James	Eccl xliiij	g þe blessynge of þe	ende crowne of glorie
	Iohun xv	a I am a verry vyne	ende be don to ȝou |
Iames, apostle	Effecies ij	f Now ȝe ben not ges	ende in þe Holi Goost f. 10ᵛ
	Mathu xx	e þanne þe modir of	ende redi of my fadir
S Anne, oure Lady modir	Proub xxxj	c Who schal fynde a	ende preise hir in þe ȝatis
	Mathu j	a þe book of þe gener	ende þat is clepide Crist
Of vij slepers	Sapiens iij	a þe soulis of iust men	ende wiþouten ende
	Luk xxj	c Whanne ȝe shuln he	ende into witnessynge
S Sampson, bish. and confessour	Eccl xliiij	d Lo þe greet prest	ende smel of swetnesse
	Mathu xxv	b As a man þat goiþ	ende ioie of þi Lord

S Felice Symplici and Faustin	Parabl xv	a þe tunge of wise	ende	be loued of þe Lord
	Luk xij	a Be ȝe ware of þe so	ende	þe aungels of God
S Abdon and Sennes	ij Corinth j	b Blessid be God and þe	ende	plenteuous in vs
	Mark xiij	b Luke ȝe þat no man	ende	schal be saf
S Germayn, bish.	Sapiens x	d þe Lord ledde forþ a	ende	þe Lord is oure God
	Mark xiij	f Se ȝe wake ȝe and prei	ende	to alle wake ȝe
August				
Lammasse day	Actus xij	d He cam to þe hous	ende	hym out of prisoun
	Mt xvj	c Ihesus cam into þe pre	ende	also in heuenes
S Steuen, pope and marter	Ebrews v	a Ech bisshop takun	ende	of Melchisedech
	Luk xix	b A worþi man went	ende	ȝede vp into Ierusalem
Finding of Steuen	Act vj	d Steuen fin	ende	þat spak
	viij	f and þei hiden	ende	he diede
	Mathu xxxiij	f Lo I sende to ȝou pre	ende	name of þe Lord
S Oswold, king and marter	Eccl xxxj	b Blessid is a man	ende	hise almesdedis
	Luk xiiij	f If ony man comeþ	ende	not be my disciple
S Sixte, Filisisime and Agapite, marters	ij Corinth j	b Blessid be God and þe	ende	also of counfort
	Luk xxj	c Whanne ȝe schulen	ende	into witnessinge
S Donat, bish. martir	ij Tymo ij	b No man holdynge	ende	heuenli glorie
	Mark xiij	f Se ȝe wake ȝe and prei	ende	to alle wake ȝe
S Ciriaci, martir, with hise felowis	Eccl ij	c ȝe dredynge þe Lord	ende	merciful is þe Lord
	Mark xvj	g Go ȝe into al þe w	ende	schulen wexe hool

Vigil of Laurence	Eccl lj	**a** Lord kyng I schal	**ende** þe Lord my God	
	Math xvj	**f** If ony man wole co	**ende** in his kyngdom	
Laurens, martir	ij Corinth ix	**c** He þat sowiþ scar	**ende** riȝtwisnesse	
	Iohun xij	**d** But a corn of w	**ende** worschip hym	
S Tiburs, martir	Ebrews xiij	**c** Nile ȝe be led awey	**ende** God is disseruede	
	Mathu xvj	**f** If ony man wole co	**ende** in his kyngdom |	
S Ypolite, martir	Sapiens iiij	**c** A iust man þouȝ	**ende** hise chosun men	f. 11ʳ
	Luk xij	**a** Be ȝe ware of	**ende** þe aungels of God	
Vigil of Assumpcioun	Eccl xxiiij	**c** Fro þe bigynnynge	**ende** myn wiþholdynge	
	Luyk xj	**e** It was don whan	**ende** and kepen it	
Assumpcioun day	Eccl xxiiij	**b** In alle þes men I	**ende** swetnesse of odour	
	Luk x	**g** He entride into a	**ende** be takun awei fro him	
Vtas of S Laurence	ij Corynth ix	**c** He þat sowiþ scars	**ende** of ȝoure riȝtwisnesse	
	Mathu x	**g** He þat loueþ dafir	**ende** not leese his mede	
Vtas of Assumpcioun	Cant iij	**g** ȝe douȝtris of Syon	**ende** clustris of grapis	
	Luk x	**g** He entride into a	**ende** be takun awei fro him	
Vigil of Bartholomewe	Prouerb iij	**c** Blessid is þe man	**ende** bi dewe woxen togidre	
	Iohun xv	**a** I am a verri vyne	**ende** schal be don to ȝou	
Bartolmew	Effecies ij	**f** Now ȝe ben not ges	**ende** in þe Holy Goost	
	Luk xxiij	**d** Strijf was made	**ende** kynredis of Israel	
S Ruphe, martir	Eccl xiiij	**f** Blessid is þe man	**ende** þe Lord oure God	
	Math x	**e** No þing is hid	**ende** þat is in heuenes	
S Austin, doctour	Eccl xlvij	**f** þe Lord haþ ȝoue k	**ende** schal be blessid	
	Mathu v	**b** ȝe ben salt of þe er	**ende** þat in heuenes	

Bihedynge of S I. Baptist	Prouerb x	g þe abidynge of iust	ende	blessynge of iust men
	Mark vj	d Heroude sente and	ende	leide it in a biriel
S Felice and Audacte	Sap iij	a þe soulis of iust	ende	wiþouten ende
	Luk xij	a Be ȝe ware of þe	ende	þe aungels of God
S Cutburgh, virgin	ij Corinth x	g He þat glorieþ ha	ende	virgyn to Crist
	Mathu xxv	a þe rewme of heue	ende	þe day ne þe oour
Septembre				
Translacioun of S Cuthbert	Eccl xliiij	d Lo þe greet preest	ende	of swetnesse
	Mt xxv	b As a man þat goiþ	ende	þe ioie of þi Lord
Vigil of Natyuyte	Eccl xxiiij	c Fro þe bigynnynge	ende	myn wiþholdynge
	Luk xj	e It was don whanne	ende	of God and kepen it
Natyuyte of oure Ladi	Eccl xxiiij	b I as a vyne made	ende	euerlastyne lijf
	Mathu j	a þe book of þe gener	ende	is clepid Crist
Fering of þe cros	Galath v	c I truste on ȝou in	ende	and I seye ȝou in Crist
	Iohun xiij	f Now is þe doom of	ende	ȝe ben þe children of liȝt
Vtas of Natyuyte	Sapiens iiij	a Hou faire is a chast	ende	be in refreischinge
	Luk xj	e It was don whanne	ende	of God and kepen it |
S Edith and Eufemye, virgins	ij Corinth x	g He þat glorieþ ha	ende	a chast virgyn to Crist
	Mathu xxv	a þe rewme of heuenes	ende	þe day ne þe oour
S Lambert, martir	Ebrews v	a Eche bisschop takun	ende	of Melchisedech
	Mathu ix	g Ihesus wente aboute	ende	into his ripe corn

f. 11ᵛ

Vigil of Math.	Prouerb iij	c Blessid is þe man	**ende** togidir bi dewe
	Luk v	f Ihesus wente out and si3	**ende** men to penaunce
Mathu, apostle	Ezechiel j	c þe liknesse of þe ch	**ende** of leite schynynge
	Mathu ix	c Whanne Ihesus passid fro	**ende** but synful men
S Maury with hise felowis	Ebrews xj	f Whiche bi feiþ ouer	**ende** witnessynge of feiþ
	Luk vj	e Ihesus cam doun fro þe	**ende** is moche in heuene
S Tecle, virgyn	ij Corynth x	g He þat glorieþ ha	**ende** a chast virgyn to Crist
	Mathu xxv	a þe rewme of heuenes	**ende** day ne þe oour
S Firmyn, bish.	Ebrews v	a Eche bisschop takun	**ende** of Mechisedech
	Mathu ix	g Ihesus wente aboute	**ende** into his ripe corn
S Ciprian and Iustyne	Sapiens v	d Iust men schulen ly	**ende** into a certeyn place
	Mathu x	d Whanne þei pursu	**ende** drede 3e not hem
S Cosme and Damyan, martris	ij Corinth j	b Blessid be God and þe	**ende** plentyuous in vs
	Luk vj	f Whanne hise i3en	**ende** moche in heuene
My3hel Archaungil	Apoc j	b He signefiede sending	**ende** synnes in his blood
	Mathu xviij	a Disciplis camen to	**ende** þat is in heuenes
S Ierom, doctour	Eccl xlvij	f þe Lord haþ 3oue kno	**ende** he schal be blessid
	Mathu v	b 3e ben salt of þe er	**ende** þat is in heuenes
S Remigius and Geruasius	Ebrews vij	f þe oþer werun mad	**ende** offrynge hymsilf
	Luk xij	f Be 3oure leendis	**ende** sone schal come

Octobir

S Leodegar, bish. and marter	ij Tymo ij iiij	c Be þou mynde but þou	ende	glorie
			ende	persecucioun
	Luk x	d He þat heeriþ 30u	ende	in heuenes
S Feiþ, virgin	Eccl lj	c My Lord God þou en	ende	Lord þou art my God
	Mat xiij	h þe kyngdom of he	ende	newe þingis and elde |
S Marcus and Marcellus and Apuley	Ebrews xj	f Whiche bi feiþ ouer	ende	witnessynge of feiþ
	Luk xxj	c Whanne 3e schuln he	ende	into witnessynge
S Denys with felows	Actus xvij	d While Poul abode	ende	Areopagite was
	Luk vj	e Ihesus cam doun fro	ende	is moch in heuene
S Geradion with felowis	Ebrews xj	f Which bi feiþ ouer	ende	witnessynge of feiþ
	Luk xxj	c Whanne 3e schuln	ende	into witnessynge
S Nichasius with felows	Ebrews x	f Haue mynde on þe	ende	lyueþ of feiþ
	Mathu x	d Whanne þei pursuen	ende	drede 3e not hem
Translacioun of S Edward, king	Eccl xxxix	c þe ri3twise schal 3e	ende	into generacioun
	Luk xj	f No man tendiþ a lam	ende	3eue li3t to þee
S Kalix, pope, martir	Ebrews xiij	c Nile 3e be ledde awei	ende	God is disseruede
	Mark xiij	f Se 3e, wake 3e and preie	ende	I seye to alle wake 3e
S Wolfrayn, bish. and confessour	Eccl xliiij	d Lo þe greet prest	ende	smel of swetnesse
	Mathu xxv	b A man þat goiþ m	ende	ioie of þi Lord
S Mi3hel in þe mount	Apocalips xij	d A greet batel was	ende	dwellen in hem
	Mathu xviij	a Disciplis camen to	ende	þat is in heuenes

f. 12ʳ (margin, beside "S Marcus and Marcellus and Apuley")

S Luk, euaungelist	Ezech j	c þe lickenesse of cher	ende	of leyte schynynge
	Luk x	a þe Lord Ihesus ordeyned	ende	is worþi is hiȝe
S xj þousand virgins	Sapiens iiij	a Hou faire is a chas	ende	be in refreischynge
	Mathu xxv	a þe rewme of heue	ende	þe day ne þe oour
S Romayn, confessour	Sapiens x	d þe Lord led forþ a	ende	euerlastynge cleernesse
	Mark xiij	f Se ȝe wake ȝe and preie	ende	to alle wake ȝe
S Crispin and Crispinian, marters	j Corinth iiij	d We ben made a spec	ende	derworþe sones
	Mathu x	c Lo I sende ȝou as sch	ende	schal be saaf
Vigil of Symond and Iude	Sapiens iij	a þe soulis of iust men	ende	wiþouten ende
	Iohun xv	b I am a vyne ȝe þe	ende	be don to ȝou
Symon and Iude, apostlis	Romans viij	f We witen þat to	ende	Crist Ihesus oure Lord
	Iohun xv	d þis is my comaunde	ende	he ȝeueþ to ȝou
Vigil of alle Halowyn	Apoc v	c I saiȝ and lo in þe myd	ende	worldis of worldis
	Iohun xvij	c Holi fadir kepe hem	ende	be in hem and I in hem
Nouembir				
Alle Halowen day	Apocal vij	b I siȝ anoþer aungel	ende	of worldis. Amen
	Mathu v	a Ihesus seynge þe pupl	ende	plentyuous in heuenes
Al Soules day	j Tessal iiij	f We wolen not þat	ende	in þes wordis
	Iohun xj	c Martha seide to Ihesus	ende	into þis world
S Lenard, abb.	Eccl xxxix	c þe riȝtwise schal ȝe	ende	into generacioun
	Luk xj	f No man tendiþ a lamp	ende	ȝeue liȝt to þee

S four crownede martris	Sapiens iij	a þe soulis of iust men	ende	regne wiþouten ende
	Luk xxj	c Whanne ȝe schulen	ende	into witnessynge
S Teodore, mar.	Eccl xiiij	f Blessid is þe man	ende	þe Lord oure God
	Mathu xvj	f If ony man wole co	ende	in his kyngdom |
S Martyn, bish. and confessour	Eccl xliiij	d Lo, þe greet preest	ende	smel of swetnesse
	Mathu xxv	b As a man þat goiþ	ende	ioie of þi Lord
S Brise, bish. and confessour	Sapiens x	d þe Lord led forþ a	ende	euerlastynge cleerness
	Luk xix	b A worþi man wente	ende	and ȝede vp to Ierusalem
S Macute, bish.	Eccl xliiij	d Lo, þe greet preest	ende	smel of swetnesse
	Luk xix	b A worþi man wente	ende	and ȝede vp to Ierusalem
S Edmunde, bish.	Eccl l	a Biholde þis is þe gre	ende	bi daies euerlastynge
	Mathu xxv	b As a man þat goiþ	ende	þe ioie of þi Lord
S Hwe, bish.	Eccl xlv	a Loued of God and of men	ende	of lijf and of techinge
	Mark xiij	f Se ȝe, wake ȝe and preie	ende	to alle wake ȝe
Vtas of Martyn	Eccl xliiij	d Lo, þe greet prest	ende	smel of swetnesse
	Mathu xxv	b As a man þat goiþ	ende	þe ioie of þi Lord
S Edmund, king	Eccl xxxj	b Blessid is a man	ende	hise almesdedis
	Luk xiiij	f If ony man com	ende	be my disciple
S Cecil, virgin and martir	Eccl lj	c Mi Lord God þou en	ende	Lord þou art my God
	Mathu xiij	h þe kyngdom of he	ende	newe þingis and elde

f. 12ᵛ

S Clement, pope and martir	Philipens iiij	a My briþeren moost	ende	in þe book of lijf
	Luk xix	b A worþi man wente	ende	3ede up to Ierusalem
S Grisogon, martir	Prouerb iij	c Blessid is þe man	ende	togidre bi dewe
	Luk x	d He þat heeriþ 3ou	ende	writun in heuenes
S Kateryn, virgin and martir	Eccl lj	a Lord kyng I schal k	ende	þe Lord my God
	Mathu xiij	h þe kyngdom of heuenes	ende	newe þingis and elde
S Lyne, pope and martir	Ebrews v	a Ech bisschop takun	ende	þe book of lijf
	Luk xix	b A worþi man wente	ende	3ede vp to Ierusalem

EXPLANATORY NOTES

These editorial notes discuss significant points regarding the textual features of the OTL, as well as its relation to WB and SM. Notable aspects of translation strategies from Latin into Middle English are also discussed. Where necessary for purposes of comparison, short passages from WB, SM, or the Vulgate (Vu) are cited. Where other collated OTL manuscripts diverge in a significant way from Bo (e.g. where they contain different lections), some sections have been edited separately and are commented on in the notes. In such cases, the edition follows the same policy as that outlined in the Introduction (§VI).

The notes follow the Editorial Policy in their use of lemmata and references. For each lection, a note indicates whether it uses LV, EV, or an independent translation, and this information can be found after the initial reference to each lection. The text has been collated with F&M, in default of a more recent comprehensive edition, and the abbreviations LV and EV refer to the text of WB as presented in F&M's edition. The scope of the collation with LV and EV in these notes is thus by necessity limited by F&M's editorial decisions. Notes on EV and LV give noteworthy variants in the version (EV or LV) which a lection uses; where it is of interest, the reading in the other version is given as well. Both Legg's and Dickinson's editions of SM have been used. Where there are differences between these two editions, a reference has been added to clarify the use of these editions in a particular note.

The editorial notes do not mention which lessons are omitted in Bo, or whether a lection is present in full or as a cross-reference, since this information can be found in the lection list (Introduction, §III). Owing to constraints of space, no attempt is made to note whether a particular lection is given as a cross-reference or in full in the collated manuscripts, except where this is of relevance to identify the relationship between individual manuscripts.

1–2 *And here bigynnen . . . al þe ʒeeris*: there is some variation between the introductory rubric in different manuscripts. Type I has a very fixed rubric which is found in all Type I manuscripts with very little variation: 'Here bigynneþ þe lessouns and pistlis of þe olde lawe þat ben red in þe chirche in al þe ʒeer aftir þe uss of Salisburi'. Type II shows more variation, but only a few OTLs of this group contain a reference to the use of Salisbury. Many rubrics for Group II A–C contain a shorter version of the one we find in Type I: 'Here bigynnen þe lessouns and pistlis of þe oolde lawe þat ben red in þe chirche bi al þe ʒeer', with some variation thereon, such as omission of 'bi al þe ʒeer' (Se, Si, x) or 'in þe chirche' (x) or addition of 'at Masse' (Se, x) or 'in sundaies and feries' (Tc). ι is unusual in that it is the only OTL to contain a rubric entirely in Latin. The two manuscripts of Group II D 2 have two extremely similar rubrics: 'Here byginnyþ the gospels and þe epistlis of alle þe festis in þe ʒeer, stondyng by ordir as þei ben redde in þe messebuk aftir þe use of salisbery' (*He*), whilst Group II D 1 has more variation. *Pl* has an extremely short rubric: 'Here bygynnen þe lessouns of þe olde lawe', but *Ar* has a rather expansive one: 'Here beginnen þe lessouns of þe olde lawe þat ben redde in þe Masse book of alle þe festis of þe ʒere aftir þe use of Salisbure'. Type III has a lengthy rubric which is similar to that of the TOLs, explaining the use of indexing letters (cf. Introduction §V.2), but here too we find a lot of variation between texts of this type.

LECTION 1

LV

3 *The first Friday . . . Isaye li capitulo*: as pointed out in the Introduction (§VI), there is a great deal of variation in the different manuscripts concerning the rubrics for each lection. Type I OTLs strive to achieve the greatest possible clarity of reference, much more so earlier Type II lectionaries. These patterns can be observed throughout the lectionaries, and not all individual instances will be commented upon in these notes, except in cases which are particularly noteworthy.

LECTION 2

LV

33 *infauntis*: 'ʒonge children' LV.

35 *seiþ þe Lord of oostis*: *not in* LV, SM, Vu.
    wheþer: this functions as an interrogative adverb and is frequently used in LV to translate the Latin adverb 'numquid'. The S-V word order follows the usual ME usage (cf. *MED* whether *adv. & conj.*, s. 2).
    seen²: *not in* LV.

40 *a*: *not in* LV.

LECTION 3

LV

42–3 *Vpon þi wallis . . . ordeynede kepers*: 'Jerusalem, Y haue ordeyned keperis on thi wallis' LV.

50 *forʒerdis*: 'hallis' LV.

52 *made herd*: a very literal translation of 'auditum fecit' in Vu, meaning 'proclaimed, declared'.

Both EV and LV

57–9 *And þere schal . . . out upon hillis*: uses EV, but the rest of the lection is in LV.
Bx uses LV for the entire lection. The first sentence in Bx is: 'In þo daies Isaie þe
prophete seide in þe laste daies þe hil of þe hous of þe lord shal be maad redi in þe
cop of hillis and schal be reisid aboue litil hillis.'

66 *hauntid*: 'exercisid' LV.

LV

72 *wheþer it is litil to ȝou*: a literal translation of 'Numquid parum vobis est' ('Is it
a small thing to you') in Vu. The sense of this sentence is somewhat obscure in the
Middle English; it is not immediately obvious that the sense of 'litil' here is 'a small
thing'.
    also: *not in* LV.

76 *þat he kunne repreue ȝuel*: a translation of 'ut sciat reprobare malum', using 'þat'
in the sense 'in order that', and 'he kunne' in the sense 'he may know how to/be
able to'.

LV

82 *fulfille*: 'fille' LV.

LV

LV

103 *clumside*: 'comelid' LV.

104 *men of litil counfort*: this functions as the indirect object of this sentence,
translating the dative 'pusillanimis' in Vu.

LECTION 9

LV

119 *reise*: here Bx is missing approximately three leaves, although the manuscript is too tightly bound to be certain of the exact number. The following lections are collated from Lt, up until Ash Wednesday.

reise in his bosum: the unusual absence of an object can be explained as a result of the translator's policy of following closely the syntax of the Latin: 'in sinu suo levabit'. Literal translations of this type are frequent throughout the Wycliffite translations.

LECTION 10

LV

134 *cloudis reyne a iust man*: there are various possible interpretations of 'et nubes pluant iustum' in Vu, including a reading of 'iustum' in a literal way as 'a just man', or less literally as 'righteousness' (in keeping with the Hebrew original). The translator here chooses a literal translation, which fits well with the language of the rest of the verse in Vu ('aperiatur terra, et germinet Salvatorem').

136 *þe Lord . . . made hym*: 'I þe Lord haue maad him of nouȝt' LV.

LECTION 11

LV

139 *of fire*: 'of the fire' LV.

140–2 *And þe flawme . . . bisidis þe furneis*: this section is not found in LV or the Vulgate, but occurs in the lection as 'Flamma autem diffusa est super fornacem cubitis quadraginta novem, et incendit quos reperit juxta fornacem de Chaldeis ministros regis qui eam incendebant' (*Missale*, ed. Dickinson, 37). OTL contains the somewhat difficult wording 'þe flawme passide held out', in the sense 'The flame, when it had passed, reached out'. The last part of the last sentence, 'ministros regis qui eam incendebant', is omitted in all other texts apart from Se.

145 *seiynge*: all Type I OTLs end this lection here, and do not contain the texts for different liturgical seasons. The same applies to Type III. Most, albeit not all, Type II OTLs contain the texts for other liturgical seasons, whilst Group II D tends to omit them.

156–97 *Thou art blessid . . . hym into worldis*: which parts of this lection are underlined can vary from manuscript to manuscript. Bo tends to underline less than Ny, but the practice of both manuscripts is not entirely regular. Bo also indicates different verses by alternating red and blue paraphs. Se does not underline any parts of this lection. Bo and Ny seem to underline to indicate differences between the Vulgate and SM. The Sarum lection abbreviates some verses in the Vulgate, and frequently omits the refrain 'laudate et superexaltate eum in saecula' which is found at the end of each of these verses in the Vulgate (*The Sarum Missal*, ed. Legg, 22). Interestingly, this practice of omitting the refrain is also found where this psalm occurs in the Divine Office at Lauds (Benedictines of Solesmes, *Antiphonale sacrosanctae romanae ecclesiae pro diurnis horis* (Paris, 1949), 4). Bo and Ny follow the Vulgate rather than SM here, but indicate the differences by underlining the relevant sections, even if the underlining practice does not accurately reflect the differences between the Vulgate and SM in all cases. This practice of underlining is similar to the one observed in other lections, where additions from the biblical text to the lection are indicated by underlining in red. Se does not underline any part of this lection.

This part of the lection in Se is very different as it translates SM directly without having recourse to the biblical text. Since the text in Se contains none of the frequent additions found in Bo and Ny, it is edited here separately in order to reflect the effect of the differences of this portion of the lection as a whole:

Thou art blessid in þe firmament of heuene, and preisable and aboue enhaunsid into worldis. Alle werkis of þe Lord, blesse 3e þe Lord. Heuenis, blesse 3e þe Lord. Aungelis of þe Lord, blesse 3e þe Lord; herie 3e hym and aboue enhaunce 3e hym into worldis. Alle watris þat ben aboue heuenis, blesse 3e þe Lord. Alle vertues of heuenis, blesse 3e to þe Lord. Sunne and moone, blesse 3e to þe Lord; herie 3e him and aboue enhaunce 3e him into þe worldis. Sterris of heuene, blesse 3e þe Lord. Reyn and dewe, blesse 3e to þe Lord. Ech spirit of God, blesse 3e þe Lord; herie 3e and aboue enhaunce him into worldis. Fier and heete, blesse 3e to þe Lord, ny3te and dayes, blesse 3e þe Lord. Li3t and derknesse, blesse 3e þe Lord; herie 3e and aboue enhaunce 3e him into worldis. Coold and somer, blesse 3e to þe Lord. Ises and snowis, blesse 3e þe Lord. Leitis and cloudis, blesse 3e þe Lord; herie 3e and aboue enhaunce 3e him into worldis. The erþe blesse þe Lord. Mounteyns and litel hillis, blesse 3e þe Lord. Alle buriounnynge þingis in erþe, blesse 3e to þe Lord; herie 3e and aboue enhaunce 3e hym into worldis. Sees and flodis, blesse 3e þe Lord. Wellis, blesse 3e þe Lord. Whallis and alle þingis þat ben moued in watris, blesse 3e þe Lord; herie 3e and aboue enhaunce 3e him into worldis. Alle briddis of þe eir, blesse 3e þe Lord. Alle wylde beestis and tyme beestis, blesse 3e þe Lord. Sonis of men, blesse 3e þe Lord; herie 3e and aboue enhaunce 3e him into worldis. Israel, blesse 3e þe Lord. Prestes of þe Lord, blesse 3e þe Lord. Seruauntis of þe Lord, blesse 3e þe Lord; herie 3e and aboue enhaunce him into worldis. Spiritis and soulis of iust men, blesse 3e þe Lord. Holy men and meke of herte, blesse 3e þe Lord; herie 3e and aboue enhaunce 3e him into worldis. Ananye, Azarye and Misael, blesse 3e þe Lord; herie 3e and aboue enhaunce 3e him into worldis. (f. 287^r)

160 *þe watris*: 'watris' LV.

162 *heuenes*: 'þe Lord' LV, 'domini' SM Vu.

177–8 *Leitis and cloudis . . . hym into worldis*: *om.* Ny

LECTION 12

EV

204 *for I þe Lord ȝoure God*: this sentence is grammatically incomplete in Middle English, as a result of a very literal translation of the Latin 'quia ego Dominus Deus vester'. The implied main verb in Latin ('I [*am*] þe Lord ȝoure God') is not reflected in EV. Here as in many other places, 'for' is chosen as a translation of 'quia'.

209 *reyn*: 'reyny' EV.

210 *a*: *not in* EV.

211–12 *And wiþouten . . . enhabitid*: 'And Judee schal be enhabited with outen ende' EV.

213 *into*: *not in* EV.

LECTION 13

LV

216 *glad*: 'be glade' LV.

217 *schal*: 'I schal' LV.
   þe²: *not in* LV.
   Many: 'and many' LV

219 *þe¹*: *not in* LV.
   for: 'that' LV.

221 *Be eche fleisch*: 'Ech fleisch be' LV.

222 *fro*: 'of' LV.

LECTION 14

Synthesis of EV and LV

225–9 *For Sion . . . þe Lord nempnede*: this translation incorporates some features of both EV and LV ('For Sion I shal not be stille, and for Jerusalem I shal not resten, to the tyme that go out as shynyng the riytwis of hym, and his saueour as a laumpe be tend. And seen shul Jentiles thi riytwis, and alle kingus thi noble; and clepid shal be to thee a newe name, that the mouth of the Lord nemnede' EV; 'For Sion Y schal not be stille, and for Jerusalem Y schal not reste, til the iust *man* therof go out as schynyng, and the sauyour therof be teendid as a laumpe. And hethene men schulen se thi iust *man*, and alle kyngis schulen se thi noble *man*; and a newe name, which the mouth of the Lord nemyde, schal be clepid to thee' LV).

229–33 *And þou schalt . . . Lord in þee*: based on EV.

LECTION 15

Translated from SM, using an independent translation for the biblical text

234–41 *On Cristemasse morewe . . . of boþe togidre*: the rubric is very similar in Bo, Ra, and La, with only minor variants such as different prepositions. However, the rubric in Se is strikingly different, and seems rather less elaborate and clear: 'On Cristemasse Ny3t at þe firste Masse a lessoun þat is sungun of tweyne togidre, þe firste verse and þe laste. But alle þe oþer oon syngeþ o vers and þe toþir anoþir, of whiche firste is text and þe toþir is a glose þeron and so is it þorou3 al þe lessoun. Þe firste vers þat boþe syngen togidere is as a preising to God at þe bigynnyng.' Similarly, the rubric in Lt is different, and perhaps less clear than the ones in Bo, Ra, and La: 'On Cristunmasse Morn at þeo furste Masse þer is songun a lessoun in þeo pulpit, of whiche þeo furste vers and þeo laste ben songen of tweyne togedre, and alle þeo oþur vers ben songen on o vers anoþir þat oþer. Þeo firste vers of þo þat arn songen of on by hymself is þeo text of Ysaye. Þeo secunde is as a glose on þeo text and so hit is þorgh þeo lessoun þeo furste vers þat is songen of boþe togedre is þis þat sueþ'.

242–4 *I schal seie . . . of his sone*: this introductory passage is translated from SM ('Laudes Deo dicam per saecula, qui me plasmavit in manu dextera, atque redemit cruce purpurea sanguine Nati'; *Missale*, ed. Dickinson, 50).

245–6 *This is þe firste vers of þo þat ben sungen of oon bi hymsilf, whiche is of þe tixte*: this is omitted in Lt. The version in Se differs from the one we find in the other collated manuscripts: 'þes þat suen þat oon syngiþ, þe firste is text of Isaye ix, þe secounde is glose'.

247 *The lessoun of Isaye þe profete*: the practice of underlining the alternating parts is largely, but not entirely, consistent in the different manuscripts. For instance, Lt switches halfway through the lection from underlining the first singer's part to the second part instead.

247–70 *The lessoun of Isaye . . . so be it*: in Type I, the independent translation of the lines from Isaiah in the Christmas lection (which is translated directly from SM in Type II) is replaced by LV. As an example of a Type I Christmas lection, the lection in La is edited below:

The lessoun of Isaie þe prophete, in which þe schynynge birþe of Crist is pro-
fecied. These þingis seiþ þe Lord, þe fadir, þe sone, þe holi goost, in whom alle
þingis ben maad, boþe hiȝe þingis and lowe þingis. The peple þat ȝede in derknessis, whom þe enemye wiþ trecherous gyle putte out of paradijs, and ledde
hem wiþ him bi þraldom into helle, say a greet liȝt. Ther schoon greete liȝtis
boþe at mydnyȝt and vnto þe heerde men. Whanne men dwelliden in þe cuntre
of schadowe of deeþ: liȝt, liȝt euerlastynge and oure verri aȝenbiynge, roos up
to hem. O þat wondirful birþe! Forsoþe, a child is born to us. But he schal be
greet Jhesu, þe sone of God, and a sone of þe hiȝ fadir is ȝouen to us fro þe
souereyn heiȝþe, as it was seid bifore. And princeheed is mad on his schuldre,
for he schal gouerne heuenes and feeldis, and his name schal be clepid: Messias,
Sother, Emanuel, Saboth, Adonay, wondirful roote of Dauiþ, and counseilour
of God þe fadir þat made alle þingis, God strong, brekynge þe strengiste closuris
of helle, a fadir of þe world to comynge, kyng almyȝti, gouernynge alle þingis,
a prince of pees bi þe worldis euerlastynge. His empire schal be multiplied in
Ierusalem and in Iurie and in Samarie. And noon eende schal be of his pees,
here and elliswhere. And he schal sette on þe seete of Dauiþ and on þe rewme
of him, and þer schal be no marke ne no teerme of his rewme, þat he conferme
it in þe wed of bileue and make it strong in doom and in riȝtfulnesse, whanne he
schal come domesman to deeme þe world. Fro henneforþ glorie, preisynge and
ioie be ȝolden vnto him and til into wiþouten eende. Worþi preisynge be sungen
vnto þe creatour of alle creaturis. Fro eest and west, norþ and souþ, alle creaturis
seie, so be it.

250 *derknesses*: Se here adds 'which þou hast maad of noȝt', which translates 'Quem
creasti' in SM (*Missale*, ed. Dickinson, 50). However, none of the other OTLs
contains this addition.

269 *ende*: uniquely amongst the collated manuscripts, Se here translates the rubric from SM ('Hic cantent simul usque ad finem', *Missale*, ed. Dickinson, 51): 'þis
vers þat sueþ is sungen of boþe togidre as þe firste'.

LECTION 16

LV. A part of this lection is the same as in the previous one, but in Type II A–C,
LV is used instead of an independent translation. Type I uses LV both for this and
the preceding lection.

271 *The secunde lessoun at þe same Masse*: 'if þer ben not tweyne to singe þis lessoun
aforseid þis lessoun suynge be rad of oon' Se; 'where þat þis lesson byfore is not
songen þis suwyng is red' Lt.

274–80 *Thou multipliedist folk . . . mete of fire*: the section which is underlined here
is material which is contained in the Vulgate, but not in SM. The same section
is omitted in Type I and in those OTLs of Type II which adhere more closely to

SM than Type II B, in particular LaSeRa amongst the collated texts. Bo marks the section from the Vulgate by underlining and with the marginal notes 'va' and 'cat' at the start and end of this section to indicate that this part of the lection is missing in SM.

282 and²: 'a' LV.

285 þat he conferme it: a translation of 'ut confirmet illud', in which the Latin 'ut' is translated as 'þat' (in the sense 'in order that he may confirm it').

LECTION 17

EV

289 The spirit of þe Lord upon me: here as elsewhere in EV, the translation is extremely literal and does not reflect the implied main verb in the Vulgate: 'The spirit of the Lord [is] upon me' ('Spiritus Domini super me').

289–90 for þat he anoyntide me: 'for that enoyntede me the Lord' EV.

290 He sente me to preche to pore men: this section is contained neither in the Vulgate nor in the Sarum lection. The Latin lection has 'Domini super me, eo quod unxerit me: ad annunciandum mansuetis misit me' (*Missale*, ed. Dickinson, 55). It is unclear why the reference to preaching to poor men is included in most OTLs (out of the collated texts, only Lt does not contain it). This might be due to the Latin exemplar the translators used, or it might be evidence of the influence of Wycliffite thought on the OTL.

    deboner: a translation of 'mansuetis' in Vu. The Latin word can have a range of meanings, including 'peaceful', but the translator here chooses 'deboner' in the sense 'gentle, meek, mild'.

294 counfort: 'coumforting' EV.

299 ȝe: not in EV.

301 hym: a form of the third-person plural accusative pronoun, used to translate 'eos' in Vu. According to *LALME*, occurrences of this form are centred on East Anglia, but 'hym' might also be a misspelling of the form 'hem', which is the usual form of the plural pronoun in the oblique case in Bo.

LECTION 18

LV

312 erþe: 'þe erþe' LV.

LECTION 19

EV

314 *Ecclesiasticus*: throughout the manuscripts *Ecclesiasticus* and *Ecclesiastici* are used as interchangeable terms. Abbreviations are here expanded in accordance with manuscript usage. References are clarified, where necessary, through editorial additions following lection titles.

315 *is wiþholdynge*: 'withholding is' EV.

317 *and as a womman . . . vndirtake him*: this section is contained in the Vulgate ('et quasi mulier a virginitate suscipiet illum'; Ecclus. 15: 2), but omitted in SM (*Missale*, ed. Dickinson, 66). La follows SM and omits this section entirely, whilst Bo underlines it to emphasize the difference.

318 *and*: 'and of' EV.
wiþ²: 'with the' EV.

322 *þe Lord*: this is not in the Vulgate or EV, but SM adds 'Dominus' here, which the lectionaries follow.

LECTION 20

Composite lection, translated independently

This lection is syntactically difficult in Middle English, as it closely translates the elliptical syntax of the composite source text. The editor's punctuation is an attempt at clarifying the Middle English syntax, but parts of the text remain ambiguous.

There is some variation between the manuscripts as to whether Ecclus. 50 ('Ecce sacerdos magnus qui in vita sua') or Ecclus. 44 ('Ecce sacerdos magnus qui in diebus suis') is given as the lection here. Some even contain both lections. Further details are given at Lection 20 in the lection list above (Introduction, §III).

327 *Siluestirs day*: 'Seynt Nicolas day Ecclesiastici xliiij' *add.* Ny.

LECTION 21

LV

350 *sprungen vpon þee*: 'risun on thee' LV, 'on thee is sprunge' EV.
þe¹: *not in* LV.

357 *heþen*: 'hethene men' LV.

LECTION 23

Composite lection, independent translation (see *The Sarum Missal*, ed. Legg, 39, for the Latin lection). Frere (*Studies in Early Roman Liturgy*, iii: *The Roman Epistle-Lectionary*, 93) details the way in which this lection is composed from different parts of Isaiah.

LECTION 24

LV

Here the lacuna in Bx ends, and this and all following lections are collated from Bx instead of Lt.

390 *and sacrifice and moiste sacrifice to oure Lord God*: this phrase is syntactically incomplete, following the Vulgate, which does not provide a main verb here ('sacrificium et libamen Domino Deo vestro?'). The translator keeps very close to the Latin source, in spite of the obscurity of the resulting translation.

LECTION 25

LV

406 *and*[3]: 'and thou' LV.

412 *and*[2]: *not in* LV.

LECTION 26

LV

420 *and*[1]: 'of' LV.

421 *fasten*: 'fastiden' LV.

428 *a day of fastynge*: 'a fastynge' LV, 'ieiunium' Vu.

434 *þe*[1]: 'thi' LV.

LECTION 27

LV

441 *þat*[2]: *not in* LV.
    not: *not in* LV, 'desieris' Vu.

442 *soule*: 'that is' *add.* LV (in some of the manuscripts collated by F&M).

LECTION 28

LV

458 *scheep*: 'that ben' *add*. LV.

464 *þe²*: *not in* LV.

469–70 *and riȝtwisnesse*: *not in* LV.

LECTION 29

LV

LECTION 30

LV

486 *in*: 'into' LV.

LECTION 31

LV

503 *and¹*: *not in* LV.

507 *and¹*: *not in* LV.

511 *mete*: 'bi' *add*. LV.

LECTION 32

LV

520 *and¹*: *not in* LV.

523 *and²*: *not in* LV.

530–3 *but etynge . . . takynge more*: this section is in the Vulgate, but not in SM. All collated manuscripts, apart from Bo and Ny, follow SM. This section is underlined in Bo to draw attention to the differences between SM and the Vulgate. It is interesting that underlining is used in Bo to indicate both deviation from the Vulgate (as in cases where extra-biblical material is underlined) and deviation from SM, even where the text agrees with the Vulgate. Underlining can thus be used for two inverse textual situations, and the text seems to assume that a reader would be able to make sense of this practice without any further explanation.

535 *his blood schal be in hym*: a translation of 'sanguis ejus in ipso erit' in Vu. The sense 'his blood shall be on his head' does not become clearly apparent in the translator's extremely literal rendering.

537–42 *etiþ not . . . he lente*: this section is in the Vulgate, but not in SM. Only Bo and Ny contain this section, and both underline it to emphasize the difference from SM. Underlining is not completely the same in the two manuscripts—for instance, Ny underlines 'etiþ not on hillis' (537) as well as the rest of this section.

542 *haþ*: 'doiþ' LV.

LECTION 33

LV

551 *The*[1]: 'Thilke' LV.

555 *þe*: 'hise' LV.

558 *In his riȝtwisnesse . . . he schal lyue*: 'he schal lyue in his riȝtfulnesse which he wrouȝte' LV.

559–60 *Where þe deep . . . weies, and lyue?*: a rendering of 'Numquid voluntatis meae est mors impii, dicit Dominus Deus, et non ut convertatur a viis suis, et vivat?' in Vu, meaning 'Is the death of a wicked man my will, says the Lord God, and not that he should be converted from his ways, and live?' The closeness of the translation to the Latin source somewhat obscures the meaning in Middle English.

566–7 *where my wey . . . weies ben schrewide?*: the unusual syntax of this sentence is a result of the translator's following the Latin source more or less word for word.

569 *vnriȝtfulnesse*: 'unriȝtwisnesse' LV.

LECTION 34

LV

579–80 *þat þou kepe and fille of al þin herte and of al þe soule*: in Middle English it is somewhat unclear what this clause refers to; the sense is 'that thou shalt keep them and fulfil them with all thy heart and with all thy soul'. The translator follows the Vulgate word for word.

580 *þe*: 'thin' LV.

582 *comaundementis*: 'comaundement' LV.

LECTION 35

LV

592 *þe*: 'tho' LV.

596 *3oure*[3]: *not in* LV.

EV

604 *þe Lord*: 'he' EV.

605 *make he*: this entire sentence uses the subjunctive mood, which explains the inversion of subject and verb here, following the same pattern as the preceding clause.

LV

610 *haue*: 'thou' *add*. LV.

CR (LaRa give the full text of this lection instead of a cross-reference)

LV

628 *þat*: *not in* LV.

634–5 *þe citee on þe whiche þi name is clepide to help*: the Latin reads 'civitatem super quam invocatum est nomen tuum', which can either be interpreted as 'the city on which thy name is invoked for protection' or as 'the city over which your name is invoked', i.e. 'the city that bears your name'. The translator chooses the former interpretation.

634 *þe*[2]: *not in* LV.

635 *teeris*: 'preiers' LV.

636 *in þi manye merciful doyngis*: the translator seems eager to express the plural which is found in the Latin 'in miserationibus tuis multis', but does not choose the word 'mercies', which would have been closer to the source text.

637 *and do*: a translation of 'et fac' in Vu, meaning 'and act'.

638 *for þi name is clepide to help on þi citee*: see comment above, on lines 634–5.

LV

643 *And*: *not in* LV.

647 *him*: *not in* LV.

LV

667–72 *Thou knowist alle þingis . . . outaken my God*: these three verses are omitted in SM, and in most collated texts as well, with the exception of the two Group II B manuscripts, Ny and Bo. As in other lections with a similar pattern, (e.g. Ezek. 18, Lection 28), this section is underlined in Bo and Ny to indicate a difference between the Vulgate and the text of the lection.

672 *of kyngis*: *not in* LV.

LV

680 *settiþ fleische his arm*: a word-for-word rendering of 'ponit carnem brachium suum' in Vu, without an attempt at conveying the sense (which is likely to be 'maketh flesh his arm', i.e. relies on human power for support).

687 *tyme²*: 'it' *add*. LV.

LV

704 *For*: 'therfor' LV.

708 *redi*: 'esi' LV, 'prospera' Vu. This might be a scribal error which is transmitted in Bo and Ny, but not in LaSeBxRa.

713 *kepen*: 'kepten' LV.

718 *sende we*: this is a difficult reading in Middle English, which can be explained in terms of the Latin ('mittamus'). In Vu the object (*eum*) is implied from the preceding clause, which explains the absence of 'hym' in the ME translation.

719 *þanne*: 'it' *add*. LV.

724 *delyuere hem*: the Latin has the singular pronoun 'eum' here, so 'hem' in the Middle English is likely to be singular.

to ȝilde to his fadir: this clause omits the object, following the Latin ('et reddere patri suo').

LECTION 44

LV

726 *Rebecca*: 'sche' LV. The name here replaces the personal pronoun to make the reference clear.

to: *not in* LV.

732 *I*: 'he' LV, 'moriatur' Vu. The variant translation in OTL derives either from a scribal error or from a misunderstanding of the Latin.

733 *also*: 'and' LV.

753 *And²*: *not in* LV.

764 *he²*: *not in* LV.

778 *also a blessynge*: 'a blessyng also' LV.

780 *wheet*: 'and' *add.* LV.

LECTION 45

LV

811 *come*: 'go' LV.

812 *his God*: 'the Lord his God' LV.

813 *þe²*: *not in* LV.

820 *waischide*: 'hym' *add.* LV.

LECTION 46

LV

831 *hous²*: 'no' *add.* LV.

835 *fillid*: 'ful' LV.

837 *ȝotide*: most of F&M's collated manuscripts have 'heldide' or 'helde' here. Manuscripts B and C have 'ȝotte', and x has 'ȝettide'.

LV

843 *and þi modir*: LV agrees with the reading in NyLaSeBxRa here.

844 *vpon*: 'on' LV.

845 *not do*: 'do not' LV.

LECTION 48

LV

872–3 *a widewe*: 'to a widewe' LV.

LECTION 49

LV

880 *puple*: 'multitude' LV.

891 *not*: *not in* LV.

891–2 *brynge out to ȝou watir of þis stoon*: 'brynge out of this stoon watir to ȝou' LV.

LECTION 50

LV

911 *in þe*: 'in to the' LV.

917 *aspien*: 'se' LV.

924 *ony man was not þere*: 'no man was there' LV.

937 *to me*: 'for me' LV.

939 *criede*: 'an hiȝ' *add.* LV.

940 *Forsoþe*: 'soþeli' LV.

965 *sche*: 'Susanne' LV.

966 *þou*: 'that' LV.

967 *þou*: 'that' LV.

981–2 *þat oon fro þat oþer*: 'oon fro the tother' LV.

982 *and*²: *not in* LV.

983 *new*: a form of 'now', translating 'nunc' in Vu.

LECTION 51

LV

1005 *strumpetis*: most LV manuscripts have 'hooris'; only one manuscript collated by F&M (I) has 'strumpetis'.

1007 *I childide at hir in a couche*: a literal translation of 'peperi apud eam in cubiculo'.

1012–13 *settid in hir bosum*: the absence of an object after 'settid' reflects the Latin 'conlocavit in sinu suo'.

1017–18 *sche seide*: the Latin 'illa', denoting the other woman, is simply translated as 'sche', which does not make it unambiguously clear which of the two women is speaking.

1023 *in*: 'into' LV.
　　half: 'half part' LV.

1024 *þe¹*: not in LV.

1027 *sche seide*: this pronoun refers to the other woman, not the one mentioned at the beginning of the verse (the real mother). See above, lines 1017–18.

LECTION 52

LV

1033 *Go þou doun*: 'Go thou, go doun' LV.

1036 *worschipiden*: 'it' *add*. LV. The absence of an object in OTL reflects the Latin ('adoraverunt').

1039 *wickidnesse*: 'woodnesse' LV.

1044 *to sle*: 'that he schulde sle' LV.

1046–7 *hast swoor bi þisilf*: a literal translation of 'iurasti per temet ipsum'.

LECTION 53

LV

1052–3 *whiche is . . . myddis of hem*: this section is omitted in LaSeBxRa as it is found only in the Vulgate but not in SM. It is underlined in Ny to emphasize that this section is missing in the Latin lection.

1063 *worschip*: 'worche' LV.

LV

1067 *awey*: 'the' *add.* LV.

1070–1 *repreue ȝe me*: a literal translation of 'arguite me'. The sense of this section is difficult to discern based on the translation in the Vulgate. Modern translations tend to render this as 'let us reason together', 'let us discuss this'.

1071 *made*: *not in* LV.

LV

1077 *euen aȝens*: a translation of 'de contra' (in the sense 'from afar').

1084–5 *Wheþer I askide my sone of my Lord?*: 'Did I not ask my Lord for a son?'.

1088 *to²*: *not in* LV.

LV

1109 *wickidnesse*: 'wickidnessis' LV.

1110 *seide*: 'to hir' *add.* LV.

1113 *turmentide*: 'also' *add.* LV.

LV

1125–6 *eritage distriede*: following the word order of the Latin 'hereditates dissipatas'.

1125 *eritage*: 'that ben' *add.* LV.

1127 *Be ȝe schewide*: translating 'revelamini', which can be variously interpreted as 'show yourselves', 'appear', or 'come into the light'.

1131 *I*: *not in* LV.

1133 *fro þe²*: *not in* LV.

1135 *þe²*: 'thou' LV.

LECTION 58

LV

1150 *in¹*: 'with a' LV.

LECTION 59

LV

1162 *gaderide togidre*: 'comun' LV.

1165 *and²*: 'he' *add*. LV.

1167 *And¹*: 'Certis' LV.

1184 *Soþeli*: 'Certis' LV.

LECTION 60

Composite lection, using both EV and LV

1191–9 *The Lord spak . . . I am Lord*: uses LV, whilst the rest of the lection uses EV.

1196–7 *The werk of þin hyrid man . . . þee til to þe morewetide*: i.e. 'do not make your hired workers wait for their pay until the next day'.

1198 *putte þing of lettynge*: 'sette an hurtyng' LV.

1200 *not²*: *not in* EV.

1203 *ne¹*: 'a' *add*. EV.

1204 *þe²*: 'a' EV.
   I þe Lord: no translation of the implied verb ('sum') in 'Ego Dominus' is provided.

1205 *þou¹*: *not in* EV.

1205–6 *þat þou haue of hym no synne*: 'lest thow haue on hym synne' EV.

1207 *on*: 'of' EV.
   I þe Lord: see above, line 1204.

1208 *My lawis kepe ȝe*: 'Kepe ȝe my lawes' EV.

LECTION 61

LV

1210–11 *neþer do awei*: 'and take thou not awei' LV, 'nether do awey thi mercye' EV.

1212 *þin holy*: a literal translation of 'sanctum tuum'.

1225 *yuel*: 'yuelis' LV.

1227 *þe roundenesse of londis*: a literal translation of 'orbem terrarum', in the sense 'all the world'.

LECTION 62

Synthesis of EV and LV; predominantly EV, but with some variants which are similar to LV

1230 *schulen*: 'shul' EV.

1233 *saue me*: 'saf mac me' EV.

1235 *folowynge þe schepherd*: 'thee shepperde folewende' EV.

1236 *riȝt was in þi siȝte*: 'riȝt in thi siȝte was' EV (following the syntax of the Vulgate: 'rectum in conspectu tuo fuit'). OTL seems to aim at making the syntax more idiomatic by moving the verb further towards the front of the sentence (in a position after the subject complement), but still preserves the placement of 'riȝt' before the verb, as in the Latin.

1236–7 *to ferdful to me*: 'to me to ferd' EV.

1237 *þou myn hope*: 'myn hope thou' EV.

1237–40 *Be þei confoundide . . . bi doubil defoulynge*: 'thei confoundid, that me pursuen, and confoundid be not Y, inwardly drede thei, and inwardly drede not Y, bring in vp on hem dai of tormenting, and with double to-treding to-tred hem' EV; 'Be thei schent, that pursuen me, and be Y not schent; drede thei, and drede not; brynge in on hem a dai of turment, and defoule thou hem bi double defouling' LV.

LECTION 63

LV

1246 *Lord, ȝeue þout tente to me*: translating 'adtende Domine ad me'.

1255 *do*: 'thou' *add.* LV.

LECTION 64

LV

1271–2 *The puple go out þat it gadere . . . þat I asay þe puple where it goiþ in my lawe*: the Middle English translation refers to the people as 'it' in the singular, following the Latin very closely (which uses the pronoun 'eum'). Such close translations of Latin pronouns are a frequent feature of OTL.

1273 *gadere þei*: 'make thei redi' LV.

1282 *Seye*: 'thou' *add*. LV.

LECTION 65

LV

1291 *moost*: 'maad' LV.

LECTION 66

LV

1302 *a tre*: a literal translation of 'lignum' in 'Mittamus lignum in panem eius'. A more likely interpretation is 'wood'. The phrase is figurative and its intended sense may be 'Let us destroy his sustenance'.

1305 *se I*: the verb is in the subjunctive, translating the Latin 'videam'.

LECTION 67

Composite lection, using both EV and LV

1308–11 *Seye ȝe to . . . and not forsaken*: this section uses LV; the following section from Isa. 63 uses EV.

1310 *hym*: this is likely to be a plural pronoun, translating 'eos'.
    Thou, forsoþe: 'Forsothe thou' LV.

1311 *a souȝt citee*: 'a citee souȝt' LV.

1315 *is þi cloþinge reed*: 'red is thi clothing' EV.

1318 *þe blood of hem is spreynt*: 'sprengd is the blod of hem' EV.

1321–2 *and myn indignacioun sauede to me myn arm and it halp to me*: this reading occurs in only a few of F&M's collated manuscripts. For further details see *The Holy Bible*, ed. Forshall and Madden, iii. 334.

1322–4 *I al to-trad . . . hem into erþe*: this verse is omitted in LaBxRa, but the reason is not clear, since neither Legg nor Dickinson notes this section as missing from the Sarum lection.

1325 *on*: 'vpon' EV.

LECTION 68

Both EV and LV

1327–31 *who bileuede to . . . we disiriden hym*: this part of the lection uses EV; the remainder of the lection uses LV.

1330–1 *he was not of siȝt, and we desiriden hym*: this is a literal translation of Latin 'non erat aspectus et desideravimus eum'. The sentence is problematic in Latin; a more likely interpretation is that 'et' subjoins 'desideravimus eum' to the preceding 'non erat' ('there was no sightliness as we felt him to be wanting').

1336 *þe lernynge*: a translation of 'disciplina'. The meaning 'chastisement' in this context is not brought out clearly by the translator's choice of words.

1343–5 *And he schal ȝeue vnfeiþful men for biriynge and riche men for his deeþ, for he dide not wickidnesse*: a literal translation of 'et dabit impios pro sepultura et divitem pro morte sua eo quod iniquitatem non fecerit'. A likely interpretation is 'he will share his grave with the unfaithful and the rich in his death even though he did no evil'.

1346–7 *If he puttiþ his lijf for synne . . . dressid in his hond*: a literal translation of 'si posuerit pro peccato animam suam videbit semen longevum et voluntas Domini in manu eius dirigetur', meaning 'if he shall offer his life for sin, he will see a long-lived seed, and the will of the Lord shall prosper in his hand'.

1347–51 *For þat þat . . . þe strong fendis*: this section is not in the Sarum lection (*Missale*, ed. Dickinson, 287) and is omitted by LaBxRa, which frequently follow Sarum more closely. The section is underlined in Ny, which demonstrates, as in many other cases, that the scribe was aware of the differences between the biblical text and the Sarum lections.

1349 *comynge*: 'kunnyng' LV.

1351 *departe*: 'the' add. LV.

1352 *felownesse men*: a translation of 'sceleratis'; 'felownesse' is a form of the adjective 'felouns', meaning 'wicked'.

1353 *it shulde not perische*: a puzzling translation, as the antecedent of 'it' is not clear from the context. The Sarum lection has 'perirent' in the plural, referring to the trespassers. It is possible that the translator misread the plural for a singular, or that his exemplar had 'periret' instead of 'perirent'.

LECTION 69

LV

1359 *sue*: a translation of Latin 'sequemur', which suggests that the meaning of 'sue' should be interpreted as 'follow' here.

LECTION 70

LV

1384 *to*: *not in* LV.

If ony þing is residewe, ȝe schulen brenne in þe fire: the Latin has 'si quid residui fuerit igne conburetis'. To make the object of the main clause unambiguously clear, the English would require the addition of a pronoun 'it', but the translator closely follows the Latin syntax.

1387 *passynge*: 'the passynge' LV.

LECTION 71

LV

1389 *firste bigynnynge*: 'firste' EV, 'bigynnyng' LV.

1398 *þe³*: *not in* LV.

1399 *on*: *not in* LV.

1403–4 *an appil tre*: the Latin has 'lignum pomiferum', 'fruit-bearing tree'. The tree is specified as an apple tree in both LV and the OTL.

1407 *þe²*: *not in* LV.

1409 *þe²*: *not in* LV.

1417 *a crepynge beest*: the use of the singular here follows the Latin, which uses a collective singular ('reptile'). This usage is somewhat obscured in English by the translation with an indefinite article.

1418 *soule lyuynge*: 'lyuynge soule' LV.

a brid fleynge: the use of the singular here follows the Latin, which uses the collective singular 'volatile'. As in the previous case, this usage is obscured by the indefinite article in English.

1419 *soule lyuynge*: 'soule lyuyng' EV, 'lyuynge soule' LV.

1425 *beestis²*: 'vnresonable beestis' LV, 'bestias' Vu.

1426 *vnresonable beestis*: there is some variation between 'resonable' and 'vnresonable beestis' in the manuscripts here. The use of the term 'vnresonable' in l. 1430, however, makes it likely that 'resonable' in l. 1426 is a scribal error.

1430 *to vnresonable beestis*: 'bestiis' Vu.

1431 *reptile*: this variant is contained in only three of F&M's manuscripts. For further details see *The Holy Bible*, ed. Forshall and Madden, i. 81. Most other manuscripts have 'crepynge beest'.
  þe: *not in* LV.

1435 *þe erþe*: 'erthe' LV.

1438 *hemsilf*: 'the' LV.

1439 *þe*: *not in* LV.

LECTION 72

LV, apart from the very beginning of the lection (**1448** *And now was . . . morewtide, and now lo*), which uses EV

1448 *And now was . . . morewtide, and now lo*: 'And now was comun the morewtide, and loo' EV, 'And the wakyng of the morewtid cam thanne, and lo' LV.

1450 *into*: 'the' *add.* LV.

1460 *as*: 'for' *add.* LV.

LECTION 73

LV

1470 *oonli þi name be clepide on vs; do þou awey oure schenschip*: a literal translation of 'tantummodo vocetur nomen tuum super nos; aufer obprobrium nostrum' ('only let us be called by your name; take away our reproach').

1474–5 *eche þat is writun in lijf in Ierusalem*: a figurative expression following the Latin closely ('omnis qui scriptus est in vita in Jerusalem'), possibly meaning 'everybody who is counted among the living in Jerusalem'.

1475–6 *if þe Lord waischip awey þe filþis of þe douȝtris of Syon, and waischip þe blood of Ierusalem*: the Latin verbs are in the future perfect tense 'abluerit' , 'laverit', whilst the ME translator chooses the present tense.

1479 *hilinge, or defendynge*: 'protectio' Vu ('shelter, defence').

1481 *of*: 'from' LV.

LV

1488 *and fillide*: the Latin has 'atque conplevit', meaning 'and finished it'. The meaning is somewhat obscured by the absence of an object in the translation.

1495 *wordis*: 'and' *add*. LV.

LV

1516 *And*: *not in* LV.

1526 *sparist*: 'sparidist' LV.

1527 *and*: 'he' *add*. LV.

1529 *Therfor*: 'wherfor' LV.

LV

1546 *and*: *not in* LV.

1547 *what is it*: translating 'quid est', meaning 'why is it' in this context.

1548 *And*: *not in* LV.

1564–67 *Also þe sones of Agar . . . on þe paþis þerof*: the English sentence is incomplete, stemming from the translator's decision to render Latin 'autem' as the co-ordinating conjunction 'but', introducing a new main clause. In the Latin version, 'filii quoque Agar qui exquirunt prudentiam quae de terra est negotiatores Merrae et Theman et fabulatores et exquisitores intellegentiae' forms the subject to the following 'viam autem sapientiae nescierunt'.

1569 *Namyde giauntis*: translating 'gigantes nominati'—in this context, 'nominati' is more likely to mean 'renowned' than 'named', but the translator settles for the latter option.

1575 *And*: *not in* LV.

1581 *into*: 'to' LV (a translation of 'luxerunt ei' Vu, meaning 'they shone for/ to him').

LV

1586–7 *Loue ȝe . . . þe erþe*: 'ȝe that deme the erthe, loue riȝtfulnesse' LV.

1587 *fele ȝe of þe Lord in goodnesse*: a translation of 'sentite de Domino in bonitate'; 'sentite' is more likely to mean 'think of' in this context.

in²: 'the' *add*. LV.

1591 *yuel*: 'willid' *add*. LV.

1596–7 *and þe sercher of his herte is trewe, and þe heerer of his tunge*: a literal translation of 'et cordis illius scrutator est verus, et linguae ejus auditor'. These clauses are grammatically ambiguous, but are likely to have as their implied subject that of the previous clause ('Deus'), so that a more likely reading is: 'and God is a true searcher of his heart, and a hearer of his tongue'.

1598 *þat¹*: 'and' LV.

LECTION 80

LV

1599 *On Trynyte Euen þe first lessoun*: LaRaSe refer to this liturgical occasion as 'þe satirday in Witson woke'.

1606–7 *þe grete day and orible of þe Lord*: the unusual syntax is due to the influence of the Latin ('dies Domini magnus et horribilis').

1607 *schal clepe*: 'clepith' LV, 'vocaverit' Vu. LV and OTL choose two different ways of translating the Latin future perfect. The lack of an equivalent tense and aspect in Middle English evidently led to different solutions to the problem: LV chooses the present tense, whilst OTL expresses the future tense by 'schal'.

LECTION 81

LV

1618 *þat is fifti daies*: this section is in the Vulgate, but is omitted in SM. LaSeBxRa follow the liturgical rather than the biblical version.

1620–1 *whiche þe preest schal reise bifore þe Lord*: this section is in SM ('quos elevabit sacerdos coram Domino'; *Missale*, ed. Dickinson, 445), but not in the Vulgate. It is interesting that Bo incorporates both elements specific to the Vulgate and those specific to SM in this verse (see next note).

1621–8 *of floure diȝte . . . falle into vse*: this section is contained in the Vulgate but omitted in the Sarum lection, as well as in most collated texts. As in many other cases, the Group B manuscripts Ny and Bo follow the biblical text rather than the lection, but Ny underlines this section to indicate that it is not part of the Sarum lection.

1624 *wiþ²*: 'in' LV.

1626 *and*[1]: 'of' LV.

1628 *into*: 'his' *add*. LV, a more accurate translation of 'in usum ejus'.

LECTION 82

LV

1641 *ledden*: 'us' *add*. LV. OTL follows the Latin text, which has 'introduxit', very closely here, whilst LV adds a pronoun to clarify the reference.

1646 *schal ʒeue*: 'ʒaf' LV, 'dederit' Vu. Like Lection 80, l. 1607, OTL here uses a construction with 'schal' to translate the Latin future perfect, whilst LV uses the present tense.

LECTION 83

LV

1648–9 *þe Lord spak . . . seye to hem*: this section is underlined in BoLaSeBx. This might suggest that the scribes checked this lection against the Vulgate, but failed to realize that unlike the rest of the lection, this section is from the preceding chapter of Leviticus.

1660 *And*[1]: *not in* LV.
    make: 'you' *add*. LV. OTL follows the Latin text, which has 'faciam', very closely here, whilst LV adds a pronoun to clarify the reference.

1662 *ete*: 'the' *add*. LV.

LECTION 85

LV

1671–2 *sendynge*: Most of F&M's manuscripts have 'sowynge' here. F&M's manuscripts FMQRSU agree with the variant in Bo.

1674 *shulen dwelle*: a literal translation of 'inhabitabunt'.

LECTION 86

LV

1689 *and þei stoden bisidis hym*: this section is in SM ('et steterunt juxta eum'; *Missale*, ed. Dickinson, 538), but not in the Vulgate. Underlining is used here to indicate a deviation from the Vulgate.

1692 *Amen*: the 'Amen' is doubled in the Vulgate, but not in SM.

1694–5 *Forsoþe Iosue . . . Iosabeth, Anan, Fallaye*: this section is omitted in the lection in SM. As usual in such cases, Type II B manuscripts are the only ones which follow the Vulgate rather than SM. Ny underlines this section, which shows that the scribe was aware of the differences between SM and the Vulgate.

1699 *he is Athersata*: this explanation in the Vulgate ('ipse est Athersatha'), which is usually interpreted as the title of a high-ranking Persian official (G. J. Venema, *Reading Scripture in the Old Testament: Deuteronomy 9–10; 31; 2 Kings 22–23; Jeremiah 36; Nehemiah 8*, Oudtestamentische Studien, 48 (Leiden, 2004), 174), is omitted in all manuscripts except Bo and Ny.

1701–2 *For al þe . . . of þe lawe*: according to Legg and Dickinson, this section is contained in SM. However, LaSeBx do not include this section, and Ny underlines it. It is possible that there was some variation in missals here as to whether this section was included or not, which would account for the differences between the OTLs here.

LECTION 87

LV

1707–8 *conuertid to þi . . . and be 3e*: this section is omitted in Ny, probably due to eye-skip.

1715 *as*: 'a' *add*. LV.

1716 *as*: 'of' *add*. LV.

1720 *þe*: *not in* LV.

1721 *dresse*: a translation of 'dirigam', in the sense 'arrange, form'.

LECTION 88

LV

1728 *holy*: 'and' *add*. LV.
    3e schulen turmente 3oure soulis: 'You shall humble/afflict your souls . . .'.

LECTION 89

LV

1740–1 *þe feries of tabernaclis*: a literal translation of 'feriae tabernaculorum'. Throughout the lection, 'tabernaculum' ('tent') is translated by the Latinate term 'tabernacle'.

1740–51 *schulen be . . . þe seuenþe moneþ*: this section is in the Vulgate, but not in SM. It is omitted in LaSeBxRa and underlined in Ny. The Group II B manuscripts are the only collated texts which follow the biblical text rather than the lection.

1744 *moost holy*: in Ny, this is followed by 'ȝe schulen not do ony seruile werk kerynne: and in seuen daies' as in verse 35, due to eye-skip.

1748 *fletynge offryngis*: a translation of 'libamenta' ('libations, drink offerings').

1749 *outaken þe Sabotis of þe Lord*: a translation of 'exceptis sabbatis Domini'.

1755 *salewis*: a translation of 'salices', meaning 'willows'.

LECTION 90

LV

1765–7 *bi oold daies . . . wondirful þingis*: this is a combination of the biblical text and the Sarum lection. The lection has 'gregem hereditatis tue habitantem in terra in salutem iuxta dies antiquos' (*The Sarum Missal*, ed. Legg, 199) and then continues with verse 16, omitting part of verse 14 and all of 15. LaSeBxRa follow the Sarum lection, whilst Ny and Bo incorporate both—with the result that 'bi oold daies' and 'bi elde dayes' occur twice in close proximity.

1768–72 *Thei schulen putte . . . schulen drede þee*: this section is part of the biblical text but not of the Sarum lection, and is omitted in LaSeBxRa. Again, the Group II B manuscripts are the only collated texts which follow the biblical text rather than the lection.

1773 *berist ouer þe synne of relifis of þin eritage*: translating 'transis peccatum reliquiarum haereditatis tuae', 'passest by the sin of the remnant of thy heritage'.

LECTION 91

LV

1791 *to*[2]: 'into' LV.
  gladnesse: 'and' *add.* LV.

LECTION 92

CR

NyLa have a cross-reference to Trinity Eve here, instead of the third Saturday in Advent.

LECTION 93

LV

1798 *regne*: 'a' *add.* LV.

1800 *tristeli*: 'and' *add.* LV.

LECTION 94

LV

1807 *men of mercy ben*: following closely the syntax of the Latin: 'viri misericordiae sunt'.

1808 *wiþ þe seed of hem contynueli*: 'contynueli with the seed of hem' LV.

1809 *bifore*: 'for' LV.
  into: 'til in to' LV.

1814–15 *Here endiþ . . . þe Propre Sanctorum*: in Type II manuscripts this rubric is variable, but in Type I it is very stable: 'Here eendiþ þe dominicals and ferials togidere of al þe ȝeer. Now bigynneþ þe rule of þe sanctorum boþe propre and comyn togidere' La.

LECTION 95

Composite lection; independent translation of Sarum lection

LECTION 96

Composite lection; independent translation, which is on the whole closer to LV than EV

1841 *to vse presthode in fredom*: a translation of 'fungi sacerdotio', 'to execute the office of the priesthood'. There is no Latin equivalent to 'in fredom' in SM.

LECTION 108

LV

1845 *lordschiper*: translating 'dominator'.

1846 *þe²*: *not in* LV.

1847 *And who schal mowe þenke*: 'And who will be able to think', a translation of 'et quis poterit cogitare'. ME 'schal' is here used to indicate future tense.

1853–4 *as þe daies of þe world and as oold ȝeeris*: a literal translation of 'sicut dies saeculi et sicut anni antiqui' (in the sense 'as in the days of old and in former years').

LV

1861–2 *þe sodeynte of heelþe vnhopide*: i.e. the suddenness of the unexpected salvation (of the righteous).

1865 *likenesse of vpbreidynge*: translating 'similitudinem improperii' ('parable of reproach').

1866 *ony*: *not in* LV.

LV

LV

1886–8 *And I seide . . . my God*: this section is in the Vulgate, but not in SM. It is omitted in LaSeBxRa and underlined in Ny.

1889–92 *þat I bringe . . . drastis of Israel*: this section is in the Vulgate, but not in SM. It is omitted in LaSeBxRa and underlined in Ny.

1891 *It is litil*: i.e. it is a small thing.

1893 *into*: 'the' *add.* LV.

1894 *þe¹*: *not in* LV.
    aȝenbier: translating 'redemptor' ('redeemer').

1895 *into*: 'in' LV.

1897 *for he is feiþful*: this section is in the Vulgate, but not in SM. It is contained only in Bo and Ny amongst the collated manuscripts.

LV

1909–10 *fer, fro þe laste endis*: a translation of 'procul et de ultimis finibus'('far and from the uttermost ends of the earth'). The ME presents a literal translation which does not attempt to capture the figurative sense of the verse.

1914 *pray*: i.e. food.

1915 *meydens*: 'handmaidis' LV.

1918 *quenche*: 'be quenchid' LV.

1924 *of*: 'to' LV, expressing the dative 'Chananaeo'.

LECTION 157

LV

This is named 'St Cyriacus' in Bo and several other Type II B lectionaries, but it is actually the lection for St Lawrence Eve.

1943–4 *fro rorers made redi to mete*: i.e. 'from those that roared, ready to devour'.

1945 *cumpassiden me*: both in the biblical text and in SM, this is succeeded by 'a pressura flammae quae circumdedit me' (*Missale*, ed. Dickinson, 857), which is not translated here.

1948 *to*: 'into' LV.

1952 *and*: 'thou' *add.* LV.
   men hatynge þee: 'hethene men' LV, 'Jentiles' EV, 'manibus gentium' Vu, 'odencium te' SM. All collated OTLs follow the Sarum lection rather than the Vulgate here.

LECTION 159

EV

1959–61 *And I hadde root . . . my wiþholdynge*: a literal translation of 'et radicavi in populo honorificato et in parte Dei mei hereditas illius et in plenitudine sanctorum detentio mea'. A more idiomatic version (using LV) appears in Lection 160, lines 1970–2.

1959 *hadde root*: this variant occurs in only four of F&M's EV manuscripts (AEGH). For further details see *The Holy Bible*, ed. Forshall and Madden, i. 169.

LECTION 160

LV; part of the text of this lection is the same as in the preceding lection, but here in LV instead of EV

1967–9 *I was gendride . . . bifore hym*: this verse is omitted in SM, and is missing in LaSeBxRa. Only Bo and Ny follow the biblical text here.

1973 *Liban*: 'and' *add*. LV.

1975 *feeldis*: 'and' *add*. LV.
    palm tre: 'plane tree' LV, 'platanus' Vu SM.

LECTION 161

Composite lection (the first part is LV, the second part (from **1994** *Thi buriownynge until the end*) is translated from the Latin lection independently)

1984 *withynne*: 'hid with ynne' LV.
    þou art ful faire[2]: The repetition of this phrase is unique to Bo. Neither the Vulgate nor SM, nor any other of the collated OTLs, contains it.

1986–9 *Thou shalt . . . þi necke*: this section is in the Vulgate, but not in SM. It is omitted in LaSeBxRa, and underlined in Ny.

1987 *my*[2]: *not in* LV.

1991–5 : *Spousesse, þi lippis . . . fruyt of appil trees*: these verses lack a main verb, which reflects the Latin syntax.

1993 *smelle*: 'odour' LV.

1994 *Thi buriownynge*: from this verse onward, the rest of the lection is translated independently. The lection is composed of different verses from different chapters of the Song of Songs, with the result that the text of the lection differs quite significantly from the biblical text. The OTL makes it clear that this is a composite lection which does not follow the biblical text in a linear way by adding the relevant chapter numbers and indexing letters to individual sections.

2003 *of his modir*: the possessive determiner 'his' translates 'suae' in 'matris suae'. In this context, 'suae' could be translated as 'his' or 'her'; the context indicates that the latter is more likely, as the text refers to the beloved (a woman).
    þe geter: translating 'genetrici suae' (i.e. 'her that bore her').

LECTION 165

LV

2012 *The*: *not in* LV.

2015 *on*: 'the' *add*. LV.

2018–20 *A gileful . . . wisdom is*: this section is in the Vulgate, but not in SM. It is omitted in LaSeBxRa and underlined in Ny.

2018 *gileful balaunce*: i.e. 'false balance'.

2020 *wisdom is*: 'is wisdom' LV.

2022–5 *Richessis schulen . . . his wickidnesse*: this section is in the Vulgate, but not in SM. It is omitted in LaSeBxRa and underlined in Ny.

2026–7 *Whanne a wickid . . . schal perische*: this section is in the Vulgate, but not in SM. It is omitted in LaSeBxRa and underlined in Ny.

LECTION 169

LV

2035 *and*: 'of' *add*. LV.

LECTION 170

LV

2047–8 *þe mynde þerof is vndedely*: i.e. 'the memory thereof is immortal' (translating 'immortalis est enim memoria illius').

2049 it²: 'and' *add*. LV.

2049–50 *þei desiren it . . . of batels vndefoulide*: i.e. 'they desire it when it has withdrawn itself, and victoriously it wins the reward of undefiled conflicts'.

2054 *þei sette vnstidfastli schulen be mouede of þe wynde*: i.e. 'as they stand insecurely, they will be shaken by the wind'.

2055 *of*¹: 'the' *add*. LV.

LECTION 171

LV

2066 *þerof*: 'and' *add*. LV.

LECTION 172

LV

2075 *a*: 'the' LV.

2080 *þo*¹: 'the' LV.

LECTION 198

LV, with some variation

2097–8 *biþenke in þe biholdynge of God in wit*: 'thenke in wit the biholding of God' LV.

2098 *in wit*: i.e. 'in his mind' (translating 'in sensu').

2099–100 *of þe watir of helpful wisdom it schal ȝeue hym drynke*: 'it schal ȝyue drynke to hym with watir of heelful wisdom' LV.

2100 *fastnede*: 'fastned' EV, 'maad stidfast' LV.

2101–2 *And it schal . . . anentis hise neiȝboris*: 'And it shal withholden hym, and he shal not be confoundid; and it shal enhaunce hym anent his neȝebores' EV; 'And it schal holde hym, and he schal not be schent; and it schal enhaunse hym at his neiȝboris' LV. On the whole this section seems to be based more on EV than LV.

2103 *and with þe euerlastynge name he schal enerite hym*: 'and schal enherite hym with euerlastynge name' LV.

LECTION 199

LV

LECTION 200

LV

2115 *The witties of a man been hoore*: i.e. 'the understanding of a man is grey hair'.

2119–2120 *Forwhi disceyuynge of . . . wit withouten malice*: this section is in the Vulgate, but not in SM. It is omitted in LaSeBxRa and underlined in Ny.

2120 *contynuaunce*: 'vnstablenesse' LV.

2123–4 *but puplis sayen . . . in þe entraylis*: this section is in the Vulgate, but not in SM. It is omitted in LaSeBxRa and underlined in Ny.

2125 *chosun*: 'chosun men' LV.

LECTION 201

LV

2127 *The*: prec. by 'Forsothe' LV.
   hondis: 'hond' LV.

2130 *þat*: Most of F&M's manuscripts have 'that that' here. Only C omits the second 'that' (*The Holy Bible*, ed. Forshall and Madden, iii. 89).

2131 *men²*: 'hem' LV.

2137 *þei*: Only F&M's MS I contains this variant (*The Holy Bible*, ed. Forshall and Madden, iii. 89).

LECTION 202

LV

2148–9 *and þe world . . . vnwitti men*: this section is in the Vulgate, but not in SM. It is omitted in LaSeBxRa but contained in Ny and Bo.

2149 *Streite sendingis out of leitis*: translating 'emissiones fulgurum' ('shafts of lightning').

LECTION 203

EV

2152 *mercies*: 'of hym' *add.* EV.

2153–4 *ʒoure mede schal not be voidide awey*: 'there shal not be voidid awei ʒoure meede' EV.

2155 *into likynge schal come to ʒou mercy*: i.e. 'mercy shall come to you for your delight'.

2157 *witiþ*: 'for' *add.* EV.
or: *not in* EV.

2158 *forsaken*: 'or' *add.* EV.

LECTION 204

LV

2162 *it*: in the original context in the Book of Wisdom, the pronoun 'it' refers to the personification of wisdom. The lection is prefaced by the addition 'God', which serves as a liturgical framing device. This addition makes the reference of the pronouns throughout this lection somewhat incongruous.

2167 *preiseden*: 'togidere' *add.* LV.
hond ouercomer: translating 'victricem manum'. In SM the lection ends with 'domine deus noster', an ending which is translated in La but in none of the other

collated texts. Here as elsewhere, Type I follows SM more closely than Type II does.

LECTION 205

LV

2178 *and*: *not in* LV.

LECTION 209

LV

2192–3 *þat fledde fro þe ire of his broþer*: omitted in SM and in all collated manuscripts, except Type II B.

2193 *broþer*: 'and' *add.* LV.

   it: the original referent of this pronoun in the Vulgate is 'wisdom'; owing to the liturgical framing of 'The Lord' this original context is obscured. For a similar case see above, Lection 204, line 2162.

2197 *is*: 'the' *add.* LV.

LECTION 210

LV

2208 *wondris aȝens kynde*: translating 'monstra' ('monstrosities, evil signs').

2212 *in*: 'to' LV.

LECTION 211

Predominantly LV, with the second part of the lection (from Ecclus. 24) translated independently

2216 *his*: *not in* LV.

   God: a somewhat puzzling translation, given that this word is not found in the Sarum lection, which merely has 'sancto suo'. This addition does not seem to fit well with the context of the following sentence—'he heriede God'. The reason for this addition is unclear, but might be connected to a misreading of 'suo' as 'Deo' in the copy of the Sarum Missal from which the translator was working.

2226–31 *Wisdom schal preise... schal be blesside*: independent translation.

LECTION 212

LV

2233–45 *I desiride . . . of Goddis frendschip*: this entire lection is underlined in Ny to indicate that it is not read after the Use of Sarum.

2235 *of it*: 'therof' LV.

2240 *honeste*: a translation of Latin 'honestas'. The Latin is ambiguous, but a more likely meaning in this context is 'wealth'.

LECTION 213

LV

2253–4 *schal counceile in hise hidde pingis*: i.e. 'he will take counsel of his (= God's) hidden mysteries'.

2254 *And*: *not in* LV.

LECTION 214

Synthesis of EV and LV. The syntax of this lection follows LV more than EV, but with some variants which agree with EV, and other variants which have no equivalent in either translation. The main deviations from LV are given in the notes below.

The entire lection is underlined in Ny, probably to indicate that this lection is not read after the Use of Sarum.

2261 *þe wey of hym*: 'the weie of hym' EV, 'his weie' LV.

2262 *seke*: 'inwardli sechen' EV, 'enquere' LV.
  plesynge: 'plesid' EV, 'plesaunt' LV.

2263 *þe lawe of hym*: 'the lawe of hym' EV, 'his lawe' LV.
  And: *not in* LV or EV.

2264 *in her spirit*: 'in the siȝte of hym' EV, 'in his siȝt' LV, 'in conspectu illius' Vu SM.

2265 *þe comaundementis of hym*: 'the hestis of hym' EV, 'hise comaundementis' LV.

LECTION 216

LV

2272 *schal herie it togidre*: a translation of 'collaudabo illud', which renders both prefix and base of the Latin verb literally.

LECTION 217

CR

The cross-reference to St Lawrence Eve is an empty reference, since the feast of St Lawrence Eve is misnamed as St Cyriacus and companions in Bo and several other Type II B OTLs.

LECTION 218

Composite lection, predominantly EV, whilst the last section of the lection (from l. 2289, *I haue ȝoue*, onwards) is translated independently

2283 *glorifien*: 'glorien' EV.

2284 *þe*[1]: *not in* LV.

2289–91 *I haue ȝoue . . . onour and grace*: this entire section, which does not follow continuously after the previous verses, is translated independently.

LECTION 219

LV

The entire lection is underlined in Ny. The reasons for this are unclear. Ny frequently underlines non-Sarum lections, but that does not apply in this case. A possible explanation is that the scribe erroneously underlined this lection instead of the preceding one, which is a non-Sarum lection and which starts with the same word.

2295 *fro þe ende til to þe ende strongli*: i.e. 'from one end of the earth to the other, with might'.

LECTION 220

LV

2302–3 *out-ioye*: 'out ioiyng' LV.

2303 *cloþ*: 'clothis' LV.

2304 *cloþ*: 'clothis' LV.
cloþide: 'compassid' LV.

2314–15 *Here endiþ . . . Ladi in Aduent*: this rubric can vary between Type II manuscripts. For Type I, it is more fixed: 'Here eendiþ þe rule of þe sanctorum boþe þe propre and comyn togidere. And here bigynneþ þe temperal þat is þe commemoraciouns of þe ȝeer' La.

LECTION 223

CR

Unlike Bo, most OTLs give a more precise reference to the Eve of Assumption Day here.

LECTION 225

Composite lection, translated independently from SM

This is the same lection which is read for Salus populi (Lection 233), and those OTLs which contain that commemoration usually give a reference here.

2333–4 *3ilden hem*: translating 'solvent' ('they will fulfil them').

LECTION 227

Composite lection, translated independently from SM

2344 *Rise up togidre*: a literal translation of both prefix and base of 'consurge'.

2347 *alle feterid men*: 'alle many weies in to oon' EV, 'alle meetyngis of weies' LV, 'omnium conpetorum' Vu. EV and LV accurately translate 'conpetorum' in the sense 'crossroads', whilst the translation 'feterid men' in the lectionary is puzzling. The reason for this odd translation is unclear, but it may be based on a confusion with the noun *captivorum* ('of the prisoners'), pointing towards scribal error in the translator's Latin source text.

LECTION 228

LV

2361 *tyme*: 'of heeling' *add*. LV.

LECTION 229

EV

BxNy give a cross-reference for this lection to the 2nd Wednesday of Lent (Lection 41). Even though both liturgical occasions use the same section from Esther 13, Bo uses two different translations, EV for the commemoration and LV for Lent. Bx and Ny do not make a distinction between the two liturgical occasions.

2371 *forsope*: *not in* EV.

2372 *ben*: 'is' EV.

2373 *wiþstondiþ*: this variant is contained only in F&M's manuscript A (*The Holy Bible*, ed. Forshall and Madden, ii. 662); to *add*. EV.

2374 *on*: 'of' EV.

2374–5 *don awey oure eritage*: 'thin eritage don awei' EV.

2375 *þou*²: 'hast' *add*. EV.

2376 *be þou merciful*: 'and merciful be thou' EV.

    lot and litil coord: translating 'sorti et funiculo'. *DMLBS* defines 'funiculum' as a 'portion (of land) allotted w. measuring rope' (sense 3). The translator clarifies this meaning by adding 'of þin eritage'.

2377 *Lord, þat we lyuynge preise þi name*: 'that liuende we preise thi name, Lord' EV.

LECTION 230

EV

2380 *do for þi name*: i.e. 'do it for thy name's sake'.

2382 *comelynge tilier*: the translator here interprets 'colonus futurus' as a 'farmer who is a newcomer/stranger'.

2384 *me*: 'come' EV.

2384–5 *Forsoþe, þou art, Lord, in vs*: 'thou forsothe in vs art, Lord' EV.

2385 *clepide*: 'inwardly clepid' EV.

LECTION 231

EV

LECTION 232

EV

2391–7 *collacioun, or spekynge togidre . . . vnbounden fro synnes*: this is a somewhat awkward translation caused by the difficult Latin syntax. I interpret verse 45 in the ME as a continuation of verse 43 (to avoid the problem of an incomplete sentence in verse 45). The ME in verse 45 is best read in the sense 'and for (=because) he biheld þat þei [who] token slepynge, *or diynge*, wiþ pite (=in righteousness), hadden best grace kept'.

2391 *collacioun, or spekynge togidre*: the Latin 'collatio' can mean both 'collection (of money)' and 'gathering'—the alternative translation 'spekynge togidre' indicates the translator's awareness of the ambiguity in meaning here.

2392 *Ierusalem*: 'for' *add*. EV.

for: 'synnes of' *add*. EV, 'pro peccatis mortuorum' SM, 'pro peccato' Vu. It may be significant in a Wycliffite context that this reference to the sins of the dead is omitted; however, the thought reappears in the last verse of the lection, which mentions that prayers for the dead will help them 'be vnbounden fro synnes' (lines 2397). Thus the omission of references to this concept is not systematic in this lection, and this single instance could simply be the result of scribal error and variable transmission of the Latin text rather than pointing to a consistent Wycliffite agenda.

2395 *diynge*: 'deth' EV.

2396 *helþful and holi*: 'holy and helthful' EV.

2398 *Here enden þe lessouns and pistlis of al þe ȝeer*: the concluding rubric can vary between OTLs. In Type III OTLs, this rubric refers to the TOL, e.g. 'Here endiþ þe kalender wiþ þe lessouns of þe olde lawe togidere' Bx.

GLOSSARY

The Glossary is selective and is intended to provide a guide for readers accustomed to Chaucerian English. A number of peculiar turns of phrase in the text stem from close translation of the Latin source. Where there is a noticeable pattern (e.g. in the translations of Latin prefixes such as *con-*), a note is included in the Glossary. Further details on peculiarities of translation from the Latin are contained in the Explanatory Notes.

Only the actual forms found in the text appear in the Glossary, not hypothetical uninflected forms. Variant spellings which are not easily referable to a headword are entered in their alphabetical place with a cross-reference. Minor spelling variants such as variation between *y* and *i* are not explicitly noted, except where confusion may arise. Glossary entries for verbs list the forms in line with the standard order of the inflectional paradigm.

Words are glossed only if their meaning departs from that of modern English or if their form within the texts is likely to cause difficulties. When one Middle English sense of a word coincides with modern English but another does not, only the second is regularly included here. Thus, the material under each headword is not a full inventory of either paradigms or senses in the texts. Phrases likely to cause difficulty are entered under the word within them that departs from its normal sense. At most four instances of a sense are given.

Throughout the Glossary, I retain the scribe's usage of *i*/*y* and *u*/*v*. In sorting forms, I include *i*/*y* variation under *i* (but the use of either initially as a consonant is treated as *j*); ȝ follows *g*, þ is interpreted as *th*. The scribes normally use *v* initially, *u* medially for both the consonant and the vowel; in the Glossary I sort them according to vocalic and consonantal usage.

ABBREVIATIONS

1 sg. first person singular	*pa.* past tense
2 sg. second person singular	*pa. p.* past participle
3 sg. third person singular	*pl.* plural
adj. adjective	*pr.* present tense
adv. adverb	*pr. p.* present participle
comp. comparative	*pref.* prefix
conj. conjunction	*prep.* preposition
fig. figurative	*pron.* pronoun
intr. intransitive	*subj.* subjunctive
imp. imperative	*superl.* superlative
inf. infinitive	*v.* verb
n. noun	*vbl. n.* verbal noun

A

abatide *v. pa. p.* diminished 656, 659

abiden *v. pl. pr.* wait for 1952, 2367; **abidynge** *pr. p.* 388; **abideden** *pa. pl.* 2360, 2361

abidynge *vbl. n.* expectation 2012, 2027

aboue *adv. frequently translating the Lat. pref.* super 148, 149, 150

aȝenbier *n.* ransomer, saviour 1894

aȝenbiynge *vbl. n.* redemption 254

aȝenbouȝt(ist) *v. 2 sg. pa.* redeemed 674, 2375; **aȝenbouȝt** *pa. p.* 54, 301, 310

aȝenrisynge *vbl. n.* resurrection 2393

aȝens *prep.* over 1454

aȝenseie *v. 1 sg. pr.* resist 1288; **aȝenseiþ** *3 sg. pr.* contradicts 1292

aȝenseiynge *vbl. n.* opposition 897

aȝenstonde *v. inf.* resist 663; **aȝenstonde** *3 sg. pr. subj.* 667

aȝenward *adv.* in reply 1017, 1026

alargide *v. pa. p.* expanded 356
aliene *adj.* foreign 47, 613, 874
alien(e)s *n. pl.* strangers 205, 1658
aliens *see* aliene
almesdedis *n. pl.* works of charity 2111
and *adv.* also 519
anentis *prep.* towards, against 1281;
before 321, 788, 2019; with respect to,
concerning 709, 2140, 2141; close to
739; among 2048²
angwischen *v. pl. pr.* trouble 1859–60
angwischis *n. pl.* tribulations 936
anoon *adv.* instantly 664, 948, 1180
answere *v. inf.* testify 2380
appliede *v. pa. p.* joined 218
arettiden *v. pl. pa.* considered, regarded
1332, 1334; **arettid(e)** *pa. p.* 1352,
1549, 2237
as *conj.* as it were 700
asaiede *v. 3 sg. pa.* tested 1503, 2133;
asay *1 sg. pr. subj.* 1272
askis *n. pl.* ashes 295
aspien *v. inf.* see 917; **aspieden** *pl. pa.*
observed 916, 922
aspiyngis *vbl. n.* plotting 2026
astonyede *v. pa. p.* upset, stupefied 517
atreet *adv.* slowly 1697
atwynny *adv.* apart 980
avoutrie *n.* adultery 2052
avowis *n. pl.* oaths 93
axe *v. inf.* ask 71; **axen** *pl. pr.* demand
recompense 423; **axe** *imp.* 69
axer *n.* extortioner 278
axyng *vbl. n.* trial 2059

B

basenet *n.* helmet 2146
bere(n) *v. pl. pr.* carry 49, **bere in** *inf.*
carry inside 1273; **bere ouer** *inf.* trans-
fer 670, **berist ouer** *2 sg. pr.* pass by
1773
bi *prep.* ~ **daies euerlastynge** for ever
(*translating Lat.* per dies sempiternos)
347
bidynge *vbl. n.* hope 2381
bifore *adv.* be ~ to be rulers 1412
biheeld *see* bihold
biheestis *n. pl.* promises 2333
bihi3te *v. 1 sg. pa.* promised 1487
bihold *v. inf.* consider 1201; **biholdeþ**
3 sg. pr. admires 2018; **biholden**

pl. pr. admire 2017; **biholdynge**
pr. p. watching 925, ~ **to** looking for
1949–50; **biheeld** *1 sg. pa.* looked 1320;
bihe(e)ld(e) *3 sg. pa.* looked 954; saw
1639, 1915; considered 2395; **bihelden**
pl. pa. looked 1284
biholders *n. pl.* observers 307
biholdynge *vbl. n.* sight 1838, 2080,
2098, 2135
biys *n.* a precious kind of linen 1922
bynde *v. inf.* wind about 426
birþuns *n. pl.* burdens 430
bischediþ *v. 3 sg. pr.* moistens 480
biseche *v. inf.* pray 2249, 2250; **bisou3te**
1 sg. pa. 2268
bisechyngis *vbl. n. pl.* supplications 632
biþenke *v. inf.* meditate 2097; **biþou3ten**
pl. pa. remembered 913
biþenkynge *vbl. n.* thinking 2393
bitook *v. 3 sg. pa.* gave 741, 1119, 1165;
bitake *imp.* 1163
blamede *v. 3 sg. pa.* reproached 702
bodyes *n. pl.* carcasses 1167
boolis *n. pl.* bulls 1219
boond *n.* ~ **of pees** covenant 881, 1124,
1489, 2365
bosum *n.* embrace 1013, 1111
botir *n.* butter 75
brasun *adj.* made of brass 125
breste *v. inf.* send forth 375
brynge *v. inf.* lead 38
buyliþ *v. 3 sg. pr.* ~ **out** boils up 2169
burioyne, buriowne *v. inf.* put forth
shoots 100, 1715, 1719; **buriowne**
pl. pr. 2053–4; **buriownynge** *pr. p.*
growing, sprouting 100, 180–1, 339,
1994
burioynynge *vbl. n.* bud 1471, 1797

C

cacche *v. inf.* take hold of 1468
caitif *adj.* captive 291
caytifte *n.* captivity 1673
calenge *see* chalange
canel *n.* cinnamon 1975
certeyn *adj.* true 2146
certis *adv.* surely 818; indeed 949, 1179
cesonable *adj.* according to the season
336
chalange *n.* accusation 544, 1195
charis *n. pl.* chariots, wagons 807, 1450,
1453

chaunge *v. imp.* ~ **merueilis** create different miracles 616–17
cheer *n.* face 1201, 1332, 2073
chees *v. 1 sg. pa.* chose 426, 429; **chees** *3 sg. pa.* 583; **chese** *imp.* pick out 51
chidingis *n. pl.* quarrelling 423
childide *v. 1 sg. pa.* gave birth 1007, 1008; *3 sg. pa.* **childide** 7
clarioun *n.* trumpet 850
cleer *adj.* magnificent 1791
cleernesse *n.* splendour 2047, 2202
clensynge *vbl. n.* expiation 1730; **clensingis** *pl.* 1727
clepe *v. inf.* call 54; **clepide** *1 sg. pa.* 7, 128; **clepide** *3 sg. pa.* 1101; **clepide** *pa. p.* 29, 75, 231, 282; **clepe** *imp.* 1101; **ynwardli** ~ (*as a translation of Lat.* invocare) called upon *1 sg. pa.* 2233, *3 sg. pa.* 2158, *pa. p.* 1636
cleuynge *v. pr. p.* sticking 1527
clumside *adj.* weak 103
collacioun *n.* gathering, collection 2391
comelynesse *n.* beauty 2143
comelynge *adj.* foreign 872, 2382
comyn *adj.* in ~ together 920
comyn *v. pa. p.* come out, are manifest 983
comoun *v. 1 sg. pr.* communicate 2243
conuertid *v. 1 sg. pa.* changed 1782
coord *n.* litil ~ little string, *fig.* share (*literal translation of Lat.* funiculus) 2376
cop(pe) *n.* peak of a mountain 58, 496
couche *n.* bedroom 1007
counceile *v. inf.* ~ in take counsel of 2253
coueiten *v. pl. pr.* desire 2038
coueitise *n.* lust 911, 915, 991
couenable *adj.* suitable 922, 2057
creauncer *n.* creditor 828
crist *n.* the anointed one 121
crokide *adj.* crippled 107
cubitis *n. pl.* cubits (measure of length) 141
culuer *n.* dove 2003; **culueris** *pl.* 1983
cumpas(se) *n.* circle, sphere 666, 2372; in ~ round about 353; **bi oure** ~ round about us 631
cumpasside *v. 3 sg. pa.* covered 740; **cumpassiden** *pl. pa.* surrounded 1945, 1949

D

damysel *n.* maid in waiting 791[1,2], 795; **damysels** *pl.* 923, 925, 930
deboner *adj.* gentle, meek 290
declaren *v. pl. pr.* proclaim 2043
defoule *v. inf.* profane 1194, destroy 1346; **defoulid** *1 sg. pa.* 1319; **defoulid** *pa. p.* desecrated 1053; destroyed 1294; abused 1335; defiled 1946; **defoule** *imp.* destroy 1239
defoulynge *vbl. n.* destruction 1240
degre *n.* position 1697
dele *v. inf.* give 1350
delicis *n. pl.* pleasures 10
delyuerynge *v. pr. p.* releasing 984
deme *v. inf.* judge 15, 63, 82, 83; **demest** *2 sg. pr.* judge 2370; **demynge** *pr. p.* exercising judgement 975, 983; **demede** *pa. p.* 1030
departen *v. 3 pl. pr.* divide up 276; **departide** *3 sg. pa.* separated 1392; **departide** *pa. p.* separated 981, 1027; **departe** *imp.* separate 980, 1023
depnesse *n.* depth 1776
derlynge *n.* beloved 1211, 1584
derworþe *adj.* honoured, noble 2116
deuydide *v. pa. p.* assigned 1819
deuouren *v. inf.* eat 1382
diȝte *v. pa. p.* prepared 1621
diligentlier *adv. comp.* more attentively 1015
disceyuable *adj.* deceitful 1930
diseseful *adj.* irksome 72–3
dispite *n.* disdain 2364
disposiþ *v. 3 sg. pr.* order 2295; **dispose** *imp.* make provision for 405
dissencioun *n.* quarelling 879
dissese *n.* pain 143
distriede *v. pa. p.* destroyed 1126, 1147, 1559
distryinge *vbl. n.* destruction 2130[1,2]
do *v. inf.* ~ **awey** destroy, take away 673, 1044, 1060; *1 sg. pr. subj.* 1040
domesman *n.* judge 267
doom *n.* judgement 13, 420, 520, 526; **domes** *pl.* matters of judgement 908
drastis *n. pl.* scum, refuse 1892
drawe *v. 2 sg. pr. subj.* ~ **vp** tear down 1879
drede *n.* fear 81, 596[1,2], 611
drede *v. inf.* fear 104, 115, 652; **dredde** *3 sg. pa.* 1463; **dredden** *pl. pa.* 992

drenchide *v. 3 sg. pa.* drowned 2164

dresse *v. inf.* place 1721; direct 2021, 2024, 2253; **dressid** *pa. p.* placed 1347

dromedis *n. pl.* dromedaries 358

droue *n.* herd 1623

drunkenede *v. 1 sg. pa.* made drunk 1323

dwellynge *vbl. n.* dwelling place 2383; **dwellyngis** *pl.* 1630

E

e(e)ld(e) *n.* age 2115; old age 980, 2114

eft(e) *adv.* a second time 508, 745, 778, 1038

egge *n.* sharp edge 517 (*here in the idiom* þe teeþ of sones ben an ~ the sons are surprised)

endynge *vbl. n.* completion 341

enforside *v. 3 sg. pa.* strove 720

enhaunce *v. inf.* raise 321; **enhaunsidist** *2 sg. pa.* 2268; **enhauncid** *pa. p.* raised, elevated 148, 1132, 1972, 1972; **enhaunce** *imp.* raise 114, 321, 417

enseelide *pa. p.* sealed up 1994

entraylis *n. pl.* bowels 1116, *fig.* emotions 1025, 2124

enuyrownede *v. pa. p.* surrounded 339, 370

equyte *n.* impartiality 84, 2147

erer *n.* plowman 1670

eritagen *v. inf.* give for a heritage 325

eþer *conj.* or 83, 697, 749

euen *adj.* straight 566[1,2]; just 2019

euen *adv.* ~ aȝens opposite 1077

euennesse *n.* impartiality 2147

euer *adj.* ~ eiþer both 1379

F

faile *v. inf.* run out 656

fairnesse *n.* beauty 101, 951, 991

fallynge *vbl. n.* ~ adoun falling into ruin 1257; **fallyngis** *pl.* ruins 9

fatnesse *n.* abundance 761

feynede *adj.* insincere 1592

feyner *n.* hypocrite 2029

feynynge *vbl. n.* hypocrisy 2118, 2243

feiþ *n.* faithfulness 87

fele *v. imp.* understand 1587

felli *adv.* treacherously 1044

felouship *n.* escort 822; company 2298

felownesse *adj.* wicked, deceitful (felonous) 1352

ferdful *adj.* terrifying 1236, 2007

feries *n. pl.* feast 1740, 1746, 1752

feterid *adj.* bound 2347

fillen *v. pl. pa.* rushed 942; ~ yn attacked 1164

fillid(e) *v. 3 sg. pa.* completed 1488, 1500; **fillid** *pa. p.* completed 765, 2121; satisfied 883–4, 2263

fillynge *vbl. n.* fulfilment 1618

filþis *n. pl.* filthiness 1058

fleischis *n. pl.* meat 1268, 1279, 1380

fletynge *adj.* ~ offryngis drink offerings 1624, 1748

fletynge *vbl. n.* ~ doun disappearing 2269

flynte *n.* stone 893

floreyns *n. pl.* gold coins 798

folk *n.* nation, tribe 65, 1040, 1895; ~ of kynde nation 1316–17

fonned *adj.* foolish 975

for *prep.* because of 73, 84

for(e)fiȝter *n.* defender (*translating Lat.* propugnator) 90, 1315

forȝerdis *n. pl.* courts 50

forsoþe *adv.* truly (*often translating Lat.* autem) 55, 704, 714, 723

forswere *v. inf.* swear a falsehood 1194

forwhi *conj.* because, for 13, 16, 278, 454

frost *n.* whiȝte ~ rime 171; blak ~ killing frost 172

ful *adj.* abounding 324

ful *adv.* fully, completely 331, 334, 335; very 739, 901, 903, 1442

fulhede *n.* abundance 2230

fulle *n.* at the ~ completely 331

fulleris *n. pl.* fullers, cloth-finishers 1849

furneise *n.* furnace 139

G

gendrid(e) *adj.* begotten 744, 769, 1504, 1526

gendriþ *v. 3 sg. pr.* begets 529, **gendride** *v. pa. p.* given birth 1016, begotten 1967

gesside *v. 1 sg. pa.* thought, considered 694, 811; **gessid** *pa. p.* considered 1582; **gesse** *3 sg. pr. subj.* think 734

gete *v. inf.* conquer 1535; **gete** *pa. p.* 1634

geter *n.* parent 2003
getynge *vbl. n.* purchasing 2063
gileful *adj.* false 2018
gird(e) *v. pa. p.* girded, surrounded 130, 1826
girdil *n.* belt 87
glade *v. imp.* rejoice 199, 216
gladli *adv.* with great pleasure 731
glorien *v. inf.* rejoice 2281
glorifien *v. inf.* praise 297, 2283; **glorifiede** *pa. p.* 2227, 2229
grees *n.* step 1688
greuouse *adj.* grave 1203
grucchen *v. pl. pr.* grumble 1278; **grucchiden** *pl. pa.* 1265
grucchinge *vbl. n.* grumbling 1277, 1281

3

ȝatis *n. pl.* gates 123[1,2], 125
ȝede(n) *v. 3 sg. pa.* went 272, 502, 511, 737; **ȝeden** *pl. pa.* 713, 790
ȝellynge *vbl. n.* wailing 783
ȝerd(e) *n.* sapling 78; rod 75, 277, 885, 889
ȝetun *v. inf.* bestow, provide 376
ȝhe *interj.* yes 669
ȝilde(n) *v. inf.* restore 724; distribute 1350; give 1911; perform, fulfil 2333; **ȝildiþ** *3 sg. pr.* make restitution 523; **ȝolden** *pa. p.* given 1247; bestowed 1325
ȝildynge *vbl. n.* recompense 105, 1320, 2136
ȝit *adv.* still 30
ȝok *n.* yoke 277
ȝolden *see* **ȝilde(n)**
ȝotide *v. 3 sg. pa.* poured 837; **ȝotun** *pa. p.* molten 1036
ȝouun *v. pa. p.* given 101, 577, 1168, 1437
ȝoxide *v. 3 sg. pa.* yawned, hiccuped 1100

H

haburiown *n.* hauberk 2145
halowe *v. inf.* sanctify 895, 1052, 1615; **halowide** *1 sg. pa.* 1871; **halowide** *pa. p.* 614, 895, 1700; **halowe** *imp.* 391
halowyngis *n. pl.* holy days 2220
han *v. pl. pr.* have 419
hard *adj.* difficult 34

hauntid *v. pa. p.* stirred, engaged 66
hawe *n.* hawthorn 987
he(e)lþe *n.* salvation 18, 23, 306, 312; prosperity 788; cure 810
he(e)riynge *vbl. n.* praise, worship 12, 1135, 360, 2274
heede *n.* notice 5
heerd-men *n. pl.* shepherds 252
heerynge *v. pr. p.* 1495; **heere** *imp.* hear, listen 20, 72, 216, 566; **heriþ** *imp. pl.* 4
heerynge *vbl. n.* hearing 83; report 1327
heestis *n. pl.* commandments 556, 582, 589, 605
heggis *n. pl.* fences 448
held *v. 3 sg. pa.* ~ out spread out 141
helþful *adj.* saving 2100, wholesome 2396
hemsilf *pron.* each other 915, 918
herburles *adj.* homeless 432
herie *v. inf.* praise 49, 307; **herieden** *pl. pa.* 144; **herie** *imp.* 156, 159, 160
heriþ *see* **heere**
hertli *adv.* cheerfully 1135
hewide *v. 1 sg. pa.* struck 1364
hiȝe *adv.* an ~ loudly 1182
hiȝede *v. pa. p.* exalted 2229
hiȝþe *n.* height 70, 256, 371
hile *v. inf.* cover 351, 358; **hiliþ** *3 sg. pr.* clothes 525, 540; **hilid** *3 sg. pa.* 492; **hiliden** *pl. pa.* 1457, 2077; **hilide** *pa. p.* 1153; **hile** *imp.* 433
hilinge *vbl. n.* protection 1479, 2162
hyre *n.* wages 1196
hondful *n.* wheatsheaf 694; **hondfullis** *pl.* 694, 1612–13, 1617
hondmaide *n.* servant 848, 1012; **handmaydens** *pl.* 1603
(h)oneste *n.* honour 2240, 2243
hool *adj.* healed 94, solid 338
hoore *adj.* grey-haired 2115
huyde *v. 1 sg. pa.* concealed 2243
huydynge *vbl. n.* refuge 1481

I

idil *adj.* empty 1390
iȝe *n.* eye 308[1,2]; **iȝen** *pl.* eyes 16, 82, 106, 311
ilis *n. pl.* islands 15
in *prep.* by 46[1,2], 1120; for 48; with 92[2], 95; upon 736; against 988, 996
inclepe *v. imp.* implore 380
into *prep.* in 70[1,2]; to 418; against 210[2]; ~ **withouten ende** *as a translation of Lat.*

usque in sempiternum *and* in aeternum
268–9, 286, 1809–10
inwit *n.* mind 604
yrun *adj.* iron 125
iustifiyngis *vbl. n. pl.* justifications 635

K

kepers *n. pl.* watchmen 43
kepyngis *vbl. n.* watches 1580
kepte *v. 1 sg. pa.* preserved 1124
kerue *v. imp.* cut, cleave 386
knouleche *v. inf.* acknowledge 1938,
1939, 2252; profess 2274
knoulechynge *vbl. n.* worship 2272
kunne *v. inf.* know 1723; **kunne** *2 sg. pr.
subj.* 1547; **kunne** *3 sg. pr. subj.* know
how to 76
kunnynge *vbl. n.* knowledge 81, 1366,
2030, 2169

L

lake *n.* pit 1166, 1167, 1173, 1174
largist *adj. superl.* most abundant 893
laste *adj.* furthest 52
lateful *adj.* late in the season 1361
laumpis *n. pl.* lights 849, 2081
le(e)ndis *n. pl.* loins 87, 1086
leche *v. inf.* heal 291
ledde *v. pa. p.* brought forth 887; ~ **out**
taken away 2049
leeneþ *v. 3 sg. pr.* lends 525
leese *v. inf.* destroy 673, 2374; **leese** *2 sg.
pr. subj.* 1879
leesynge *vbl. n.* falsehood 869, 1941,
1947; loss, perdition 330
lei3he *v. inf.* laugh 1926
leit *n.* lightning 2082, 2083; **leitis** *pl.*
flashes of lightning 177, 2149
lendis *see* **le(e)ndis**
lernynge *vbl. n.* lesson 1336; discipline
1825; knowledge 2299
lesewis *n. pl.* pastures 463, 465, 1128
lettynge *vbl. n.* hindrance, obstacle 1198
liban *n.* tree from which incense is
derived 2289
li3tnede *v. pa. p.* enlightened 349, 2156;
li3tne *imp.* give light 1411
ligge *v. inf.* lie down 466
likenesse *n.* example 1865
likynge *vbl. n.* delight 2155

liknede *v. 1 sg. pa.* made like 128
lynage *n.* tribe 12; **lynagis** *pl.* 762
litil *adj.* insignificant 72
looues *n. pl.* loaves of bread 741, 1268,
1271
lords(c)hip *n.* power 117, 663; rule 2328
lordschiper *n.* ruler 1845
lot *n.* heritage 675

M

magiste *n.* power 667, 2373
maydenhode *n.* virginity 317
make *v. inf.* ~ **large** magnify 2221;
made *pa. p.* contrived 969
malice *n.* severe punishment 1158
mantel *n.* robe 295
mark *n.* limit 265
mede *n.* reward 53, 117, 300, 1309
medelide *v. pa. p.* sprinkled 279; mixed
2290; having sexual intercourse 933,
960
meynealis *n. pl.* servants 1914, 1921
meynees *n. pl.* household, servants 1371
mekiden *v. pl. pa.* humbled 421
mele *n.* flour 650, 653, 656, 659
merueilis *n. pl.* miracles 616–17, 1188,
1224, 2107
mete *n.* food 47, 280, 1172, 1438; meal
917
mette *v. 3 sg. pa.* measured 1114
myche *adj.* generous 475
mylde *adj.* meek 1300
mylte *v. inf.* melt 17
mynde *n.* memory 2040
mynystrid *v. 1 sg. pa.* served 1968;
mynystride *3 sg. pa.* provided 698
myssel *n.* leper 1334
more *adj.* older 752; greater 1148
morwetide *n.* morning 434, 1384, 1398–9
mossel *n.* small piece 648
mou3þe *n.* moth 22, 1295
moun *v. pl. pr.* are able to 891; may
1374, 2065

N

nameli *adv.* in particular 951
namyde *v. pa. p.* renowned 1569
nempnede *v. 3 sg. pa.* named 229
new *adv.* now 983
ny3(e) *adj.* close 14, 473, 904, 1292

ny3(h)e *v. inf.* approach 421; nei3eþ *3 sg.*
pr. 522; ny3ynge *pr. p.* 1948; ny3ede
3 sg. pa. 716, 749, 1082; ny3eden
pl. pa. 817; ny3e *imp.* advance, move
close 1283, 1293
nyle *v. imp.* do not (do sth) 20, 104, 115,
424
nobeley *n.* dignity 228
nol(le) *n.* neck 1038, 1492
noumbre *v. inf.* count 1616

O

occasiouns *n. pl.* grounds for hostility
804
odour(e) *n.* smell 758, 1625, 1717, 1976
of *prep.* by 91; from 1033
on *prep.* above 153; upon 704; for 1025;
behind 1094[1,2]
oneste *see* (h)oneste
oon *adv.* only 1504
oostis *n. pl.* hosts 27, 30, 33, 35
oppresse *v. inf.* attack 1196; oppresside
3 sg. pa. smothered 1011
ordeyneden *v. pl. pa.* agreed upon 920
ournement *n.* adornment 1444
ourneþ *v. 3 sg. pr.* adorns 2169; ournede
3 sg. pa. arranged 2220; ournede *pa. p.*
adorned 2305; honoured 2226
outaken *prep.* except 616, 672, 924, 1009
out-ioie *n.* gladness (*translating Lat.*
exultatio) 101, 276, 1134–5, 1472
ouerabundaunce *n.* excess 541
ouercomer *n.* victor 2167; ouercomeris
pl. 275
ouercomeþ *v. 3 sg. pr.* conquers 2294;
ouercomynge *pr. p.* conquering 2050

P

paye *v. inf.* fulfil 93
panyer *n.* basket 1170, 1636
passynge *adv.* exceedingly 369
passynge *v. pr. p.* ~ forþ going away
1363; passe *imp.* enter 50[1,2], come 2038
passynge *vbl. n.* flowing 336
perauenture *adv.* perchance 853
perdis *n. pl.* leopards 1987
perdiscioun *n.* destruction 1184–5, 1940
perseyuede *v. 1 sg. pa.* discovered 1015;
perseyue *imp.* take notice 637, 803,
1546, 1881

perteneris *n. pl.* partakers 2245
pesible *adj.* peace-loving, gentle 2068;
peace-making 860, 1626; calm, peaceful
2208
pite *n.* compassion 81; wiþ ~ in
righteousness 2396; pitees *pl.* deeds of
righteousness 1807
pitte *n.* well 1997
playn *adj.* even 51
platis *n. pl.* coins 798
plentee *n.* abundance 1268, 2284
posterne *n.* side door 928, 942
pray *n.* provisions 1914
prechide *v. pa. p.* declared 2004
preien *v. pl. pr.* ask 420
preisable *adj.* praiseworthy 150–1
preisynge *vbl. n.* object of praise 45;
praise 242, 367, 373, 585
pressouris *n. pl.* wine presses 202
preue *v. inf.* test 854; preuest *2 sg. pr.*
test 1304; preue *1 sg. pr. subj.* have
proof 749
pry *n.* reward 276
priueli *adv.* by himself 705; secretly 777
pryuy *adj.* hidden 126, 1083, 1203
priuytees *n. pl.* secrets 126
profiten *v. pl. pr.* avail 720
puple *n.* people 12, 34, 37, 39; puplis *pl.*
nations 14
purueie *v. inf.* provide 1517

Q

queemful *adj.* merciful 1045
quenche *v. inf.* extinguish 1918
quicke *adj.* living 883, 1023, 1025; ~
hegge a row of shrubs 1328
quikene *v. inf.* revive 571, 802, 1358

R

raunsomed *v. pa. p.* redeemed 243
raunsomer *n.* redeemer 2356
raueyn *n.* spoils 279, 539; raueynes *pl.*
532
rauyschide *v. 3 sg. pa.* stole 777
rebel *adj.* rebellious 891
redi *adj.* unimpeded 1845
refreischynge *vbl. n.* solace 2060, 2113
rehed *n.* reed 2137
reherside *v. 3 sg. pa.* recited 345

reynes *n. pl.* loins 87, 1385; kidneys, *fig.*
the heart 689, 1304
reise *v. inf.* lift up 66, 119, 1620; reisid
pa. p. lifted up 1627; attentive 1687;
reise *imp.* lift up 51; stir up 617; reisiþ
imp. pl. raise 16; ~ awey *imp.* take
away 1302–3
relifs *n. pl.* remnants 34, 1773
rennynge *vbl. n.* ~ aboute running to
and fro 2081
represue *v. inf.* rebuke 64, 76, 83, 84
rerid *v. pa. p.* ~ out lifted up 59; ~ vp
lifted up 2348
residewe, residue *adj.* left 1384, 1474
residewe *n.* remainder 841
restorid *v. 3 sg. pa.* returned 1180
rewme *n.* kingdom 151, 230, 285
ri3tful *adj.* just 567, 903, 1723, 1801
ri3tfulli *adv.* properly 1079
ri3tfulnesse *n.* justice 19, 84, 86, 135
ri3twise *adj.* righteous 1818, 1832
ri3twisnesse *n.* justice 40, 200, 267, 297
ri3twisse *n.* the just one 226
rikened(e) *v. pa. p.* counted 1867, 2114
rootide *v. 1 sg. pa.* took root 1970
rope *v. pa. p.* gathered 2000
rorers *n. pl.* the roaring ones 1943

S

sad *adj.* strong 468
say *v. 1 sg. pa.* saw 412, 694, 1173; *3 sg.
pa.* 1164; *pl. pa.* 272
sak *n.* sackcloth 1150; sackis *pl.* 1148
salewis *n. pl.* willows 1755
saltnesse *n.* salty wasteland 682
schaken *v. pl. pa.* shook 851
schapli *adj.* beautiful 1313
scharis *n. pl.* plowshares 65
schede *v. inf.* pour out 1057, 1600, 1604;
schedist *2 sg. pr.* pour out 441; schede
imp. pour out 618
scheltrun *n.* battle formation 2007
schende *see* schent
schenschip *n.* destruction 395, 401, 2363;
reproach 630–1, 1470; schenschipis *pl.*
reproaches 21
schent *v. pa. p.* harmed, destroyed
1225[1,2], 1290, 2157; confounded 1230,
2042; schende *imp.* confound 1222
schewe *v. inf.* reveal 345, 915, 963;
schewide *1 sg. pa.* 1299; schewide
3 sg. pa. 1084; schewe *imp.* 382, 610

schynynge *adj.* radiant 247
schynynge *vbl. n.* radiance, brightness
226, 353; schynyngis *pl.* 444
schrewide *adj.* crooked 567; wicked 688
schrewis *n. pl.* evildoers 2016
schul(e)n *v. pl. pr.* shall 15[1,2,3], 17, 31,
48[1,2]
seeld *v. 3 sg. pa.* sold 1924; seeld *pa. p.*
sold 2198
seeþ *v. imp. pl.* look 16
seew *n.* stew 741
seyntuarie *n.* holy place 575, 632–3
seiþ *v. 3 sg. pr.* says 4, 27, 30; sey(e) *imp.*
say 102, 115, 299
seitis *n. pl.* habitations 462
semely *adj.* beautiful 1983, 2008
sende *v. imp.* cast 718
sendingis *n. pl.* ~ out emissions 2149
seruage *n.* servitude 780
set *v. pa. p.* placed 1170
sette *v. inf.* make 1131; settiþ *3 sg. pr.*
makes 680
si3t(e) *n.* sightly appearance 1330; vision
2081
signe *n.* banner 51
sikelis *n. pl.* sickles 65
sikirnesse *n.* security 1481
siþis *n. pl.* scythes 65
siþis *n. pl.* vij ~ seven times 809, 820,
1100
sle *v. inf.* kill 86, 845, 946, 985
smertli *adv.* vigorously 1997
smyte *v. inf.* strike 1130
snobbingis *vbl. n. pl.* sobbing 2354
sodeynte *n.* suddenness 1862
sode(n) *adj.* boiled 766, 1382
softnesse *n.* gentleness 1823
soler *n.* upper chamber 1111, 1118
somer *n.* summer heat 169
soone *adv.* quickly 1035
sooþ *adj.* true 1121
sorie *adj.* painful 143; upset 523
soþeli *adv.* truly 530, 654, 720, 750
sou3t *v. pa. p.* longed for 55, 1311
souereyn *adj.* supreme 256; ~ to pre-
eminent over 1429
sparklis *n. pl.* sparks 2136–7
spousesse *n.* bride 394, 1985, 2297, 2305
spousynge *vbl. n.* marriage 1981
spred *v. 3 sg. pa.* ~ abrood spread out
1114
spreynt *v. pa. p.* sprinkled 1318
sprungoun *v. pa. p.* risen 254

steynede *adj.* coloured, dyed 1313
stie *v. inf.* grow 79, 1328; mount 1711;
  stiede *3 sg. pa.* went up 489, 1095,
  1099; stiede *pa. p.* ascended 492; stie
  pl. pr. subj. let us ascend 60; stie *imp.*
  ascend 113, 486
stiynge *vbl. n.* ascending 341
stille *adj.* silent 43, 44, 222, 225
stirid *v. pa. p.* moved 783, 989
stirten *v. pl. pa.* ~ out flowed out 1997
stonyinge *vbl. n.* astonishment 769
stool(e) *n.* robe 324, 1314
streem *n.* torrent 209; streemes *pl.* 109
stryuyngli *adv.* rebelliously 1492–3
strumpetis *n. pl.* prostitutes 1005
studies *n. pl.* labours 868, 871, 1300
sue *v. inf.* follow 1359; suen *pl. pr.* 4,
  1221, 2049; suede *3 sg. pa.* 1090;
  sueden *pl. pa.* 1458
suffre *v. inf.* submit to 15; suffride *3 sg.*
  pa. 993
suget *adj.* subservient 122
susteynede *v. pa. p.* supported 1113;
  susteyneþ *imp. pl.* wait 2152
sweuene *n.* dream 693, 699, 700, 701;
  sweuenes *pl.* 698
swoor *v. 3 sg. pa.* swore an oath 45

T

tabernacle *n.* tent 881, 1480, 1663, 1965;
  tabernaclis, tabirnaclis *pl.* 1741,
  1760, 1761
take *v. inf.* overtake 1671 [1,2]
tarie *v. imp.* delay 637
teerme *n.* limit 265; te(e)rmes *pl.* borders 595, 1656
teetis *n. pl.* breasts 1989
tend *v. pa. p.* lighted 227
tente *n.* consideration, attention 1246
terrid *v. pa. p.* provoked 1782; terre
  pl. pr. subj. 1499
testament *n.* covenant 1809, 1836, 1839–
  40, 2255
þankyngis *vbl. n. pl.* thanksgiving 11
þenken *v. pl. pr.* ~ on remember 44;
  þou3ten *pl. pa.* intended 716
therebynte *n.* turpentine tree 2291
þerf *adj.* unleavened 1381
thilke *adj.* that 519
thilke *dem. pron.* that (one) 1348
þo *dem. adj.* those 57, 69, 89

þo *dem. pron.* those 400
þraldom *n.* captivity 251
tilier *n.* farmer 2382
tymful *adj.* early in the season 1361
tobrokun *v. pa. p.* torn 17; broken 1226
togidre *adv.* bi hemsilf ~ to each other
  915, 986, 994
togidre *adv.* translating the Lat. prefix
  com-, con- 64, 1252, 1848, 2005
to-rentist *v. 2 sg. pa.* tore from top to
  bottom 806; to-rente *3 sg. pa.* 802;
  to-rente *pa. p.* 805
to-trad *v. 1 sg. pa.* trampled 1322
toukers *n. pl.* fullers, cloth-finishers 1849
translatide *v. 3 sg. pa.* moved 2163
trauailide *v. 1 sg. pa.* laboured 1886;
  traueilid *pa. p.* laboured 48, 1348;
  afflicted 2132
trauel *n.* labour 1639; traue(i)l(i)s *pl.*
  1860, 2161, 2194
tre *n.* wood 1302
tresouren *v. inf.* heap treasure 325
treuþe *n.* truth 29, 408, 528, 1776
trifelynge *vbl. n.* extravagance 2119
tristeli *adv.* confidently 1800
troon *n.* throne 151
troubler *n.* oppressor 89
tungen *n. pl.* tongues 108
turmente *v. inf.* humble, afflict 426,
  1728, 1735, 1781; turmentid *pa. p.*
  afflicted 442, 1731; turmente *imp.*
  injure 618
turmentynge *vbl. n.* affliction 1237
turne *v. inf.* ~ a3en return 95, 482;
  turneþ *3 sg. pr.* ~ ouer turns away
  2120; turnede *3 sg. pa.* ~ a3en
  returned 509, 1092, 114; turneden
  pl. pa. ~ awey perverted 912; turnede
  pa. p. ~ a3en turned away 909, 1156
tur(ne)ment *n.* torment 2127, 2129

U

vnabitable *adj.* uninhabitable 683
vnbile(ue)ful *adj.* unfaithful 891, 2260
vnbounden *v. pa. p.* liberated 2397
vndedely *adj.* immortal 2048
vndedlynesse *n.* immortality 2132
vndirnyme *v. imp.* rebuke 1205
vndirtake *v. inf.* receive 317
vndirturnede *v. pa. p.* destroyed 1146
vneþe *adv.* scarcely 764

vnhilide *adj.* uncovered 950
vnmesurable *adj.* immoderate 2171
vnpite *n.* hard-heartedness 429
vnpiteuous *adj.* wicked 2179
vnresonable *adj.* unreasoning, not
    endowed with intelligence 1426
vnriȝtfulnesse *n.* injustice 569
vnriȝtwisli *adv.* unjustly 1200
vnwisdom *n.* foolishness 1572
vnwitti *adj.* foolish 2149
vpbreidynge *vbl. n.* reproach 1865
vtas *n.* octave 362
vtmest *adj.* furthest reaches 299
vtterli *adv.* ~ not not in any way 142–3

V

vagaunt *adj.* wandering, homeless 2384
vendage *n.* vintage, ripe grapes 1652
vermyloun *n.* bright red 1072
verri *adj.* true 254
vertues *n. pl.* powers 162
vyner *n.* vineyard 1675, 1916
voide *adj.* empty 833
voidide *v. pa. p.* ~ awey taken away
    2153
volatil *n.* bird 1421; volatils *pl.* 1430,
    1436

W

wannesse *n.* bruising 1337
waxe *v. inf.* grow, increase 1834; woxen
    pl. pa. 2071; wexe *imp.* 1422
wed(de) *n.* pledge 266, 523, 539, 539
weeld(e) *v. inf.* rule 220, 592, 1048, 1634
weigoer *n.* wayfaring man 2383
weile *v. inf.* cry 1862
weilynge *adj.* weeping 294[1,2]
weilynge *vbl. n.* weeping 295, 386, 2377
weyward *adj.* wicked 1589, 2018, 2022
weywardli *adv.* wickedly 1068
welle *v. inf.* melt 64
wellynge *vbl. n.* ~ togidre melting 1849
wemme *n.* flaw 1375, 1623, 1985, 2105
werk *n.* crime 938
whanne *conj.* as, since 902

wheete *n.* wheat 47, 399, 1718
where, wheþer *interr. adv. introducing
    a question expecting a negative answer
    (often translating Lat.* numquid) 35, 72,
    425, 533
whette *v. inf.* sharpen 2147
wielde *adj.* overgrown 1765
wilnynge *v. pr. p.* intending 344, 723
wit(te) *n.* thought 912; consciousness
    1091; mind 2098; understanding 2233
wite *v. inf.* know 204, 219, 1226; woot
    1 sg. pr. know 1291; woost *2 sg. pr.*
    667, 1235; woot *3 sg. pr.* 389, 1155;
    wite *pl. pr. subj.* 1054; wite *imp.* 800
wiþholde(n) *v. inf.* preserve 320, 2101;
    wiþholdynge *pr. p.* possessing 315
wiþholdynge *vbl. n.* abode, dwelling
    1961, 1972
wiþout *prep.* ~ wey impassable 98
wlappide *v. 3 sg. pa.* enfolded 1456
wlatid *v. pa. p.* felt disgust with 2359
wode *adj.* mad 1865
wole *v. 3 sg. pr.* signifies 702; wolen
    pl. pr. want 419, 421, 1846; wolde *1 sg.
    pa.* wanted 483, 734, 747; wolde *3 sg.
    pa.* wanted 738, 963
wondris *n. pl.* miracles 1604, 1641, 1822;
    ~ aȝens kynde monstrosities 2208
wonyinge *v. pr. p.* dwelling 253, 1957
wood(e)nesse *n.* passion 1156; wrath
    1317, 1322; madness 1866
worche *v. inf.* perform 562; worchen
    pl. pr. perform 1941, 2014; work 2042;
    wrouȝtist *2 sg. pa.* committed 983
worchinge *vbl. n.* works 1951
world *n.* fro þe ~ and til into þe ~ for
    ever and ever (*translating Lat.* a saeculo
    usque in saeculum) 875, 214; til into
    þe ~ for ever 2256 (*translating Lat.* in
    saeculum)
worschipful *adj.* honourable 905
worschipide *adj.* honoured 1959–60
woxen *see* waxe
wraþfulnesse *n.* anger 1832
wrong *n.* injury 541
wrongful *adj.* unjust 278
wrooþ *adj.* enraged 810, 1039, 1041

INDEX OF PROPER NAMES

The index lists all the proper names in the Old Testament Lectionary, with the following exceptions. I do not index the names of God (God, Lord, Christ, Holy Spirit, Trinity, Sabaoth, Emmanuel, etc.). I also do not index liturgical seasons (Advent, Lent, Easter, etc.) or liturgical terms (Proprium Sanctorum etc.). The index contains names of biblical books but does not include references to biblical books which are added by the editor for clarification, marked by square brackets in the text. Where the same name occurs several times in a single line, I give the line number only once. Uninflected forms are given as headwords except in cases where only inflected forms of a name are found in the text. Line numbers in **bold** refer to rubricated headings of lections, which are represented by bold type in the edition. The spellings of names given in brackets are the modernized English versions following the Authorized Version, as being generally familiar and current forms. Occasionally, for additional clarity, modern forms of some names have been included where they differ from biblical spellings. Short explanations have been added for purposes of clarification. Cross-references indicate cases where further explanations can be found in the Explanatory Notes. In sorting forms, I include *i/y* variation under *i*.

Sus(s)an(ne) (Susanna, wife of Joachim) 901, 909, 935, 939, 944, 946, 947, 949, 956

Vr (Hur, companion of Moses and Aaron) 491

Theman (region of Edom) 1564, 1565

Trenorum (Threnorum, Book of Lamentations) 2343

Zacharie (Zechariah) 26, 215, 1779